GREEN M

Nature, Culture and Literature
06

GREEN MAN HOPKINS

POETRY AND THE VICTORIAN
ECOLOGICAL IMAGINATION

John Parham

Amsterdam - New York, NY 2010

The paper on which this book is printed meets the requirements of "ISO 9706:1994, Information and documentation - Paper for documents - Requirements for permanence".

ISBN: 978-90-420-3106-7
E-Book ISBN: 978-90-420-3107-4
©Editions Rodopi B.V., Amsterdam - New York, NY 2010
Printed in the Netherlands

Printed by Printforce, the Netherlands

For Elaine and Isaac

Contents

Acknowledgements

There are many people whose contribution I would like to acknowledge.

The project was supported, in the first place, by funding awarded by the University of East London. It is underpinned, at least at its foundations, by the encouragement and practical support I received from the following people: Bob Chase, Jim Harris, Frank Mort, Alan O'Shea, Ken Parker, Susannah Radstone and Bill Schwarz. I received further external advice from Roger Bromley and Chris Mulvey and benefitted, also, from the support, academic and social, of Anita Biressi and Heather Nunn. Most especially, however, I owe an enormous debt to Andrew Blake for his advice and ideas, for reading various drafts of the material, and for always trusting me to get on with it.

I also owe, more recently, a debt of gratitude to the Faculty of the Arts at Thames Valley University, not least for the funding received from its Research Committee. This enabled attendance at several conferences where I spoke about Hopkins as well as a period of research leave. I would acknowledge, in particular, the direct support offered by Jeremy Strong and Francis Pott. It is also the case that I would have found it considerably more difficult to continue without the day to day support offered by Angie White and Maria Pennells, and the interest taken by friends such as Judy Coulton, Donovan Synmoie, and Pete Smith. In fragmented conversations in the office (or even walking across the car park), Pete taught me more about critical and aesthetic theory than I have ever learnt in most conferences or symposia.

I owe more specific thanks to other friends – to Nick, who offered perhaps the most substantial support of all in procuring several of the primary texts for me; and Eve Poole and Tony Ramsey who plugged gaps in my knowledge of theology and classics respectively. The same applies to Pete Thornton, at the University of Worcester, who helped me out with IT problems during the production of this book.

Recognition is due, more generally, to the members of the ecocritical community, both worldwide and in the British branch of the Association for the Study of Literature and Environment (ASLE-UK). Many of them have supported my work, either indirectly or by providing opportunities to speak at conferences, but I should mention in particular Simon Estok and Won-Chung Kim, and Matt Jarvis, for invitations to speak about Hopkins at Sungkyunkwan University in Seoul and the University of Wales (Lampeter); and to Simon (and Yeon-hee) and Matt for exceptionally generous hospitality in each case. Likewise, Molly Westling, who commented on the initial proposal for this book, and, especially, Terry Gifford who has, both at the beginning and end of the process, notably in proofreading it, provided both enormous practical help and valuable encouragement.

On similar lines I would of course like to acknowledge the support and advice provided by the series editors at Rodopi, notably Hubert van den Berg and Axel Goodbody. In particular, Axel's scrupulous and sympathetic reading of the drafts helped improve the clarity of the book. Their guidance has been consistently valuable as has that of Christa Stevens who has overseen and helped me through the production process.

Acknowledgement is due to Oxford University Press for permission to reproduce the cover image. I would particularly like to thank Ben Kennedy at OUP and Philip Endean and Jed Clapson at the British Province of the Society of Jesus for their help in my enquiries towards tracing the copyright as well as my friend and colleague Sean Dodson for helping scan the image to a professional quality. I am grateful, likewise, to Ashgate Publishing for permission to reproduce, in chapter two of this book, material that appeared, in an earlier form, in John Parham (ed.) *The Environmental Tradition in English Literature* (2002); and to Taylor & Francis, and the editors of *Nineteenth-Century Contexts*, especially Professor Keith Hanley, who previously published a short summary of some of the arguments made here and who allowed me to re-use the 'Green Man Hopkins' title (see 2003, 25(3): 257-76).

Finally, most importantly, I must of course thank my partner, Elaine, and son, Isaac, who never complained about the late evenings, late mealtimes, and writing holidays engendered by this book. It is dedicated, as it should be, to the two of you.

John Parham
Crystal Palace
2010

Chapter 1

Muddying the Waters:
Towards a Humanist Ecocriticism

Gerard Manley Hopkins was born in Stratford, East London in July 1844. Situated just beyond the metropolitan boundary, then, as now, the area was changing rapidly. With the arrival of the Great Eastern Railway's locomotive works it was "cut up in all directions by branches of railways" (Olsen 1976: 275-6) but also suffered, as Norman White points out, as a consequence of London's environmental diligence. The Metropolitan Buildings Act passed that same year restricted "offensive" trades in Central London but left Stratford a refuse for industries such as soap-works, bone boilers, varnish makers, and chemical manure. While the 1852 Metropolitan Water Act compelled water companies to filter water for domestic use, being outside the metropolitan boundary this did not apply to Stratford with the result that cholera raged through the neighbourhood (1992: 13).

Research for this book entailed occasional trips to a library located just off The Grove, Stratford's main thoroughfare, where the Hopkins family lived. With the construction of the Channel Tunnel rail-link, Stratford, albeit in the name of urban regeneration, was once again being "cut up" by railway lines not least along the traffic-congested road that The Grove had now become. The house is gone, replaced (for now) by a local government office. The site is unmarked. Further up the road, however, where Stratford turns into Maryland, is a public house, *The Goldengrove*. Taking its name from the poem 'Spring and Fall'

> Márgarét, áre you grieving
> Over Goldengrove unleaving?

the pub remains the one obvious reference in this place to Hopkins.[1] The name is predictable enough, given the road name and that 'Spring and Fall' is one of Hopkins' better-known poems, yet still a little incongruous, in this most urban of environments, unless also read as testimony to an enduring cultural inheritance of the romantic love of nature. In which case Hopkins stands as a representative of that tradition as, indeed, he is generally regarded.

Yet to base an ecological reading of Hopkins on his nature writing alone would be unnecessarily limiting, a fact which can be demonstrated with reference to a further biographical example taken from the other end of his life. Hopkins died in June 1889, prematurely at the age of forty-four. The last five years of his life were spent in another insalubrious environment, the Catholic University College in Dublin. Here, dilapidated college buildings were afflicted by a combination of dry rot, sanitation problems, poor drainage and rats rife with infectious disease. Hopkins died from typhoid fever which attacking his body, afflicted him with pain and sleeplessness and disrupted his digestion. Consequently his two most recent biographers have both conjectured that he was killed as a result either of a lack of proper sanitation, or by water or food contamination (Martin 1991: 370-71; White 1992: 454-5). Whatever the precise cause, Hopkins' death was the result of an urban environmental hazard.

Near to the beginning of *The Environmental Imagination* Lawrence Buell describes his subject, Thoreau, as "more my base of operations than my main subject" (1995: 2). In part this might apply here in that I will be proposing Hopkins as a representative of a more general Victorian ecological tradition. It is, nevertheless, the case that his life and work, while illustrative of that wider context, have also, in themselves, shaped the argument of this book. That argument is concerned, more widely, with broadening the scope of existing studies in literature and ecology – ecocriticism – beyond a prevailing focus on romantic nature writing and with suggesting, specifically, that literature has the capacity to illuminate the full range of ecological theory, including the environmental impact society has on its human as well as nonhuman inhabitants. Prior to the outline of a 'Victorian ecology', and the application of this to Hopkins, this opening chapter will lay the foundations for my argument by establishing ecology as the specific framework that underpins the reading of Hopkins and by outlining, in more detail, the ways in which literature

---

[1] My thanks to Julian Corder of Laurence Tring Architects for corroborating this information.

might shape an ecological awareness in the fuller sense of the word implicit from his life.

1. Definitions: preservation, conservation, environmentalism, ecology

Critical studies of literature and the environment have been somewhat lax in their terminology. To give examples, Buell turns to Anna Bramwell's *Ecology in the Twentieth Century* in order to establish a theoretical basis for an "*environmental* imagination" while, conversely, the British critic Jonathan Bate's *Romantic Ecology* is sub-titled "Wordsworth and the *Environmental* Tradition". While this may sound pedantic, equivalent work in other disciplines, from environmental science to political theory, reveals a great deal of debate about the parameters of connected terms such as ecology and environmentalism and the philosophical differences between them. The importance of establishing the appropriate paradigm prior to any application to literary study rests upon the fact that each can provide, as Greg Garrard has put it, "the basis for a distinct ecocritical approach with specific literary or cultural affinities and aversions" (see 2004: 16). In what follows ecology will be differentiated from three other prominent philosophies within green studies: conservation, preservation and environmentalism, each of which, with the possible exception of the second, represents both a scientific and a social paradigm.

The first two, conservation and preservation, can be understood in relation to each other. In their book *Environmental Science* William P. Cunningham and Barbara Woodworth Saigo make a distinction between "Pragmatic Resource *Conservation*" and "Moral And Aesthetic Nature *Preservation*" (1997: 6-7), a distinction that has been expanded upon by Michael Allaby:

> In modern scientific usage conservation implies sound biosphere management within given social and economic constraints, producing goods and services for humans without depleting natural ecosystem diversity, and acknowledging the naturally dynamic character of biological systems. This contrasts with the preservationist approach which, it is argued, protects species or landscapes without reference to natural change in living systems or to human requirements. (2004: 95)

Understood in this way the first term, conservation, refers to a management of natural resources for human benefit based upon scientific understanding. As such it has been defined by Tim O'Riordan as "a utilitarian notion, the orderly exploitation of resources for the greatest good to the greatest number over the longest time" (1981: 12). While this corroborates that conservationism is, indeed, connected to human self-interest, that interest has been interpreted in quite a specific way.

Conservation foregrounds, in its very name, notions of limitation. In this respect it is best exemplified by the 1960s concept "Spaceship Earth" which posits that an over-populous humanity has consumed, polluted and destroyed so much of its resources that the earth has become a closed system in which inputs have to be controlled and regulated like the atmosphere of a space capsule. This is an approach that derives histo-rically from Malthus' argument that while "population, when unchecked, increases in geometrical ratio [...] subsistence increases only in arith-metical ratio" (Wall 1994: 118). In turn, Malthus' conclusion, that "the power of population is indefinitely greater than the power in the earth to produce subsistence for man" (Wall 1994: 118), appears to have shaped a conservationist pre-occupation with population that is articulated in early writings such as Garrett Hardin's 1968 essay 'The Tragedy of the Commons' and Paul Ehrlich's 1972 book *The Population Bomb*.

The effect of these has been to translate a concern to protect human resources into the anti-humanist sentiment that runs throughout such work. Hardin argues, for instance, that to grant everybody equal right of access to finite natural resources would be to "lock the world into a tragic course of action" (see VanDeVeer and Pierce 2003: 369). It becomes apparent, furthermore, that the victims of such an approach would be the poor. At a symposium in New York Hardin is reported to have said:

> we should go lightly in encouraging rising expectations [among the poor] [...] for if everyone in the world had the same standard of living as we do, we would increase population by a factor of 20 [...] Therefore it is a questionable morality to seek to increase the food supply. We should hesitate to make sacrifices locally for the better-ment of the rest of the world. (see O'Riordan 1981: 30)

In connection with his subsequent notion of a "lifeboat ethics" Hardin also "advocates", as O'Riordan puts it, that survival will require the deliberate "jettisoning [...] of an undetermined number of the present earthly community for the good of 'humanity'" (O'Riordan 1981: 31). It is little wonder that conservationist ideas have been seen to couple, as Richard Neuhaus writes, a "moving reverence for the 'seamless web of life'" with "shocking indifference to the weaker and less convenient forms of human life" (O'Riordan 1981: 31).

Preservation can be regarded as a predominantly cultural ideal con-cerned, specifically, with preserving existing environments. These sometimes include built environments, as in the work of the National

Trust in the UK, but more commonly, as exemplified by the Sierra Club in the United States, preservationists are concerned with the veneration and defence of 'natural' or 'wilderness' areas:

> those [...] "whose priority is wilderness" are much better described as preservationists, since they may be more or less indifferent to the ecological character of wilderness and interested chiefly in its cultural and recreational values. (Phillips 2003: 122)

So much as it can be described as a social philosophy, preservationism is, most accurately, the cultural equivalent of conservationism in that it is premised upon a corresponding notion of limitation, this time in terms of advocating limited access to wilderness or other such areas so as to preserve the integrity of a supposedly natural state. As a result preservationist sentiment frequently seems to at least imply the denial of access to all but a socially privileged minority, an instinct which has on occasion been supported or articulated by literary figures. Such a perspective is evident, for instance, in Wordsworth's campaigning in 1844 against the proposed Kendal and Windermere railway, a campaign partly motivated by anxiety about the influx of the masses into the Lake District, or in the policy shift by which the Sierra Club (founded by John Muir amongst others) altered its bylaws so as to emphasise preservation over "accessibility", a change that has led critics to regard the organisation as politically conservative (see Cohen 1988: 118).

The two remaining concepts, environmentalism and ecology, both of which adopt, broadly speaking, a more humanist emphasis, can also be defined in relation to each other. Allaby offers a succinct definition of scientific environmentalism when he describes it as the study of the specific "physical, chemical and biological surroundings in which organisms live", a study that encompasses "changes wrought by human activities". This he contrasts with ecology defined, simply, as the scientific framework that underpins such study (2000: 2, 9). In terms of a social philosophy, Allaby goes on to make an analogous distinction between pressure groups such as Friends of the Earth or Greenpeace who work to prevent "environmental damage" to specific places and a broader ecological social philosophy which "no longer demands piecemeal reform to achieve environmental amelioration, but calls for a radical restructuring of society and its economic base" (2000: 9). This distinction, between a reformist environmentalism and a more revolutionary ecology (see Giddens, in Pepper, Webster and Revill 2003: IV, 271), appears to have been widely accepted. The political theorist Andrew

Dobson argues, for example, that "ecologism seeks radically to call into question a whole series of political, economic and social practices in a way that environmentalism does not" (2000: 201). The end result of this has been that environmentalism is now often regarded, in the familiar terms established by Arne Naess, as a "shallow" philosophy that priori-tises what we might have expected from conservationism, human survival and well-being, in contrast to which there exists a *"deep*, long-range ecological movement" (see Sessions 1995: xii, 151-5). As I will be arguing in this book that it was, specifically, ecology which Hopkins anticipated, this will now be defined in greater detail both as a scientific and a social philosophy.

The genesis of the word ecology can be dated with precision to its coinage in 1866 by the German zoologist Ernst Haeckel and to his subsequent development of the term when, in 1870, he described ecology as

> the investigation of the total relations of the animal both to its inorganic and organic environment; including above all, its friendly and inimical relations with those ani-mals and plants with which it comes directly or indirectly into contact. (see McIntosh 1985: 7-8)

The conjunction Haeckel makes between two quite different nineteenth-century scientific frameworks – natural history which, in the main, posits a stable, hierarchical 'balance of nature' and evolutionary theory, a mode of progressive, dynamic alteration – is one broadly accepted by theorists and historians as representing the origins of ecological science (see Allaby 2000: 13; Bramwell 1989: 45-8; Hayward 1995: 25-6; Simmons 1993: 22-3; Worster 1994: 192-3).

Derek Wall, to give one example, describes the natural theologians of the seventeenth century as carrying out "the first systematic attempts to understand the environment" (1994: 104). This is a view informed by Donald Worster who in *Nature's Economy* refers to an eighteenth-century belief in nature as "the grand organisation and government of life on earth: the rational ordering of all material resources in an interacting whole" wherein "each species serves to support others as it earns its own living" (1994: 37, 35). This has, however, been a problematic legacy. For while the second idea posited here, of co-operation or interaction, remains central to ecological theory the first, "organisation and govern-ment", derives, as Tim Hayward has pointed out, from a pre-modern, largely Christian conceptualisation of the natural world as a hierarchical 'chain-of-being', a conception which has been criticised as unscientific and as offering a "naively idyllic view of nature" (1995: 25-6; and see Allaby 2000: 9). While such ideas, most notably the related concept of balance, do persist in the popular perception of ecology, influenced by paradigms such as Frederick Clements' notion of climax ecosystems which have evolved into a state of stability, these are now largely disregarded by the scientific community.

Juxtaposed to the natural history tradition is an emphasis on "inimical relations" which, originating from Malthus, also underlies conservationism and the grimmer forecasts of potential environmental catastrophe (Pepper 1996: 172-80; Wall 1994: 116-19; Worster 1994: 150-4). Malthus' significance in an ecological context resides mainly, however, in his influence on Darwin and on the theories of evolution and natural selection; Darwin's own significance lies in the fact that he laid the foundations for scientific ecology by effecting a synthesis between natural history and Malthusian theory (see Wall 1994: 5-6; Worster 1994; and see also Pepper 1996: ch. 4).

Worster points out that Darwin, though profoundly influenced by Malthus, tempered his theories of natural selection and species competition by means of a background and interest in natural history and botany (1994: 149; and see Pepper 1996: 183-4). These, in turn, fostered a regard for other species as "living organisms" on which many of his most prominent ideas – notably adaptation, variation, and descent – hinged (Desmond, Moore and Browne 2007: 12, 89). In *The Origin of Species*, Darwin sought, then, to reconcile struggle with balance:

> Battle within battle must be continually recurring with varying success; and yet in the long run the forces are so nicely balanced, that the face of nature remains for long periods of time uniform, though assuredly the merest trifle would give the victory to one organic being over another. (Wall 1994: 112)

Haeckel was a notable "disciple" of Darwin (see McIntosh 1985: 8; Worster 1994: 192) and so it was, therefore, Darwin's encapsulation of a creative and dialectical tension between species competition and interdependence which, from the start, defined scientific ecology.

A fundamental extension to Haeckel's conception, one that enhanced its dialectical aspect, came, however, with a shift of focus from species classification and biological systems to the physics of energy systems (Hayward 1995: 27; Simmons 1993: 22-3). This shift was encapsulated in the development of ecosystems theory defined in 1935 by Arthur Tansley and subsequently refined by scientists such as Raymond Lindeman and Eugene Odum (see Hayward 1995: 24-31; Phillips 2003: 61-5; Worster

1994: 301-4). Nowadays, ecosystems are more commonly understood as "discrete units", albeit complicated by the fact that "Ecosystem principles can be applied at all scales" (Allaby 2004: 136). As Daniel B. Botkin and Edward A. Keller put it, "The term *ecosystem* is applied to areas of all sizes, from the smallest puddle of water to a large forest or the entire global biosphere" (2005: 47). The more fundamental significance of ecosystems theory has, however, been to transform scientific ecology from relatively static, Clementsian models of biological interrelationship, to a theory in which those same relations are structured, as Tansley suggested, by the movement of energy:

> All relations among organisms can be described in terms of the purely material exchange of energy and of such chemical substances as water, phosphorus, nitrogen, and other nutrients. (see Hayward 1995: 27)

Ecosystems theory incorporated into scientific ecology the laws of thermodynamics which as a consequence became, alongside evolutionary theory, its single most important theoretical foundation. The first law, that energy is neither independently created nor destroyed, emphasises that species only receive energy in exchange with other species or abiotic (non-living) sources. Energy gets lost (as heat) but is replaced by solar energy that is transformed by plants through photosynthesis and passed along the food chain. Energy's tendency to spread out and become disordered (the second law – entropy) means, however, that ecosystems function, and are sustained, only where that energy is used efficiently. Understood in this way ecosystems theory equates to a network of energy exchange that encompasses and interconnects all the levels alluded to above, from the gene and the cell to the individual organism, communities of creatures, geographical regions (bioregions), the earth, the surrounding abiotic environment, and, one assumes, the universe. While it is this, ubiquitous nature of ecosystems theory which extends ecology from a science to a social philosophy, in order to better understand the specific social formation that might emerge from this we must first clarify the philosophy of nature to which scientific ecology gives rise.

Exacerbated by the development of ecosystems theory, ecological science has taken on an increasingly dialectical quality. The culmination of this has been what is often called 'postmodern ecology', a thesis well epitomised by Daniel B. Botkin's influential (1990) book *Discordant Harmonies*. Botkin argues that "change appears intrinsic and natural at many scales of time and space in the biosphere" (10) and, therefore, that nature, ecosystems, never remain stable. These arguments have been drawn upon by critics, including literary critics such as Garrard and Dana Phillips, to argue that there is no ultimate "truth" in nature. This, in turn, has engendered the valuable idea that humanity, rather than following an unstable nature which it cannot, by definition, understand, should seek to assume responsibility for constructing its own conceptions of nature. The theological writers David M. Lodge and Christopher Hamlin argue, for example, that contingency "magnifies the inescapability and enormity of moral decisions about how humans should live, because we must give up a concept of a nature that would guide us" (2006: 7); Garrard, likewise, that "the contingency and indeterminacy" of postmodern ecology will bring about the replacement of a "poetics of authenticity", in which we judge ourselves and human institutions against an ideal (and externalised) standard of the natural, with a "poetics of responsibility" whereby we take responsibility for the paradigms or models by which we construct our attitudes to and relationship with the rest of the natural world (2004: 178-9). A potential difficulty here, as Terry Gifford has pointed out, is that the notion that there is no "truth" in nature runs the very real risk, if taken too far, of enticing us simply to "indulge in debating deferred meanings" during which time the environmental crisis may, presumably, deepen (2006: 11). Garrard, in turn, has defended the point, asserting that by postmodern ecology he merely meant "a revitalising scepticism towards certain supposed 'truths' of popular ecological discourse" as opposed to an "enervating scepticism towards truth in general" (illustrated through Baudrillard) (2007: 23). However, while his book, *Ecocriticism*, does (in fairness) take that line, in the absence of the subtlety of Garrard's analysis, the risk remains that the idea that there is no truth in nature will engender, at worst, despair in the face of the urgent, anxiety-provoking nature of ecological crisis and, at best, the temptation to invoke Kwame Anthony Appiah's question, concerning the equally nebulous concept of 'African identity', of when to "endorse the ennobling lie?" (1992: 175).

One can, then, make sense of the debate between a postmodern and (what might be called) realist ecology by connecting it to a much longer running debate in evolutionary theory, one in which Hopkins himself participated. This debate is between a dogmatically materialist understanding of nature as continual flux which, driven by the random motivations of the gene, defies theory (arguably the stance of postmodern ecology) and a less materialist evolutionism that seeks to identify the emergence of pattern and organisation in the natural world. The second of these is a position that has been advocated, most recently, from within the complexity sciences. A good understanding of what it entails can be gathered from Brian Goodwin's book *How the Leopard Changed its Spots: The Evolution of Complexity* (1994).

Goodwin argues that there has emerged from the "sciences of complexity" a sense of unity in diversity (see 1994: xi). He makes the argument by taking issue, in the first place, with the replacement, in much evolutionary theory, of organisms by genes as the fundamental component of biological reality (ix). Conceding that "extreme diversity" is exhibited in the behaviour of genes, Goodwin nevertheless argues that their interactions are "limited so that distinctive types of order arise". Constituting, themselves, alternative levels of biological reality, these types of order include "organismic behaviour" (xi). Organisms, he suggests, "are as real, as fundamental, as irreducible, as the molecules out of which they are made" (xii). This also means that organisms are, in effect, "not random assemblages of working parts, the results of trial and error tinkering by natural selection. They reflect a deep pattern of ordered relationships" (98; and see Wheeler 2006: 72). From this Goodwin goes on to posit the existence of complex, overarching "dynamical systems" which both shape and emerge themselves from "the integrated behaviour" of different types of organisms (xi-xii).

Wendy Wheeler has equated this "deep interconnectivity" to ecological science (2006: 72). Indeed, the two-part argument that Goodwin makes to support the principle of unity in diversity – concerning the integrity of the organism and the propensity of natural phenomena to coalesce into "dynamical systems" – coincides with what has emerged as the consensus within ecological science. Kevin J. Gaston and John I. Spicer argue, for example, that, notwithstanding doubts about their categorical limitations, species are, on the whole, readily identifiable. This, in turn, leads them to posit "organismic" or species diversity as "the most fundamental element of biodiversity" (2004: 15, 6), a central tenet of ecological science seen as fundamental to the functioning of ecosystems (101-3). Townsend, Begon and Harper concur, arguing in greater detail that the number of species is the most important component of biodiversity (2003: 468) because "the activities of organisms profoundly influence the patterns of flux of chemical matter" (384). Even Botkin ultimately leaves in place the more fundamental ecological principles. These include an awareness of the dialectical interrelatedness of all species that encompasses our own (human) dependence on the continuation of complex (if never stable) ecosystems (1990: 8) and, beyond that, a recognition that humanity's consumption of 'natural' resources ought to be dictated by the limits and constraints generally referred to under the rubric of 'sustainability' (see Botkin and Keller 2005: 8).

One can overstate, that is to say, the degree of contingency that post-modern ecology imposes upon ecological theory. Saying that ecosystems are never stable is not the same thing as saying that there are no fundamental truths to which, ultimately, we have to adhere. What, on the other hand, Goodwin's assessment of evolutionary theory helps us perceive is not a return to the static organic unity of balance, or the climax ecosystem, but something closer to what Eric Wilson has described as a new organicism of "agitated processes" shaped by mutually antagonistic forces of chaos and order (2000: 4). Writing essentially about postmodern ecology, Wilson asks:

> does this mean that the universe is anarchy? If life is as much chaos and order, are there no laws, no stable structures? No, for the abyss—again—*plays*; that is, manifests itself as necessity as well as chance, follows rules as well as breaks them [...] Mere order and necessity would stiffen into rock; simple chaos and chance would dissolve into a formless mass. Imbricated, these forces generate tumultuously coherent organisms participating in a cogently turbid planet. (12-13)

This idea that chaos precedes and engenders complex reorganisation can be traced in Hopkins in the course of his own engagement with evolutionary theory. Accordingly, the middle-ground posited by the sciences of complexity – of a fundamentally dialectical but, at the same time, realist ecology – will inform my study.

One final thing to emerge from the complex evolutionism expounded by Goodwin is the basis of a transition from science to social philosophy. Goodwin argues that the recognition, on the one hand, of the organism as a distinct biological entity and, on the other, that each organism exists within an overarching dynamical system confers an understanding that we are, ourselves, "biologically grounded in relationships [...] with other species" an understanding that ought to shape human values for such relationships "operate at all the different levels of our beings as the basis of our natures" (1994: xiv). He continues:

> These are not romantic yearnings and utopian ideals. They arise from a rethinking of our biological natures that is emerging from the sciences of complexity and is leading towards a science of qualities which may help in our efforts to reach a more balanced relationship with the other members of our planetary society. (xiv)

As Mary Midgley has indicated, this argument connects to ecological philosophy via James Lovelock's 'Gaia hypothesis' (2006: 280). A paradigm that, in many ways, brings ecosystems theory to its logical conclusion, Lovelock's hypothesis is also a good example of a human construction of nature that, while necessarily metaphorical (see Lovelock 2000b: xvi; and Garrard 2004: 174), is grounded in a realist conception of the conditions that underlie human being.

Lovelock posits the notion of the earth as a single ecosystem or what he calls a "superorganism" in which "the entire range of living matter on earth, from whales to viruses, and from oaks to algae, could be regarded as constituting a single living entity [...] [with] powers far beyond those of its constituent parts" (2000: 9). He expands the complexity position by introducing the dimension which ecological theory, in the context of environmental crisis, specifically offers – a clearer sense of our own, human vulnerability. Lovelock explains that Gaia continually adapts to changing environmental conditions by manipulating the atmosphere so as to find those physical and chemical properties "optimal for life" (2000: 9). It is a process of modification which means, in the first place, that "'Earth's fragile shield' is a myth. The ozone layer certainly exists today, but it is a flight of fancy to believe that its presence is essential for life" (2000b: 84). The additional implication is that any adaptations made might leave behind those species unable to survive under new climatic or chemical conditions; in other words, that changes in environmental conditions, including those wrought by human activity, might activate adaptations "good for the biosphere as a whole but bad for man as a species" (2000: 9).

Lovelock nevertheless leaves aside the misanthropic conclusions that might have been drawn from his hypothesis by suggesting that 'Gaia' presents an "alternative" not only to the "pessimistic view of nature as a primitive force to be subdued and conquered" but also to the "equally depressing picture of our planet as a demented spaceship" (2000: 11). He rejects, that is, the conservationist notion of limitation, which envisages the earth as a closed system preferring, instead, an ecological concept of the earth as an open system. This applies the logic of ecosystems theory: that when we extract energy from fossil fuels we are not acting on an abstract nature but, rather, performing our role in activating the flow of energy around that system (Simmons 1993: 23). While, then, on the basis of our vulnerability, and mutual dependence on other living and abiotic forms, we need to think sensibly and creatively about our use of re-sources, we do have a choice, as he suggests in his later book, *The Ages of Gaia*, as to how we go about this: "If we see the world as a superorgan-ism of which we are a part [...] we could have a long time ahead of us and our species might survive for its 'allotted span'; however "so long as we continue to change the global environment against her preferences, we encourage our replacement with a more environmentally seemly species" (2000b: 239). His conclusion that "it is up to us to act personally in a way that is constructive" (2000b: 239) forms, I will now argue, the basis for an ecological social philosophy.

2. 'Deep' versus 'social' ecology

The translation of scientific ecology into a specific social philosophy has, however, been no easy task. This is mainly because ecology has been bedevilled by the dichotomy between a respect for nature's integrity which as Tim O'Riordan describes it "preaches the virtues of reverence, humility, responsibility and care" and a belief in the power of human management solutions (including scientific and political paradigms) to address ecological problems (1981: 1). A dichotomy widely recognised in ecological theory – and variously labelled romantic–rational, arcadian–imperial, ecocentric-technocentric (see, respectively, Pepper 1996: 38; Worster 1994: 2; O'Riordan 1981: 1-19) – each of these theorists perceives, as O'Riordan puts it, that "the contradictions that beset modern environmentalism reflect the divergent evolution of two ideological themes" (1) and insists upon the need for the two approaches to be reconciled.

This dichotomy has taken a particular hold on ecological theory in the shape of two divergent, sometimes antipathetic philosophies, 'deep' and 'social' ecology. The central tenet of the first, deep ecology, is a belief in the value of all nonhuman life, a belief that encompasses not only other species but also "rivers (watersheds), landscapes, ecosystems" (Naess 1995: 67). It is a philosophy which has been transcribed into Arne Naess and George Sessions' eight principles for a Deep Ecology platform the first of which states that

> The well-being and flourishing of human and non-human life on Earth have value in themselves (synonyms: intrinsic value, inherent worth). These values are independent of the usefulness of the non-human world for human purposes. (see Sessions 1995: 68)

Subsequent principles broadly assert that human needs (notably population levels) must be tailored to take into account the intrinsic value and "richness and diversity of life forms" and countenance the need for fundamental changes in the policies that govern society. The eighth principle states, for example, that "those who subscribe" to deep ecology "have an obligation directly or indirectly to try to implement the necessary changes".

Nevertheless, deep ecology has tended towards the "indirect" component of that injunction and is usually seen as concerning, in Michael Tobias' words,

> those personal moods, values, aesthetic and philosophical convictions which serve no necessarily utilitarian nor rational end. By definition their sole justification rests upon the goodness, balance, truth and beauty of the natural world, and of a human being's biological and psychological need to be fully integrated within it. (1988: vii)

As a movement deep ecology has, then, been accused of invariably displacing political action "into the realm of ethical ideals" which leaves it open to accusations of political ineffectiveness in that it fails to offer, so Timothy Luke has argued, any "concrete theory of the state, ideology, technology, or the economy" (1997: 24). In fact, even where deep ecology has engaged directly with social philosophy this has often been in the form of what might more accurately be described as preservationism, illustrated, in Luke's account, by features that include an "unusual fetishization of wilderness" and an "anachronistic fascination with pre-agricultural peoples" (1997: 33). While deep ecology clearly is of relevance to Hopkins and will form part of my reading of his work, I will now consider social ecology in more detail because part of the aim of this book will be to elucidate the neglected, complementary dimension that social ecology, as represented by Hopkins and most other major Victorian writers, offers to ecological literary studies and ecological theory in general.

Social Ecology is a predominantly American concept synonymous, albeit contentiously, with the name of Murray Bookchin (see Light 1998; Watson 1996). It will be used in this book, however, in a more general sense that will incorporate the work of other writers, including British writers such as Tim Hayward or Kate Soper, working in the largely same tradition. Difficult to pinpoint (see Watson 1996: 13-14), Bookchin argues, on the one hand, that "to separate human beings and society from nature is to dualize and truncate nature itself" (1988: 27) and, on the other, that "our image of nature is formed by the kind of society in which we live and by the abiding natural basis of all social life" (1987: 59; see also Light 1998: 6-7; Watson 1996: 14). The philosophical foundation of social ecology is, then, a belief, defined by Bookchin, in the "deep-seated continuity between nature and society" (1987: 59).[2] Social ecology is, then, dialectical but is also, in Tim Hayward's words, a "realist ontology" one in which, Hayward elaborates, "the social structure is embedded in, conditioned by, and in turn acts back upon the rest of nature; it thereby acknowledges the specificity of the social but without perpetuating the dichotomous opposition between society and nature" (1995: 48-9). In this sense, social ecology can be regarded as a philosophy that amplifies the fundamental premise of Marxist economics – that society and social structures embody the way in which we choose to organise the labour by which we extract 'natural resources' (see Hall 1977: 315) – with the idea that labour is humanity's specific contribution to the input and output of energy in and around the ecosystem.

Because of this emphasis on the continuity of nature and society, social ecology has adopted a largely pragmatic position. This centres, in particular, on two areas, the first of which is a greater faith in technology. While accepting that "mechanization" is one of the factors that has contributed to the ecological problems facing contemporary society (Clark 1997: 7), social ecologists such as Janet Biehl tend to stress that the majority of technologies are "morally neutral" (with the exception, she says, of nuclear power) and "merely magnify the consequences of the social relations in which they are embedded" (1998: 97). There is, then, a belief, highlighting social ecology's intrinsic technocentrism, that just as human inventiveness, in the shape of technologies such as birth control and food production, helped alleviate (if not absolutely) the problems Malthus foretold, so too this can be harnessed in ways consistent with ecological imperatives. Bookchin, for example, has advocated an "ecotechnology", or "people's technology", driven by sustainable sources such as sun and wind that would be small-scale, durable and non-polluting (1980: 69; 285); Biehl, speaking of renewable energy, even argues that in reducing toil, and increasing free time, technology has the

---

[2] This perspective will shape how I use the word 'nature'. Jhan Hochmann makes a distinction between 'nature' as an overriding principle – understood, by Raymond Williams, as an "inherent force that directs either the world or human beings or both" (1984: 219) – and 'nature' as a collective name for "individual plants, nonhuman animals, and elements" (see Coupe 2000: 3). Following the implications of ecosystems theory, as adapted into social ecology, that we cannot but regard humanity as embedded within 'nature', I will here employ the word to refer to Hochmann's first sense, i.e. to a 'natural economy' in which humanity is included; elsewhere, when referring to individual elements of that economy, I will distinguish, where necessary, between 'human' and 'nonhuman nature'.

potential to allow people to "participate in political life as well as enjoy rich and meaningful personal lives" (1998: 98-9).

The second element comprising social ecology's pragmatism is a focus on the political philosophies and structures that might best guarantee the "constructive" and sustainable use of technology. Consistent with a broadly Marxist understanding of natural and social economy, most social ecologists have concluded that this means some form of left-wing politics. While, as Ulrich Beck has noted (1995: 41), the perception of ecological crisis has led some critics, such as Robyn Eckersley (2004: 1-8), to re-assert the "strong hand" of the state, the more common emphasis has been on decentralised forms of government. This couples a distrust of central government with a belief that localised decision-making would be more "sensitively tailored to its natural ecosystem" (Bookchin, cited in Luke 1997: 190), an emphasis articulated, in the United States, around notions such as "eco-communitarianism" (Clark 1997: 3-4) or "libertarian municipalism" (Biehl 1998: viii).

Social ecology also adds, or possibly resurrects, a dimension that has been missing from more conventional socialism. Demonstrating a commitment to social justice (see Light 1998: 7-8; Luke 1997: 188; Watson 1996: 15), a stress which has arisen on the need for an equitable redistribution of resources is broadly equivalent to traditional socialist demands for a redistribution of wealth. Yet, advocated primarily as an alternative to conservationist solutions, this also emphasises the need to prevent future resource conflicts such as, one might suggest, the two Gulf wars. Accordingly, a concern with the use of the earth's resources, not least in the face of the development of hitherto less industrialised countries and the expansion of global consumerism, has resulted in a re-appraisal of the notion of 'quality of life' away from a focus on material prosperity usually accepted even within socialism. Shaped by books such as E. F. Schumacher's *Small is Beautiful* (1973), which posits material consumption as the "antithesis of freedom", because it increases "dependence on outside forces over which one cannot have control and [...] increases existential fear" (1974: 31), a number of influential paradigms have placed this re-conceptualisation of quality of life close to the centre of a social ecological philosophy. Including René Dumont's 1975 'Manifesto of an Alternative Culture' and Jonathan Porritt's 'Green paradigm' (1984) (see Wall 1994: 247-9, 8-9) these principles are currently embedded in the UK Green Party's 'Statement of Core Principles':

The success of a society cannot be measured by narrow economic indicators, but should take account of factors affecting the quality of life for all people: personal freedom, social equity, health, happiness and human fulfilment.

The pragmatism central to social ecology emanates, as already stated, from a realist ontology. The guiding principle, which underwrites both its ideas about the use of technology and the drive for appropriate political solutions, is sustainability. Sustainability is a slippery and contested concept around which a variety of different interpretations indicates "tensions between competing socio-political projects with different rationalities and different political implications" (Becker and Jahn 1999: 15). Deep ecologists, in particular, are often hostile to it and, in particular, to the associated concept of 'sustainable development' or 'sustainable economic development'. Raymond Rogers criticises this, for example, as an instrumental philosophy "less to do with conservation, and more to do with striving [...] to add an immortal aspect to exploitation" (1994: 169; see also Grumbine 1995: 376-96; Snyder 1995: 167-8; Worster 1995: 417-27). Yet the relationship implied here, between conservation and human resource use, also unwittingly highlights that what informs the concept of sustainability is precisely the dialectical paradigm suggested by both scientific and social ecology.

Apparent in what must surely be the most familiar definition of the term, that offered by the 1987 Brundtland Report of the UN World Commission on Environment and Development (and cited by the International Institute for Sustainable Development)

Development that meets the needs of the present without compromising the ability of future generations to meet their own needs (see http://www.iisd.org/sd/)

this sense of sustainability has been elaborated into a paradigm advanced by John Robinson and Jon Tinker. They link sustainability to three interconnected imperatives:

the ecological imperative, to remain within planetary bio-physical carrying capacity; the economic imperative, to ensure an adequate material standard of living; and the social imperative, to provide social structures, including systems of governance, that effectively propagate and sustain the values that people want to live by. (see Eichler 1999: 183)

In her own slight adjustment to that paradigm, Margrit Eichler makes an ecologically salient point concerning the primacy of the first of these: "If we were to represent this model graphically, we would draw a series of smaller overlapping circles (the human sub-systems) within a larger circle (the biosphere)" (1999: 201). Her subsequent suggestion, that, understood in this way, sustainability infers "a condition in which all human imperatives are met subject to the constraints imposed by the ecological imperative" (1999: 201), will be taken here as a succinct summary both of sustainability and social ecology itself.

I have gone into some detail because the ecological reading of Hopkins offered in this book will be based upon the two-fold definition of ecology outlined above: as a scientific philosophy constructed around ecosystems theory; and as a corresponding theory of society organised around the sustainable use of that energy. In order to ground, in turn, the related examination of Hopkins' literary practice, the remainder of this chapter will survey existing work in ecological literary theory. Drawing attention to a prevailing deep ecological bias, I will argue, in the first place, that the value of those perspectives lies partly in the development of paradigms of 'ecopoetry' which can, up to a point, be applied to Hopkins. However, given that Hopkins also went on to transcend this, in directing his poetry towards an essentially social-ecological critique, I will, in the closing section of this chapter, outline the parameters for and possibilities of an alternative 'social ecocriticism'. The initial question this raises, however, is, why turn to literature at all?

Though it has been repeatedly stated that ecology's dialectical quality presupposes multidisciplinary research, literature has tended to be neglected in such discussions. To take one example, Ted Benton and Michael Redclift, in *Social Theory and the Global Environment*, have illustrated diagrammatically how "research on the environment occurs at different points of convergence between disciplines" and demonstrated that the study of an environmental issue such as pollution brings together natural and social scientific disciplines. Yet despite identifying one of those environmental concerns as "the competing claims of 'nature' and 'nurture'", indisputably a cultural question, they find no place in their paradigm for the arts and humanities (see 1994: 11-13). An alternative model is offered, however, by Cunningham and Saigo. They argue that the concept of environment should be informed by natural, technological, social and cultural components and do incorporate the study of literature into this process. Their reason for doing so is that for "an increasing number of environmental issues, the difficulty is not to identify remedies. Remedies are now well understood. The problem is to make them socially, economically and politically acceptable" (see 1997: 4-5).

This is the argument that has most frequently been offered by literary critics themselves. The British ecocritic Terry Gifford writes, for example, that "the difference between what is politically preferable and what is politically possible indicates that the environmental crisis is actually a cultural crisis" (1995: 188). An American counterpart, Cheryll Glotfelty, claims, somewhat more dramatically, that "literature acts on people, and people act on the world" (1996: 230). Such arguments are suggestive of what James Robertson calls the "pre-political", a process of "creative thinking and dissemination of ideas" that brings about the changes in sensibility necessary before more pragmatic or political acts (1998: 76-7).

In this context such arguments have the potential to indicate the value of reconciling deep and social ecological approaches: a deep ecological assertion of the intrinsic value of (nonhuman) nature and of our psychological dependence on it might inform social ecology's more pragmatic attempts to reconceptualise what is meant by quality of life. While this will be a central rationale for studying a Victorian literary culture in which certain writers, I will argue, made precisely those links, I also wish to raise the stakes by suggesting that literature, even poetry, that most cerebral of forms, has a more pragmatic capacity to inform critique, even shape solutions, a capability which can be inferred when the environmental historian Carolyn Merchant writes that "new social concerns generate new intellectual and historical problems. Conversely, new interpretations of the past provide perspectives on the present and hence the power to change it" (1982: xvi). Both of these (directly and indirectly) pragmatic dimensions have, however, been neglected in an ecological literary studies that has so far been derived, more or less exclusively, from a deep ecological perspective.

3. Deep ecocriticism

The emergence of a literary ecocriticism in the 1990s was stimulated by the growing perception of environmental crisis. It took the specific form, in key books such as Bate's *Romantic Ecology* (1991) and Buell's *The Environmental Imagination* (1995), of a backlash against the tendencies of critical and literary theory to abstract the natural referent and/or minimize the interest shown by canonical texts in their surrounding environment (Buell 1995: 9-10). Early ecocritics were, then, often hostile to the post-structuralist or post-modernist theories regarded by the poet, essayist and farmer Wendell Berry as exemplifying a "diseased" contemporary consciousness (1983: 42). Buell complained, for example, that texts are analysed through "layers of mediation", something he illustrated by his own teaching of one of Berry's poems, "On the Hill Late at Night" as "structured" by cultural and literary conventions: the machine-in-the-garden, the neoclassical prospect poem, the Ovidian metamorphosis plot. He asked despairingly "must literature always lead us away from the physical world, never back to it?" (1995: 10-11). Bate, in *Romantic Ecology*, took issue with a 1980s new historicism marked, he wrote, by the assumption that "the economy of human society is more important than [...] 'the economy of nature'". He picked up, in particular, on Alan Liu's remark that "there is no nature except as it is constituted by acts of political definition made possible by particular forms of government" (1991: 9; 18-19). The most significant paradigm advanced to represent ecocriticism's break from prevailing literary theory has, however, been 'place'.

Designed to contest the post-modern abstraction of 'space', critics have sought to re-assert the importance of belonging in place as a pre-requisite to understanding the impact humanity is having upon the earth and as a desirable aspiration in the re-affirmation of an ecological ethic. Berry writes "Without a complex knowledge of one's place, and without the faithfulness to one's place on which such knowledge depends it is inevitable that the place will be used carelessly, and eventually de-stroyed" (cited in Buell 2001: 252-3); Freya Mathews, that a feeling of "re-enchantment [...] bound up with the recovery of place" (2000: 10) is necessary to an environmental activism that will otherwise seem to be "a chore, a burden, an abstract cause [...] best delegated to the very authorities who are in fact overseeing the regime of development that has ravaged the natural world" (2000: 8). In one of the most explicit state-ments of this position, John Elder, in *Imagining the Earth*, asserts that "to start from the soil again is the task when human culture has become impoverished" (1985: 40). Offering, thereafter, a firm foundation for the somewhat nebulous concept of place, Elder posits the notion of "Rein-habitation" to encapsulate the idea that a return to place can foster environmental or ecological awareness: "a culture harmonious with the cycles of nature must be attuned to the various characters of the regions in which people live. A natural culture is thus a localized culture" (37-8). This he illustrates through various sources in which place is largely equated to the rural landscape. These include Gary Snyder's evocation of pre-agricultural life and Berry's "self-definition [...] as a farmer" (1985: 41, 51).

This foregrounding of a sense of place as central to ecological literature has been supported by an attempt to delineate what Bate refers to as
the "historical continuity of a tradition of environmental consciousness"
(1991: 9). Bate and Buell have installed, respectively, Wordsworthian
Romanticism and its American derivative, nineteenth-century transcen-
dental nature writing, as pivotal to that tradition, a move followed by
several critics – Karl Kroeber, Laurence Coupe, James C. McKusick,
Kate Rigby – who have gone on to demonstrate, in more detail, the
environmental and/or ecological credentials of Romanticism or variously
identified post-Romanticisms. In *Green Writing*, to give the most obvious
example, McKusick offers an extended argument that "the English
Romantic poets [...] inaugurated a radically new conception of humankind's relationship to the natural world" which was then "more explicitly
developed by the American nature writers of the later nineteenth century"
(2000: 27-8). This has since been extended to encompass European
Romanticism (Rigby 2004), elements of twentieth-century critical theory
– Leavis, Adorno and Horkheimer, Heidegger – that have been seen to
represent a "complex, self-conscious kind of post-romanticism" (Coupe
2000: 62) and the identification of contemporary literary figures around
whom, it is perceived, the romantic tradition has been updated to reflect
environmental concerns. These include, in the US, Edward Abbey, Terry
Tempest Williams, Gary Snyder, A. R. Ammons (see Buell 1995: 63-4,
71-4; Scigaj 1999: xii-xiii; Tallmadge 1998: 197-8, 206-7) and, elsewhere, names such as Ted Hughes, Basil Bunting or Les Murray (see
Bate 2000).

In *The Environmental Imagination* Buell, seeking to establish his
terms, draws directly from O'Riordan's definition of "ecocentrism". In
that O'Riordan himself traces that philosophy to "the romantic transcen-
dentalists of mid-nineteenth-century America" one can understand why
Buell's "history of Thoreauvian nature writing about the American
natural environment" became an attempt "to imagine a more "ecocentric"
way of being" (1995: 1, 425). What, however, he offers is, on
O'Riordan's own terms, only one-half of ecological philosophy. While
Buell has moved on in subsequent books and has expanded his notion of
ecocriticism to incorporate more technocentric, social ecological
perspectives (see 2001, 2005), elsewhere ecocentrism continues to exert a
disproportionate influence, an influence which, furthermore, has become
fully theorised in what might be called the works of phenomenological
ecocriticism. The most prominent examples of these are David Abram's
The Spell of the Sensuous (1996) and Bate's *The Song of the Earth*

(2000). These will be examined now in detail because while they illuminate the full extent of deep ecological criticism, both also conclude, one implicitly the other explicitly, that the appropriate medium for a deep ecological literature is poetry. What emerges from that are the foundations for an ecopoetry that I will, in turn, develop and expand through Hopkins.

Abram's central argument is that we need to re-kindle, prior to a more systematic ecological realignment, an awareness of humanity's embeddedness in what he calls the "more-than-human" world. The conceptual framework he brings to this is bioregionalism, a paradigm of place which refers to the division of the earth into discrete geographical regions bounded by natural features such as watersheds, mountain ranges or the particular characteristics of a terrain. Its derivative philosophy, bioregionalism, is, in turn, the belief that political and economic units should be structured around and according to the dictates of the local bioregion (see Pepper, Webster and Revill 2003: II, 197). It "aspires", Paul Lindholdt writes, "to replace arbitrary political jurisdictions with integrated native regions; to allow watersheds, ecoregions, and larger bioregions to become the basis of analysis, planning, and resource management" (1996: 126). Lindholdt also suggests that a bioregional agenda would be the most profitable way to revive a "literary activism" that by returning our attention to "the biological processes that nourish us" might then "form the foundation of the sustainable culture" (1996: 122). Seemingly apparent in the writers who, as detailed above, make up the canon of American environmentalist nature writing a fuller elaboration of what Lindholdt is advocating is, essentially, the project that informs Abram's book.

Beginning with a critique of western culture, Abram argues that we are "deaf" and "blind" to other species and to "the animate landscapes they inhabit" (1996: 27-8).

> To shut ourselves off from these other voices, to continue by our lifestyles to condemn these other sensibilities to the oblivion of extinction, is to rob our senses of their integrity, and to rob our minds of their coherence. We are human only in contact, and conviviality, with what is not human. (22)

Seeking, then, to rediscover a lost relationship, Abram turns to phenomenological philosophy. He suggests, in the first place, that Edmund Husserl's conceptualisation of the "world of experience (the 'phenomenal' world) as a thoroughly subjective realm" offers an alternative to "the apparently mechanical world of material 'facts' [...] constructed by the objective sciences" (36). Addressing the inevitable criticism, that Husserl's concept might potentially imprison us within "solitary experience", Abram explains that what he is envisaging is an understanding of experience that would open up an "intersubjective" relationship between nonhuman "bodies and one's own" in terms of an "associative empathy" that would make us aware of "the interweaving of our individual phenomenal fields into a single, ever-shifting fabric, a single phenomenal world or 'reality'" (39).

He elaborates this by turning to Maurice Merleau-Ponty's *Phenomenology of Perception*, a book which has been seen to expand Husserl's abstract ideas into a fuller philosophy of the relationship between "the 'lived body' and its surrounding world" (see Small 2001: xxi). Through Merleau-Ponty, Abram develops the idea of experiential relationship into the more specific notion of a sensual "reciprocal exchange between the living body and the animate world that surrounds it" (73), an idea spelt out as follows:

> To touch the coarse skin of a tree is [...] to experience one's own tactility, to feel oneself touched *by* the tree [...] *We* can experience things—can touch, hear, and taste things—only because, as bodies, we are ourselves included in the sensible field, and have our own textures, sounds, and tastes. We can perceive things at all only because we ourselves are entirely a part of the sensible world that we perceive! We might as well say that we are organs of this world, flesh of its flesh, and that the world is perceiving itself *through* us. (68)

If sensual reciprocity with a "more-than-human" nature is what we need to rediscover so as to become re-attuned to the ecological condition of human existence, the secondary idea of ourselves as "organs of this world" implies, not least of all given the direction in which Abram develops his argument, that humanity has the capacity, indeed the responsibility, to communicate such an awareness.

Abram suggests that the "organic, interconnected structure" of language is an "extension or echo" of a natural world "relational and weblike in character" (84-5). He believes, therefore, that language has the capacity to reawaken us both to the "rhythms of dawning and dusk, its seasons of gestation and bud and blossom" (272-3) and to that sense of ourselves (as quoted above) as "part of the sensible world that we perceive". It is this awareness that can bring about a "recuperation of the living landscape in which we are corporeally embedded" (65). The problem, however, is that in "Western civilization language seems to deny or deaden that life, promoting a massive distrust of sensorial experience while valorizing an abstract realm of ideas hidden behind or beyond the sensory appearances" (70-2). On that basis, Abram shuts out, illuminating the deep ecological premise to his argument, any pragmatic response to the problems he describes. This includes "philosophical principles and legislative strictures" (69) as well as "huge centralized programs, global initiatives, and other 'top down' solutions [that] will never suffice to restore and protect the health of the animate earth" (268). Ultimately, Abram believes, highlighting in turn the preservationist dimension to deep ecology, that a language bioregionally "attuned […] to the contour and scale of the local landscape […] to the visual rhythms of the local topography" (140), can only be found, nowadays, in "indigenous, oral peoples" (57) a point he exemplifies through Apache storytelling and Aboriginal songlines.

While Abram conveys, therefore, a strong sense that the "reciprocity" being advocated is impossible in an apparently monolithic Western civilization, he does leave behind one clue as to where we might find such a thing. What he is seeking, Abram explains, is a language that will *"allow our words to emerge directly from the depths of our ongoing reciprocity with the world"* (56), a mode of writing that articulates "things *as we spontaneously experience them,* prior to all our conceptualisations and definitions" (56). He believes, furthermore, that this lies within what he, as did Hopkins, refers to as speech, for it is spoken words and phrases, which Abram describes as "active sensuous presences afoot in the material landscape", that embody, in contrast to the written word, natural processes. Though he is evidently referring here to "indigenous, oral peoples", the emphasis on spontaneous language coupled with the suggestion that "only if words are felt, bodily presences, like echoes or waterfalls, can we understand the power of spoken language to influence, alter, and transform the perceptual world" (89) also infers, it seems to me, a form of writing – romantic poetry – that explicitly emphasises both these things.

While poetry is not explicitly foregrounded in *The Spell of the Sensuous*, other writers have indicated the role that it might play in re-awakening a sense of our connection to the "more-than-human" world. Len Scigaj suggests that "Poets grounded in the real world are still the antennae of the race" (1999: 79). Karl Kroeber has written that "the imaginativeness essential to poetry is the primary human capability enabling us to interact in a responsible manner with our environment" (1994: 21). He regrets, though, that such a capacity rests upon rediscovering an "organic attunement to the local earth" that has more or less disappeared from Western consciousness (267). Elder has argued that the ethic of "Reinhabitation" can be learnt from our "contemporary poets of nature". For those poets

> who so often focus on a chosen landscape [...] dig [...] more deeply into the soil and into themselves. And finding their lives sustained as they grow out of the earth, they attain a reverence for nature informed by the most precise observation and familiarity. (39)

One of the more detailed outlines of poetry and ecology offered so far appears, however, in the introduction to J. Scott Bryson's edited collection *Ecopoetry: A Critical Introduction* (2002). Bryson identifies "three primary characteristics" of ecopoetry: "an ecocentric perspective that [...] leads to a devotion to specific places and to the land itself, along with those creatures that share it"; a "humility in relationships" with both human and nonhuman (although his explanation focuses only on the latter); an "intense skepticism" towards rationalism and "an overtechnologized modern world" (2002: 5-6). While the definition seeks, then, to indicate the potential poetry has to re-awaken a deep ecological consciousness, it is, nevertheless, primarily thematic and at no point offers any explanation or analysis of what ecopoetry actually does or of the devices it might employ to realise those aspirations. A fuller, more technical account of this is, however, what we get in Jonathan Bate's *The Song of the Earth* in which a phenomenological perspective, much the same as Abram's, is worked up into a fully-fledged 'ecopoetic'.

Though not without its problems, *The Song of the Earth* is, nevertheless, the most theoretically sophisticated work of British ecocriticism published so far. Lying at its heart is the belief, Bate explains elsewhere, that "the whole Enlightenment project – democratic politics and rational discourse, the political and scientific strands which have gone together – is now falling apart and alternative ways are being invoked" (see Wallace 1997). Concerned with tracing and elaborating those ways, Bate argues that prominent within what has been an ongoing "critique of Enlightenment" is the Romantic tradition. Identifying three central strands – Wordsworthian Romanticism; twentieth-century criticism; contemporary environmental literature – Bate summarises that tradition as follows:

> Romanticism declares allegiance to what Wordsworth in the preface to *Lyrical Ballads* called 'the beautiful and permanent forms of nature'. It proposes that when we commune with those forms we live with a peculiar intensity, and conversely that our lives are diminished when technology and industrialization alienate us from those forms. It regards poetic language as a special kind of expression which may effect an

imaginative reunification of mind and nature, though it also has a melancholy awareness of the illusoriness of its own utopian vision. I have re-described this broadly
conceived Romanticism as an 'ecopoetic'. (2000: 245)

The related belief that it is "poetic language", specifically, that can
reunite us to nature derives, Bate makes clear, from a romantic principle
that "poetry is something that happens at a particular time and in a
particular place" and for which "Wordsworth remains the founding
father" (205-6). He, too, is working therefore from the basis of the
importance of place, which Bate theorises through 'dwelling', an
inflection of 'place' that has been particularly prominent in British and
European ecocriticism (see also Coupe 2000; Goodbody 2007; Kerridge
2002).

Derived initially from Heidegger, the use of "dwelling" in an ecocritical context has, to a large extent, been stimulated by Robert Pogue
Harrison's book *Forests: The Shadow of Civilization* (1992). In his
critique of our alienation from nature, Harrison argues that "for reasons
that remain altogether obscure, western civilization has decided to
promote institutions of dislocation in every dimension of social and
cultural existence" (1992: 198). Framing this with reference to Vico's
"order of human institutions" – which begins with the forest, where
humanity, after the ice age, initially settled as a domestic agricultural
species and which continues through the hut, village, city, academy,
economy, media, ideology – Harrison suggests that these institutions have
incrementally brought about an "oblivion of the meaning of dwelling"
(see 11, 197-9). Bate draws on Harrison because in the attempt to
recapture an understanding of what, for humans, it is to dwell in place, he
returns, like Abram, to the question of human language.

For Harrison the concept of dwelling articulates not the desire to
return to nature, in any simplistic sense, but an innate human condition
characterised by estrangement from the earth (265). This "estrangement",
he argues

manifests itself in the phenomenon of language, which does not belong to the order of
nature. Language is a differential, a standing-outside of nature, an *ecstasis* that opens
a space of intelligibility within nature's closure. Understood not merely as the linguistic capacity of our superior intelligence but as the transcendence of our manner of
being, language is the ultimate "place" of human habitation. Before we dwell in this
or that locale, or in this or that province, or in this or that city or nation, we dwell in
the *logos*. (200)

While, then, we cannot return to nature, because we are always estranged from it, the language in which we dwell nevertheless "opens a space of intelligibility" that transcends "our manner of being" and in which we can, therefore, understand or articulate, for example, the intrinsic value of other species or our mutual dependence on them. In relation to the latter, Harrison makes it clear that this remains a dialectical relationship by recovering an original meaning in which "logos" refers not only to "language" but also to "relation". He suggests that while "we dwell not in nature but in the relation to nature" (201), language nevertheless

> binds, gathers, or relates. It binds humans to nature in the mode of openness and difference. It is that wherein we dwell and by which we relate ourselves to this or that place. Without *logos* there is no place only habitat [...] no dwelling, only subsisting. In short, *logos* is that which opens the human abode on the earth. (200)

Notwithstanding the fact that that "estrangement" is often embodied in the technological or rationalist modes of language which enframe nature, Harrison argues that it is in language, in the 'logos' within which we dwell, where we might also find alternative institutions of civilisation that can offset impending ecological "oblivion" (201). Inferring from this a potential role for poetry, Bate develops the idea further by connecting it to Heidegger's notion of *poiesis*.

He begins with Heidegger's distinction between a pre-modern, Greek understanding of technology and a modern (i.e. post-Enlightenment) thinking which has transformed technology into a mode that converts 'nature' into something other than itself. The first, Bate explains, was designed to reveal the presence of and truths about things in nature. Encapsulating a sense of wonder it represented "one of the distinctively human ways of being-in-the-world". To illustrate the second Bate cites Heidegger's comparison between a bridge (which does not alter the essential being of a river) and a hydroelectric plant that transforms that river into a water reserve. Suggesting that modern technology transforms, reorders, or as Heidegger puts it, "enframes" nature, Bate argues that the "history of technology" has become "a history of the loss of wonder, a history of disenchantment" (2000: 253-6).

Heidegger, as Bate goes on to point out, sought, however, to reincorporate *physis* – "the arising of something from out of itself", and originally a mode of revelation encompassed by technology – back into human understanding by means of the (connected) act of the artist (or artisan) "bringing-forth into presence". In Heidegger's own words "There was a time when the bringing-forth of the true into the beautiful was called *techne*. The *poiesis* of the fine arts was also called *techne*" (257). Suggesting from this that "poetically man dwells on this earth", Heidegger was arguing that while technology is one distinctive mode of human existence, language is another. Therefore, if technology has alienated us from the natural world then perhaps language holds the potential to "effect an imaginative reunification of mind and nature".

What Bate does, then, is connect Heidegger's belief that "poetically man dwells on this earth" to Harrison's elaboration of language as the specific human mode of dwelling. He goes on, therefore, to offer poetry as the particular "institution" by which we can, once again, "relate ourselves" to place and a renewed sense of our ecological relationship with nature even arguing, in the words with which he ends the book, that poetry can offset the "oblivion" of humanity or nature: "if poetry is the original admission of dwelling, then poetry is the place where we save the earth" (283). In conceptualising this, and in answering his own question, "What are Poets For?" Bate offers the most detailed outline yet as to what might constitute an ecopoetic.

Bate establishes three governing principles. Considered in turn, these are as follows:

- that poetry is activated by the phenomenological moment at which nature impacts upon the human consciousness, a moment it then attempts to re-convey;
- that the recreation of the phenomenological moment is rendered possible by the predominately aural quality of poetry.
- that this aurality offers a mode of writing juxtaposed to other – descriptive, representational or rhetorical – modes all of which attempt to enframe nature.

Through Wordsworth Bate suggests that poetry is activated by the desire "to reanimate the [phenomenological] moment" and of "reawakening the momentary wonder of unconcealment" (258). It is a view also closely related, as he makes clear, to that of Gary Snyder:

> the work of poetry […] has to do with bringing us back to our original, true natures from whatever habit-molds that our perceptions, that our thinking and feeling get formed into. And bringing us back to original true mind, seeing the universe freshly in eternity, yet any moment. (Snyder 1980: 72)

Bate substantiates the paradigm, however, by referring back, like Abram, to phenomenology. Drawing in particular on the work of Gaston Bachelard he suggests that it is the peculiar quality of poetry that it "reverberates" on the individual consciousness, producing, in Bachelard's words, a "duality of subject and object [that] is iridescent, shimmering, unceasingly active in its inversions" (154). In doing this we are returned to the phenomenological moment, the encounter with other nature which, in romantic poetry at least, is seen to activate the writing. Bate summarises this as follows:

> The consciousness which experiences the poetic image becomes 'naïve' in Schiller's sense of being at one with, not self-reflexively apart from, the world. Through the poetic image, oneness with the world can be experienced directly rather than yearned for elegiacally in nostalgia [...] or the imagined good life of primitivism. (154)

An even more specific sense of the way in which poetry does this is elaborated by means of reference to Paul Ricoeur's essay 'Writing as a Problem for Literary Criticism and Philosophical Hermeneutics'.

For Ricoeur, Bate explains, the problem with most writing is that "it detaches the 'said' from the act of 'saying', the 'meaning' of an utterance from the 'event' of an utterance" (249). In this removal we are denied any possibility that language, as Abram puts it, can act as an "extension or echo" of the natural world. Sharing that perspective, Bate refers to Ricouer's positing of the need for an alternative, non-descriptive mode of writing that, in Ricoeur's words, "liberates a power of reference to aspects of our being in the world which cannot be said in a direct descriptive way". It is only through such a language, Bate suggests, that "we can start to imagine what it might be like to live differently upon the earth" (250-1).

Bate finds this language in poetry because of its predominately aural quality. The foundation for that argument lies in a reference, earlier in the book, to Merleau-Ponty's essay, 'Eye and Mind'. Merleau-Ponty had written "We speak of 'inspiration' and the word should be taken literally. There really is inspiration and expiration of Being" (166). What this means, Bate explains, is that "the poet breathes in the being of the world" and in words, rhythm, metre – that is, in the spoken sound – the poet "expires" that being. He illustrates this quality, which belongs to poetry alone, by means of the scholar Ludwig von Pigenot's re-arrangement of some lines of prose into poetry (see 258-61). Bate asserts that

> In lovely blue the steeple blossoms with its metal roof. Around which drift swallow cries, around which lies most loving blue

is not the same as

> In lovely blue the steeple blossoms
> With its metal roof. Around which
> Drift swallow cries, around which
> Lies most loving blue.

This, he argues, is because of the differentiation – in the space on the page and in the pause "for breath in […] reading" – between poetic and prosaic modes. "The white of the page or the second of silence" enfold us, we enter those spaces by dwelling poetically finding "that they are not only 'lovely' but 'loving'" (260-1). It is this aural quality – which conveys rather than describes, and which demands, in turn, "a mode of reading that is a listening rather than an interrogation" (154) – that, for Bate, enables verse-making to be "language's most direct path of return to the oikos, the place of dwelling" (76). He suggests that metre, in particular, is "an answering to nature's own rhythms, an echoing of the song of the earth itself" (76) which in its quite literal act of enveloping brings about a fresh understanding of our place on the earth as a whole.

Returning to Heidegger's terms, Bate asserts then that poetry, more or less uniquely in contemporary culture, has the capacity both of *poiesis* – "bringing-forth into presence" – and *physis* – "the arising of something from out of itself", an alignment necessary in order to re-awaken us both to the integrity of nonhuman nature and to our interrelationship with it, a point reiterated in a series of statements:

> By disclosing the being of entities in language, the poet lets them be. That is the special, the sacred role of the poet.

> the poet can unconceal the being of things … the *poet* more than anyone else, because our distinctive being – our *Dasein* ["mode of being in the world"] – is in language, and the poet is the guardian, the treasurer, the primary maker of language. (258, 272)

This idea that poetry "lets them [other beings] be" because it conveys rather than explains or enframes nonhuman phenomena – that, as Heidegger puts it, "poetry is the original admission of dwelling because it is a presencing not a representation, a form of being not of mapping" (262) – brings us to the third and final principle of Bate's "ecopoetic", the rejection, like Abram, of technocentric modes. This focuses on two aspects in particular: aesthetic convention and pragmatic, politicised writing.

Bate's rejection of aesthetic convention comes by means of an extended comparison of writings on the Wye Valley by Wordsworth and the artist and writer William Gilpin (see 139-52). For Gilpin, in formulating the principles of the picturesque, the landscape was there to be processed, organised and mastered, something which Bate, via Adorno, compares to the modern day tourism industry. Wordsworth, in contrast, is described as having eschewed the scientific, the researched and the reductive. So, in composing his poem, 'Lines written a few miles above Tintern Abbey' Wordsworth neither took out his notebook nor wrote anything down until he returned. As a result, the poem was, Bate suggests, impressionistic, written in a "meditative spirit" (148-9), and Wordsworth, by this understanding, represents "a way of imagining the world that begins in feeling and not in judgement", and which, in "submitting [...] to an inner vision [...] enables one to 'see into the life of things'" (139, 146). This process, which Bate reads, specifically, as a necessary correction to the "Cartesian error" by which "the eye was master of the heart" (141), appears to rule out any notion that ecopoetry might articulate, and therefore help us understand, scientific or other rational modes of describing nature, a distinction which, as we shall see, runs contrary to Hopkins' practice.

Bate similarly rejects any notion of a politicised poetry. In *Romantic Ecology* he had argued that it was "time for literary criticism to politicise itself in a new way" and that "ecology has to be an attitude of mind before it can be an effective set of environmental policies" (1991: 4, 83). To the extent that any of this appears in *The Song of the Earth* it is in relation to bioregionalism and to the description of Wordsworth as a poet whose sense of nation emanates from a "tradition of local defence of liberty" (218-19). Seemingly mindful now of Heidegger's Nazi affiliations and of Anna Bramwell's link between deep ecological values – organicism, land-based self-sufficiency, idealisation of the peasantry – and an equivalent flirtation with Nazism by British nature writers between the wars (Lawrence, Tolkein, Henry Williamson) Bate retreats instead to the view that "there is no straightforward path from scientific to political ecology" (40) and thereby restricts ecopoetry's role to, at best, a prompting of Robertson's "pre-political" changes in sensibility. He concludes, in several similar quotes, that "ecopoetics must concern itself with consciousness. When it comes to practice, we have to speak in other discourses" (266); or, that

> Ecopoetry is not synonymous with writing that is pragmatically green: a manifesto for ecological correctness will not be poetic because its language is bound to be instrumental, to address questions of doing rather than to 'present' the experience of dwelling. We will, then, need to hesitate over the complex of intersections and contradictions between ecopoetics and eco-politics. (42)

The value of the ecopoetic set out by Bate in *The Song of the Earth* will be demonstrated later where it will be used as the foundation for that constructed around Hopkins. Yet ultimately that ecopoetic, and the arguments by which it is formed, are weakened by the limitations of the deep ecological agenda which has shaped it (see 138-9). Including a somewhat foreshortened view of romanticism itself, which I have discussed in Chapter Two and elsewhere (see Parham 2008: 29-30), this encompasses, for example, the fact that having supposedly disregarded enframed forms of knowledge, Bate nevertheless draws upon outdated versions of ecological science, deploying, for instance, the largely discredited notion of the climax ecosystem to argue, via Snyder, that poetry, is "an especially efficient system for recycling the richest thoughts and feelings of a community" (246-7). Correspondingly, having skilfully conceptualised his ecopoetic as "pre-political", which would allow (in some circumstances) for the implication that "consciousness" can lead to "practice", the uncompromising position taken on enframing makes it difficult to envisage this ever actually happening. All of which leaves Bate's approach at the impasse more or less acknowledged when he talks of the romantic tradition's "melancholy awareness of the illusoriness of its own utopian vision". The inadequacies of this otherwise valuable approach will now be addressed by means of mapping out an alternative, social-ecological literary criticism.

4. Towards a social (and humanist) ecocriticism

Towards the end of the last decade Louise Westling identified two central tasks facing an 'Ecocriticism for the Millennium': to respond to accusations of naïve idealism by developing complex, theoretical approaches to the representation of nature; and to establish a dialogue with other, more emancipatory discourses so as to enhance ecocriticism's pragmatic and political dimension (see Parham 1999: 123). Each of these have now begun to happen and, taking each in turn, we can see that such developments form the basis for a social ecocriticism that might complement, rather than counteract, the deep ecological agenda which has prevailed so far.

One of the problems with earlier ecocritical work was, as Westling writes elsewhere, a tendency to presume "unmediated access to an essentialized natural world" (2002: 2). Such a tendency has gradually been addressed by attempts to conceptualise nature in ways that appear consistent with ecological imperatives, an attempt which, in the UK at least, has been informed by the philosopher Kate Soper's book *What is Nature?* (1995) (see, for example, Coupe 2000; Ryle 2002; and, also, Love 2003: 7-8).

Critical of sub-Foucauldian positions, Soper argues that we must acknowledge the "extra-discursive reality of a nature [...] which is *not* a cultural formation" (1995: 8). She advocates, like Hayward

> a 'realist' perspective [in which] nature refers to limits imposed by the structure of the world and by human biology upon what it is possible for human beings to be and do, at least if they are to survive and flourish. It is an order of determinations that we infringe only at the cost of a certain 'loss' of self or 'alienation' from what is true to ourselves, and in this sense provides the essential gage by which we may judge the 'liberating' or 'repressive' quality of human institutions and cultural forms, including those through which we relate most directly to the environment and other creatures. (1995: 34)

While arguing then, in relation to this, that a "realist position" offers "the only responsible basis from which to argue for any kind of political change" (8), Soper nevertheless makes it clear that it is only possible to apprehend nature, and the grounds of our (human) incorporation into it, by means of human concepts and constructions (8). "It is inevitable", she writes, "that our attitudes to nature will be 'anthropocentric' in certain respects since there is no way of conceiving our relations to it other than through the mediation of ideas about ourselves" (13; see also Dobson 2000: 51). Such ideas have gradually begun to filter into ecocritical work due to a recognition that literature is one of the key places where we mediate ideas about nature, self and society.

The most radical articulation of this approach comes in Dana Phillips' book *The Truth of Ecology: Nature, Culture, and Literature in America*. Asserting that phenomenological "purity" is a "fiction" because knowledge supposedly derived from "perception", "experience" or "awareness" is always, inevitably, socially and culturally constructed (2003: 215), he argues not only that all artistic visions or expressions are supplemented by "thought" (2003: 218) and by the theories or enframings – scientific, literary or political – that inform and shape that thought but that theories, paradigms, and structures are, themselves, a distinctive part of human nature. "Our sense of things is, and will remain, analytic", Phillips writes (2003: 15), an argument that offers the most outright defence yet of the type of literature, such as Hopkins', where a depiction of nonhuman nature has first been underpinned by an intellectual process of conceptualising what is meant by 'nature' itself.

A further sense of why, in this context, literature is important is set out in Gifford's 1996 essay "The Social Construction of Nature". Making clear and conscious advances towards critical theory, in the wake of Bate's *Romantic Ecology*, Gifford seeks to legitimate the view that literature, in addition to its capacity to foster an ecocentric love of nature, might also inform the rational, conceptual thought processes (i.e. the technocentric modes) by which we can understand our place in, and live more productively with, the rest of nature.

Gifford returns, initially, to the Alan Liu statement, quoted by Bate, that "there is no nature" but suggests, in a more conciliatory manner, that while Liu was in fact correct to emphasise that nature is always mediated he was "wrong to deny the general physical presence that is one side of that mediation" (1996: 32). In this connection he makes the point that ecological theory challenges the postmodern belief that there are no longer any "grand narratives" by asserting the real facts, such as "growth and decay", that govern nature (1996: 32). Yet Gifford concedes, like Soper, that concern for the environment must be underpinned by a conception both of what nature is and of "which notions are most useful to our survival and that of the planet" (1996: 32). It is, he concludes, this process of establishing "which notions are most useful" that might best be informed by literature and he offers, as an example, a contemporary, more ecologically aware nature poetry epitomised by writers such as Sorley Maclean or Seamus Heaney (1996: 33). This conjunction, between the realism that lies at the heart of ecology and the constructivism required in order for us to understand how we might live within a dialectical natural economy, is one that has now been broadly accepted within ecological literary studies:

> [we must avoid] reductionism at the level of formal representation, such as to compel us to believe either that the text replicates the object-world or that it creates an entirely distinct linguistic world. (Buell 1995: 13)

> ... green studies does not challenge the notion that human beings make sense of the world through language, but rather the self-serving inference that nature is nothing more than a linguistic construct. (Coupe 2000: 3)

> The challenge for ecocritics is to keep one eye on the ways in which 'nature' is always in some ways culturally constructed, and the other on the fact that nature really exists, both the object and, albeit distantly, the origin of our discourse. (Garrard 2004: 10)

Westling's second point, concerning the need to establish a dialogue with other emancipatory discourses, extends into the more general principle that ecocriticism requires a pragmatic, political direction. This has been suggested by several critics. Michael P. Cohen argues, for example, that too much emphasis, within ecocriticism, has been placed on personal narratives and individual enlightenment to the detriment of any real attempt to confront the socio-political factors – global capitalism, the ideology of consumerism – that have brought about ecological problems (see 2006: 16; and Cohen 2004: paras. 63-8); Gifford talks of the need to translate "empathy" into "responsibility" and into both an individual and collective activism (2006: 12). Perhaps the most sustained exploration of how this more pragmatic dimension might be developed occurs, however, in Glen Love's 2003 book *Practical Ecocriticism*.

From the very start of the book Love consciously places himself in opposition to the deep ecocritical approaches described above. We see this, for example, in an emphatic assertion that "Environmental issues *can* respond to rational means of solution" (16). *Practical Ecocriticism* is particularly insightful, however, in that Love connects the need for pragmatism to Westling's first point, the need to conceptualise what we mean by nature; indeed, he takes this further by indicating one of the main sources to which we might turn. "The key to this new awareness", Love suggests, "is the life sciences" (2003: 6, 8). Having made the point he then advocates a criticism which "acknowledge[s] the biological sciences as not just another human construction" and which seeks to tie knowledge of science to a recognition of the "human connection with nature and the rest of organic life" (8). While one might question the degree of faith Love places in biological science (see 166) he does nevertheless succeed in establishing a model for the type of criticism that can transcend philosophical investigation and help move us towards a more "pragmatic awareness" (a model which, in its specifics, is very similar to the 'Victorian ecology' outlined in Chapter Two). If one of the aims, then, of Love's "practical ecocriticism" is to engender a specific, political ecocriticism, a clearer indication of the types of literature that might nourish this can be formulated through a paradigm highly appropriate to what is being proposed, John Clark's notion of a "social ecology of the imagination".

In his article 'A Social Ecology' Clark argues that "every social institution contains organizational, ideological, and imaginary aspects". The first, he explains, refers to "a mode of organizing" people, groups, activities and practices and to the utilization of "material means for economic ends". The second relates to the "mode of discourse, and [...] system of ideas" by which an institution "understands itself and seeks to legitimate its ends and activities". The third is what he calls a "system of socially shared images by which the society represents itself to itself" (1997: 20). While social ecologists must investigate all three it is to the last of these that literature can, in all likelihood, contribute.

Clark goes on to explain that this "social ecology of the imagination" should be comprised, primarily, of two components – a "concrete and experiential investigation of the existing imaginary" and the offering of contributions to "the creation of an ecological imaginary" (1997: 20). Regarding the latter, essentially the possibility that literature might nourish an imagination of the sustainable society, one example would be so-called "ecotopian fiction", books such as Ernest Callenbach's *Ecotopia*, Kim Stanley Robinson's *Pacific Edge* or Marge Piercy's *Woman on the Edge of Time* (see Garforth 2002). Another might be earlier, historical equivalents of such work, including perhaps the vision of more sustainable, communitarian societies offered by Victorian critics and writers such as John Ruskin, John Stuart Mill or William Morris. While such examples demonstrate the existence and possibility of a literature that can guide us pragmatically towards "the creation of an ecological imaginary" (something also seen in Hopkins' work), it is probably the case that the majority of literature (and literary criticism) will feed into the other clause of Clark's paradigm, the "concrete and experiential investigation of the existing imaginary". An example of this might be literature that charts or describes the impact of processes such as deforestation or pollution, for instance (if we take the British context) Brian Clarke's 2002 novel *The Stream*. However, while damage to nonhuman nature is, it goes without saying, a central concern of ecocritical work, such an approach would already be covered by deep ecological criticism. What, specifically, a social ecological perspective would offer is an "investigation" that would explore, through literary representation, the impact of non-sustainable practices on human and nonhuman alike. It takes, that is, the first of these as a legitimate object of analysis in what might then be regarded as an extension from a social to a humanist ecocriticism.

The possibility of a humanist ecocriticism has not, to my knowledge, been outlined anywhere else. An indication of what it might entail can, however, be garnered from two brief incursions by the British critic Martin Ryle. Writing in the journal *Green Letters* Ryle has noted the dominance, in ecological literary studies, of writing that celebrates the "special places in which we can enjoy an intense and memorable encounter with the natural world". He suggests, however, that if we wish "to relate eco-critical work to green politics in its widest sense" we need to acquire "critical, as well as affirmative, knowledge" which means looking at representations of the "negative reality of destructive economic and social forces and practices" (2000: 11-12). How this might be done becomes clearer when, in a later piece, Ryle suggests that "ecocriticism, like green politics, must be centrally concerned with the historical development of 'human nature'" (2002: 13) and when, in that piece, he also suggests that such a development might be traced through representations of the human body.

Gretchen Legler has pointed out that very little ecocritical work has been done on the body because, she argues, the nature writing which has dominated so far is not "self-conscious of body politics". In attempts to render themselves "pure", Legler continues, nature writers have paid little attention to "the political specificity of their [own] *being* in the natural world" (1998: 72). Abram, of course, does describe a sensual "reciprocal exchange between the living body and the animate world that surrounds it" (73) but has no apparent interest in exploring the social dimension to this. Some discussion of the body has appeared fleetingly in American 'environmental justice' ecocriticism, for example in Terrell Dixon's analysis of Jane Smiley's *A Thousand Acres* and Don DeLillo's *White Noise* (1996), Buell's notion of "toxic discourse", by which he means literary representations of human health in a toxic environment (see 2001: 42-54), and in Rachel Stein's work on the depiction of lead poisoning in Barbara Neely's novel *Blanche Cleans Up* (see 2002: 201-7). Yet these primarily descriptive examples have occurred in lieu of any real theorisation of what might be gained from ecocritical research in this area.

One way in which such work might be theorised would be through recent cultural studies research on the body which, having been described as a response to the 'linguistic turn' that seeks to return a degree of materiality to cultural theory (see Howes 2005: 1), already has implicit parallels to ecocriticism. Encompassing, to offer some of the more prominent examples, the work of the French philosopher Michel Serres, the historian Roy Porter's book *Flesh in the Age of Reason*, and the development of biosemiotics, a field which "presupposes the axiomatic identity of the semiosphere with the biosphere" (see Cobley 2001: 164; Wheeler 2006: 19), a particularly useful argument in this context is offered, again, by Soper.

Consistent with a "realist" perspective, Soper takes issue, in *What is Nature?*, with the notion of the human body as a cultural construction (6-7). Arguing that cultural theorists often "refuse to allow that there is any natural dimension at all to human subjectivity" she suggests that this has resulted in a denial of "our biological dependency upon the eco-system" (1995: 129-30). In a parallel to Bate, she even cites as evidence of such tendencies the philosopher Susan Bordo's remark that "there *is* no 'natural' body" (1995: 129) in response to which Soper develops an argument about the corporeal that is in keeping with the alignment between constructivist and realist dimensions.

Soper argues that the body is not so much constructed as transmuted (136), a process of change and modification that is, simultaneously, both naturally and socially conditioned. There is, on the one hand,

> nature as matter, as physicality: that 'nature' whose properties and causal processes are the object of the biological and natural sciences [...] and whose forces and causal powers are the necessary condition of every human practice, and determine the possible forms it can take. (132-3)

On the other, there is a society and culture that "goes to work and inscribes its specific and mutable gender text" on this "extra-discursive and biologically differentiated body" (133). Taking our lead from this, what should form the basis for ecocritical research in this area is an examination of the body's literal incorporation of the dialectical relation-ship between self, society and nature and, in particular, an examination of the extent to which the sustainability or otherwise of that society is written upon the body. This, as the environmental justice ecocriticism clearly implies, is an awareness that could be fostered by literature (see Adamson, Evans and Stein 2002).

The question this, in turn, raises is what genres, periods or literary modes might best illustrate a proposed social-humanist approach. Ryle's suggestion here is to incorporate within ecocriticism sources like the "classic texts of fictional realism and naturalism" (2000: 12). In fact, a social ecology of the imagination would open up several potential areas of research which might include postcolonial literature (see Campbell and Somerville 2007; DeLoughrey, Gosson and Handley 2005), the urban novel (including Victorian novelists such as Dickens, Gaskell, or Gissing) and more politicised forms of travel writing (Wilfred Thesiger or Iain Sinclair). All of these contrast with the major preoccupations of ecocriti-cism thus far – prose non-fiction nature writing (primarily in the US) and Romantic (or post-Romantic) nature poetry – by foregrounding the impact of inequitable, often unsustainable political economies on human communities and individual human beings (see Parham 2008: 34-6). However, the only detailed illustration of this as yet has been a discussion by Ryle of Thomas Hardy's *The Woodlanders*.

Hardy has generally been seen, ecocritically speaking, from a bioregionalist perspective, as a writer who encapsulates the notion that culture should be "intimately related to physical setting" and to a belonging in place (see Bate 2000: 13). Yet there is also a deeper recognition in his work that human nature belongs to, and is transmuted by, nature and society alike. One sees both, for example, in the character of Elizabeth-Jane in *The Mayor of Casterbridge* whose face is "possessed" both of an "under-handsomeness […] struggling to reveal itself through the provisional curves of immaturity, *and* the casual disfigurements that resulted from the straitened circumstances of their lives" (1993: 23 (my italics)). Ryle's analysis of Marty South, in *The Woodlanders*, develops this perspective further.

Noting the impact of her (semi-skilled) labour in coppice work and forestry on the surrounding environment Ryle highlights in addition the alterations that same labour has effected upon Marty's body:

> The young woman laid down the bill-hook for a moment and examined the palm of her right hand which, unlike the other, was ungloved, and showed little hardness or roughness about it. The palm was red and blistering, as if her present occupation were as yet too recent to have subdued it to what it worked in. As with so many right hands born to manual labour, there was nothing in its fundamental shape to bear out the physiological conventionalism that gradations of birth show themselves primarily in the form of that member. Nothing but a cast of the die of destiny had decided that the girl should handle the tool; and the fingers which clasped the heavy ash haft might have skilfully guided the pencil or swept the string, had they only been set to do it in good time. (see 2002: 19-20)

Ryle suggests that while "the social uses to which the hand is put will always 'subdue' nature" so, too, the hand itself has been "subdued, within the division of labour" (not least in the description of it as "red and blistering") indicating, in turn, that Marty herself is "constrained and the development of her character limited by her subordinate economic place (a fateful social contingency which has nothing to do with her 'nature')". While he adds here the possibility of an emancipatory political dimension, in acknowledging the potential "to transcend any particular subduing", what we find, all the same, is a useful notion – of Marty's body as an index of a society that "subdues" human and nonhuman alike (20-1). While it is this approach I will apply in the discussion of Hopkins' social verse in Chapter Five, it should also be remembered that what I am really seeking to do is to bring the two approaches – deep and social ecology – together. As part of this, I wish to suggest that the notion of a pragmatic, political ecocriticism might also be extended so as to encompass poetry.

While poetry has already been acknowledged as significant in terms of literature's ability to shape an ecological awareness, it has largely been associated, as we have seen, with the deep ecological component of that philosophy. In virtually all of the most prominent conceptions ecopoetry has been connected, explicitly by Bryson and Bate, to nature poetry (see 2002: 2). One book which does, however, offer an alternative approach is Len Scigaj's *Sustainable Poetry: Four American Ecopoets*. For while Scigaj also works from Merleau-Ponty, he nevertheless offers a paradigm that broadly succeeds in attempting to reconcile phenomenological philosophy with social critique.

Scigaj begins by establishing a theory he calls 'référance', designed, as its name suggests, as an alternative to Derrida's 'différance' (broadly interpreted as the deconstruction of presence in language and the absence of the original referent) (1999: 35-8). Accepting that our conceptions of nature are culturally constructed to some extent, Scigaj states, nevertheless, that Merleau-Ponty identified a pre-reflective stage of cognition – prior to the intervention both of the egocentric 'I' and cultural convention. On that basis he argues, like Bate, that the initial stimulus to our representations of nature, such as the writing of a poem, emanates from a pre-reflective moment of response to natural phenomena: "Language and nature under *reference* constitute two opposite but interdependent systems, with the former (language) only temporarily deferring the latter, nature, where language had its origin" (38).

Scigaj goes on to suggest that one way in which to address "the worldwide degradation of planetary ecosystems" would be to re-assert the "relationship of poetic language to its referential source" (17). This begins, in the first place, with Scigaj going even further in incorporating phenomenology than do Abram or Bate. In what is a reminder of Harrison's view that language is a mark of our "estrangement" from nature Scigaj suggests that language is, indeed, a limited system (xiv) unable to fully describe or explain "the ecological processes of nature" (11). He regards this, however, as a positive thing because it means that, rather than being dominated by the human mind, "nature retains its autonomy" (80-1): "the reader's gaze is thrust beyond language back into the less limited natural world that language refers to, the inhabited place where humans must live in harmony with ecological cycles" (38). Nevertheless, though language functions imperfectly it remains, he argues, the "most flexible tool humans have created to convey their experiences and perceptions" (80). At this point, Scigaj returns to the constructivist dimension that is the other side of référance settling, as he does so, on a poetic version of Love's "practical ecocriticism".

Attending to what he sees as the dualistic nature of poetry, Scigaj, citing Horace, argues, in his preface, that literary criticism must "consider both the *dulce* and the *utile*, the aesthetic delight *and* the practical instruction value of literature" (xvi). He draws attention to the dilemma this creates for "Environmental poets and ecopoets" in suggesting that they subscribe to the twin truths that while "the Eye altering alters all" (Blake, "The Mental Traveller") at the same time "where there is no vision, the people perish (Proverbs 29: 18)" (22). Consequently, Scigaj arrives at the view, due to the pressing nature of the impending environmental crisis (which he proves with a plethora of statistics), that poetry simply must engage pragmatically.

Scigaj offers, therefore, much the same argument as Glen Love when he suggests that ecopoetry should draw upon a knowledge of environmental science so as to help us "understand, respect, and cooperate with the laws of nature that sustain us" (81). Scigaj sees as emerging from this a poetry which, in distinctly ecological terms, "persistently stresses human cooperation with nature conceived as a dynamic, interrelated series of cyclic feedback systems" (37). Though rejecting any conception of poetry as "propaganda or taking stands on particular social issues" (30), Scigaj nevertheless concludes that "sustainable poetry" must "contain an activist dimension [so as] to foreground political acts of environmental degradation and degraded planetary ecosystems" (21). What is needed, he asserts, is a "biocentric [and] politicised poetry that responds to global environmental degradation" (9).

Scigaj's paradigm of a "sustainable poetry" that is simultaneously phenomenological and pragmatic meets the aspiration for a criticism that unites deep and social ecology. It is, in this context, the ideal model through which to interpret Hopkins' work. For Hopkins modified, without ever abandoning, a deep ecological poetic, largely conforming to that envisaged by Bate, by means of adding a conceptual and pragmatic dimension. This becomes apparent in his nature writing where his own scientific awareness engenders what can be regarded as a proto-ecological poetry. Yet in turning to write about the impact of society Hopkins then extends the scope of a social ecology of the imagination by drawing on phenomenological characteristics seemingly available only to poetry, in verse which, in its emphasis on sound, enables us to *feel* the modifications being wrought, on nonhuman and human nature, by an unsustainable Victorian political economy. He draws, that is, on the full resources of poetry offering an all too rare example of a writer who, in the reconciliation of deep and social ecological perspectives, helps bring about an ecological awareness in its fullest sense. His ability to do this also came about, however, as a result of the context in which he was writing – a post-Romantic Victorian literary culture which had sought itself to bring a pragmatic dimension to the love of nature it had inherited. It is with this that the analysis outlined below begins.

5. Outline of the book

Highlighting the parallels between Victorian literary culture and contemporary ecological thinking, and a proximity to its origins which gave that culture a distinctively ecological flavour, my second chapter lays out the parameters for a 'Victorian ecology'. I will argue, first, that literary figures of that period were interested in precisely those elements, evolutionary theory and thermodynamics, that combined to form scientific ecology and, correspondingly, that they were closely connected to the emergence of an "early green politics". It will then be argued that while these Victorian writers shared with contemporary social ecology the perception of risk, responding with what Marshall Berman has identified as a "dynamic and dialectical" approach to modernity, they also share with us a critical problem. For at "a time when the assumptions of both Descartes and Wordsworth have to be doubted" (Johnson 1968: 12-13) there arose an ambivalent attitude towards their Romantic inheritance and the ways in which the romantic sensibility might be adapted to pragmatic ends, that is echoed in contemporary ecological thought. Suggesting that a Victorian literary ecology which displayed both an anticipation of ecosystems theory and of the politics of sustainability offers a historical precedent to the task of attempting to reconcile ecocentric and technocentric approaches, the remainder of the chapter explores this through a number of case-studies which will include both transitional examples, Tennyson's *In Memoriam* and Carlyle's *Past and Present*, and writers in which this perspective is more fully developed. Looking, in particular, at a development in John Ruskin's work from a "moral economy of nature" to a "political economy" of "Pure Air, Water, and Earth", this will be explored in conjunction with William Morris and (briefly) John Stuart Mill to illustrate that the differing approaches taken by these writers offer usefully contrasting ways that can help us negotiate our own dichotomy between eco- and technocentric imperatives.

The remainder of the book draws upon the paradigm of 'Victorian ecology' to offer Hopkins as a prime example of a Victorian writer who held an essentially ecological perspective. Chapter Three traces his intellectual influences. Highlighting three non-literary interests – art, architecture and science – central to the development of an intellectual framework it will be shown, in particular, that Hopkins' interest in nature was informed by a contemporary science that was gradually shifting from more static models – natural history, botany – to an understanding of nature as an energy system characterised by movement and flux. In this light, Hopkins' journal will be examined as a post-Romantic attempt at constructing an ecological economy of nature founded not on place but on theories, concepts, and epistemologies formed largely in his undergraduate essays. Hopkins' development of the twinned concepts of 'inscape' and 'instress' will then be seen as representing the creation, in advance of his poetry, of an aesthetic paradigm analogous to the two components of ecosystems theory – physical being and the energy that holds it together. The chapter concludes with a discussion of the influence of the medieval theologian Johannes Duns Scotus whose work enabled Hopkins to harmonise ecological understanding to Catholic theology bringing to his nature writing a distinctively Gaian emphasis.

Chapter Four examines how Hopkins translated the ecological aesthetic established in the journal into a corresponding poetic practice. Beginning with a discussion of his early poems and literary influences (pastoral, Romantic, dialect writing) as frustrated attempts at finding an authentic voice for representing nature, it will then be suggested that Hopkins gradually moved towards a phenomenological verse that was, nevertheless, underpinned by the scientific knowledge examined in Chapter Three. The chapter goes on to consider Hopkins' development, while teaching Rhetoric to Jesuit novices, of a stress-based verse, sprung rhythm, designed specifically to represent motion and energy in nature. The second half of the chapter offers examples of the sustainable poetry which resulted from this: in 'Pied Beauty' an anticipation of biodiversity; 'Hurrahing in Harvest', which exemplifies the (Scotist) reconciliation of ecology and theology; his air poem 'The Blessed Virgin compared to the Air we Breathe'; and, to conclude, an analysis of the 'water poem', 'Inversnaid', in which, it will be argued, a preservationist emphasis on "wilderness" is replaced by a specific ecological understanding of "wet-ness".

Chapter Five traces the development in Hopkins' writing from an ecological perspective on nature towards a social philosophy premised upon sustainability. Establishing, in the opening section, that a critical engagement with modernity was conducted through his two vocations, priesthood and poetry, the social-ecological dimensions of that critique, and the ecopoetry by which he articulated it, will be explored in relation to three areas. First of all, a sensitivity to the last of the three elements comprising Ruskin's ecological political economy, "Earth", will be examined through the depiction of industrial processes polluting the soil in 'God's Grandeur' and of deforestation in 'Binsey Poplars'. I will then argue that air quality was central to Hopkins' ecological critique, as we can see from his letters, and that it led, furthermore, to a humanist concern with the impact of Victorian industrialisation on health. This will develop the concept, as outlined above, of a humanist 'corporeal ecology' by examining Hopkins' awareness of the dialectical integration of the body into the ecosystem, contrasting the depiction of productive muscular energy in 'Harry Ploughman' with one of tuberculosis in the urban poem, 'Felix Randal'. Having examined, therefore, the extent to which Hopkins was provoked by his own ecological critique into a wider questioning of Victorian political economy I will conclude, nevertheless, by arguing that he drew back from the incipient social ecology implicit in his thinking retreating, as had Ruskin, into semi-feudal solutions.

While this book offers an argument for Hopkins as a prototypical ecological writer, that reading is predicated not upon what Cohen has called the "'praise-song' school" of ecocriticism (2004: para. 63) but a more nuanced account of how Victorian writers negotiated the same dichotomies as those that bedevil contemporary ecology. My concluding chapter examines, therefore, the factors which undercut Hopkins' ecological perspective focusing, in particular, on a gradual shift towards theological orthodoxy, in which a Scotist, sacramental understanding (equivalent to that advocated by contemporary ecotheologians) was replaced by an increasingly redemptive theology, as well as at the overly utilitarian nature of Victorian post-Romanticism as a consequence of which Hopkins became increasingly disillusioned with his vocation. In the process, as we will see, he lost sight of one side of the ecological equation – respect for the integrity of nonhuman nature – but, aware of his own failing energy, not the other – an understanding of energy as the central fact of existence. I conclude by suggesting that Hopkins rediscovered his ecological perspective once he tempered his own pragmatism with a return to a love for nature. This offers a partial corrective to the main thrust of the book – that we must not lose sight of the ecocentric dimension even while trying to make this, in light of the urgency of ecological imperatives, more pragmatic. Uneven though Hopkins' engagement with ecological ideas might therefore have been the extensiveness of this study should justify E. P. Thompson's acknowledgement of Hopkins as "one of the few men who [...] (whenever he dared to look) registered in the depths of his being the impact of the truths of his society" (1977: 142).

Chapter 2

The Trajectory of a Victorian Ecology

Superficially there is plenty of evidence for a 'Victorian ecology': Haeckel invented the term in 1866; in 1871 John Ruskin was writing about the link between deforestation and drought (1903-12 (27): 92); the term 'acid rain' has been in use since 1872 (Park 1987: 6; Wall 1994: 133-5); in 1874 George Perkins Marsh discussed both recycling and deforestation in *Man and Nature*; and in the 1880s the 'Back to the Land' movement was advocating subsistence based lifestyles while the Nobel Prize winning physicist Svante Arrhenius was studying global warming (Gould 1988; Lovelock 2000b: 70). These miscellaneous examples are, however, more than coincidental; they are symptomatic, in fact, of a more general 'Victorian ecology' which, in terms of how it was conveyed in the literature of that period, will be outlined in this chapter. The attempt to define a Victorian literary ecology is founded in the first place, though, on a re-thinking of the two juxtaposed paradigms, modernity (or the Enlightenment) and romanticism, around which the pre-existing deep ecological criticism, described in Chapter One, has been established.

1. Re-thinking romanticism[1]

To regard the Enlightenment from a solely negative perspective is somewhat misleading. Historians, critical theorists, even environmentalists have argued that the rational modes of thinking by which it is characterised encompass, as well as a dominant instrumental thinking, counter critical tendencies. The historian Norman Hampson reminds us of these more liberating qualities when he argues that many Enlightenment

---

[1] In this book I will talk in terms of a lower case 'romanticism' (which denotes the ongoing tradition of romantic ideas) except where I am making specific reference to the period (or the writers of the period) that gives the philosophy its name, in which case, as here, I will use the upper-case 'Romanticism'. This will also apply where I am discussing the historically-located phenomenon of Victorian 'anti-' or 'post-Romanticism'.

philosophers "would have been horrified [...] if anyone had predicted to them the monstrous unreason that was to degrade the twentieth century". He even cites, somewhat aptly, Condorcet's qualified statement, in 1793, that the one "limit [...] to the improvement of human faculties" is "the duration of the globe where nature has set us" (1984: 232-3).

Critical studies of the nature of the Enlightenment, which is generally regarded as having continued into and throughout the historical period referred to as 'modernity', divide into two contrasting emphases. The first of these stresses its failure. Alan O'Shea cites as an example of this Weber's belief that modernity has created an "instrumental rationality" a belief subsequently embodied in the notion of an "iron cage" that, Weber wrote, "determines the lives of all individuals [...] with irresistible force" (1996: 9). However, O'Shea reminds us, critics such as Jürgen Habermas and Marshall Berman are merely the most recent examples of a parallel, competing tradition which has continued to claim the potential for liberation in, and through, these same rational modes, a tradition which encompasses science and technology, on the one hand, and political concepts such as democracy on the other (1996: 9). Consistent with emphases in social ecology, this more critical rationalism is, then, apparent in elements of ecological theory. As Hayward puts it, "if the enlightenment project is understood as one of critique rather than of domination it is not necessarily anti-ecological" (1995: 39-40).

The problem, however, if one is seeking to draw from literature eco-logical ideas reflective of this more critical modernity, is that literature has generally been identified as part of an alternative tradition of anti-modernity. A good example here is Raymond Rogers' book *Nature and the Crisis of Modernity*. Rogers draws on Gramsci's notion of "residual forms" to argue, via Raymond Williams (21), that there is a "residual history of modernity which can best inform the current environmental crisis". Identifying three key moments during which, he says, there emerged an apprehension of "danger" in modernity's development – "the emergence of English agrarian capitalism [...] the expansion of the Industrial Revolution in England [...] the current movement towards the globalisation of the world economy", Rogers suggests, in a trajectory much like Jonathan Bate's, that each of these moments was represented by literary forms of resistance – Shakespearean Tragedy, Romanticism and "radical environmentalist commentaries". Rogers thereby equates literature, specifically romantic literature, with a withdrawal and separation from modernity, as clarified when he quotes David Morse: "What romantic discourse foregrounds as a problem is the incommensurable: there is no common measure between [...] the poet's vision and the everyday, between the values of the past and the values of the present" (1994: 99-100). Given that romanticism remains central to ecological thinking, as the cultural origin of a regard for the integrity of nonhuman nature, and cannot simply be jettisoned, the way to break free of this impasse is to acknowledge that there are alternative, plural conceptions of it (see Day 1996: 1-6; Larrissy 1999: 2; Wu 1996: ix-xi).

Perhaps the most conventional understanding of romanticism is the view that it is comprised of two main criteria, "a turn to nature", usually identified with Wordsworth, and a "subjective idealism" commonly associated with Coleridge or Shelley (Perry 1998: 7-8; and see Williams 1987: 30). Although, as Seamus Perry suggests, there is a "likely conflict between these definitions" (1998: 7), they are, in fact, brought together in deep ecology in that they underpin a primarily philosophical mode of thinking which combines, in Tobias' definition, a non-utilitarian appreciation of the "beauty of the natural world" with a human need, as much psychological as it is biological, to be "fully integrated" in that nature. Yet with a different conception of romanticism it is possible to extend those sentiments into a consideration of the human place in nature and, from there, to the type of society which might arise from that.

These alternative readings tend to see romanticism as continuous from the Enlightenment. Exploring what he calls "the questioning tendency of the Enlightenment" (72), Aidan Day notes that many of the preoccupations of romanticism, including "the political rights and psychological capacities of the individual" and an understanding of "the importance of nature itself", were "fundamentally Enlightenment preoccupations" (1996: 76). This alternative tradition divides, furthermore, into two arguments that mirror the basis of the social ecocriticism outlined in Chapter One: that nature writing is underpinned by processes of conceptualisation; and that the understandings generated might be applied pragmatically to social critique and/or the imagination of better ways of living.

An argument that our attempts to conceptualise nature might be sanctioned from within the romantic tradition can be made in relation to Marilyn Butler's re-interpretation of Wordsworth's much quoted definition, in the Preface to the *Lyrical Ballads*, of poetry as "the spontaneous overflow of powerful feelings". Butler explains that while Wordsworth's statement is generally read as favouring the creative over the rational mode, this is only because his remarks have been taken out of context and, in fact, that what Wordsworth actually argued was that though this be true, Poems to which any value can be attached, were never produced on any variety of subjects but by a man who being possessed of more than usual organic sensibility had also thought long and deeply. For our continued influxes of feeling are modified and directed by our thoughts, which are indeed the representatives of all our past feelings; and [...] by contemplating the relation of these general representatives to each other we discover what is really important to men. (1981: 60)

The passage, Butler concludes, "stresses the controlling activity of the writer's intellect and moral sense", thereby legitimating rational and enframing modes as a component of the romantic tradition (60; and see Day 1996: 77-8). Indeed, as Butler also demonstrates, Wordsworth even argued that poetry should have "a worthy *purpose*" (see 60) which sanctions, in turn, a pragmatic notion of poetry, opening up the possibility that "feeling" might also be channelled into social and political engagement.

It is precisely this that is argued in Nicholas Roe's *The Politics of Nature*, in which he challenges the more conventional conceptions of romanticism by attributing to it "a greatly increased interest in the common feelings and common destiny of human beings" (2002: xi). Towards the end of the second edition of the book (2002), Roe underlines, apparently in response to ecocriticism's emergence since the first edition (in 1992), exactly why it might be important to re-discover this broader romantic tradition, namely that "we are at a time when an understanding of how the Romantics sharpened and sustained their political, social and human commitments is urgently needed" (197). This, Roe clarifies, is because we live in a period in which "The bondages of oil 'reserves', nuclear 'capability', and the imminence of ecological disaster combine to emphasize that human survival depends upon a restored awareness of 'the common feelings and common destiny of human beings'", as well as of each other's self-realization, values which romanticism has been seen to nurture (2002: 198). In order, however, to engender this awareness, ecological literary critics need to urgently broaden their approach both to romanticism itself and to the possibilities that lie within later post-Romantic traditions. A paradigm that can help us in that endeavour, and indeed lead us towards one of those traditions, is Raymond Williams' notion of the "Romantic Artist".

Williams is a significant figure in the context of literature and ecology. A key aspect of that relates to his influence, in books such as *The Country and the City* (1973), *Politics and Letters* (1979) and *Problems in Materialism and Culture* (1980), on subsequent discussions concerning "the social construction of nature". It was Williams, after all, who was insisting, thirty years ago, that "it is necessary to recall an absolutely founding presumption of materialism: namely that the natural world exists whether anyone signifies it or not" (1979: 167). The theory of the "Romantic Artist", outlined in *Culture and Society* (1958), is also important, however, in the more pragmatic sense suggested by Roe, for through this we can define and trace the nature of romanticism's central presence within the alternative tradition of modernity as a "critical project".

Williams ventures that the development of democracy and the impact of industrialisation (1987: 31) brought about "a radical change", in the Romantic period, "in ideas of art, of the artist, and of their place in society" (32). While he concedes that part of the Romantic challenge to industrial values comprised of a somewhat exclusive emphasis on "the special nature of art-activity as a means to 'imaginative truth', and [...] the artist as a special kind of person" (36), this, he believes, is moderated in that the work of the Romantic poets also encompassed other tendencies that, importantly, belie their "supposed opposition between attention to natural beauty and attention to government, or between personal feeling and the nature of man in society" (30). Elaborating on this, Williams suggests that the Romantic artists experienced and internalised the impacts of industrialisation "on the senses: hunger, suffering, conflict, dislocation". Neither "marginal nor incidental", this was "a large part of the experience from which the poetry itself was made" (31). In doing so he highlights what was a new conception whereby art was one place in which the experience of modernity would be documented and challenged. Furthermore, in ways markedly similar to Clark's social ecology of the imagination, Williams explains that in practice this amounted to an assessment of what this new type of society meant, most evidently in its industrial processes, "on the ground" – in terms of changes to working methods, human relationships, and in what was being done to nature (1987: 30-1). This, in turn, brought about an "attention" to questions of "the nature of man in society" and of "government" (1987: 30-2).

One other respect in which Williams is a significant figure in this context is that his later work began, as did that of E. P. Thompson, to link left-wing politics to a developing ecological politics, in ways evidently nourished by romantic literature. This is implicit when, in *Towards 2000*, he described the need for a new conception of quality of life in

a broader sense of human need and a clearer sense of the physical world. The old orientation of raw material for production is rejected, and in its place there is the new orientation of livelihood: of practical, self-managing, self-renewing societies, in which people care first for each other, in a living world. (1983: 203-4)

The link between ecological socialism and his earlier interest in romanticism becomes, however, explicit in a revised 'Foreword' to *Culture and Society* which Williams wrote in 1987. In this he identifies, confirming the notion of an extended critical romantic tradition, "startling connections" between the writers he'd studied in that book and "the new ecological and radical-ecological movements":

as the crisis of our own years has continued, the openness, the diversity, the human commitments of these earlier writers came through, in a majority of cases, as the voices of fellow-strugglers rather than of historically outdated or periodised thinkers. The depth and extent of the crisis [...] was something we could readily share from our own world with even the earliest of these contributors, and we were still, with them, looking for answers, having returned, by the sheer weight of events, to many of the same questions. (1987: vii-viii)

Williams makes the same argument here as Carolyn Merchant: that confronted by "new intellectual and historical problems", such as ecological concerns, we seek out "new interpretations of the past" so as to "provide perspectives on the present and hence the power to change it" (1982: xvi). What is of equal interest, however, is the trajectory identified by Williams. For what he also analysed in *Culture in Society* was the historical development of the "Romantic Artist" into Victorian literary culture.

The remainder of this chapter proposes, therefore, a 'Victorian ecology' which, continuous from, rather than antagonistic to, 'romantic ecology', will be presented as a historical precedent to a social ecology of the imagination. Prior to a discussion that will demonstrate the existence of ecological concerns in some major Victorian writers, the following section outlines four elements that constitute the paradigm of 'Victorian ecology'. The first two elaborate on the proximity of Victorian literary culture to the origins of ecological science and social ecology respectively; the second two suggest that contemporary ecological theory's attempts to reconcile the dichotomy between ecocentric and technocentric might be informed by an equivalent Victorian attempt to adapt their Romantic inheritance to pragmatic ends.

*

2. Parameters of a Victorian ecology

Recent research on Victorian literature and science, though largely neglecting ecological science, has demonstrated the extent to which newly developing scientific paradigms shaped Victorian literary culture. In *Literary Darwinism* Joseph Carroll notes the impact "scientific revelations about geological time and evolutionary transformation" had on literary plot, in the span, for example, of H. G. Wells' work from 'A Tale of the Stone Age' to the depiction of the earth millions of years ahead in *The Time Machine* (2004: 94). Gillian Beer's groundbreaking *Darwin's Plots* argues not only that *The Origin of Species* had a considerable thematic impact on the Victorian novel but that evolutionary theory was assimilated into the narrative structure of books such as *Middlemarch* (1985: 6). In the same spirit, George Levine suggests that even in novelists not directly influenced by science there was an "absorption and testing of Darwinian ideas and attitudes" (1988: 2-3).

In her later work Beer also suggests that energy physics in its various forms – heat, light, sound – and in concepts such as conservation and thermodynamics was, itself, "transforming Victorian perceptions", a fact often obscured, she adds, by the attention given to evolutionary theory (1996: 269, 243). Much the same argument is offered by Greg Myers. Similarly of the opinion that there was "a revolution in nineteenth-century physics contemporary with the revolution brought about [...] by the concept of evolution by natural selection" (1989: 307), Myers suggests that as a consequence of the mutual exchange of ideas between scientific "popularizers" like John Tyndall and James Clerk Maxwell and "social prophets" such as Carlyle and Ruskin, theories of energy conservation and dissipation "became available for popular and very broad social use" (1989: 307-9). Furthermore, he adds that these ideas were not only reflected in but propagated by Victorian literary culture. Myers offers here Carlyle's metaphor, in *Sartor Resartus*, of the universe as a steam engine as an example of what he calls the "rhetorical commonplaces" that emerged from the formulation of the first law of thermodynamics in the 1840s. However, he also argues that while it was this theory that had established "energy as an elementary entity in nature", the later, related theory of the conservation of energy, had, as Tyndall pointed out at the time, already been anticipated in *Sartor*, in which an abundance of "such passages [...] might justify us in giving Carlyle the credit of poetically, but accurately, foreshadowing the doctrine" (1989: 314; and see Beer 1985: 5; 1996: 8).

In more general terms energy physics appears to have had two con-
flicting areas of influence on Victorian literary culture, both of which
shadow ecological science. In the first place it offered an alternative to
what was often seen as the materialist or reductive nature of Darwinian
science. Evidently dialectical, in its emphasis on flux and instability,
physics was seen, nevertheless, to offer a holistic, organic model which
posited all phenomena as manifestations of what John Stuart Mill called
"one and the same force" (cited in Brown 1997: 194). On the other hand,
the discovery of the second law of thermodynamics (entropy) bequeathed, as Peter A. Dale has argued, a preoccupation with degeneration
(1989: 206-7). Dale traces this in Hardy's later novels and poems while
Beer identifies an anxiety about 'heat-death', or the 'death of the Sun', in
books such as *Middlemarch, The Time Machine* and Richard Jefferies'
After London (1996: 219-41). A paradoxical situation in which the
concept of productive energy exchange was counteracted by a threat of
dissipation which prompted disorientation and anxiety ran, then, through
Victorian literary culture. While this would sometimes lead, as we shall
see, to a revulsion and resistance towards science, it remains the case that
so far as Victorian writers were interested in science they were interested
in precisely those components – evolutionary theory and thermodynamics
– that would come to form ecological science. Given the trajectory of
development thereafter from thermodynamics to ecosystems theory it
would be no great leap of faith to suggest that these writers intuitively
understood the concept of ecosystems.

The second reason for proposing Victorian ecology lies, analogously,
in its proximity to the origins of environmental activism and ecological
politics. In their book *Environmental Groups in Politics* Jane Goyder and
Philip Lowe point out that it was the Victorians who established the first
nature conservation, building preservation and anti-pollution pressure
groups, the initial wave of which, emerging sometime around the 1880s,
included The Selbourne Society for the Protection of Birds, Plants and
Pleasant Places; The Society for the Protection of Ancient Buildings; The
Commons, Open Spaces and Footpaths Preservation Society; and The
Coal Smoke Abatement Society (now the National Society for Clean
Air). James Winter, in his book *Secure from Rash Assault: Sustaining the
Victorian Environment* points out that such examples of nineteenth-
century environmental protest were nourished and articulated by the
literary and cultural protestations of figures such as Wordsworth, Carlyle,
Dickens, Ruskin, Gaskell and George Eliot (1999: 8-9). While such
studies clearly indicate the origins in the Victorian period of an environ-

mentalist critique, questions have been raised about whether this constitutes a movement as such and, if so, the extent of its connection with a deeper, more radical ecological movement. The evidence with regard to the first is unclear. For while Winter appears to conclude that such groups were largely disparate and localised (see McKusick 2003: 288) Goyder and Lowe argue that mutual co-operation and an often shared membership was evidence of a common environmentalist ethos and of a movement "seen, by those involved, to be part of a common cause" (1983: 18). If that is so, it remains nevertheless the case, as Peter Gould has argued, that these groups, in themselves, "posed no threat to the continuance of the existing social order or the direction that it was taking" (1988: 16).

James McKusick, in a review of Winter's book, does suggest that there emerged from this burgeoning environmental movement a broader awareness of ecological themes such as the "law of unintended consequences" and the "ecosystem concept" (289-90). Elements of this may, in turn, have fed into the more radical political movement which Gould traces in his book *Early Green Politics*. Gould regards the emergence of this, in the years between 1880 and 1900, as the most significant period in ecological politics prior to the 1980s (viii). Its origins lay in what he describes as a "Back To Nature and Back to the Land" movement influenced by figures such as Carlyle and Ruskin. In that this tended towards advocating a return to feudalism (1988: 16-17) Gould regards this as signifying an essentially defeatist act of withdrawal (32-3) but goes on to argue that similar sentiments were transformed into a radical, populist agenda as a response, during the 1880s, to economic depression and social unrest. Taking the form of a critical examination of three particular features of Victorian modernity – the philosophy of industrialism, the relationship of the individual to their social and physical environment, and the function of the city (1988: viii) – it was from this that there emerged an "early green politics", a precursor to social ecology that aligned the romantic sensibilities of "Back to Nature and Back to the Land" to an early socialist movement itself open to alternative points of view (1988: 29).

According to Gould's account, two movements, in particular, epitomised this early green politics. The first of these was the Social Democratic Federation (SDF). Formed as a radical group in 1881 the SDF adopted a socialist programme two years later. This was a programme influenced by a faction, including William Morris, who argued that production would have to be adapted to take into account social and environmental consequences (1988: 31). It took the form of an advocacy of decentralised, autonomous land-based politics (1988: 62-3) not dissimilar to that in contemporary social ecology. For a short time, therefore, ecological ideas gained a degree of prominence on the British political left until such tendencies became subsumed into an orthodox centralist and industrialist Marxism (1988: 62-3), the moment of opportunity being lost completely when, in 1884, the SDF split. A further example of an early green politics arose ten years later around Robert Blatchford's north of England newspaper *The Clarion*. This brought to a working-class readership a politicised romanticism that translated love of literature and nature into specific campaigns against water and air pollution as well as a more general critique of industrialism. In repeated condemnations of the immorality, wastefulness and environmental consequences of laissez-faire capitalism, Blatchford politicised the ecological critique arguing, for example, that "to make the slum child love and long for Nature is to sow the seed of revolution" (1988: 39-40). The newspaper's popularity ensured, as Gould puts it, that "if only for a relatively short time" such ideas "received popular treatment and enjoyed [...] widespread support" (1988: 36).

What, between them, these examples of an early green politics indi-cate is not just the proximity of literature and literary figures to the origins of environmental activism and ecological politics, but also the contribution such figures made to those movements. They also indicate, however, a spirit of vigorous and ecological engagement with modernity from which the contemporary ecological movement might learn. That this, too, was nourished by literature – where writers were seeking to imagine and demonstrate how romantic ecocentrism might be harnessed to a technocentric pragmatism – brings us to the third reason for propos-ing a Victorian ecology, which is that the Victorian literary response to modernity counteracts, to a large extent, the notion of literature as "residual critique" and corresponds, therefore, with the counter-tradition that emphasises the emancipatory possibilities of modernity. This can be demonstrated, in the first place, by highlighting the parallels between Victorian literary culture and the thinking of two contemporary theorists of modernity, Ulrich Beck and Marshall Berman, both of whom have engaged with ecological ideas.

The Victorian ecological critique corresponds with the two central theses, 'risk' and 'reflexive modernization', that comprise Beck's highly influential *Risk Society: Towards a New Modernity*. Beck argues that the scientific and industrial progress of the latter part of the twentieth century has been responsible for the creation of unprecedented 'risks' and 'hazards' such as radioactivity, toxins, or pollutants which have the potential to do irreversible harm to plants, animals, human beings and the ecological system (1992a: 22-3). The occurrence of such risks, along with others associated with global terrorism, health pandemics, or the financial and job insecurity brought about by globalisation, has, in turn, prompted a 'reflexive modernity' which Beck defines as an ongoing mode of critical reflection on, and scrutiny of, the assumptions and institutions of modernity. Encompassing scepticism about both the claims to truth advanced by science and technology, and the ability of political institutions to arbitrate on these (see 1992a: 14; 1992b: 98), reflexive modernization has, Beck argues, prompted a re-activation of the 'public sphere' (1992b: 119), but one in which the primary ground of social conflict has shifted from wealth production to hazard production (1992b: 111). He suggests that "what *was* until now *considered unpolitical becomes political*" and cites as examples of this themes consonant with ecological politics such as the processes of industrial production and the destruction of forests (1992a: 24), a point developed in his subsequent book *Ecological Politics in an Age of Risk* (1995).

Notwithstanding an all too brief acknowledgement that the germ of this dual thesis lies in the nineteenth century (1992a: 12), Beck regards reflexive modernization as a fundamental epistemological change prompted by the unprecedented nature of contemporary risks and hazards. He even seems to differentiate it from a previous critique, located in the nineteenth century, that Scott Lash and Brian Wynne, in their introduction to the English translation of *Risk Society*, refer to as "simple modernity" (1992a: 3). That response, Beck suggests, sought merely to temper industrialised modernity by means of a return to a "fading feudal agrarianism" and "traditional" hierarchical structures, an invocation of "the horizon of experience of *pre*-modernity" that would prove to be particularly ineffective (1992a 9-10). The difference, Beck argues, with the contemporary context is that "Modernization *within* the paths of industrial society is now being replaced by a more radical modernization *of the principles* of industrial society" (i.e. risk society) (1992a: 10). The retreat backwards, towards an advocacy of essentially feudal patterns of social organisation, was indeed a feature, as we shall see, of aspects of the Victorian ecological critique including (in places) that of Hopkins. Yet in other regards Beck is, I believe, mistaken in the linearity of his views. For while the risks intrinsic to Victorian industrialisation probably did not carry the same degree of hazard as nuclear, genetic or biotechnology, Victorian literary culture certainly did display a comparable level of 'risk anxiety' as is apparent in the apocalyptical tendencies of Jefferies' *After London*, Wells' *The Time Machine*, or Swinburne's poem 'The Garden of Proserpine' (Myers 1989: 312). This translated, furthermore, into a reflexive social and environmental criticism that questioned the principles of industrial society anticipating, as it did so, alternative, ecological forms of society. Described in detail later in this chapter, this is precisely what Berman identifies as a key characteristic of Victorian literary culture.

In *All that is Solid Melts into Air*, Berman describes the twentieth-century response to modernity as characterised by "passivity and helplessness". Encapsulated, he argues, in Foucauldian adaptations of Weber's "iron cage" (see 1982: 27-8; 34-5) – and also, as it happens, in the Heideggerian strand of ecocritical work – Berman regards this response as a "travesty of the nineteenth-century modern tradition" before then writing "I want to bring the dynamic and dialectical modernism of the nineteenth century to life again" (35).

What underlay this "dynamic and dialectical modernism" was the escalation within the Victorian period of the industrial impacts experienced ("on the senses") by the "Romantic Artist". Industrialisation and urban expansion created environmental problems – poor sanitation, air quality, deforestation, pollution – all of which added to equivalent problems in areas such as housing, working conditions, unemployment, or disease. As a consequence of this escalation of risk, Victorian literary culture became characterised by a conspicuous sense of social responsibility – observation, analysis, investigation – which, in turn, helped prompt a spirit of campaigning, political intervention, and legislation to which literary figures, and literary work, contributed. In that context Berman goes on to directly compare the "dynamic and dialectical modernism of the nineteenth century" with a contemporary environmental movement exemplified through roads protestors (see 171). Naming names, he argues that the major Victorian critics, in what must surely be a paradigm of reflexive modernization, combined "critical bite" with an optimism he calls the "romance of construction":

> The great modernists of the nineteenth century all attack this environment passionately, and strive to tear it down or explode it from within; yet all find themselves remarkably at home in it, alive to its possibilities, affirmative even in their radical negations.

Marx and Nietzsche – and Tocqueville and Carlyle and Mill and Kierkegaard and all the other great nineteenth-century critics – also understood the ways in which modern technology and social organization determined man's fate. But they all believed that modern individuals had the capacity both to understand this fate and, once they understood it, to fight it. Hence, even in the midst of a wretched present, they could imagine an open future. Twentieth-century critics of modernity almost entirely lack this empathy with, and faith in, their fellow modern men and women. (19, 27)

Berman suggests, finally, that "we can make their visions our own, and use their perspectives to look at our own environments with fresh eyes [...] Remembering the modernisms of the nineteenth century can give us the vision and courage to create the modernisms of the twenty-first" (36). This argument brings Victorian literary culture firmly into the tradition of an emancipatory modernity. One aspect of that culture particularly instructive in this context, and worth exploring further because of its relevance to Hopkins, is, as both Berman and Gould identify, an experience of the city which focused and radicalised that critique (see Berman 1982: 18-19).

Ecological theory is habitually characterised by a tradition of anti-urbanism which, perhaps owing something, historically speaking, to William Cobbett's famous metaphor of London as "the Wen", is typified by the philosopher Theodore Roszak's description of the city as the "most incorrigible of waste and polluters" and as "an imperialistic cultural force that carries the disease of colossalism in its most virulent form" (see Brennan 1995: 205). A further literary example occurs in *Romantic Ecology* where Bate locates the origin of an "ecological ethic" in the transition in Wordsworth's *The Prelude* from book seven ("Residence in London") to book eight ("Retrospect: Love of Nature leading to Love of Mankind"). Though he argues that "For Wordsworth, the distinction between being in the city and being in nature is cardinal" and that "the move from book seven to book eight is from negative types to positive ones" (1991: 21), a more considered view has arisen within ecological theory.

The ecological scientists Botkin and Keller accept the propensity of cities to detrimentally alter "the relationship between [the] biological and physical aspects of the environment" (2005: 612), examples of which they give as an erosion of green space, which kills plants and animals and interferes with the water cycle, and the problems caused by pollutants in the air, notably smog (see 2005: 612-15). However, they also emphasise the need to engage with, rather than withdraw from, the urban environment on the basis that the city "exports ideas", even a "spirit of civilization" that can, at the social level, help us address those problems (see 2005: 604). In the same manner Tim Elkin and Duncan McLaren have noted that the city is the prime site of human production, consumption and exchange, impacting upon the entire surrounding environment to such an extent that human and nonhuman alike can be said to live within an "urban system". However, they likewise argue that the city "house[s] decision-makers in politics and industry" and is the place "where people and social groups principally interact and new styles and movements evolve" (1991: 5) before suggesting, therefore, that we can only realistically achieve an ecological social state by working towards "sustainable urban development" (see 1991: 4-9).

These are views that would appear to be consistent with the approach taken by Victorian writers. B. I. Coleman, like Gould and Berman, identifies anxieties about the city as the catalyst for a Victorian literary critique (1973: 12). What we find, furthermore, notwithstanding the sometimes near apocalyptical tone of such writing, is that this was founded upon a recognition, consistent with scientific ecology, that the physical environment is connected to other – cultural, economic, social, and moral – components of society and, ultimately, to political organisa-tion, a view articulated by Charles Kingsley in his 1857 lecture, "Great Cities and their Influence for Good and Evil":

> The social state of a city depends directly on its moral state, and [...] the moral state of a city depends – [...] to an extent as yet uncalculated, and perhaps incalculable – on the physical state of that city; on the food, water, air and lodging of its inhabitants. (see Coleman 1973: 146)

The Victorian approach to the city was, therefore, a particularly signifi-cant element both of its "dynamic and dialectical" engagement with modernity and of the distinctively ecological character of that engage-ment. It suggests a need to confront, rather than denigrate or ignore, the "urban system" in which the majority of us live. What is particularly instructive, however, were the new modes of writing that that experience generated, a fact acknowledged by Berman and, before him, by Williams.

Returning to Wordsworth, Williams, in *The Country and the City*, traces a pragmatic and humanist post-Romantic trajectory. Though we find in *The Prelude* a renunciation of the "perpetual flow/Of trivial objects, melted and reduced/To one identity" in the city there is also, Williams reminds us, a contrary belief that "oftentimes was seen/Affectingly set forth, more than elsewhere [...] the unity of men". Where Bate directed his discussion of Wordsworth towards Ruskin and an anti-industrial tradition of post-Romanticism (see 1991: 81-3), Williams turned to Dickens and argues that in his novels "the physical world is never [...] unconnected with man. It is of his making, his manufacture, his interpretation. That is why it matters so much what shape he has given it" (1985: 161). Consequently, these urban novels perform the technocentric function of presenting a "crisis of choice; of the human shape that should underlie the physical creation" (1985: 161). Williams is not, though, advocating here the type of didactic literature rightly criticised by Bate (see Bate 2000: 199-200), but a more subtle mode of representation that dwells upon the impact that social and political organisation, whether in the country or the city, has on human and nonhuman nature alike. Rendered, in the example of Dickens, through novelistic literary devices such as metaphor, symbolism, narrative and characterisation, this can also translate, as we shall see, into the poetic modes of representation utilised by Hopkins.

Where Williams argues that new modes of writing developed as a result of the urban experience, Berman suggests, in the context of a discussion of Baudelaire's prose poem 'The Loss of a Halo', that there developed, also, an entirely new conception of the artist. Having acknowledged that the city stimulated a post-Romantic impetus towards more socially engaged literature, Berman's argument is essentially that suggested when, returning to the theme two years later in an article published in *New Left Review*, he writes that a "reduction of the modern artist to an ordinary mortal can open up new lifelines and force fields through which both artists and the public can grow" (1984: 122). What, specifically, Berman is describing, in reference to Baudelaire's portrayal of the poet and "ordinary man" encountering each other in the city (1982: 155), is the notion of an art not so much grounded in but ignited by the artist's everyday immersion in that environment, a notion also exemplified by the poems which emerged from Hopkins' experience as a priest in the city. It was these two things, the formation of new modes of writing generated from the experience of being in the city, that epitomised, and motivated, the Victorian literary engagement with modernity. That engagement was, however, not as straightforward as it might at first appear.

The final reason for studying Victorian literary culture relates, in this context, to a shared critical problem, of how, precisely, to align romanticism with the imperative of engaging with modernity. For rather than being the linear development perhaps implied above, in which ecocentric sentiment developed seamlessly into more pragmatic (technocentric)

modes of writing, the difficulty of doing this, coupled with the persistence of contrary, romantic elements such as the temptation to withdraw
from society, created a considerable degree of confusion, a confusion
which, because it mirrors the paradoxical lines of development of deep
and social ecology, is worth examining here.

Victorian modernity, in the shape of new scientific paradigms and
fundamental social changes, threw into confusion the greater certainties
of Romanticism. Victorian literature became characterized, in the first
place, by what Wendell Stacy Johnson has described as a "deep feeling of
ambivalence about the sea, the sky, the seasonal trees, flowers, and fruits
[...] about the whole Romantic landscape" (1968: 44). Johnson identifies
in particular a dichotomy whereby new scientific understanding and
modes of conscientious, accurate description were counteracted by
increasingly symbolic representations of nature. In these the largely
positive associations attached to a Wordsworthian sense of human
meaning in the landscape became frequently replaced with ambivalent or
negative ones, exemplified by the "grotesque wastelands" (as Johnson
describes them) of Tennyson's 'The Vision of Sin', or James Thomson's
City of Dreadful Night (1968: 31-3), or a dystopian literature preoccupied, albeit in a language furnished by contemporary science, with
degeneration or heat-death.

The same applies, in a sense, to the Victorians' social thinking though
in a dichotomy which, as described by Williams, also partially characterised the "Romantic Artist". In this context, Walter Houghton, in his
formulation of a "Victorian frame of mind", noted a constant oscillation
between "Optimism" and negative moods – worry and ennui, isolation,
loneliness and nostalgia – grouped, generically, under the heading
"Anxiety". Accordingly, a situation in which feelings of social responsibility and of the "morality of art" are constantly undermined by "a sad
contemplation of withering faith and an unprecedented fear of encroach-
ing materialism", which gave rise in turn to "world fatigue" and self-
consciousness, can be seen as the defining characteristic of what Jerome
Hamilton Buckley labelled "Victorianism" (1969: 9-12).

An inevitable consequence of this ambivalence towards modernity
was that the Victorians began to doubt their Romantic inheritance and to
regard it with a degree of suspicion shared with some contemporary
ecological theory. With regard to the latter, David Pepper has suggested,
for example, that as one of the "roots of ecocentrism" (see 1996: 188-92),
romanticism is problematised both by a concentration on "the isolated
individual" (190), which runs contrary to ecology's holistic nature, and

by a failure to "contemplate rationally the nature of social, political and economic structures" (1996: 229). Likewise, Andrew Dobson has argued that if we regard the Green movement merely in terms of "a resurgence of romanticism", which he describes in much the same terms, "then we are blind to the enormous range and influence of rationalist attempts" at addressing ecological issues (2000: 11-12). Such critiques call to mind, as already implied, a mid-twentieth-century literary criticism which, in writers like Houghton, Buckley, Raymond Chapman and E. D. H. Johnson, drew attention to Victorian literature's conscious differentiation from a Romantic sensibility summarised by another critic, Mario Praz, as one in which "the essential is the thought and the poetic image and these are rendered possible only in a passive state. The Romantic exalts the artist who does not give a material form to his dreams" (1970: 14-15).

It is Buckley, however, who developed this argument furthest, when he labelled the Victorians as "Anti-Romantics" suggesting, in particular, that they rejected both the perceived "naturalism" of their Romantic predecessors and the pre-eminence of feeling over thought which Praz describes as a "sharp individuality" and "self-expression for its own sake" (see 1969: 14-23). As Buckley makes clear, the anxieties wrought by the rapid state of modernisation coupled with doubts about romanticism's ability to address those concerns also brought about a deeply confused literary writing which Buckley, via a discussion of Tennyson, refers to as the "two voices".

At Cambridge, he explains, Tennyson's innate introspectiveness was tempered by brief membership of the Cambridge Apostles, "a group devoted to the discussion of serious philosophical subjects" including politics, science and religion (Martin 1983: 86) and one of whose members, R. C. Trench, later Dean of Westminster, is reported to have told him, "Tennyson, we cannot live in art" (1969: 73). Thereafter, his poetry, as captured in the poem "The Two Voices", was characterised by contradictory impulses in which a sense of duty in the form of public pronouncement, what Buckley calls a "'national' art centred upon immediate actualities" (1969: 83), was recurrently countered by a "taste for "escapist" art" or "an isolated art for art's sake" (73, 77).

While the dichotomy of the "two voices" ran throughout Victorian literary culture, the way in which the majority of writers attempted to quell the allure of withdrawal was by seeking, as E. D. H Johnson has argued, external objectives that would establish a meaning and purpose to their work (1963: 217-18). In this context Victorian literary culture built upon the political interventions of the Romantic writers by theorising and

conferring upon the "Romantic Artist" the more public role countenanced
by Tennyson, a role captured, most prominently, in Carlyle's "Man of
Letters" (see below, and Heyck 1982: 193). Such an enhancement of the
pragmatic element of literary activity led, not infrequently, to the
abandonment of literature and other creative modes for what were
perceived to be more utilitarian forms of engagement. Matthew Arnold,
for instance, forsook poetry in favour of "essays in criticism", Ruskin,
increasingly, turned from art to social criticism, while Hopkins sporadically
neglected poetry in deference to his parochial responsibilities. From this
notion of a socially responsible art driven by external objectives, there
emerged, in juxtaposition to the "residual critique" described by Rogers, the
"dynamic and dialectical" ecological engagement outlined below. Yet even
leaving aside the continual counter-emphasis towards withdrawal, this,
again, was not so straightforward.

On the one hand, the modes of engagement were not always particularly appropriate. An example of this was an interest in medievalism
inherited from Romanticism that has been examined in Alice Chandler's
A Dream of Order: The Medieval Ideal in Nineteenth-Century Literature.
Discussing its double-edged character, Chandler argues that as a form of
critique Victorian medievalism "forced man to imagine a totally different
society instead of merely acquiescing in his own [and] to question his
own conventional existence and the mechanistic assumptions on which it
was based". Useful up to a point, fears about political violence, ingrained
by the French Revolution, nevertheless led critics such as Carlyle and
Ruskin to resort to an advocacy of neo-feudal political solutions (1971:
8). So while the allure of medievalism represented a symptom of the
Victorian engagement with modernity, the ensuing retreat to feudalism
also bears out, where it did occur, Beck's argument that a "simple
modernity" preceded our own more radical reflexive modernization.

The other, converse problem was that Victorian "Anti-Romanticism"
sometimes gave rise to an overly-utilitarian slant to the engagement of
Victorian literary figures with modernity. For the tendencies, in some
writers, to forsake imaginative modes for seemingly more practical forms
of engagement were by no means an unmitigated success. While, as we
shall see, Ruskin's sophisticated art criticism did give way to intelligent
and rhetorically powerful social and ecological critique, the practical
proposals which came after were, in no uncertain terms, a failure.
Hopkins, similarly, remained tormented by what he believed to be the
impossibility of a pragmatic poetry even where his work demonstrated
precisely the opposite. What this indicates is one of the most important

lessons to be learnt from Victorian literary culture: that while an insistence upon the possibility of translating romantic sensibility into pragmatic critique is important, and necessary, we should not forget, as some of these writers did, the importance of retaining an ecocentric or romantic sentiment, and equivalent modes of writing, for it is these that would, in this context, motivate and serve to maintain an ecological philosophy.

In the light of this my preferred conceptual framework for encapsulating the Victorians' sometimes confused response to Romanticism and modernity is one developed by the Hopkins critic Alison Sulloway. Describing herself as a self-professed "disciple" of Houghton and Buckley, Sulloway identifies a post-Romantic "Victorian specificity" (1984: 63) which she defines as an attempt to utilize Romantic sensibility into "a new empiricism from which emerged a new pragmatism or utilitarianism" (1984: 63). Captured in Matthew Arnold's desire "to see the object as in itself it really is", its purpose was to direct the empirical knowledge gained to practical ends (1984: 63-4) largely through scientific understanding. At the same time, Sulloway concedes that the post-Romantic project was often "wearying to the spirits" and would leave Victorian writers "adrift in moral ambiguities". These, as is clear from Arnold's 'Preface' to *Poems* (1853), were also an effect of modernity: "the calm, the cheerfulness, the disinterested objectivity have disappeared [he wrote]; the dialogue of the mind with itself has commenced; modern problems have presented themselves" (see Sulloway 1984: 65).

In bringing these emphases together into one paradigm Sulloway crystallises precisely what this "Victorian specificity" might offer to our own ecological thinking. For in stating that Victorian post-Romanticism anticipated a "conflict" in the twentieth century between "the claims of objective, empirical, utilitarian science [...] with disciplines trying to protect the unquantifiable, yet equally utilitarian demands of the human spirit" (1984: 78), Sulloway captures the critical conundrum that troubles contemporary ecological thought. If a central task of that thought is to reconcile competing eco- and technocentric tendencies, a historical precedent is, therefore, available in the thorough (and conscious) reworking of romanticism towards social ecology that occurred within and throughout Victorian literary culture and which will now, in the remainder of this chapter, be examined.

*

3. The transition towards a Victorian ecology

In strictly chronological terms, the concept of a 'Romantic ecology' is somewhat problematic, at least given the dialectical quality now attributed to scientific ecology. We might consider this in relation to two examples. In his article "What did Wordsworth mean by 'Nature'?", Laurence Lerner describes the poet's bewilderment, in 'The Redbreast Chasing the Butterfly', when confronted with what became known as natural selection. Describing the poem "as a protest against what the poet sees", a Darwinian struggle for existence "which does not fit his preconceptions", Lerner describes Wordsworth's uncertainty as he struggles to retain a moral order premised upon the balance of nature (1975: 306-8).

In 'Section First' of *The Guide to the Lakes* Wordsworth imagines himself suspended from a cloud "midway between" the mountains of Great Gavel and Scafell, the "common centre" of what is depicted as a diverse ecosystem. In his description each facet of the landscape – the "bold and [...] savage shores" of Ennerdale that give rise to the stream "the Ehen or Enna, flowing through", and, in turn, the "soft and fertile country [as it] passes the town of Egremont", which is nourished by the Enna – complements and helps sustain the whole (1977: 22-3). Yet beyond this Wordsworth appears to lack the scientific paradigm or language by which to describe the scene, specifically, ecologically, in terms of a "material exchange of energy". With no perception of the Lakes networked within a wider ecosystem, he speaks instead, in a bioregionalist sense, of a boundary imposed by the "powers of nature" and falls back on another paradigm – preservation – which is not the same thing at all. Further to this, condemnation of the "discord [...] bewilderment [...] deformity" caused by an invasion of non-native species – larch plantations and "whole acres of shrubbery and exotic trees" introduced by new settlers – translates into an attempt to preserve both a natural and neo-feudal social order (1977: 84-5). This environment, Wordsworth suggests, cannot be "comprehended [...] without processes of culture [educated nobility] or opportunities in some degree habitual [rural peasantry]" (1977: 151). Speaking of the need to protect the environment against both the philistine middle class and, as seen in his protest against the Kendal-Windermere railway, the mass influx of the industrial working class, there is little sense, here, of the democratic sentiments that have shaped social ecology and its late Victorian equivalent.

What these brief examples indicate is that in predating the more substantial development of Darwinian and thermodynamic theory, Wordsworth was chronologically excluded from the reconciliation of balance and conflict that Haeckel achieved through his definition of ecology, and, even more so, from the developments in physics that might have enabled him to see a landscape, and its human inhabitants, in terms of an economy of energy exchange. What Wordsworth "meant" both by nature and humanity's relationship to it was something fundamentally pre-ecological.

Where Wordsworth had sought to deny evolutionary theory, no such option was available, however, to Victorian writers confronted by early works about evolution such as Lyell's *Principles of Geology* (1830-3) and Chambers' *Vestiges of the Natural History of Creation* (1844). Because the changes in perception these brought about happened gradually, arguably only achieving full currency (and notoriety) with the publication of *The Origin of Species* in 1859, there was, ahead of the more fully formed 'Victorian ecology' examined below, a transitional phase which displays the gradual, incremental process by which Romanticism slowly developed into an ecological understanding which shaped the perspectives of that later work. Two figures who exemplify, respectively, a nature writing being altered by new scientific paradigms and a social critique that attempted, in part, to deal with the escalating environmental realities of Victorian modernity were Tennyson and Carlyle.

The dichotomy Johnson sees as characterising Victorian nature writing is exemplified clearly by Tennyson. Robert Bernard Martin refers, for instance, to an "ambivalent attitude" towards science which "unsettled" Tennyson's faith, even while Thomas Huxley had been stating, on the basis of the perceived factual accuracy of his poems, that "We scientific men claim him as having quite the mind of a man of science" (1983: 36, 462). It is a dichotomy epitomised particularly well by *In Memoriam* (1850) in which we find, in the first place, passages of carefully observed, detailed natural description.

> Sweet after showers, ambrosial air,
>   That rollest from the gorgeous gloom
>   Of evening over brake and bloom
> And meadow, slowly breathing bare
>
> The round of space, and rapt below
>   Thro' all the dewy-tassel'd wood,
>   And shadowing down the horned flood
> In ripples, fan my brows and blood

> The fever from my cheek, and sigh
>> The full new life that feeds my breath
>> Throughout my frame […] (lxxxvi.1-11)

In these lines Tennyson clearly seems to anticipate ecological science, most specifically in an understanding of the atmosphere as a sustainable energy system. For not only is the air, in this passage, "slowly breathing" energy into the environment, in referring to the energy in his "blood" and "throughout my frame", Tennyson even moves to incorporate the human within that ecosystem.

What follows, however, is a valuable ecocritical lesson as Tennyson, eschewing ecological representation, turns away from the surrounding environment and lets his "fancy fly":

> Throughout my frame, till Doubt and Death
> Ill brethren, let the fancy fly
>
> From belt to belt of crimson seas
>> On leagues of odour streaming far,
>> To where in yonder orient star
> A hundred spirits whisper 'Peace'. (lxxxvi. 11-16)

Looking now towards the mystic east and seeking out the abstractions of spiritual peace, Tennyson turns increasingly towards the compulsive, even morbid, symbolism of the environment that Johnson describes.

> Witch-elms that counterchange the floor
>> Of this flat lawn with dusk and bright;
>> And thou, with all thy breadth and height
> Of foliage, towering sycamore;
>
> How often, hither wandering down,
>> My Arthur found your shadows fair (lxxxix.1-6)

Here the "witch elms", that like the trees in the earlier passage shadow and protect the surrounding countryside, become displaced into a metaphor for Tennyson's late friend Arthur Hallam. The result is that the proto-ecological understanding of the natural environment, displayed in the earlier lines, quite literally recedes:

> The hills are shadows, and they flow
>> From form to form, and nothing stands;
>> They melt like mist, the solid lands,
> Like clouds they shape themselves and go.

> But in my spirit will I dwell,
>> And dream my dream, and hold it true;
>> For tho' my lips may breathe adieu,
> I cannot think the thing farewell. (cxxiii.5-12)

The first of these stanzas bears, of course, a notable similarity to Marx's remark about the disorientation of modernity that "all that is solid melts into air"; the second implies a retreat into memories of a lost, imagined nature. Similar anxieties, also founded on evolutionary theory's undermining of religious certainty, appear in Matthew Arnold's 'Dover Beach' which was probably composed the following year though not published until 1867. Here Arnold makes his famous analogy between inhospitable nature – "the grating roar/Of pebbles which the waves draw back, and fling" (9-10) – and the decline of organized religion (in an image of the "melancholy, long, withdrawing roar" (25) of "The Sea of Faith") before declaring that the world

> Hath really neither joy, nor love, nor light,
> Nor certitude, nor peace, nor help for pain;
> And we are here as on a darkling plain. (33-5)

Arnold's despair and Tennyson's alienation occur in lieu of any alternative to balance, as is implied by Tennyson's "I cannot think the thing farewell". Eventually provided by ecological theory's dialectical reconciliation of balance with competition, the perspectives being offered from within the developing theories of evolution and energy physics would, in time, facilitate the enhanced scientific veracity, and pronounced anticipation of ecological science, seen in later Victorian writers such as Hopkins.

Equivalent to, and co-existent with, the problematic attempt at re-conceptualising 'nature' was that of developing a critique and political philosophy capable of responding to the impact of industrialisation on the surrounding environment. Here again Tennyson and Arnold are important figures in understanding the ambiguities of this transitional phase of Victorian post-Romanticism. Tennyson's response in *In Memoriam* to the uncertainties of Victorian modernity was to "dwell" in "my spirit" and "dream my dream". Arnold, likewise, retreats in 'Dover Beach' to a weak, romanticized "love, let us be true/To one another!" Neither is especially useful and though Arnold was arguably more attuned than Tennyson to the inadequacies of this response, it was Carlyle, of all the early Victorian writers, who most significantly adapted romantic sensibility towards a new social pragmatism out of which a Victorian ecological critique developed.

Carlyle's *Past and Present* (1843), based around a juxtaposition between medieval and Victorian England, encapsulates both the sense of risk and the "critical bite" that Berman attributes to Victorian culture:

> For the times are really strange; of a complexity intricate with the new width of the ever-widening world; times here of half-frantic velocity of impetus, there of the deadest-looking stillness and paralysis.
>
> We have quietly closed our eyes to the eternal Substance of things, and opened them only to the Shews and Shams of things [...] All the Truth of this Universe is uncertain; only the profit and loss of it, the pudding and praise of it, are and remain very visible to the practical man. (1845: 24, 115)

Recognising the difficulty, in a Victorian culture "heartworn" or "weary" (1845: 283), of developing "critical bite" into more systematic social critique, Carlyle introduced an insistence that any impulse towards those traits Houghton categorises as "Anxiety" must be rejected. Having described in *Past and Present* "all misery" as "faculty misdirected, strength that has not yet found its way" (1845: 388) this impatience with any suggestion of overwrought subjectivity was well epitomised in an essay, "Varnhagen von Ense's Memoirs", which concerns the memoirs of a nineteenth-century German writer and diplomat. Here he suggests that

> they do not suit us at all. They are *subjective* letters [...] the grand material of them is endless depicturing of moods, sensations, miseries, joys and lyrical conditions of the writer; no definite picture drawn, or rarely any, of persons, transactions or events which the writer stood amidst: a wrong material as it seems to us. To what end, to what end? we always ask. (1869 (3): 245)

In his 1831 essay "Characteristics" Carlyle developed a more general critique concerning "the diseased self-conscious state of Literature" which "does [...] like a sick thing, superabundantly 'listen to itself'" (1869 (2): 212). While this seems dismissive of literature, Carlyle actually believed that, in the context of the Victorian decline in faith, literature had the capacity to become "a branch of Religion" within which writers might take up the role of moral, social, or cultural leadership previously assumed by the priesthood. For notwithstanding its present "diseased [...] state", Carlyle saw literature, relatively speaking, as "in our time [...] the only branch that still shows any greenness; and, as some think, must one day become the main stem" (1869 (2): 211-12). Counselling the need for writers or artists to socially engage – "Not by looking at itself, but by looking at things out of itself, and ascertaining and ruling these, shall the mind become known" (1869 (3): 245) – Carlyle gave substance to his belief through the figure of a "Man of Letters" (or "man of utterance"), a revised conception of the "Romantic Artist" by which, "Literary men", as he wrote elsewhere, might become

> the appointed interpreters of this Divine Idea; a perpetual priesthood, we might say, standing forth, generation after generation, as the dispensers and living types of God's everlasting wisdom, to show it in their writings and actions, in such particular form as their own particular times require it in. (1869 (1): 49-50)

What Carlyle bequeathed to Victorian literary culture, and to literature in general, was, therefore, a redefinition of its purpose, a belief that literature has the capacity both to develop an empirical "strength" in the perceptive faculties and to apply this to utilitarian ends. One "particular form" of the "wisdom" required in his time was, as Carlyle implicitly understood, ecological. Perhaps a result of his familiarity with the commonplaces of Victorian science, this was certainly due to an instinct towards aligning nature and society that Carlyle shares with social ecology. In this regard, *Past and Present*, in particular, foreshadows the ecological quality of later Victorian writing.

In the book Carlyle placed an emphasis on the importance of the surrounding environment on our material relationship with the rest of the ecosystem: "This England of the Year 1200", he wrote, "was no chimerical vacuity or dreamland, peopled with mere vaporous Fantasms [...] but a green solid place, that grew corn and several other things" (1845: 59). He also developed a stark critique issuing dire warnings as to the possible consequences of the existing political economy. In Book III, 'The Modern Worker', Carlyle identifies a "plague-spot", a "universal Social Gangrene, threatening all modern things with frightful death" (1845: 186). Ostensibly referring to a lack of religious faith, analogous references to nature throughout this chapter make it evident that he is also talking about the perils of neglecting basic, ecological principles. Carlyle describes, for example, a nation that will "advance incessantly towards the land's end; you are, literally enough, 'consuming the way'" (1845: 195) and shortly before offers an even direr warning:

> Nature's Laws, I must repeat, are eternal: her small still voice, speaking from the inmost heart of us, shall not, under terrible penalties, be disregarded [...] Shew me a Nation fallen everywhere into this course, so that each expects it, permits it to others and himself, I will shew you a Nation travelling with one assent on the broad way [...] Not at happy Elysian fields, and everlasting crowns of victory, earned by silent

> Valour, will this Nation arrive; but at precipices, devouring gulfs, if it pause not. (1845: 193)

Measuring an abstract Victorian modernity against the "realist ontology" he finds in medieval England, Carlyle even arrived at a quality of life critique resonant with contemporary social ecology:

> We have sumptuous garnitures for our Life, but have forgotten to *live* in the middle of them. It is an enchanted wealth; no man of us can yet touch it. (1845: 6)

> It is not to die, or even to die of hunger, that makes a man wretched [...] It is to live miserable we know not why; to work sore and yet gain nothing; to be heartworn, weary, yet isolated, unrelated, girt in with a cold-universal Laissez-faire. (1845: 283)

The only divergence, in Carlyle's writing, from contemporary social ecology is that he personifies the shift back towards a "simple modernity". For in the end his "Man of Letters" translated logically enough, in that he regarded this as a "perpetual priesthood", into an advocacy of pre-modern hierarchical political solutions, most specifically a return to feudalism.

> Aristocracy and Priesthood, a Governing Class and a Teaching Class: these two, sometimes separate, and endeavouring to harmonise themselves, sometimes conjoined as one [...] There did no Society exist without these two vital elements [...] Man, little as he may suppose it, is necessitated to obey superiors. (1845: 324)

Carlyle's writing did, all the same, bequeath an essentially ecological foundation to later work that would be strengthened in its empiricism by the development of new scientific ideas and which was (in some cases) brought closer to the politics of social ecology by more democratic political formations. To fully delineate the parameters of the Victorian ecology in which my reading of Hopkins will be grounded, I will now consider the two writers – John Ruskin and William Morris – both influenced by Carlyle, who most clearly illustrate both an incipient Victorian ecology and the contrasting directions that it took.

4. John Ruskin

Ruskin may not appear to be an obvious candidate for a Victorian ecology in that he was somewhat sceptical about science and scientists. He became increasingly hostile, for instance, to evolutionary theory, particularly as it developed ever further away from natural theology, while, with reference to physics, he regarded Tyndall somewhat cynically (see Hewison 1996: 37-9; Myers 1989: 315-16). At the same time he had, under the influence of Wordsworth, retained a romantic emphasis on instinctive knowledge which he consciously opposed to the more rationalist mode of science. In *The Elements of Drawing*, for example, Ruskin puts forward the notion that "The whole technical power of painting depends on our recovery of what may be called the *innocence of the eye* [...] a sort of childish perception" (1903-12 (15): 27), before suggesting that the "highly accomplished artist has always reduced himself as nearly as possible to this condition of infantine sight. He sees the colours of nature exactly as they are" (1903-12 (15): 28). Yet in reality, as Michael Wheeler has made clear, Ruskin's beliefs were more ambivalent, for

> While Ruskin protested against what he perceived to be a changing intellectual climate which threatened certainty itself, he was also – paradoxically and thus, for him, typically – drawn to the very language of flux and inconstancy associated with the new science. (1996: 13)

In fact, Ruskin established a post-Romantic approach that aligned rational study of nature with romantic perception or insight. It was this that brought about an essentially ecological understanding of natural economy which, in turn, fed into a critique of Victorian political economy the extensiveness of which suggests that Ruskin exhibited, more than any of his contemporaries, the main facets of a Victorian ecology.

The development of Ruskin's ecological ideas can be traced back to the unfolding volumes of *Modern Painters*. In these he gradually shaped a fascination with lakes, rocks and clouds, inherited from Wordsworth, into what might be called an aesthetic of the eye. Ruskin believed that the artist should be able both to instinctively recognise natural beauty (i.e. "the *innocence of the eye*") and to reflect the natural world faithfully in their work, an insistence that prompted a concern with the technique of painting (he wrote *Elements of Drawing* in response to readers' requests for a practical manual). His broader purpose, however, was not reproduction but, rather, an uncovering of the deeper truths of nature which, he believed, would be latent in works that conformed to his principles (see White 1992: 75-6).

The section, in volume 1 of *Modern Painters*, which outlines these principles is "Of Ideas of Truth". Here Ruskin distinguishes between "imitation", which refers merely to the object depicted, and "truth" (the conceptive faculty) which encompasses "emotions, impressions and thoughts". Truth, he writes may be stated by any signs or symbols which have a definite signification in the minds of those to whom they are addressed [...] Whatever can excite in the mind the conception of certain facts, can give ideas of truth, though it be in no degree the imitation or resemblance of those facts. (1903-12 (3): 104)

By "truth" Ruskin refers to an underlying Platonic notion, which is acknowledged when he writes that "there is a moral as well as material truth" (1903-12 (3): 104). Like Carlyle, and Hopkins, what he meant by this was ultimately a recognition of God: he was to declare this openly in the first chapter of *The Laws of Fésole* (1877-1878), the lessons in drawing he later revised and published under the title "All Great Art Is Praise" (see 1903-12 (15): 351). Yet in having founded that recognition on aesthetic study of the forms and structures of the natural world, Ruskin also indicates that the artist would, simultaneously, arrive at the complementary "material truth" suggested in his quote, by which he meant the underlying principles, including ecological principles, that govern the universe. As Wheeler puts this, in a paradigm equally applicable to Hopkins, "the demands of the eye and those of the moral sense [...] were inextricably linked" (1995: 2). Hence, what we see in *Modern Painters* is the emergence of a nature writing that, like Tennyson's, anticipates the "truth" of an ecological ontology in which a nature alive and interdependent is characterised by energy exchange:

all soil whatsoever, whether it is accumulated in greater quantity than is sufficient to nourish the moss or the wallflower, has been so, either by the direct transporting agency of water, or under the guiding influence and power of water. All plains capable of cultivation are deposits from some kind of water; some from swift and tremendous currents, leaving their soil in sweeping banks and furrowed ridges; others, and this is in mountain districts almost invariably the case, by slow deposit from a quiet lake in a mountain hollow, which has been gradually filled by the soil carried into it by streams [...]

the peculiar characters of bark [...] express the growth and age of the tree; for bark is no mere excrescence, lifeless and external, it is a skin of especial significance in its indications of the organic form beneath; in places under the arms of the tree it wrinkles up and forms fine lines *round* the trunk, inestimable in their indication of the direction of its surface; in others, it bursts or peels longitudinally, and the rending and bursting of it are influenced in direction and degree by the undergrowth and swelling of the woody fibre, and are not a mere roughness and granulated pattern of the hide. (1903-12 (3): 428, 585)

This perception of an underlying "truth" in nature brought about, in turn, a critical appraisal of Victorian society in terms of its adherence (or lack of it) to those truths. Ruskin establishes the basis of that connection in the distinction between "typical" and "vital" beauty found in volume 2 (1846) of *Modern Painters* (see 1903-12 (4): 76-207). "Typical beauty", underlining the natural dimension to his ideas, relates to the outer form and is appraised by means of aesthetic rules of "Proportion" derived from nature. To aid an understanding of this Ruskin instructed artists to copy the line of the horizon between sea and sky (79), the graceful symmetry of chestnut leaves or rhododendron shrubs (126), or "the lines and gradations of unsullied snow" (146). "Vital beauty" refers to an "inner goodness" or roundedness of character, that is to personal or spiritual beauty. The link between them is that a person's ability to perceive "typical beauty" is dependent upon their possession of "vital beauty". While, at an aesthetic level, this applies to an ability to discern underlying truths in nature, and to the representation of those truths in art, the broader implication, as Raymond Williams points out, was that art became a barometer for the moral health of society because if social organization is wrong, the conditions for an artistic way of seeing cannot exist (1987: 136). Presenting Ruskin, on this basis, as an epitomisation of the "Romantic Artist", Williams argues that aesthetic "standards of perfection" translated, in Ruskin's work, into social attempts to "establish [...] the conditions of perfection in man" (1987: 135); "typical beauty" became, that is, the basis of Ruskin's art criticism, "vital beauty" of his social criticism.

Because of this connection of art, and the moral and material truths within art, to a proper understanding of nature, Ruskin's critique, when he turned to social questions, was inevitably focused on the Victorian relationship with, and attitudes to, the surrounding environment. That critique begins, in many ways, with a chapter, "The Moral of Landscape", in volume 3 (1856) of *Modern Painters*. Here, in a discussion of Wordsworth's "Tintern Abbey", Ruskin both differentiates himself from Romanticism and proposes, specifically, the necessity of a more pragmatic nature writing.

Suggesting, in general terms, that Romantic literature had been characterised by an "inability to define" what he calls the "character of [...] emotion", by which he means the ideas that underlie the feelings being expressed, Ruskin offers Wordsworth's poem as an example. He suggests that when we try to find a definition of the thoughts contained within the poem all we get told is that they comprise "A mingled sentiment/'Twixt resignation and content" (1903-12 (5): 355) and that what thoughts we do find are "languid" and "in such a state [...] not good for much". As an alternative to this he declares his own belief that the imaginative faculty is capable of conjuring up a "spiritual or second sight" (1903-12 (5): 354-5), by which he means religious, moral or social thought. Placing this firmly in the context of nature writing, in expressing the belief that "a curiously balanced condition of the powers of the mind is necessary to induce full admiration of any natural scene" (1903-12 (5): 357), it is this that moves Ruskin's analysis closer to ecological critique.

Ruskin acknowledges that what is, in effect, ecocentric sentiment is "necessarily connected properly with the benevolence and liberty of the age; that it is precisely the most healthy element which distinctively belongs to us" (1903-12 (5): 379). However, while arguing that "our love of nature had been partly forced upon us by mistakes in our social economy" he also suggests that this has, regrettably, "led to no distinct issues of action or thought" (1903-12 (5): 354). In other words, while Ruskin sees "love of nature" as the basis for social critique, he also believes that this has not actually happened, an unfulfilled potential also alluded to by Carlyle. Nevertheless, there can come about, from this, a mode of writing that addresses Victorian modernity. Offering instances of it when he argues, for example, that prosperity depends "in no wise" upon "iron, or glass, or electricity, or steam", and in contrasting modern leisure pursuits, horse-racing, fashion and music, with "real and wholesome enjoyments" – "to watch the corn grow [...] to draw hard breath over ploughshare [...] To read, to think, to love, to hope, to pray" (1903-12 (5): 381-2) – Ruskin writes:

> out of it [the "love of nature"] results will spring of an importance at present inconceivable; and light arise, which, for the first time in man's history, will reveal to him the true nature of his life, the true field of his energies, and the true relations between him and his Maker. (1903-12 (5): 379-80)

It is in his later work, however, that we find the full development of these "truths" about nature within a specific ecological perspective and critique.

Two particular stages of transition served to develop this "second sight" into social and ecological critique: from art to architectural criticism, from the 1840s onwards; and, from the 1870s, towards a more explicit engagement with social and environmental questions. In the first of these, Ruskin, in books such as *The Seven Lamps of Architecture* (1849) and the three-volume *The Stones of Venice* (1851-3), drew upon Gothic architecture's reproduction of natural pattern to criticise Victorian taste and ethics before then deploying architectural criticism, as did other Victorians such as Pugin and Morris (see Williams 1987: 130-2), towards a discussion of the ways in which Victorian society was re-shaping both its 'natural' and human environments. In the later phase, Ruskin developed a social critique that, belying the uniqueness of a contemporary reflexive modernity, foregrounded "hazard production" as the most significant "conflict field" of Victorian social and political debate. Two pieces, in particular, indicate the ecological critique that emerged: "The Storm-Cloud of the Nineteenth Century", an apocalyptical lecture that exemplifies Victorian anxieties about 'risk'; and "The White-Thorn Blossom", a critique of Victorian political economy which Ruskin ultimately developed into a blueprint for ecologically-oriented political change.

"The Storm-Cloud of the Nineteenth Century" is, in fact, two lectures Ruskin gave at the London Institution in February 1884. Given an environmental reading by Wheeler (1995), these mark the development of the "moral of landscape" into what might be called a moral of energy economics. Ruskin believed, as Sulloway puts it, that motion was the source of "as much variety as a world of sharply individuated things and creatures" (1972: 80). He initially translated this interest, in *Modern Painters* I, into a fascination with clouds. Writing first, about clouds, that it is "impossible to establish truth" because they are "impossible to draw" (358), Ruskin eventually finds "consistency in their great outlines, which give system to the smaller curves of which they are composed" (373) as well as, anticipating ecological science, an "appearance of exhaustless and fantastic energy which gives every cloud a marked character of its own, suggesting resemblances to the specific outlines of organic objects" (1903-12 (3): 373). The subsequent transition from an interest in observing clouds to a social critique based on those observations comes about, in part, as a result of science.

His fascination with motion and with the possibilities of being able to structure it derived from a familiarity with the commonplaces of contemporary physics. Ruskin's interest in this extended, despite the cynicism noted earlier, to an acquaintance with the main principles, the conservation and dissipation of energy, that lay behind the theory of thermodynamics. Myers points out in this context the similarity, up to a point, of "The Storm-Cloud of the Nineteenth Century" to William Thomson's 1852 essay "On a Universal Tendency in Nature to the Dissipation of Mechanical Energy". Thomson's essay, forecasting "heat death" (entropy), and suggesting that "within a finite period of time to come the earth must again be unfit for the habitation of man" (1989: 318-19), had left a deep impression on Victorian culture. Reiterating similar anxieties, having read Thomson's description second hand (Myers 1989: 318), Ruskin indicts Victorian political economy with changing the weather. He observes, for instance a ceaseless, "calamitous" gradually increasing wind (31) possessed of what he calls a "malignant quality" (34); he relates having experienced the "devil's darkness" of "the most terrific and horrible thunderstorm" (37) as well as a blanching, as opposed to reddening, of the sun (38); and he describes the storm cloud, more generally, as "the plague-wind of the eighth decade of years in the nineteenth century" (31).

Myers notes, however, that where Ruskin differed ("bitterly") from Thomson was in his rejection of the "irreversibility" and despair attached to the concept of universal dissipation (1989: 318-19). For while there were, in the debates about entropy, parallels to the conservationist "Spaceship Earth" metaphor, notably in the suggestion that in destroying energy the Earth will eventually become a "closed system", Ruskin held out the hope, as Myers puts it, that "the world will be redeemed by a new moral order". He had written, in *Modern Painters* IV, that "the universe presents itself continually to mankind under the stern aspect of warning, or of choice, the good and the evil set on the right hand and the left" (1903-12 (6): 416). Here, likewise, at the close of the first lecture, Ruskin advocates a reorientation of cultural values, grounded in the equation between "typical" and "vital beauty", as the means towards living in a more benevolent ecosystem:

> Whether you can affect the signs of the sky or not, you *can* the signs of the times. Whether you can bring the *sun* back or not, you can assuredly bring back your own cheerfulness, and your own honesty [...] The paths of rectitude and piety once regained, who shall say that the promise of old time would not be found to hold for us also? (1903-12 (34): 41)

The suggestion here, that a shift in cultural values might prompt a re-adjustment of political economy towards greater ecological sustainability, is one Ruskin then took forward in "The White-Thorn Blossom", the fifth of ninety-six "Letters to the Workmen and Labourers of Great Britain" published as *Fors Clavigera* between 1871 and 1884.

Fors Clavigera represents the culmination of the post-Romantic trajectory as it was worked through by Ruskin. In an archetypal statement of Victorian pragmatism he had declared, in personal letters written at the time, "I simply cannot paint, nor read, nor look at minerals, nor do anything else that I like [...] because of the misery that I know of" and that "the day has come for me to cease speaking, and begin doing, as best I may" (1903-12 (27): xviii-xix). "Possessed", his editors write, "by the instinct and passion for practice to realise the conditions of the good and beautiful in the actual world" (1903-12 (27): xviii-xix), these letters were addressed to all parties interested in working towards changing society, including, Ruskin explained, "masters, pastors, and princes" as well as the working man (1903-12 (27): xxiii). Touched upon in *Romantic Ecology*, where Bate describes its "prescience" in highlighting the dangers of pollution and deforestation (1991: 59), "The White-Thorn Blossom" is open, I believe, to a detailed reading in the light of the Victorian ecology paradigm.

The letter begins with what, on the surface, is a classic anti-Enlightenment argument. Ruskin complains about a lecturer at the Kensington Museum who had asserted that "there was no such thing as a flower" on the grounds that, technically, flowers are leaves. Drawing here a parallel with those who regard humans as merely "a transitional form of Ascidians and apes", he describes this as

> the most perfect and admirable summary given you of the general temper and purposes of modern science. It gives lectures on Botany, of which the object is to show there is no such thing as a flower; on Humanity to show there is no such thing as a Man; and on Theology, to show there is no such thing as a God. No such thing as a Man, but only a Mechanism; no such thing as a God, but only a series of forces. (1903-12 (27): 83-4)

While Ruskin's remarks are clearly characterised by anti-scientific sentiment, the "realist ontology" that he seeks to reassert is, nevertheless, then applied effectively in what becomes a thorough ecological examination of Victorian industrial society.

Ruskin writes, as the letter continues, of an England where "you have shut the sun out with smoke" (86); he criticises deforestation, referring to a blasting of the valley between Buxton and Bakewell which had "heaped thousands of tons of shale into its lovely stream" (86). He describes river pollution, and he hints at acid rain, writing that society has "turn[ed] every river of England into a common sewer, so that you cannot so much as baptize an English baby but with filth, unless you hold its face out in the rain; and even *that* falls dirty" (92); and, in characteristically apoplectic language, Ruskin condemns air pollution:

> You are vitiating [the air] with foul, chemical exhalations; and the horrible nests, which you call towns, are little more than laboratories for the distillation into heaven of venomous smokes and smells, mixed with effluvia for decaying animal matter, and infectious miasmata from purulent disease. (1903-12 (27): 91)

Consequently "The White-Thorn Blossom" shares an apocalyptical quality with "The Storm-Cloud of the Nineteenth Century", Ruskin again warning, for instance, that "you can vitiate the air by your manner of life, and of death, to any extent. You might easily vitiate it so as to bring such a pestilence on the globe as would end all of you" (1903-12 (27): 91).

Yet, possessed by the "romance of construction", Ruskin also argues that we do have a choice in such matters. Having described, in such detail, what "*modern* Political Economy" is doing to the environment, he then proceeds to advocate a need for precisely the "radical restructuring of society and its economic base" that Allaby contrasts to the "piece-meal" quality of an *environmental* social philosophy:

> There are three Material things, not only useful, but essential to Life. No one "knows how to live" till he has got them
>   These are, Pure Air, Water, and Earth.

Continuing with what is an adaptation of Wordsworth's *The Excursion*, he also writes:

> There are three Immaterial things, not only useful, but essential to Life. No one knows how to live till he has got them
>   These are, Admiration, Hope, and Love. (1903-12 (27): 90)

Out of this radical revision of Romanticism, towards an assertion that "Life" depends on a political economy premised upon humanity's embeddedness within the ecosystem, Ruskin goes on to advocate a range of alternative options and measures. The threat of deforestation, for example, engenders a choice, between "planting wisely and tending carefully" and creating "drought [...] by ravage of woods and neglect of soil". Air pollution, similarly, might be solved "by dealing properly and swiftly with all substances in corruption; by absolutely forbidding noxious manufactures; and by planting in all soils the trees which cleanse and invigorate earth and atmosphere". And, at a more generalised level, Ruskin argues that society must decide how it wishes to consume natural resources: "you can destroy them at your pleasure or increase, almost without limit, the available quantities of them" (1903-12 (27): 91-2). Divulging a belief in 'natural economy' as an open system Ruskin offers not only an ecological perspective but also a model of the "vision and courage", or, in his words, "Hope, and Love" required to put this into action.

It is, however, precisely at this point, where the ecological perception is strongest, that the social vision turns backwards. For Ruskin ends the letter by proposing his medieval Guild of St George, promising to tithe one-tenth of his income ("you shall see the accounts") to a practical initiative for buying land "which shall not be built upon, but cultivated by Englishmen, with their own hands, and such help of force as they can find in wind and wave" (95). He continues:

> We will try to take some small piece of English ground, beautiful, peaceful, and fruitful. We will have no steam-engines upon it, and no railroads; we will have no untended or unthought-of creatures on it; none wretched, but the sick; none idle but the dead. We will have no liberty upon it; but instant obedience to known law and appointed persons: no equality upon it; but recognition of every betterness that we can find, and reprobation for every worseness. (1903-12 (27): 96)

Though the Guild represented an attempt to tackle Victorian modernity, this Carlylean regression, "back to nature" and to a feudal social organization, was ill-equipped to deal with Victorian hazards in the face of the highly developed modernity the period was witnessing, a context which also included political shifts – parliamentary reform, capitalist social organisation, new democratic movements – within which the urban working class were already pro-actively voicing ecological concerns. Indeed, when Ruskin instigated the Guild, run on feudal lines with himself as master, it soon collapsed, mainly through lack of support (Batchelor 2000: 260-1). If this is the point at which many contemporary observers would wish to separate from Ruskin's otherwise powerful ecological critique, an alternative trajectory, in terms of the development of Victorian post-Romanticism into an ecological social philosophy, is available in the work of William Morris.

5. William Morris

A member of the Social Democratic Federation, the organisation at the forefront of an "early green politics", Morris identified the source of his beliefs as "a deep love of the earth and the life on it, and a passion for the history of the past of mankind" (1993: 382). Indicative of the romanticism which stimulated and, to a large extent, maintained that critique, this could sometimes be, E. P. Thompson has suggested, a troubling legacy. For example, romantic elements in earlier poetic works, that were heavily influenced by Keats, such as *The Life and Death of Jason* (1867) and *The Earthly Paradise* (1868-70), "nourished pessimism", Thompson suggests, and an impulse to use art as a "means of escape" (1977: 12; 808-9). It was, all the same, a preoccupation with the conservation of architecture, essentially a desire to defend tradition, which led Morris, in the first place, to more active social engagement.

That activism largely centred around the early environmental groups identified by Goyder and Lowe. A founder member of the Society for the Protection of Ancient Buildings, Morris also became involved in early manifestations of the Council for the Protection of Rural England, the National Trust and The Commons, Open Spaces and Footpaths Preservation Society as well as in campaigns to enforce the Smoke Act. Evidence, therefore, of Goyder and Lowe's contention that the shared membership of such groups was indicative of a movement "seen, by those involved, to be part of a common cause", Morris nevertheless bears out Gould's point that such organisations were "no threat to the continuance of the existing social order". For with an "analysis of society", Thompson argues, "far too profound to suppose that these efforts would do more than scratch the surface" (1977: 257), he converted to a socialism that impacted both on his activism and his writing.

These developments were summarised, by Morris himself, in the 1894 essay 'How I Became a Socialist'. Much of this essay is the standard matter of Ruskinian social critique. He describes, for example, the "eyeless vulgarity which has destroyed art", the "mastery […] and waste of mechanical power", and a "stupendous organization" designed "for the misery of life!" before describing the foundation of his socialism as a "hatred of modern civilization". Acknowledging that the need for an alternative form of society had been fostered in him by Ruskin (381), Morris nevertheless distanced himself from Ruskin's conclusions when he wrote that becoming a "practical Socialist" absolved him from being "a mere railer against 'progress'" and "from wasting time and energy" in fruitless schemes or, even, from "a fine pessimistic end of life" (382).

The pivotal point, in terms of this transition, appears to have been when Morris was prompted to read *Capital* by a realisation that working conditions dictated by the economics of industrialism made it impossible for Victorian craftsmen to restore ancient buildings in ways identical, or faithful to, their original design (Thompson 1977: 239). He concluded that any restoration of architectural and environmental standards would be dependent upon a re-direction of Victorian society and eventually drew the conclusion, through Marx, that the possibility of such a transformation resided in the apparently revolutionary potential of the industrial working class; as Morris writes, demonstrating the sense of possibility lauded by Berman, "amidst all this filth of civilization the seeds of a great chance, what we others call Social-Revolution, were beginning to germinate" (1993: 382).

Morris' interpretation of socialism did not, however, conform to conventional understandings of that philosophy. For the outcome of a work, and life, dedicated to drawing out the full potential of what Thompson describes as a "transformed romantic tradition" in which "the long romantic breach between aspiration and action was healed" (1977: 273), was a form of social ecology that foreshadowed, first of all, an understanding of sustainability:

> what I mean by Socialism is a condition of society [...] in which all men would be living in equality of condition, and would manage their affairs unwastefully, and with the full consciousness that harm to one would mean harm to all – the realization at last of the meaning of the word COMMONWEALTH. (379)

He also appeared to reconceptualise quality of life in a way, as discussed in Chapter One, integral to social ecology. For towards the end of the essay notions of art and beauty are given equal emphasis, and seen as mutually dependent on, material need. Morris argues, for instance, that while "civilization has reduced the workman to such a skinny and pitiful existence that he scarcely knows how to frame a desire for any life much better than that which he now endures", it is, nevertheless, the "province of art to set the true ideal of a full and reasonable life [...] a life to which the perception and creation of beauty, the enjoyment of real pleasure that is, shall be felt to be as necessary to man as his daily bread" (1993: 384). In his implicit understanding that the dual aim of preventing social inequality and environmental depletion is dependent upon the fostering of a revised notion of quality of life Morris, as has been acknowledged, was to become a primary influence on contemporary social ecology (see Bookchin 1988: 13; Hay 2003: 12; Luke 1997: 178; Parham 2008).

While Morris put these beliefs into practice through membership of the SDF, he also represented them in the novel *News from Nowhere* (1890) a depiction of a utopian sustainable society which comes as close as any novel to presenting an "ecological imaginary". Based around its central character, William Guest, who wakes up one morning to find himself in the year 2102, *News from Nowhere* offers, in the first place, both a social and environmental critique of Victorian society. When, for example, one of its characters asks

> don't you find it difficult to imagine the times when this pretty little country was treated by its folk as if it had been an ugly characterless waste, with no delicate beauty to be guarded, with no heed taken of the ever fresh pleasure of the recurring seasons, and changeful weather, and diverse quality of the soil [...]

and follows this up by asking "How could people be so cruel to themselves?" the answer given is "'And to each other,' said I" (1993: 208). Morris duly characterises Victorian Britain as a world in which people have got "used to living in dung" (125) and in which a global capitalised economy, where what is being produced are poor or useless goods, exploits the people by taking "their natural products in 'exchange'" (125-6). Against this he depicts a future society of clean, clear water where salmon swim in an unpolluted Thames, urban London is designed along Italian architectural lines and in which the countryside is a garden to be cultivated by all. In this world where the population barely age and where they live a life free of law and government there would be, Morris envisaged, "delight in the life of the world; intense and overweening love of the very skin and surface of the earth on which man dwells" as well as "a nature bettered and not worsened by contact with mankind" (159). In *News from Nowhere* Morris achieves, therefore, an imaginative and utopian representation of what had been the central (and successful) aspiration of his political thought, the squaring of a romantic view of nature with a socialist ecological restructuring of human society.

6. Conclusion

Morris' life and work represents, then, probably the most fully realised example of a paradigmatic Victorian ecology in which an ecocentric love of nature has been successfully translated into a technocentric political philosophy. Especially helpful in the context of the coincidence noted earlier between a Victorian engagement with Romanticism and contemporary ecological theory's ecocentric-technocentric dichotomy, the full utility of Victorian literature lies, nevertheless, in its offering a diversity of ecological perspectives and approaches any of which might, in their different ways, help us negotiate that dichotomy.

There must, of course, be boundaries. I have argued that as a result of their cultural climate (i.e. new scientific and social ideas) Victorian writers intuitively understood the central tenets of ecology. Consequently, the criteria for studying writers in accordance with a Victorian ecology should be an intuitive understanding of nature as a dialectical ecosystem and/or an attempt to translate that understanding into some form of social philosophy premised upon sustainability. Filtered through the lens of post-Romanticism, as it is described by Sulloway, these common threads unite writers as diverse as Ruskin, Morris, Tennyson, Arnold, Carlyle, Gaskell, Dickens, Mill, Hardy, and Hopkins.

A more extensive study of 'Victorian ecology' might, then, to give an example, continue to explore the ways in which romantic sensibility can be applied to technocentric, pragmatic ends. In this context both Ruskin and Morris would deserve fuller study: Ruskin, in terms of a fuller elaboration of the trajectory outlined in this chapter, one that might, for instance, incorporate other works such as *Unto this Last*; Morris, in terms of a closer, more detailed analysis of why he became a socialist, a transition particularly worth examination in the context of current debates concerning the precedence that ameliorative environmental actions which are commonly imposed as responsibilities on the individual consumer – recycling, carbon off-setting, the minimisation of plastic bag use – are often given over more radical and systematic political solutions (see Bookchin 2003: 276, 277).

Also of interest in this respect would be John Stuart Mill, a writer whose ideas broadly conform, as I have argued elsewhere (see Parham 2007), to social ecology. In the first place, his essay 'Nature' offers a still useful conceptualisation of that term which can inform our own attempts to understand it. Mill carefully balances an insistence that nature has a primary meaning independent of human construction with the belief that understanding the human place in 'nature' rests, nevertheless, upon analytical and conceptual faculties that are, themselves, a part of 'human nature' (1969: 379-80). Particularly useful here is a notion of "intelligent action", by which he meant that the shape of both human social organisa-tion and the surrounding environment rests (in part) on "intelligent" choices as to how we live within the ecosystem (1969: 375). Anticipating Lovelock, Mill writes that "by every choice that we make either of ends or of means, we place ourselves to a greater or less extent under one set of laws of nature instead of another" (1969: 379-80).

Mill is also enlightening, however, as a writer whose development of his philosophy came about, in a notable reversal of Morris, by means of a tempering of rational, technocentric thought with romantic, ecocentric feeling. Educated by his father, the utilitarian philosopher James Mill, into a strict conformity with those principles, Mill, at the age of 21, experienced "a crisis in my mental history". Interpreted by most critics as a form of depression brought about by the perceived inadequacies of the Enlightenment mind-set, he turned, in the midst of that crisis, to the poems of Wordsworth. Initially read for consolation, his discovery of Romanticism altered Mill's entire way of thinking (see Mill 1964: 115-16). In particular, Wordsworthian ideals of solitude and meditation, and "of natural beauty and grandeur", re-animated his economic philosophy towards an advocacy of anti-growth subsistence economics, which, as encapsulated in *The Principles of Political Economy*, have become, Derek Wall writes, "a swift and sure way of separating Green ideology from environmentalism" (1994: 116). For what Mill referred to as the "stationary state" was motivated by a concern about population which, as much romantic as it was utilitarian, was premised upon a re-imagining of quality of life that shifted this concept away from the materialist basis that underlay Victorian notions of progress:

> A population may be too crowded, though all be amply supplied with food and rai-ment. It is not good for man to be kept perforce at all times in the presence of his species. A world from which solitude is extirpated, is a very poor ideal. Solitude, in the sense of being often alone, is essential to any depth of meditation or of character; and solitude in the presence of natural beauty and grandeur, is the cradle of thoughts and aspirations which are not only good for the individual, but which society could ill do without. Nor is there much satisfaction in contemplating the world with nothing left to the spontaneous activity of nature; with every rood of land brought into cultiva-tion, which is capable of growing food for human beings [...] (1920 [1848]: 750)

The other obvious way in which Victorian literary sources might inform a contemporary social ecology would be through the critical but imaginative representation of Victorian political economy's impact on nonhuman and human alike. Many writers, novelists in particular, offer depictions of the hazards created by Victorian society on the surrounding environment. Disraeli, for example, pictures, in *Sibyl*, a landscape "interspersed with blazing furnaces, heaps of burning coal, and piles of smouldering ironstone" albeit that "patches of the surface" were "cov-ered, as if in mockery, with grass and corn". Yet he conveys this with the careful deliberation of a writer keen to properly understand nature. Describing a "dingy rather than dreary region", the selection of the adjective here is highly significant. For "dingy" – preferred to the more aesthetic, and more environmental, metaphor "dreary", and meaning soiled, sullied, tarnished – connotes, in the description of a land conta-minated, a deeper, ecological mode of analysis. This is likewise apparent when he records an example of soil erosion: "the subterranean operations [of the mining] were prosecuted with so much avidity that it was not uncommon to observe whole rows of houses awry, from the shifting and hollow nature of the land" (1980 [1845]: 177).

Victorian literature was equally preoccupied with the risk 'toxic' conditions posed to the human population. Apparent in the writings of the Victorian social investigators – Booth, Mayhew, Engels – a further example might be found in George Gissing's *Demos*, in the description of

Hoxton as "a region of malodorous market streets, of factories, timber-yards, grimy warehouses, of alleys swarming with small trades and crafts" that focuses not so much on condemnation of that environment, but on the nature of the streets as receptacles carrying disease into "filthy courts and passages leading into pestilential gloom" (1982 [1886]: 26). Dickens, similarly, describes in *Little Dorrit* a London where "Melancholy streets, in a penitential garb of soot, steeped the souls of the people who were condemned to look at them out of windows, in dire despondency" and where there is "Nothing to see but streets, streets, streets. Nothing to breathe but streets, streets, streets" (1985 [1857]: 67-8). Here again aesthetic, environmental description gives way, as implied in the "Nothing to breathe", to an ecological and also humanist critique of sanitary conditions:

> Fifty thousand lairs surrounded him where people lived so unwholesomely that fair water put into their crowded rooms on Saturday night, would be corrupt on Sunday morning [...] Miles of close wells and pits of houses, where the inhabitants gasped for air, stretched far away towards every point of the compass. Through the heart of the town a deadly sewer ebbed and flowed, in the place of a fine fresh river. (1985 [1857]: 68)

Finally, as is consistent with the development suggested in Chapter One, other Victorian writers revealed the extent to which this socially determined physical environment is inscribed upon the human body. In *Tess of the D'Urbervilles*, Hardy depicts the impact of a non-sustainable political economy both on the rural ecosystem and on its people. Here both the machine that reaps in circular motions pushing "rabbits, hares, snakes, rats, mice" into an "ephemeral refuge" and inevitable death in the middle of the field, and the threshing machine that shakes Tess "bodily by its spinning" and into an "incessant quivering, in which every fibre of her frame participated" serve a distant metropolis that exploits land and people alike (1978 [1891]: 137, 413-14). Elizabeth Gaskell is similarly attentive, in novels such as *Mary Barton*, to the human health implications of the Victorian urban ecosystem and the literal embodiment of it on the human population. This appears, for instance, in detailed descriptions, near the beginning of the book, of the "little feeble twins, inheriting the frail appearance of their mother" (1985 [1848]: 42) and later, more substantially, in Gaskell's

> thorough specimen of a Manchester man [...] born of factory workers, and himself bred up in youth, and living in manhood, among the mills. He was below the middle size and slightly made; there was almost a stunted look about him; and his wan, colourless

face, gave you the idea that in his childhood he had suffered from the scanty living consequent upon bad times. (1985 [1848]: 41)

Hopkins, though, has been selected as the subject of this study because his work adds an extra dimension to 'Victorian ecology'. That dimension is his utilisation of a deep ecological poetic, designed to reconvey the phenomenological moment and to enable us to feel the rhythms and processes of nature, towards a social ecopoetic in which we might feel, experience, and understand the transformations wrought by society on its human and nonhuman inhabitants. That poetic is to be found in the midst of a wider body of writing in which even the briefest of surveys would uncover many ideas that might loosely be called ecological: journal descriptions of 'harmony' and nativity – such as observations in the Alps of the "Beauty of the sycamores here, native to the soil" and "gracefully" shaped by "the valley winds" (JP 16/7/68: 175; 18/7/68: 176) – are one example as is a description of ecological imperialism in, Hopkins thinks, Australia: "the English trees introduced had driven out the natives, mostly different kinds of gum-trees […] In particular our furze, which thrives wonderfully and grows into great hedges, has driven the native vegetation before it" (JP 30/4/69: 190). We find further instances in the poetry: in the praise of wilderness in 'Inversnaid', in the protest against tree-felling in 'Binsey Poplars', in the complaint, in 'God's Grandeur', that "all is seared" and "smeared" by trade; and, likewise, in the assertion, in a letter to his mother, of the universal right of access to nature:

> No one is ever so poor that he is not (without prejudice to all the rest of the world) owner of the skies and stars and everything wild that is to be found on the earth. (FL 1/3/70: 111)

Yet as unconnected fragments these tell us little about whether Hopkins had the deeper understanding of ecological truths exhibited by writers discussed in this chapter. Accordingly, the next chapter highlights and outlines the ecological ontology that did frame his thinking and which was encapsulated and articulated in his nature journal, a piece of writing absolutely pivotal to a 'green' reading of Hopkins.

Chapter 3

Ways of Understanding Nature:
Ecology in Hopkins' Intellectual Formation

The development of Hopkins criticism points logically towards an ecocritical study. Early responses to his work, from supporters and detractors alike, dwelt, however, on its supposed peculiarity. This originated in the preface to the first edition of *The Poems of Gerard Manley Hopkins*, where his friend and editor Robert Bridges catalogued "faults of style" in sections titled "Obscurity", "Oddity", "Mannerism" etc. An impression cemented with the publication of a major two-part study by W. H. Gardner (editor of the third and fourth editions), entitled *Gerard Manley Hopkins: A Study of Poetic Idiosyncrasy in Relation to Poetic Tradition* (1944, 1949), it has persisted more recently with an interest in Hopkins' "intensity" or personal eccentricities in books such as John Robinson's *In Extremity* (1978) and Robert Bernard Martin's *Gerard Manley Hopkins: A Very Private Life* (1991). Nevertheless this had begun to change in the 1930s with a re-appraisal of Hopkins' work by critics such as I. A. Richards, William Empson and F. R. Leavis. Their emphasis on close reading of the text demonstrated that Hopkins' choice of language was not idiosyncratic but, rather, determined by the meaning and intention of the poems themselves (Roberts 1987: 19). Around this time, G. W. Stonier also complained that "there are two facts about Hopkins—that he was a Victorian in style, outlook and feeling, and that he was a Catholic priest who wrote poetry to the glory of God—these facts have been recognised by no critic whom I can trace" (see Roberts 1987: 227). The achievement of the approach taken by Leavis and others was to open up the possibility of seeing Hopkins in relation to each of these two contexts.

Religion was the first of these to be addressed. When John Pick, for example, opened his 1942 book *Gerard Manley Hopkins: Priest and Poet* with the statement that "interest in Hopkins the technician has been disproportionately great" (1) he was articulating just such an appetite for an understanding of the contexts and beliefs that shaped Hopkins' work, an appetite satisfied, in the 1930s and 40s, by a flurry of articles and books by critics such as Christopher Devlin, Fr. John Keating, W. A. M. Peters and Herbert Read. Asserting the centrality of faith to his work, such studies, claims Gerald Roberts, transformed the perception of Hopkins from a "devotional" to a more substantially theological poet (see 1987: 32-4).

Consideration of the other clause to Stonier's remark remained largely neglected until the 1960s when critics such as Alison Sulloway and Wendell Stacy Johnson began to relate Hopkins to the broader studies of the "Victorian temper" or "frame of mind" discussed in Chapter Two. The impact of this work can, in turn, be traced through the publication of even more detailed studies that have examined Hopkins in relation to particular aspects of Victorian culture. Including philology (Milroy 1977), Tractarianism (Johnson 1997), masculinity (Najarian 2002), and English Catholicism (Muller 2003), these represent an incremental narrowing of the critical focus that has extended to encompass further studies that point specifically towards an ecocritical reading. Stemming from the growth of research into Victorian literature and science, two books dealing, respectively, with evolutionary theory and energy physics – Tom Zaniello's *Hopkins in the Age of Darwin* (1988) and Daniel Brown's *Hopkins' Idealism: Philosophy, Physics, Poetry* (1997) – highlight an interest in precisely the ideas that would underlie the origins of ecological science (see, furthermore, Banfield 2007; Beer 1996; Nixon 2002). Similarly, with Sulloway already having established Hopkins within the paradigm of Victorian post-Romanticism, a subsequent study of his social thought, Sjaak Zonneveld's *The Random Grim Forge* (1992), pushes him towards the radical end of that critique thereby opening up a connection to Peter Gould's "early green politics".

Neither Sulloway nor Zonneveld sought, however, to establish the connections between Victorian post-Romanticism and ecological politics made by Berman or Williams. Correspondingly, none of the work on Hopkins' interest in science has made what appear to be obvious connections to ecological science. While the analysis, in the course of the next four chapters, addresses this, it should first be acknowledged that Hopkins himself has so far merited very little attention in ecocritical literature (see, however, Bellanca 2007; Nixon 2006; Parham 2003). I would suggest that one possible reason for this is the difficulty of relating him to the trope of place that has dominated such writing. Hopkins was constantly moved by the Jesuits and lived in nine different places in his twenty-one years in the Society. Memorably describing himself as "fortune's football" (RB 26/7/83: 183), lasting attachments were denied him. While the argument of this chapter will be that Hopkins arrived at an ecological mode of perception primarily by means of his intellectual formation, nevertheless place was not wholly insignificant in the formation of those ideas and interests.

1. Hopkins as not a poet of place

Born in East London, Hopkins actually spent most of his childhood in Hampstead in North London. This was, and probably still is, the antithesis to Stratford. On the edge of open country, Hampstead Heath had streams and ponds in which the family bathed. The Oak Hill development, where they lived, the recipient of an award at the Great Exhibition, was backed, not by the wooden hovels of railway workers, as at Stratford, but by fields of oak, hawthorn and elder trees, and wild rose and woodbine, where the family walked and sketched. Most significantly, while Metropolitan London's refuse was being exported eastwards, Hampstead was not only supplying the city's water, there had even been plans to "pipe its fresh air into the city centre" (White 1992: 14). At the same time, that centre was ever present – in his father Manley's occupation (as an Average Adjustor), in the visibility of St Paul's Cathedral from the Heath, and in the proximity of art galleries that Hopkins always enjoyed visiting. Hampstead had also, by this time, acquired an artistic reputation. Keats and Constable had lived there, Ford Madox Brown was resident, and between 1863 (when Hopkins went to university) and 1873 the publisher George Smith regularly entertained the likes of Thackeray, Millais, Trollope, Browning and Gaskell (see White 1992: 15-16).

Hopkins' next two experiences of place, at university in Oxford and at the Jesuit novitiate in Roehampton, West London, largely mirrored that at Hampstead. At university Hopkins frequently filled empty afternoons with excursions around the Thames Valley. Enjoying the countryside on an array of possible routes, walking was, at the same time, a social activity where friendships and connections were formed including, in his case, somewhat divergent friendships with Walter Pater, Fellow of Brasenose College and the controversial advocate of a philosophy of aestheticism, and Henry Parry Liddon, a charismatic clergyman and public speaker who, at the time, exerted a considerable influence on high church undergraduates. Reflecting the combination, here and at Hampstead, of an enjoyment of nature with social and cultural interests, it is apparent from his journal not only that much of Hopkins' walking involved visiting churches and manor houses but, in general, that the landscapes he most valued were those that incorporated both 'natural' and human (or 'built') features:

> most charming views from Elsfield [...] A plain lies on the opposite side to Oxford with villages crowned with square church-towers shining white here and there. The lines of the fields, level over level, are striking, like threads in a loom. Splendid trees—elms, and [...] great elliptic-curve oaks. Bloomy green of larches. (JP 14/4/64: 23)

The pattern was repeated at Roehampton, at the time regarded, like Hampstead, as "one of the highest and healthiest suburbs in London" (White 1992: 171). For while Hopkins clearly appreciated the forty acre grounds of Manresa House (see FL (Baillie) 6/5/82: 249) with its numerous species of trees, secluded landscape walks, farm and kitchen garden, as well as, on one occasion, "a remarkable show of buttercups" of which "you would not see the like in Italy" (RB 15/5/82: 144), the evidence of his letters suggests that he appreciated it also for its accessibility to London and his university friends (see RB 27/6/68: 23; 7/8/68: 24; FL (Baillie) 6/5/82: 249).

Hopkins did not really experience the countryside proper until 1870 when he began a three year course in 'philosophy', as part of his training for the priesthood, at St Mary's Hall, the Jesuit seminary situated at Stonyhurst in Lancashire. His immediate response unsurprisingly indicates an unfamiliarity with such environments. Writing to his mother "I feel the strangeness of the place" Hopkins was, all the same, fascinated, lingering, in his letters, on the landscape and the cold, and telling his university friend Alexander Baillie that it is "very bare and bleak [...] But nevertheless it is fine scenery, great hills and 'fells'" (FL 10/9/70: 112; 10/4/71: 234; see also RB 2/4/71: 26). In 1874 Hopkins went on to study theology at St Bueno's College in North Wales. Here he was immediately enraptured. Given five weeks to acclimatise, he took walks around the rivers, hills, woods, mountains and villages surrounding the college and felt his spirits immediately lift. He tells his father that "The air seems to me very fresh and wholesome" (see FL (Father) 29/8/74: 124) and he is captivated by a landscape of mountains and sky:

> The heights by Snowdon were hidden by the clouds but not from distance or dimness. The nearer hills, the other side of the valley, shewed a hard and beautifully detached and glimmering brim against the light, which was lifting there. All the length of the

valley the skyline of hills was flowingly written all along upon the sky. (JP 6/9/74: 258)

The diversity of places in which Hopkins lived (most of his later experience was, as described in Chapter Five, in the city) and the alien quality of his response to wild or rural environments suggests that Hopkins was not a poet of place in the way conventionally understood. Specific locations are mentioned in some of his titles – 'Binsey Poplars', 'Ribblesdale', 'Inversnaid', for example – yet the named place is often there merely to add authenticity. The only time at which place appears to assume any importance in his work was when, in his final years, Hopkins was exiled, as he saw it, to Dublin. There he yearned for England longing to see Epping Forest and the New Forest (see FL (Mother) 17/5/85: 171) and giving his poems specific English settings such as Fairlop Fair in Essex for a discarded stanza of 'On the Portrait of Two Beautiful Young People' and the River Hodder in Lancashire for the bathing place in 'Epithalamion'. Yet, as suggested by the fact that these poems remained incomplete, these are, in the end, merely the exceptions that proved the rule – that a poetry of place was alien to Hopkins.

Place did, as it happens, have some significance in his work, but in a less obvious way than would conventionally be associated with nature poetry. Jude V. Nixon suggests that Hampstead in particular "informed Hopkins' […] attitude to nature" (2006: 193). This he bases on a parallel to Constable, who had also lived there and whose interest in sky and clouds and light was, it seems, influenced by his observations of the sky around Hampstead. While offering no direct evidence of this, beyond the basic parallel, Nixon is, I believe, correct in his assertion but not in the specifically romantic sense that might be construed from his article (2006: 208). In actual fact, the influence of Hampstead on Hopkins was more in keeping with the area's epitomisation of a Victorian garden suburb.

Depicting Hampstead Village itself as a place where "Wordsworthian escape can […] be domesticated, stabilized, brought in close", Walter L. Creese defines the garden suburb, in more general terms, as "shaped by two very different impulses—the one, emotional or aesthetic, retained the Romantic wish to flee into woodland alleys and places of nestling green; the other, communal in emphasis, stressed the values of social cohesion and interdependence" (1977: 52-3). This conveys, at one level, what Hopkins got from Hampstead, as well as from Oxford and Roehampton: the enjoyable co-existence of a 'natural' environment with cultural amenities. However, it can also be translated, in a more abstract sense, to

something connected to Hopkins' intellectual formation. For where
Creese infers, here, the notion of the "two voices" – in the tension
invoked between a withdrawal and escape associated with the Romantic
attachment to nature and something "communal" and interested in "social
cohesion and interdependence" – Hopkins succeeded in unifying these
through what can be regarded as the suburban perspective that underlay
his nature writing.

   Reflective of Hopkins' upbringing was a perspective in which nature
was understood and articulated through cultural forms. There also came,
conversely, the recognition, taught by Ruskin, that culture itself should be
founded on, and pay deference to, nature. At one level this simply
amounted to a nature writing generated by the (sub)urban environment –
"Odd white-gold look of short grass in tufts: noticed it especially on the
opposite bank of the G.N.R. [Great Northern Railway] at Muswell Hill"
(JP 9/8/67: 150). More fundamentally, it also encapsulated a relationship
whereby what Hopkins gained from place was a reinforcement of generic
ideas that had been initially formulated through his intellectual interests.
That this equates to much the same ecological awareness as that aspired to
in the dominant ecocritical place-based paradigms can be inferred when
John Piper points out that Hopkins was "a *particularizer* in observation [...]
who by nature centred and converged on the local and the special as giving
the best evidence of the whole and of God" (JP: 455 (second italics mine)).
This can, however, be proven by means of a more extensive examination of
those intellectual interests, in which we find that Hopkins, in seeking to
establish a post-Romantic understanding of nature, arrived at an
ontological framework equivalent to that posited by an impending
ecological science.

2. Hopkins' intellectual formation: three major influences

One of the things indicated by the scope of the more recent studies of
Hopkins is the full extent of his intellectual interests, as indeed is
apparent from his diaries, journal and letters. *The Journals and Papers of
Gerard Manley Hopkins* contains, for example, "books to read" lists that
encompass literary works, philology, church history, theology and church
architecture (JP 1864: 35-6; February-March 1865: 56; Spring 1865: 60)
and a general content that points towards an even more bewildering array
of interests including etymology, botany, physics, art, Egyptology, and
current affairs. Though there may be some justification therefore for
Paddy Kitchen's description of Hopkins as one of those Victorians

preoccupied with "miscellaneous pieces of esoteric knowledge" (1978: 21), it was the convergence of three of the more prominent of those interests that brought him to a conception of nature and society that anticipated ecological theory. As described below these are: an interest in art which led him towards the development of a Ruskinian aesthetic of nature; an interest in architecture that brought about the conservatism of his religious and political beliefs, and an understanding of how Victorian society was re-shaping its natural and human environments; a familiarity with contemporary science that gave an unmistakeably ecological quality to his understanding and representation of nature.

Hopkins' earliest interest appears to have been sketching, which he honed initially in the fields around Hampstead, at his grandparents' home in Croydon, and at his aunt's house in Epsom. At school he studied drawing as an additional subject (Martin 1991: 13) while we know from his letters that Hopkins took a lively interest in his brothers' pictures (two out of four of whom became artists or illustrators) and, from a remark to Baillie, that he had "once wanted to be a painter" (FL 12/2/68: 231). Critical assessments of Hopkins' drawings, a selection of which are reproduced in *The Journals and Papers*, suggest, however, that he would have been unlikely to have succeeded and imply, in fact, that his drawings "do not show the response of a painter but of a scientific natural philosopher who uses drawings as a secondary, subordinate process to his main purpose" (White 1975: 90; see also White 1992: 20; JP: 454). The "main purpose" to which Norman White refers was a Ruskinian attempt to understand the underlying "truths" behind nature. Destined to become the primary motivation behind his writing, this interest, derived from Ruskin, was the most substantial outcome of Hopkins' interest in painting.

While there is little evidence as to how much Ruskin Hopkins actually read, circumstantially the signs of his influence are irrefutable (see Ball 1971: 104; Bergonzi 1978: 6, 20; Sulloway 1972: 64-9). In 1863, in a letter to Baillie – written when he was just eighteen – Hopkins confirms both his interest in painting and a great ad miration for Ruskin that extended to the deployment of both a Ruskinian methodology and philosophy. He tells Baillie "I am sketching (in pencil chiefly) a good deal. I venture to hope you will approve of some of the sketches in a Ruskinese point of view" (FL 10/7/63: 202). He adds, in a second letter, that he regards Ruskin as a critic whose "whole powers [...] are perhaps equal to those of the men whose work he criticises" (FL 6/9/63: 203). Praising Millais, again in distinctively Ruskinian terms, for "at last arriving at Nature's self, which is of no school—inasmuch as different schools represent Nature in their own more or less truthful different ways, Nature meanwhile having only one way" (FL 10/7/63: 201-2), Hopkins concludes the first letter by corroborating that his primary interest lay in observing and recording the natural world:

> I think I have told you that I have particular periods of admiration for particular things in Nature; for a certain time I am astonished at the beauty of a tree, shape, effect etc, then when the passion, so to speak, has subsided, it is consigned to my treasury of explored beauty, and acknowledged with admiration and interest ever after, while something new takes its place in my enthusiasm. The present fury is the ash, and perhaps barley and two shapes of growth in leaves and one in tree boughs and also a conformation of fine-weather cloud. (FL 10/7/63: 202)

The reference here to a "treasury of explored beauty" which will be "acknowledged [...] ever after" corroborates that what motivated Hopkins' interest in trees and leaves and clouds was the attempt to establish an underlying "truth" behind nature. Inevitably then, Hopkins followed Ruskin's suggested methods for arriving at that truth. Most notably, Ruskin's insistence that the artist should reproduce the natural world faithfully was a key principle by which he assessed artists or works of art. George F. Rosenberg is criticised, for example, because "he has definitely given himself to a mannered tree touch" (JP 2/7/66: 142). Observations made in the journal supported this practice, offering direct means of comparison. A description of the sea, written in the Isle of Man in 1872, fed into Hopkins' assessment of a painting ('Rough weather in the open, Mediterranean') by Henry Moore, the contemporary seascape specialist, two years later:

> The overflow of the last wave came in from either side tilting up the channel and met halfway, each with its own moustache.
>
> a coast-scene with wave breaking, but there the moustache of foam running before the wave or falling back to it seemed a little missed or muddled. (JP 16/8/72: 225; Spring 1874: 247)

This was a basis for judgement that Hopkins would extend to poetry. Swinburne is criticised because he "does not see nature at all or else [...] overlays the landscape with such phantasmata, secondary images, and what not of a delirious-tremendous imagination" (RB 1/1/85: 202). Conversely, Hopkins admired his friend Richard Dixon's poems for possessing "so astonishingly clear an inward eye to see what is in visible nature" (RWD 13/6/78: 9) while nevertheless monitoring Dixon's adherence to that principle. He is admonished, in one letter, for making roses redder than poppies and because "the rain could never be wooed by the rainbow which only comes into being by its falling" (RWD 26/9/81: 61; 10/3/79: 20).

The most significant element, however, of Ruskin's influence on Hopkins was to incorporate him into what Patricia M. Ball describes as a "nineteenth-century tradition of factual observation" (115). Referring to Ruskin's famous distinction, in "The Moral of Landscape", between science proper and a "science of the aspects of things" – defined in the claim, about natural phenomena, that "it is as much a fact to be noted in their constitution, that they produce such and such an effect upon the eye or heart […] as that they are made up of certain atoms or vibrations of matter" (1903-12 (5): 387) – Ball is slightly dismissive in relation both to Ruskin, in whom she sees a "science of aspects" as leading to a "pathetic fallacy" that theologises nature (100), and, to a lesser degree, Hopkins. With regard to Hopkins, Ball finds in the journal "an imaginative logic at work based on visual analogy, rather than a more strictly scientific process of thought" before concluding that "His science, in short, is Ruskin's: the science of aspects" (119). Robert Hewison, however, has argued that this Ruskinian paradigm actually represents a useful alignment between the "discipline imposed by the emphasis on accurate observation as the foundation of all knowledge" and the imaginative dimension, not least "in terms of man's moral relationship with nature", that can be supplied to science by the arts; an "even more pressing" need, he points out, in the context of environmental concern (1996: 43-4). While such an argument usefully justifies a "science of the aspects of things" and does indeed describe an element within Hopkins' approach, it is also worth pointing out that the Ruskinian aesthetic was, in Hopkins' work, submitted to, and modified through, new ways of seeing nature that became available as a result of contemporary science. Before considering this, however, one further direction in which Hopkins followed Ruskin was through his interest in architecture.

This interest was initially fostered when, at the age of thirteen, Hopkins was given, as a present, J. H. Parker's *Introduction to the Study of Gothic Architecture*. White describes Parker's book as "perhaps the most lastingly influential book in his early education" (1992: 21) and certainly architecture was a notable feature of Hopkins' earliest writing. His first known poem, "The Escorial", which won him the Poetry Prize at Highgate School, describes the monastery and palace built near Madrid in the sixteenth century by Philip II (now a UNESCO World Heritage site).

His 'early diaries', written while at Oxford, also highlight this interest. They indicate further reading on the subject, including a list of things to show visitors that is dominated by Gothic buildings (JP 1864: 21 (310), 30-1, 32-3); and see FL (Baillie) 20/7/64: 214), and numerous detailed descriptions, precise measurements (see JP 1/9/68: 187-8; 15/8/74: 253), and judgements about the architecture of churches, abbeys and cathedrals. That stringent evaluation implies, as White goes on to argue, that Hopkins' interest in this area, as with his interest in art, formed tastes "which went well beyond architecture" (1992: 21). In fact, two things appear to have developed out of it. The first was an awareness that from buildings we can judge the nature of humanity's impact on the environment, an idea which conforms to Ruskin's paradigm of typical and vital beauty; secondly, Hopkins began to develop from this a social philosophy which would, in due course, inform and structure his critique of society. Discussed in more detail in Chapter Five, the origins of that philosophy can, nevertheless, be outlined here.

Sharing Parker and Ruskin's Gothic prejudices a notable feature of Hopkins' descriptions was a preference for old over new architecture. Occasionally confusing the former with what was, in fact, restored work (see JP 4/8/72: 221; 1/9/74: 257), the judgements Hopkins made nevertheless indicate a particular preference for medieval architecture. He admires the Lady-chapel at Ely Cathedral that had prompted Pugin to burst into tears; he describes the "flow of the main lines" of tracery and foliation in a medieval tomb at Exeter Cathedral as "original, flush, sweet, and tender, and truly classical, as befits and marks a flush and hopeful age" (JP 1/9/68: 187-8 (400); (15/8/74): 253); and, on the same basis, Hopkins championed the architect William Butterfield, heavily associated with the revival of Gothic, whose buildings he frequently visited and from whom, in 1877, he requested and received a list of commissions. Praising Butterfield's "beautiful and original style" Hopkins told the architect "I do not think this generation will ever much admire it. They do not understand how to look at a Pointed building as a whole having a single form governing it throughout" (cited in White 1992: 277). What, however, Hopkins was actually seeking was the development of a "modern spontaneous Gothic, as in [the] middle ages" (JP: 13).

Central to his preference for medieval work was a belief in the idea of historical permanence or continuity. Hopkins dismissed, on this basis, Alfred Waterhouse's new Balliol College buildings (completed in 1868) because "there seems to be no conservative spirit at work"; he later tells

Bridges that "in architecture it heightens one's admiration of a design to know that it is old work, not new; in itself the design is the same but as taken together with the designer and his merit this circumstance makes a world of difference" (FL (Mother), 13/4/67: 100-1); RB 14/8/79: 88). These architectural preferences were symptomatic of his social values. For what, in this context, the combination of a "modern spontaneous Gothic" and his emphasis on permanence and continuity amounted to was something consistent with Chandler's depiction of Victorian medieval-ism, a critique of modernity that fell back upon the desire to reassert conservative values. This initially took the form, in Hopkins' case, of an adoption of High Church beliefs at Oxford where in fact the principal High Church Society, the Brotherhood of the Holy Trinity, had been founded on the demise, a decade earlier, of the Oxford Architectural Society (Martin 1991: 57). Hopkins' involvement with this faction began almost as soon as he had arrived at Oxford. In May 1863 he heard Liddon speak and took notes (White 1992: 63). Subsequently, Liddon became his confessor. Though Hopkins declined an invitation to join the Brother-hood, by the spring of 1864 he was involved in the formation of the Hexameron Society "an essay group devoted to conservative principles in the church" (Martin 1991: 73-4). Oxford cemented, in other words, a conservatism which had developed out of his interest in architecture, a principle which, as discussed in Chapter Five, found its culmination in Hopkins' conversion to Catholicism and subsequent decision to become a Jesuit.

His interests in art and architecture created the foundation, therefore, for a framework in which an assessment of humanity's impact on the environment (whether 'natural' or built) would be converted into a consideration of the social and political solutions designed to mitigate that impact. Though, as implied, this was perhaps more environmental than ecological at this point, Hopkins' ideas about both nature and society were to become more sharply defined by the third key interest, science, which brought greater ecological precision to his thinking.

Several writers, as noted, have drawn attention to Hopkins' interest in science. Both Beer and Zaniello have pointed out, for example, that he was a keen reader of *Nature* and *The Academy*, the latter a journal, consistent with the interdisciplinary character of Victorian scientific discourse, divided equally between science, natural philosophy, theology and language (Beer 1996: 244, 254; Zaniello 1988: 134). Zaniello notes, furthermore, that scientific study was a not insignificant component of Hopkins' education, given that Oxford was undergoing something of a scientific revolution at the time, and, later, that as a Jesuit he twice came into contact with a burgeoning scientific culture at Stonyhurst (in the form of a group known as the Stonyhurst Philosophers) (see 1988: 2, 79, 89). There is, likewise, considerable evidence in Hopkins' prose testifying to his interest in science. He wrote in an undergraduate essay that science is "more vigorous than ever before and asserting its claim to new ground continually" and that its advancement had given a "fresh knowledge of facts in the same way as a trade is advancing which is widening its connection" (see Brown 1997: 52-3; Zaniello 1988: 132). He tells Dixon of wanting to write "a sort of popular account of Light and the Ether", claiming confidently that "no such account exists and scientific books, especially in English, are very unsatisfactory". He complains to Bridges of his failure to write even material consistent with his duties "like scientific works" and, highlighting a value placed on science for its own sake, criticises another poet friend, Coventry Patmore, for his suggestion that "the only real use of natural science is to supply similes and parables for poets and theologians" (RWD 7/8/86: 139; RB 12/1/88: 270; FL 20/1/87: 377; and see Nixon 2002: 148). There is also evidence of an at least passing interest in climatology and meteorology. This is seen in instances of astronomy in his theological writing (SD: 198, 307-8), in observations made at the Stonyhurst Observatory (see RWD: 161-6; JP 29/11/71: 217; 22/5/72: 220: Zaniello 1988: 61), and in four letters to *Nature* about the phenomenon of beams of shadow "in the eastern sky about sunset" and the remarkable sunsets caused by dust particles released into the air from the eruption of Krakatoa in August 1883 (see RWD: 161-6). The last of these letters (discovered and published by Ball) even highlights the surprising extent of Hopkins' faith in scientific practice itself. Discussing speculations about an increase in the power of the sun, Hopkins wrote that if this "is going on [...] this ought to be both felt and measured by exact instruments, not by the untrustworthy impressions of the eye" (Ball 1971: 148).

If the argument for Hopkins' interest in science is, then, irrefutable, it is also the case that this interest converged around the areas which were to form scientific ecology. In the first instance, Hopkins was interested in the two components, natural history (in particular botany) and evolutionary theory, that comprise Darwinian theory. Both Norman MacKenzie and Mary Ellen Bellanca have noted that his writing was informed by his reading and consulting of natural history texts and that Hopkins often visited botanical gardens and exhibits, notably Kew Gardens which was near to Manresa House (see Bellanca 2007: 202-3; MacKenzie 1993: 86).

Hopkins' interest in botany is, furthermore, flagged up by his attendance, while an undergraduate, at Charles Daubney's lectures on "Shrubs of the Ancients" – to which, Humphrey House observes, "GMH paid considerable attention" (JP 1865: 61 (336)) – and by several journal references, such as the following, to botanical classification: "Floral 'sit' of beech leaves, the knots in fact realising green flowers, as in other cases explained by botanists" (JP 22/5/68: 165).

Corresponding evidence as to Hopkins' familiarity with evolutionary theory, and with Darwin, while not explicit, is, like that concerning Ruskin, readily apparent. While Hopkins only wrote twice, and then only in letters, about Darwin, he agonised like many Victorians about the implications of Darwinian ideas. In the second of these letters Hopkins commented to Bridges on a discussion, in *The Origin of Species*, about the hexagonal structure of beehives. Darwin regarded this structure as a good example of natural selection because, optimal for saving wax, it left greater opportunity for the production of honey. Without disputing those facts, Hopkins nevertheless challenges Darwin's explanation by attributing this to design and by suggesting that it had "nothing to do with mechanics" (RB 18/8/88: 281). This indicates that for Hopkins the difficulties posed by Darwinism lay not so much with the theories themselves, but in the tendency of those theories towards a purely materialist explanation. Marie Banfield has noted that "Evolution at this time was a contested area" and that "Lamarckian evolution, suggesting purposeful adaptation rather than the random process of natural selection, continued to be a force after *The Origin of Species*" (2007: 179). Hopkins' preference for just such an alternative is apparent from the first of the two letters in which, as Banfield notes, he recommended to his mother the work of the Catholic scientist St George Mivart.

In *On the Genesis of Species* (1871), the book Hopkins recommended, Mivart attempted to square the theory of evolution with Catholic orthodoxy (FL (20/9/74): 128). Jill Muller notes that this entailed an acceptance of natural selection but one tempered by a qualification of the materialist tendencies within Darwinian theory – notably its privileging of the atomistic dimension as the core truth about nature – and by the belief that this was only one of a number of laws, some of which remained to be discovered, governing life on earth (2003: 83). This is alluded to by Hopkins prior to his recommending Mivart's work to his mother.

I do not think, do you know, that Darwinism implies necessarily that man is descended from any ape or ascidian or maggot or what not but only from the common ancestor of apes, the common ancestor of ascidians, the common ancestor of maggots, and so on. (FL (20/9/74): 128)

Though the "common", primary cause to which Hopkins alludes is that of Catholic belief – Hopkins describes Mivart as "an Evolutionist though he combats downright Darwinism and is very orthodox" – it might also be seen in terms of ecological theory because Mivart has, in fact, been claimed by at least one commentator as a "neglected" originator of such ideas.

Writing in *The Ecologist*, G. N. Syer, noting that Mivart was both a convert (at the age of 16) to Catholicism and a professional biologist, regards his ecological thinking as having emerged from an attempt to reconcile the two. Syer argues that Mivart modified Darwinism by means of an "intense aesthetic appreciation of the beauties of natural things" and through an emphasis, primarily seen in a further book, *Nature and Thought*, on the interrelationship of animals and plants with humans. This was, furthermore, a co-dependence which Mivart felt was in the process of being undermined by social practices that included deforestation and what has since become referred to as 'ecological imperialism':

> Let a new land be discovered with a peculiar fauna and flora full of scientific interest, and straightaway the European purposely introduces his thistles, his sparrows, his rabbits or his goats, and the harmonious balance which has resulted from the organic interplay of ages is at once destroyed. Downright evil is often the result. Forests are recklessly felled, and arid, rainless wastes or dismal fever-laden swamps ensue. (1971: 13-14; and see Wall 1994: 6)

The ecological connotations here are not incidental. The reconciliation in Mivart's work, between a materialist evolutionary theory and an idealist sense of underlying interdependent relationship, forms part of a tradition of evolutionary theory which, as discussed in Chapter One, has been more recently developed by the complexity sciences into an ecologically inflected notion of unity in diversity. Influenced by Mivart, this was the brand of evolutionism that entered into Hopkins' thinking.

In *Hopkins' Idealism*, Daniel Brown offers corresponding, and de-tailed, evidence concerning Hopkins' interest in and knowledge of several of the key areas and concepts of Victorian physics. These include mechanics, optics, the conservation of energy and hydrodynamics. Beer (1996) makes much the same point when she argues that Hopkins was familiar with the work both of John Tyndall (whom he had met briefly in the Alps) and, almost certainly, Hermann von Helmholtz, whose writing on thermodynamics and on the laws of optics and acoustics related closely to Hopkins' interests. While, again, a great deal of circumstantial evidence can be presented that testifies to his interest in physics, more substantial proof rests in the particular, and more fundamental, ways in which this interest came to shape Hopkins' intellectual framework.

As with evolutionary theory, physics posited a paradigm of flux, in this case through an emphasis on the flow and exchange of energy. At the same time, however, as Stephen Brush has argued, the first law of thermodynamics, the conservation of energy, also "provided an organising principle for the science of the realist period [which followed]" (cited in Brown 1997: 194). While one attraction, therefore, of physics was the principle of order that it bestowed upon flux another, Brown suggests, was that it conferred "mechanistic content" (1997: 194-5), or materiality, on "the grand ontological unity envisaged by the romantics" (1997: 193). What physics offered Hopkins, in other words, was a further extension to the post-Romantic process by which he sought to perceive and reconcile a sense of underlying truth with 'Being' or materiality.

That process would lead Hopkins to what were, in this context, significant conclusions. These are considered below. It should, first of all, be conceded, however, that one can overstate the extent to which Hopkins was informed by science. Zaniello points out that he never worked within any of the established modes of scientific practice such as carrying out experiments or writing scientific reports or articles (79, 81). He also points out that Hopkins often did treat science metaphorically (130-1, 134). Hopkins also struggled, on occasion, with scientific facts, especially botanical ones. He failed, for instance, to identify "ox-eye-like flowers", most probably those of the camomile plant, so that we see, in the journal, passages such as the following: "the head of a spike has, let us say, eight flowers, the nibs of which—I do not know the botanical name—point outwards" (JP 7/7/66: 144 (363); 2/9/67: 155). J. S. L. Gilmour, enlisted, as the Director of the Botanical Garden in Cambridge, to unpick the scientific errors in the journal, concludes that, as with his interest in art and architecture, Hopkins' real interest lay beyond scientific knowledge itself.

> GMH looked at plants with the eye of an artist rather than of a botanist. He possessed remarkable powers of close observation from his own very personal angle, but as this 'angle' was far removed from the normal botanical one, and as the language he used in his descriptions was highly individual, it is not always easy to be sure of what plant—or what part of a plant he had before him. (JP: 364)

Yet however incomplete Hopkins' understanding of science might have been, the only conclusion that can be drawn from the evidence presented is that he did have a receptiveness to, and commonplace acquaintance with, Victorian science. Indeed, composed as this interest was of various elements, Hopkins' work would bring, Brown suggests, "disparate areas of science together in a single conception, and so engenders a radically new form of knowledge" (1997: 52-3). Given that that "conception" emerges from the convergence of older disciplines (natural history, botany) with more modern paradigms (evolutionary theory and energy physics), it would be no great supposition that this "radically new form of knowledge" amounted to a prototypical ecological ontology. This is implied when Beer writes that Hopkins was "drawn to natural history by its prinked exactness of observation, to physics by its changed meteorological interpretations and its insistence on waves, vibrations, patterns" (1996: 255) and is even more explicit when Brown summarises what, exactly, Hopkins gained from physics:

> Physics was, at the time that Hopkins was writing, a much more apt source of metaphors for (and indeed examples of) integral being and specific identity than biology […] The[re was a] shift at this time to inorganic phenomena in order to illustrate differentiated unity […] Inorganic and organic phenomena have an affinity in Hopkins' ontology that allows them to keep each other 'company'. They share a 'force', a common principle which suggests the modern conception of a convertible principle of 'energy'. (1997: 201-2)

The ecological connotations here are unmistakeable. Yet throughout the work that has addressed Hopkins' interest in science there remains barely an acknowledgement of that. To give another, noteworthy example, Banfield, without any mention of ecological science, describes Hopkins as having posited a "dynamic but unified universe". She even infers the Gaia hypothesis in noting, in this connection, Tyndall's comparison of the universe to a single organism: "It is as if the body of Nature [wrote Tyndall] were alive, the thrill and interchange of its energies resembling those of an organism" (see 2007: 182). Yet as Hopkins developed his intellectual framework this anticipation of ecological science only becomes more obvious. Enacted ultimately in the journal, which is examined in the second half of this chapter, it was in his undergraduate essays that such ideas first began to really take shape.

3. Beginnings of an ecological philosophy: undergraduate essays

The cluster of essays and notes written at Oxford, where Hopkins studied between 1863 and 1867, reveal two major preoccupations: a desire to understand and assert the presence of an ontological truth governing nature; and the attempt to develop a "scientific basis of aesthetical criticism" capable of articulating that truth. It is the second of these which Hopkins began to sketch out in one of the earliest and most important of his undergraduate essays 'On the Signs of Health and Decay in the Arts'.

This essay, written in 1864, underlines, in the first place, the Ruskinian basis to his ideas. Hopkins begins the essay by reiterating the conventional Romantic argument that the "lawful objects of art" are "Truth and Beauty" (JP: 74). This occurs in conjunction, however, with a post-Romantic distinction that "Art differs from Nature in presenting Truth; Nature presents only beauty" (JP: 74). While this appears at first to diminish nature, that is rectified, to a large extent, by the "aesthetical criticism" Hopkins then sets out. He suggests, to begin with, that the "preponderance" of either truth or beauty "to the setting aside of the other" would destroy "the balance and therefore the success of Art" (JP: 76). What Hopkins argues here is that while the pursuit of "Truth" remains primary, that can and must be prompted by beauty, by which he means, effectively, the initial phenomenological stimulus. Hence, the expression of truths first glimpsed through nature remain the foundation, Hopkins believes, of art.

What, however, he means by differentiating "Truth and Beauty" is that the identification of the former, while motivated by the phenomenological moment, has to lie, ultimately, within the human mind. This Hopkins makes clear when he writes that "truth" might be established by means of any one of the following range of comparisons: "(i) of existence with non-existence […] (ii) of a thing with itself so as to see in it the continuance of law […] (iii) of two or more things together […] (iv) of finite with infinite things" (JP: 74). Arguing that "Art" is primarily "concerned with the last two of these classes" (JP: 74), Hopkins concludes, more generally, that the pleasure to be gained from art resides in an intellectual process of establishing truths about and within nature:

> The pleasure given by the presence of Truth in art may, if the classification above be rightly made, be referred to the third head. It lies in a (not sensuous but purely intellectual) comparison of the representation in Art with the memory of the true thing; and the truer it is, the more exact the parallel between the two, the more pleasure is perceived. (JP: 74-5)

Hopkins also established in this essay that any inability, as displayed through art, to understand or apprehend nature accurately would be indicative of a society un-attuned to truth, a line of argument which follows, of course, Ruskin's connection between typical and vital beauty. Hopkins writes "The arts present things to us in certain modes which in the higher shape we call idealism […] The character of these idealisms is the best guide to the health of any age of Art"; and, in a pointed reference to Victorian modernity, that "with genius abounding and in a time of national health, there would be no degeneracy" in art (JP: 78-9). Hopkins formulates then, in this essay, the two aesthetic principles that would guide his work. The first of these – that writing, having been prompted by the phenomenological moment, then moves towards a conceptualisation of nature founded on the comparison of phenomena – became the basis for his journal and for the nature poetry examined in Chapter Four; the second, that the health of art is indicative of the "health" of the "age of Art", implies, and shapes, the later development from aesthetic to social critique covered in Chapter Five. Further to this, it was Hopkins' other concern, to understand and assert the precise form of the ontological truth governing nature, that preoccupied the majority of his undergraduate writing.

That concern was motivated by the desire, as has been alluded to, to incorporate the philosophies of atomism and flux into a fresh conception of underlying reality. The particular shape Hopkins gave to this engagement with prevailing Darwinian philosophy is most apparent in an 1867 essay 'The Probable Future of Metaphysics'. Opening with the remark that as "The Positivists foretell and many other people begin to fear, the end of all metaphysics is at hand", Hopkins goes on to suggest that Positivism has come to "over-power" Victorian culture and that "a form of atomism like a stiffness or sprain seems to hang upon and hamper our speculation" (118, 120). Demonstrating, though, an at least partial receptiveness to new ideas, Hopkins attempts a degree of resolution. Outlining "three great seasons in the history of philosophy" – Greek, the Enlightenment, nineteenth-century historicism – Hopkins, though conceding that "philosophy must not so much speak of right and wrong in systems but must acknowledge its history and growth to itself", suggests that Positivism and metaphysics "differ in kind" so that "neither can be made to fall under the other" (JP: 118).

Seeking not to deny but merely redress what he saw as an over-privileging of the materialist mode of Victorian science, this took the form in the first place, consistent with his later interest in Mivart, of an objection to the downgrading of the organism, or of species, that had resulted from Darwin's location of the unit of heredity in the atom. As a key aspect, that is, of his "challenge [to] the prevalent philosophy of continuity or flux", Hopkins questioned the mutability of species. Asserting here that "certain forms which have a great hold on the mind [...] are always reappearing and seem imperishable", he illustrates this, analogously, with reference to the perpetuity of artistic styles "such as the designs of Greek vases and lyres" before stating, more substantially, that while "to the prevalent philosophy and science nature is a string all the differences in which are really chromatic but certain places in it have become accidentally fixed", for him

> forms have in some sense or other an absolute existence. It is maintainable [...] that species are fixed and to be fixed only at definite distances in the string and that the developing principle will only act when the precise conditions are fulfilled. (JP: 120)

While the science here is not entirely convincing, and the critique of mutability perhaps exaggerated by the presence of a theological component, nevertheless the defence offered of the integrity of species would lead Hopkins towards an intuition of concepts such as biodiversity and, in the end, to the ecological ethic (as Goodwin writes) that we are "biologically grounded in relationships [...] with all other species".

Working, then, in the tradition of a not entirely materialist science, Hopkins goes on to establish the secondary understanding that overarching "dynamical systems" will emerge from "the integrated behaviour of organisms". For his response, in the essay, to "atomism" was to argue that "it will always be possible to shew how science is atomic, not to be grasped and held together, 'scopeless', without metaphysics: this alone gives meaning to laws and sequences and causes and developments" (118-20). On this understanding, Hopkins therefore advocates the need for a correction of the atomistic principle that the "history of growth [...] mounts from the part to the whole" so as to "once more maintain that the Idea is given [...] from the whole downwards to the parts" (JP: 120-1). He therefore speculates that Platonism "or to speak more correctly Realism, is perhaps soon to return". While one dimension of the "Realism" he'd go on to elaborate would be theological, another complementary "sense" in which Hopkins perceived this "absolute" principle was, as we shall see, through an essentially Gaian notion of the earth as a living, continually emergent ecosystem.

The beginnings of that understanding are signalled in another piece 'On the Origin of Beauty: A Platonic Dialogue'. Probably not an undergraduate essay (see JP: xxii-xxiii), this is, in fact, a largely fictional dialogue comprised of three characters – a Professor, scholar, and artist – who, accidentally meeting in New College Gardens in Oxford, discuss the relationship between beauty and the "presence of law" (JP: 90) in nature. It can, in that sense, be regarded as an informal attempt to work through the implications of Ruskinian post-Romanticism as it had been augmented by Hopkins' scientific interests.

Through the character of the Professor, who holds a "newly founded chair of aesthetics" and is apparently based on Ruskin, Hopkins defines a concept of beauty founded, in the first place, on a combination of "likeness and difference":

> 'Then the beauty of the oak and the chestnut-fan and the sky is a mixture of likeness and difference or agreement and disagreement or consistency and variety or symmetry and change.'
> 'It seems so, yes.' (JP: 90)

We begin to see here the realisation of the intellectual process established in the 'Health and Decay' essay. For Hopkins suggests that studies which would have taken the form, in the first instance, of a comparison of "a thing with itself so as to see […] the continuance of law" inevitably progress towards, first, the comparison "of two or more things together" and from there to deeper ontological principles – Hopkins' fourth heading in that essay, the comparison of "finite with infinite". This impulse to pursue the infinite is conveyed here through the interjections of the undergraduate Hanbury who wishes to consider whether "there is in the higher forms of beauty [...] something mystical, something I don't know how to call it" (JP: 95). Seeking this out, Hanbury ends up, however, merely expressing a frustration borne from the same confusion as Tennyson's "I cannot think the thing farewell". This happens because Hopkins, prior to his conversion to Catholicism, had not, at this stage, come close to resolving the theological question of the "infinite" (due to which Hanbury's speculations remain unanswered). Continuing, though, with a development of the comparison of "two or more things together" he does reach an alternative, non-theological conception of "higher forms" broadly akin to ecological thinking when the Professor, making an analogy with the balance of masses in painting, concludes that "Beauty" resides in the "relation" between phenomena:

> 'Does not then the beauty lie in the relation between the masses?'
> 'It seems it does.'
> 'Beauty then is a relation.'
> 'I suppose it is.'
> 'And things which have relation are near enough to have something in common, but not near enough to be one and the same, are they not?'

'Yes.' (JP: 94-5)

What Hopkins established, out of the Professor's insistence that the "truth" manifest in beauty resides in a dialectical interrelatedness of species, is a fundamentally ecological paradigm, a reconciliation between difference, even competition, and balance or interdependence. Only sketched out here, this emerging paradigm is developed further in some later, fragmentary 'Notes on the History of Greek Philosophy'.

One of the sections of these notes, that which begins "All words mean either things or relations of things" (see JP: 125-6), can be seen as a response to Walter Pater's criticism of Greek philosophy for a tendency to prioritise logical truths over other forms of knowledge (see Brown 1997: 165-6). In 1866 Hopkins had been sent to be coached by Pater in preparation for his finals. While he liked Pater – on later returning to Oxford as a priest he wrote "Pater was one of the men I saw most of" (FL (Baillie) 22/5/80: 246) – his tutor's influence, in terms of the development of his thinking, was to problematise the aesthetic principles Hopkins had inherited from Ruskin and Wordsworth. For though both Hopkins and Pater "stressed", writes Bernard Bergonzi, "the importance of the individual moment, the sudden insight or illumination" (1978: 18-19), they drew, from this, sharply contrasting arguments.

In the notorious, but remarkable conclusion to his *Studies in the History of The Renaissance* (1873) Pater, drawing from an acquaintance with contemporary science (see Beer 1996: 305, 248; Fletcher 1971: 26), celebrates the "prevailing" principle of ongoing flux:

> Every moment some form grows perfect in hand or face; some tone on the hills or sea is choicer than the rest; some mood or passion or intellectual excitement is irresistibly real and attractive for us,—for that moment only [...] To burn always with this hard gem-like flame, to maintain this ecstasy, is success in life. (1986: 152)

Though the external stimulus is momentary, and destined to dissolve into "impressions—colour, odour, texture—in the mind of the observer", for Pater that "moment", the moment of perception, was nevertheless primary, on which basis he rejected any attempt to "order" or theorise those perceptions:

> Gathering all we are into one desperate effort to see and touch, we shall hardly have time to make theories about the things we see and touch. What we have to do is to be for ever curiously testing new opinions and courting new impressions, never acquiescing in a facile orthodoxy. (1986: 152)

Due to the perceived secularism of his vision, and the potential connotations of immorality in his advocacy of ever more intense forms of "ecstasy", Pater was condemned for the conclusion and, indeed, professionally compromised (he was blocked, for example, from various posts at Oxford such as Professor of Poetry (see Aldington 1948: 9; Small 1979: xvi)). Hopkins was less censorious, but much of his undergraduate writing nevertheless appears to have been designed, consciously or otherwise, as a response to Pater's controversially modern arguments albeit conducted, as we can see from these notes, in a spirit of compromise.

Pater's view that experience, sensation, "ecstasy" amounted to "success in life" provoked anxiety in Hopkins because it more or less completely shattered the relationship between beauty and morality. His response, in these notes, is predictable, in that Hopkins sought to reassert the priority of "the idea" as emphasised in 'The Probable Future of Metaphysics'. Yet what is interesting about them is not the repetition of a belief in "the unity of the whole" (JP: 126), but a corrective adjustment back towards the materialist emphasis. This is established in subsequent notes on the philosopher Parmenides, also of interest because they contain the first reference to Hopkins' twinned concepts of inscape and instress.

In these notes Hopkins considers the implication of what he describes as Parmenides' "great text, which he repeats with religious conviction [...] that Being is and Not-being is not" (JP: 127). The emphasis here, as might be inferred from the similarity to Heideggerian terms, is on the material dimension which, Hopkins thereby deduced, must have value. His thinking corresponds, in this respect, with Pater's essentially phenomenological stress on the momentary "impression" for value is perceived, in the first place, through the impression that Being leaves on the individual observer, an impression so powerful than even after the act of observation it remains "to the mind's eye as fast present here; for absence cannot break off Being from its hold on Being" (JP: 128). Hopkins expands on that value by suggesting that knowledge can only be founded, ultimately, by means of a succession of separate phenomenological experiences. Without these "there would be no bridge, no stem of stress between us and things to bear us out and carry the mind over: without stress we might not and could not say/ Blood is red/ but only/ This blood is red" (JP: 127). This notion that a "stem of stress" between us and other species will "carry the mind over" means, at one level, that being has once again been submitted to the metaphysical dimension: "I have often felt when I have been in this mood and felt the depth of an instress or how fast the inscape holds a thing that nothing is so pregnant and straightforward to the truth as simple *yes* and *is*" (JP: 127). Nevertheless, the primacy given to being in the formation of understanding remains relatively unique in western intellectual culture, and was to give rise, in turn, to an ecological ontology at variance with that tradition, as we shall see, shortly, when we look at Hopkins' journal.

In this alignment of the material to the metaphysical the notes on Greek philosophy bring to a culmination the central (interconnected) purposes of Hopkins' undergraduate writing. In the first place, he corroborates the aesthetic, put forward in the 'Health and Decay' essay, whereby the initial phenomenological moment stimulates a writing which seeks, in turn, to conceptualise the truth about nature. This is formalised in a distinction, made in the first set of notes, between

> two kinds of energy, a transitional kind, when one thought or sensation follows another, which is to reason, whether actively as in deliberation, criticism, or passively, as in reading etc; ii) an abiding kind for which I remember no name, in which the mind is absorbed (as far as that may be), taken up by, dwells upon, enjoys a single thought: we may call it contemplation. (JP: 125-6)

In the second place, Hopkins established the essentially ecological nature of that ontology. For although the "truth" to which he was grasping is, of course, religious what Hopkins actually achieved in these notes was the amalgamation, in today's terms, of a deep ecological emphasis on the intrinsic value of being with a wider ecological recognition of the interrelatedness of all nature. As he writes, in Parmenides' conception of the phenomenal world "the distinction between men or subjects and the things without them is unimportant" (JP: 130).

Before considering his elaboration, in the journal, of that ontology a proviso ought to be added. Gillian Beer suggests that for the Victorians "the troubled urgency of sense-experience seeks an intelligible form in science, a sacralized in religion: the two patterns [...] sometimes cohere, sometimes lurch apart" (1996: 244). Accordingly, Hopkins walked a theologically "dangerous borderland" because of his interest in science (1996: 251), a danger of which he was all too aware. Not always confident of his ability to ensure that the two did not "lurch apart", Hopkins occasionally discharged the scientific view of nature, even nature itself, from his framework of beliefs.

There existed, in his thinking, a continual pull towards pre-modern, resolutely unscientific modes of knowledge, as well as frequent lapses into religion, supernaturalism or folklore, that are suggestive of a contrary impulse to retreat backwards. He wrote to Bridges, for example, about the need to establish truth not through "grammar and tropes" but via "mystery" and "prayer" (see RB 24/10/83: 186-7; 19/1/79: 60), a position consistent with Catholic theology and with a more widespread Victorian dismissal of the need for "evidences of Christianity". He clung to the literalness of Adam and Eve and other biblical stories, flying in the face of contemporary biblical criticism (SD: 308-9; FL (Patmore) 25/10/83: 323; (Patmore) 6/12/83: 342); he demonstrated a sporadic fascination with Catholic visionaries such as Marie Lataste and Sister Catherine Emmerich, miracles or miracle cures (RB 3/4/77: 40), and stories of ghosts, witches, pixies or fairies (see JP 22/3/70: 197-8; 29/8/67: 153-4; 4/9/67: 156 (372); 19/6/68: 185; 17/9/72: 226). These tendencies were encapsulated, more fundamentally, in a further undergraduate essay, 'The Origin of Our Moral Ideas', also written for Pater, in which Hopkins established a distinction that gave categorical priority to the unity of "moral excellence" over the diversity of beauty (JP: 80). Each time these ideas recurred, they would counteract or undermine his ecological thinking, as will be examined in Chapter Six. In the journal, however, Christianity and science did "cohere", almost perfectly. For Hopkins, as it happens, was testing and applying an essentially ecological understanding of nature just at the time at which he was also working out his religious beliefs.

4. The development of an ecological philosophy: journal writing

After converting to Catholicism in 1866 Hopkins abandoned poetry in May 1868, burning the poems he had written (see RB 7/8/68: 24). This was a decision apparently connected to his subsequent decision to follow a religious vocation and to become, in September of that year, a Jesuit (see JP 11/5/68: 164 (383); 7/5/68: 165 (383); RWD 5/10/78: 14). Hopkins believed that poetry would "interfere with my state and voca-tion" (see RB 7/8/68: 24) and "resolved", as he later told Dixon, "to write no more, as not belonging to my profession, unless it were by the wish of my superiors" (RWD 5/10/78: 14; see also JP 11/5/68: 165 (383), 537-9). This resolution held until 1875 during which time he trained as a priest, undergoing strict religious discipline and theological instruction. However, during that period Hopkins also kept a journal, predominantly of nature description, which enabled him, Alan Heuser has argued, "to record the laws and forms of nature, thereby building up materials for a philosophy of beauty" (1958: 18). That "philosophy" was the ecological understanding of nature which had begun to form in his undergraduate writing.

Consistent with the view, established in the 'Parmenides' notes, that the perception of phenomena (or 'being') would "carry the mind over" towards broader ontological truths, the starting point of that philosophy can be seen in repeated descriptions of beautiful, unusual, or arresting examples of natural phenomena. These are conspicuous in the journal. Hopkins observes, for example, in the Isle of Man "rocks, which [...] coated with small limpets, discolour the coast all along with a fringe of yellow at the tide-mark and under water reflect light *and make themselves felt*" (JP 8/8/72: 222 (my italics)); at Roehampton he records that "In the Park in the afternoon the wind was driving little clouds of snow-dust which caught the sun as they rose and delightfully took the eyes" (JP February 1870: 195-6); and, in Wales, in an archetypal example of the phenomenological emphasis on drawing the observer in, he describes how "The sight of the water in the well as clear as glass, greenish like beryl or aquamarine, trembling at the surface with the force of the springs, and shaping out the five foils of the well quite drew and held my eyes to it" (JP 8/10/74: 261). Such passages exemplify what Abram (through Husserl) describes as the sense of "associative empathy" essential to an ecological understanding that we exist within "a single phenomenal world or reality" (see 1996: 38-9). However, Abram's connected belief, that this quality has to be founded upon "things *as we spontaneously experience them*, prior to all our conceptualisations and definitions" (56), was not shared by Hopkins. For in the journal he attuned himself to nature by unifying the primary aesthetic experience to the conceptualisations that he was, at that time, developing.

This was a gradual process, for in earlier entries strikingly visual descriptions of natural pattern often failed to progress beyond long lists of sense impressions, some of which are strangely sensual:

> Mealy clouds with a not brilliant moon. Blunt buds of the ash. Pencil buds of the beech. Lobes of the trees. Cups of the eyes. Gathering back the lightly hinged eyelids. Bows of the eyelids. Pencil of eyelashes. Juices of the eyeball. Eyelids like leaves, petals, caps, tufted hats, handkerchiefs, sleeves, gloves. Also of the bones sleeved in flesh. Juices of the sunrise. (JP 1866: 72)

Though Hopkins seems not yet to have been able to theorise such impressions, some sense of process, even of an ordering principle, was implicit in the active verbs that characterised his descriptions at the time:

Cowslips *capriciously colouring* meadows in creamy drifts [...] Swallows *shooting*, blue and purple above and *shewing* their amber-tinged breasts reflected in the water [...] Peewits *flying*. Towards sunset the sky partly *swept*, as often, with moist white cloud, *tailing off* across which are morsels of grey-black woolly clouds. Sun seemed *to make* a bright liquid hole in this, its texture had an *upward northerly sweep* or *drift* from the W, *marked softly* in grey. Dog violets. Eastward after sunset range of clouds *rising* in bulky heads *moulded softly* in tufts or bunches of snow—so it looks—and *membered* somewhat elaborately, rose-coloured [...] Apples and other fruit trees *blossomed* beautifully. (JP 3/5/66: 134 (my italics))

Awaiting, at this point, a broader theory of nature, this was to be accomplished by a convergence of the significant intellectual interests – art, architecture and science – detailed above.

Heuser makes the logical enough suggestion that Hopkins' interest in nature derived, in the first place, from his interest in painting (1958: 9). He points out that colour is a notable feature of the early journal entries in particular and that Hopkins employed techniques from painting, such as scales of colour, to establish a sense of perspective designed to aid the structuring process:

There were two scales of colour in this picture—browns running to scarlet [...] and greys to blue.

Charming to see in the Garden Quadrangle the strong relief of the dark green and the balls of light in the close grass and the mixture of sunlit leaf and dewy shadow in the chestnuts high up and moving in the wind. Squares of green out-of-doors, as a window or garden-door, are delightful and the green then suggests rose in an unusually recondite way, as if it were a translation of rose or rose in another key.

Match of white grey sky, solid smooth lawn, firs and yews, dark trees, below, and chestnuts and other brighter-hued trees above. (JP May-June 1874: 244-5; 18/5/66: 137; 6/5/66: 135)

Developed out of this interest in painting, what then shaped Hopkins' journal writing was, more precisely, the post-Romantic "tradition of factual observation" that he had adopted from Ruskin.

Following through the methods of this essentially Ruskinian mode of analysis, we find that natural phenomena not only "caught" but also, consistent with Hopkins' use of active verbs, guided the eye:

All was sad-coloured and *the colour caught the eye* [...] snow quite white and dead but yet *it seems as if some blue or lilac screen masked it somewhere between it and the eye: I have often noticed it*. The swells and hillocks of the river sands and the fields were sketched and gilded out by frill upon frill of snow—*they must be seen* [he draws them]

[...] this is only to shew which way the curve lies [...] In the whitest of things the sense of white is lost, but *at a shorter gaze I see two degrees in it.*

a heavy fall of snow [...] The limes, elms, and Turkey-oaks it crisped beautifully as with young leaf. Looking at the elms from underneath *you saw every wave in every twig* [...] and to the hangers and flying sprays *it restored, to the eye*, the inscapes they had lost. (JP 19/12/72: 228; 12/3/70: 196 (my italics))

This seeking out of general principles is also apparent in that Hopkins would return, where necessary, to make comparisons. He did this when looking at elm leaves (JP 23/8/67: 152) and in an analysis of the oak tree that demonstrates clearly what Ball describes as a "prolonged programme of visual research, cumulative in its rewards" (1971: 122). Here, on his first visit, Hopkins describes the tree, with an implication of technical precision, by means of a geometrical language of planes and "tangents", and compares its shape to that of other trees.

Oaks: the organisation of this tree is difficult. Speaking generally no doubt the determining planes are concentric, a system of brief contiguous and continuous tangents, whereas those of the cedar would roughly be called horizontals and those of the beech radiating but modified by droop and by a screw-set towards jutting points. But beyond this since the normal growth of the boughs is radiating and the leaves grow some way in there is of course a system of spoke-wise clubs of green—sleeve-pieces [...] Oaks differ much, and much turns on the broadness of the leaf, the narrower giving the crisped and starry and Catherine-wheel forms, the broader the flat-pieced mailed or shard-covered ones, in which it is possible to see composition in dips etc [...] But I shall study them further. See the 19th. (JP 11/7/66: 144-5)

Notwithstanding such detailed description, Hopkins continued to puzzle over the "organisation" of the oak tree until, having fulfilled his promise to "study them further", he writes:

I have now found the law of the oak leaves. It is of platter-shaped stars altogether; the leaves lie close like pages, packed, and as if drawn tightly to. But these old packs, which lie at the end of their twigs, throw out now long shoots alternately and slimly leaved, looking like bright keys. All the sprays but markedly these ones shape out and as it were embrace greater circles and the dip and toss of these make the wider and less organic articulations of the tree. (JP 19/7/66: 146)

Such passages epitomise the alignment of romantic perception with empirical analysis that characterises Victorian post-Romanticism. However, while Hopkins compares, in the example above, "a thing with itself" in order "to see in it the continuance of law", what characterises the journal as a whole is the ongoing comparison of "two or more things together" – "Aspens thick in leaf but not so the sycamores", or the respective trajectories of the boughs of ash and oak (see JP 6/6/66: 139; 19/6/66: 140) – through which, ultimately, he would seek to establish an ontological understanding of nature.

Hopkins, like Ruskin, came to the realisation that a particular difficulty in the development of general principles would lie in attempting to isolate and explain the movement and flux characteristic of nature. He foregrounded flux in a preoccupation with clouds, that most mutable of phenomena, as seen in repeated descriptions of "flying", "scudding", "edgeless" or "transparent" cloud formations (see, for instance, JP: 140-3). However, he also attempted to structure these, and other examples of mutable phenomena, into a more "specific outline", for which purpose Hopkins utilised metaphors from another of his key interests, architecture.

long bows of soft grey cloud [...] spanning the skyline with a slow entasis

White-rose cloud formed fast [...] in perspective it was vaulted in very regular ribs with fretting between

the sky in the west was in a great wide winged or shelved rack of rice-white fine pelleted fretting. (JP 14/3/71: 205; 21/4/71: 207; 16/9/71: 216)

Hopkins came, therefore, to accept energy and flux as the principles that defined nature while also finding ways in which to trace pattern and intuit evidence of law. Some of these ways were less than subtle. Increasingly confident, for example, in his descriptive structuring of natural phenomena Hopkins began to order clouds via rigid, military analogies:

swaths of fretted cloud [that] move in rank, not in file

great bars or rafters of cloud [...] all the day marching across the sky in regular rank and with equal spaces between.

Very clear afternoon; a long chain of waxen delicately moulded clouds just tinged with yellow/ in march behind Pendle. (JP 21/4/71: 207; 9/5/71: 208; and see 1/5/71: 208)

Yet there was also, at the same time, a more refined sifting of movement into geometric lines or systematic classifications in which pattern emerged in descriptions that all the same retained the flux and dialecticism of nature. In "broken blots of snow", he wrote, focusing on one of Ruskin's own examples for tracing typical beauty, "I could find a square scaping [...] which helped the eye over another hitherto disordered field of things"; likewise, when he "caught sight of a little whirlwind which ran very fast careering across our pond", Hopkins finds not only that the circle is "regular" but that "Each tail of catspaw seemed to fling itself alive into its place in turn, so that something like the scale A B C D was very rapidly repeated all round the ring" (JP 14/3/71: 205; 29/4/71: 208). Yet architecture was, in the end, only really an enabling metaphor. For, ultimately, Hopkins developed this architectural trope of organisation into a scientific, ecological trope of complexity.

Ball, as is noted above, applied her partial critique of Ruskin's "science of the aspects of things" to Hopkins' journal writing. Yet many of the passages in the journal draw upon a knowledge of contemporary science about which Hopkins was far more conciliatory (and knowledgeable) than Ruskin. This applies particularly in relation to his interest in physics. The development which occurs in the descriptions of the oak leaves – from organisation and composition in the first passage to movement ("throw out", "dip and toss") in the second – alludes, for instance, to an attempt to explain the energy or force that holds or links organisms together. Physics also began to furnish a "commonplace" vocabulary by which Hopkins described pattern or motion as in a description of "tretted mossy clouds [that] have their law more in helices, wave-tongues, than in anything else" or in the description of the foot of the Grindelwald glacier, in Switzerland, "swerved and inscaped strictly to the motion of the mass" (JP 2/7/66: 142; 20/7/68: 178). Most substantially of all it also offered, as Brown explains, two paradigms that gave greater precision to Hopkins' conception of nature: the notion of "stress", a term whose "meaning and currency [...] extended greatly from the 1840s"; and Maxwell's "concept of a pervasive dynamic medium" of energy operating in fields of force, a concept with which Hopkins was familiar (see 1997: 210, 240-1).

The most obvious application of those paradigms occurs in a passage written at Stonyhurst which, stimulated by observations of Lenten chocolate, serves to highlight Hopkins' abiding fascination with science. As Nixon puts it, "Hopkins could not suppress the intrigue of thermodynamics even during a liturgical event" (2002: 135). Here – in a series of analogies that encompass boiling chocolate, water and candle flames – he traces the relationship between a "dynamic principle" and the essential being of a thing (see JP Spring 1871: 203-4). This relationship, Hopkins suggests, is epitomised by the simultaneous conduction of and resistance to heat which, in each of the phenomena described "result[s] in the manifestation of a substantive 'film'" (Brown 1997: 209-10). Hopkins regards this as representing both the extent to which "the heat has overcome the resistance of the surface" and the remaining presence of the "unconsumed substance" in the "part-solidity" of the smoke from a flame or "the soft bound of the general motion" in the film of vapour from chocolate by which "the side [of the chocolate] lurches into some particular pitch". For Hopkins 'pitch' denoted the existence and expression of individual being. What, therefore, he gained from studying the interaction between energy and individual phenomena was a sense of the dialectical quality that shapes all being. 'Stress', the particular term by which Hopkins encapsulated the balance between Being and motion, and within which all phenomena were drawn together in a "monistic ontology" (Brown 1997: 197), was, furthermore, equivalent to the ecological paradigm of 'tension'.

This understanding of "law" as a dialectical relationship between energy and Being was corroborated when Hopkins, in the same entry, broadens his attention towards the structure and movement of clouds:

> however solid they may look far off [clouds] are I think wholly made of film in the sheet or in the tuft. The bright woolpacks that pelt before a gale in a clear sky are in the tuft and you can see the wind unravelling and rending them finer than any sponge till within one easy reach overhead they are morselled to nothing and consumed. (JP Spring 1871: 204)

At one level, clouds, in a propensity to be "morselled and consumed", serve as a further example of flux, that is of the prevalence of energy and motion within the economy of nature. Yet there is also, in this description, the same qualification or counterbalance as seen in his descriptions of film. This is apparent when Hopkins speculates that the consumption of the cloud "depends of course on their size" and that their origin might even lie in a "crystal". Implying here that a core reality underlies all phenomena of nature, what Hopkins recognises, in a more general sense, is that while energy may prevail, while the ecosystem does enfold us, the resistance and endurance of substantive being testifies, conversely, to the intrinsic value of each and every instance of Being as an active agent within nature:

> one large flake [...] moving too slowly to be seen, seemed to cap and fill the zenith with a white shire of cloud. I looked long up at it till the tall height and the beauty of the scaping—regularly curled knots springing if I remember from fine stems, like foliation in wood or stone—had strongly grown on me. It changed beautiful changes [...] (JP Spring 1871: 204)

In unifying Ruskinian aesthetics with science Hopkins began to perceive the interplay between Being and energy that characterises ecological theory.

Nevertheless, he remained frustrated, for quite a long time, by the fact that this understanding was, in the familiar post-Romantic conundrum, too vague to fully satisfy the broader purpose underlying his journal writing, that of comprehending and articulating, in a specific sense, the ideal, the "One", shaping nature. It was a frustration Hopkins articulated when twice complaining about "the want of a canon":

> the warm greyness of the day, the river, the spring green, and the cuckoo wanted a canon by which to harmonise and round them in e.g. one of feeling.

> To see the long forward-creeping curls of the newly-leaved trees, in sweeps and rows all lodged one with another down the meadow edge, beautiful, but distraction and the want of the canon only makes these graceful shapes in the keen unseasonable evening air to 'carve out' one's thought with painful definiteness. (JP 6/5/66: 135; 15/5/66: 136)

Once Hopkins succeeded in the development of a "canon", by means of his own twinned concepts of inscape and instress, he achieved a fully recognisable Victorian ecology, one which emerged independently from, but in anticipation of, Haeckel's.

5. Inscape and instress

It is testimony to Hopkins' reputation that these two terms, 'inscape' and 'instress', now appear in the *Oxford English Dictionary*. This defines them respectively as

> the individual or essential quality of a thing: the uniqueness of an observed object, scene, event, etc.

> the force or energy which sustains an inscape.

The definitions imply, therefore, a paradigm in which apprehension of inscape leads us to perceive the nature of the underlying reality carried by instress. Having introduced the terms in the 'Parmenides' notes, this is precisely how they do evolve once Hopkins refined and put them into practice.

Inscape appears, on first impression, to function at a purely phenomenological level:

> From a height in Richmond Park saw trees in the river flat below inscaped in distinctly projected, crisp, and almost hard, rows [...]

End of March and beginning of April—This is the time to study inscape in the spraying of trees, for the swelling buds carry them to a pitch which the eye could not else gather [...] in these sprays [...] there is a new world of inscape. (JP 21/10/68: 189; Spring 1871: 205)

This becomes more evident when Hopkins, on a visit to the Swiss Alps, began to employ the term with greater regularity. His very first observation here was that the "Swiss trees are, like English, well inscaped" (JP 7/7/68: 170) which suggests that inscape is most easily perceived when the shape is strongest. This was then corroborated in subsequent passages: two plants, possibly species of Lady's Mantle and Potentilla (Hopkins isn't sure), have "strongly inscaped leaves"; the largest fall of the Reichenbach is "from halfway down the whole cascade [...] inscaped in fretted falling vandykes" (JP 16/7/68: 174 (393); 18/7/68: 177). Hopkins is struck, likewise, by the angular structure of the mountains. He used, for example, a variant of "quoins" – meaning "wedge-shaped blocks (usually of stone or wood)" or the external angle of a building (see JP: 392) – to describe the "straight quains and planing of the Alps" or "sharply quained" sycamores; he notes, in much the same vein, the "planing" of rocks which looked "as if they had been sawn" (JP 9/7/68: 171; 18/7/68: 176; 19/7/68: 177).

Yet even in these descriptions, inspired by the grandeur of the mountains, we see more or less immediately that phenomenological perception gets routinely extended into an enframed way of seeing most evident in the emphasis Hopkins placed on form: "the Monte Rosa range appeals to the eye solely by form, the sense of size [...] becoming irrelevant" (JP 23/7/68: 181). In such cases, which are indicative of the dialectical aesthetic being developed, the observation of strikingly shaped phenomena – "swells of ice rising through the snow-sheet and the snow itself tossing and fretting into the sides of the rock walls in spray-like points" (JP 20/7/68: 178) – led (or would "point") Hopkins towards a perception of the presence of the underlying force or energy to which his second term, instress, refers.

Instress, Ball argues, has two particular, though related, meanings. In the first place, it refers to "the determining energy of that object, the force which makes the thing itself, creating its design or inscape" (1971: 110). We see in this the direct derivation of instress from the term stress in energy physics, the operation of energy on being. For, as Isobel Armstrong puts it, instress, in this context

implies physical pressure and force. At the same time it cannot be materialised. It thus brings together and fuses the material and the non-material, spirit and sense, form and matter, and it brings them together *dynamically*. Like a charge of electricity. (1993: 422-3)

Replete, then, with ecological and theological connotations Hopkins would seek to establish, as we shall see, what, exactly, that "determining" force or energy was.

Ball explains the secondary meaning by quoting W. H. Gardner: "*instress* is not only the unifying force *in* the object; it connotes also that impulse *from* the 'inscape' which acts on the senses and, through them, actualizes the inscape in the mind of the beholder" (1971: 109). Both these senses are readily apparent from journal entries.

> The blue [of the sky] was charged with a simple instress

> Beeches rich in leaf, rather brown in colour, one much spread—: Tall larches on slope of a hill near the lake and mill, also a wychelm, also a beech, both of these with ivory-white bark pied with green moss: there was an instress about this spot—:

> The blue colour/ of light beating up from so many glassy heads [of bluebells], which like water is good to float their deeper instress in upon the mind (JP 22/4/71: 207; 17/8/74: 253; 11/5/73: 231)

Due to its double-sided quality the concept of instress offered, simultaneously, the reinforcement of a concept of nature analogous to the ecological notion of dialectical interdependence – i.e. the idea that living forms are "upheld" (sustained) by "force or energy" – and an aesthetic principle designed to convey that truth. That principle, to be more exact, was the belief that an awareness of force or energy is made available to us through the perception of inscape, either by means of our own direct study of nature or as this might be fostered by art. Having already established the first point, that inscape (being) is "upheld by instress" (energy) (see JP: 127), Hopkins became increasingly preoccupied with the secondary notion of instress as an aesthetic and ontological principle and with the idea, specifically, that continued study would enable him to establish the precise character of the reality being conveyed.

This was articulated by means of a subsidiary concept, "running instress". Encountering a "cross road" in Hampshire that he had seen once before, Hopkins notes that on recognising it "it lost its present instress" and that he began to see it in terms of "previous knowledge". He asks:

> what is this running instress, so independent of at least the immediate scape of a thing, which unmistakeably distinguishes and individualises things? Not imposed outwards

from the mind as for instance by melancholy or strong feeling: I easily distinguish that instress. I think it is the same running instress by which we identify or, better, test and refuse to identify with our various suggestions. (JP 14/9/71: 215)

The concept of running instress formalises the continual cross-referencing, the post-Romantic process of corroboration and refinement, that occurs throughout the journal. Writing from the Isle of Man, Hopkins records, across a nine-year interval, that "looking from the cliff I saw well that work of dimpled foamlaps—strings of short loops or halfmoons—which I had studied at Freshwater years ago" (JP 10/8/72: 223). Describing in Lancashire "the greatest stack of cloud [...] I ever can recall seeing", he remarks that "the instress of its size came from comparison not with what was visible but with the remembrance of other clouds: like the Monte Rosa range [seen] from the Gorner Grat" (JP July 1871: 212). Though Hopkins would suggest elsewhere that the perception of instress was dependent in part on factors ranging from "mood" to "good health or state of the air" to a lack of "distraction" or solitude – "with a companion the eye and the ear are for the most part shut and instress cannot come" – (see JP: 127; FL (Baillie) 10/9/64: 216; JP 15/5/66: 136; 12/12/72: 228) he regarded the recognition of instress, more generally, as the reward to be gained from sustained study.

Hopkins, then, slowly refined his ideas about nature. This can be illustrated by comparing two passages in the journal both of which describe "chestnuts in bloom". In the first, he writes, "The blooms are, as one feels, not straight but the tips bent inwards: then being thrown in some cases forwards, a good deal out of the upright, the curved type is easily seen in multiplicity which in one might be unnoticed" (JP 14/5/66: 136). While detailed enough, the later description, focusing on the spikes of the chestnut, is much more precise. Dispensing with any reference to what "one feels", Hopkins, returning initially to the concept of inscape, demonstrates that he has now mastered "motion":

> The chestnuts down by St. Joseph's were a beautiful sight: each spike had its own pitch, yet each followed in its place in the sweep with a deeper and deeper stoop. When the wind tossed them they plunged and crossed one another without losing their inscape. (Observe that motion multiplies inscape only when inscape is discovered, otherwise it disfigures) (JP 14/5/70: 199)

Immediately after this he writes "Great brilliancy and projection: the eye seemed to fall perpendicular from level to level along our trees, the nearer and further Park; all things hitting the sense with double but direct instress" (JP 18/5/70: 199). Hopkins reiterates, in this notion of instress "hitting the

sense", that with an accumulative process of observation, comparison, record and re-conceptualisation comes the ability to structure a nature characterised by incessant motion. As Heuser puts it, "every fixed form in nature pointed to an underworld of ideal reality" (1958: 21).

If the exact identity of that "ideal reality" remains unspecified in the passages quoted above it does become tantalisingly implicit in other passages including the following:

> Nov. 17 there was a very damp fog, and the trees being drenched with wet a sharp frost which followed in the night candied them with ice [...] [I] found every needle edged with a blade of ice made of fine horizontal bars or spars all pointing *one way*. (JP 17/11/69: 193 (my italics))

Soon after the later of the passages on chestnuts in bloom there appears a further entry where we find that the law, the "One", to which inscape was pointing was, so it would seem, the Christian God:

> I do not think I have ever seen anything more beautiful than the bluebell I have been looking at. I know the beauty of our Lord by it. It[s inscape] is [mixed of] strength and grace, like an ash [tree]. The head is strongly drawn over [backwards] and arched down like a cutwater [drawing itself back from the line of a keel] (all Hopkins' brackets). (JP Spring 1870: 199)

Thereafter we see, increasingly, a Christian recognition in the journal entries. Hopkins described, for example, the Northern Lights as like "a new witness to God" and notes an "instress of trinity" in the "three-light lancets" at Netley Abbey (JP 24/9/70: 200; 15/9/71: 215). Perhaps the best example, however, of what had become an enhanced ability to submit phenomenological observation to an enframing dimension can be seen by referring once again to the passage quoted earlier in which "The sight of the water in the well as clear as glass [...] held my eyes to it". For while this does exemplify, at one level, a markedly phenomenological description, the passage was in fact recorded after a visit to Holywell where the apparent healing powers of the water supposedly derive from the martyrdom of St Winefred. With this in mind, Hopkins offers an immediate extension whereby the phenomenon observed becomes interpreted religiously. He talks of "the sensible thing so naturally and gracefully uttering the spiritual reason of its being" before going on to describe "the spring in place leading back the thoughts by its spring in time to its spring in eternity". Explicitly, he "wonder[s] at the bounty of God in one of His saints!" (JP 8/10/74: 261). Hopkins achieved, therefore, through the twinned "canon" of inscape and instress, what had been, according to Heuser, the purpose of his journal all along – the establishment, that is, of a "philosophy of beauty". While this was connected to his Catholicism, and indeed came to fruition just as Hopkins was preparing to take the vows that would bind him to the Society of Jesus, it was nevertheless resonant, at the same time, with an ecological conception of nature.

Because Hopkins' Catholic ontology was constructed, to a large extent, out of an analysis of nature he did not immediately drift, subsequent to his ordination, away from the natural world. On the contrary, he produced in the journal something broadly akin to the contemporary concept of 'ecotheology' which, as described by Roger Gottlieb, in direct reference to Abram, posits the Christian, "ecological self" as embedded within a "more-than-human" world:

> The experience that we get in any form of collective religious practice [...] is to be extended to a glimpse of new flowers in spring, the sound of ice cracking on a bitter winter night, the magic of birdsong. Enlarging our powers of imagination, insight, and vibrant feeling enables us to see God in places where for too long She was absent. (2006: 42)

In Hopkins' own sacramental theology we see a similarly close correspondence with ecological ideas. This primarily came about, as noted, because of the derivation of instress from stress. Seen, for example, at Holywell where, in addition to connecting the "water in the well" to eternity and to "the bounty of God", Hopkins also described "the stress and buoyancy" of that water, the correspondence between grace and energy (see Nixon 2002: 137-8) is captured even more precisely when, in a passage recorded a few months after his observations on the bluebell, we see a convergence of the Latin acclamation "Praise be to God!" with a scientific language of "lateral motions":

> Laus Deo—the river today and yesterday. Yesterday it was a sallow glassy gold at Hodder Roughs and by watching hard the banks began to sail upstream, the scaping unfolded, the river was all in tumult but not running, only the lateral motions were perceived, and the curls of froth where the waves overlap shaped and turned easily and idly. (JP 20/10/70: 200)

This convergence of two philosophies, Catholicism and ecology, ran throughout the later journal entries and, ultimately, Hopkins' nature poetry. However, before this could be fully realised in the poems, Hopkins was first compelled to confront an official Jesuit teaching which derived from Aquinas' incorporation into Christianity of the Aristotelian separation of mind from matter and the living world.

6. Duns Scotus and Hopkins' ecological theology

Hopkins professed to admire Aristotle but only, he told Baillie, "so far as I know him or know about him" (FL (Baillie) 12/2/68: 231). This coolness was because the separation of mind from matter that is central to Aristotelian philosophy ran counter to the emphasis on being as evidence of the ideal that Hopkins had developed from his interest in Parmenides. Parmenides was fundamental, as Brown and Armstrong have conclusively demonstrated, to the construction of Hopkins' ontology. Yet one can exaggerate the extent of an influence that appears to have been relatively short-lived. Indeed, in his notes on Parmenides, Hopkins even rebukes the philosopher's "undetermined Pantheist idealism" (JP: 127). This points to the fact that however central material being might have been to Hopkins' ontology this was, nevertheless, expected to take Catholicism into account. Hopkins found the reconciliation he sought between the ideal and the material in the medieval scholar Johannes Duns Scotus, a figure ultimately of far greater significance in the establishment of his intellectual framework.

Hopkins, as he notes in the journal, discovered Scotus' work at Stonyhurst in 1872:

> At this time I had first begun to get hold of the copy of Scotus on the Sentences in the Baddely library and was flush with a new stroke of enthusiasm. It may come to nothing or it may be a mercy from God. But just then when I took in any inscape of the sky or sea I thought of Scotus. (JP July 1872: 221)

The initial "enthusiasm" did not "come to nothing". He was subsequently to make "the acquaintance of two and I suppose the only two Scotists in England" (JP 9/7/74: 249) and would even declare to Bridges "I [...] read Duns Scotus and I care for him more than even Aristotle and more *pace tua* than a dozen Hegels" (RB 20/2/75: 31). In broader terms the significance of Scotus' influence was that it enabled Hopkins to align his interest in inscape to a Catholic frame of reference.

Contemporary advocates argue that Scotus merits recognition alongside Aquinas as "the greatest of the medieval theologians" (Cross 1999: 3). However, he had by the nineteenth century become a marginal figure as is apparent from Hopkins' reference to "the only two Scotists in England". Antoine Vos suggests that this occurred because Scotus' work would have been construed as representing a retreat into pre-modern notions of abstract unity, notions out of step with a materialist scientific culture, or what Vos refers to as the "Aristotelian scientific canon" of the nineteenth century (2006: 1, 6). What, conversely, Scotus offered Hopkins was two things that reinforced and helped refine the proto-ecological understanding of nature he had been developing in the journal: a materialist emphasis on being which, in addition, gave theological justification to the love of nature; and a support for his insistence on the need for intellectual coherence.

Scotus reinforced, in the first place, Hopkins' belief that material being can guide us towards an understanding of universal principles or law. This occurred because Scotus placed being at the centre of his own adaptation of orthodox theology. The theological rationale for this was a speculation that Christ might have had a bodily presence at the beginning of creation, in order, as later explained by Hopkins, to glorify God by means of his own sacrifice:

> Why did the son of God go thus forth from the Father […] ?—To give God glory and that by sacrifice, sacrifice offered in the barren wilderness outside of God, as the children of Israel were led into the wilderness to offer sacrifice […] The sacrifice would be the Eucharist [Christ's bodily presence], and that the victim might be truly victim like […] it must be in matter. (see SD: 197 (307))

According to this conception of what is referred to as "God's first kingdom" or "commonwealth" (see SD: 62), human and non-human creatures were, furthermore, created to share in the glorification of Christ's "Great sacrifice":

> In going forth [Hopkins wrote] to do sacrifice Christ went not alone but created angels to be his company, lambs to follow him the Lamb, the flower of the flock, 'whithersoever he went', that is to say, first to the hill of sacrifice, then after that back to God, to beatitude. They were to take part in the sacrifice and he was to redeem them all, that is to say / for the sake of the Lamb of God who was God himself God would accept the whole flock and for the sake of one ear or grape the whole sheaf or cluster; for redeem may be said not only of the recovering from sin to grace or perdition to salvation but also of the raising from worthlessness before God (and all creation is unworthy of God) to worthiness of him […] (SD: 197)

Consequently, Hopkins came to believe, the materialisation of Christ was likewise designed to bring about "the efflorescence or natural consummation of the creative strain; [in which] men's minds and wills would have risen spontaneously and harmoniously from creatures to God" (SD: 290).

Scotus believed, on this basis, that the Incarnation may have been pre-destined even before original sin (see Cross 1999: 127-8; SD: 113-14) and that only after the Fall did it become connected to redemption. As Christopher Devlin writes "as a result of sin, natural values went astray and Christ had to perform a violent readjustment of them by his redemptive suffering" (SD: 290). After this human "minds and wills" could only ascend to God via conscious affirmation, good deeds, or the absence of sin, all directed by the teachings of the church. Scotus did, however, retain a belief that the being of non-human nature could still "affect" us towards a perception of God. It was this view, held by Hopkins for most of his adult life, that brought about a theology close to that advocated by contemporary 'ecotheologians', wherein the redemptive element would be balanced by its sacramental equivalent.

Scotus similarly reinforced Hopkins' belief that truth could be arrived at not only through the observation of phenomena but also in the enframing of those observations within intellectual thought. Scotus was "convinced", Richard Cross argues, of the necessity for a rational basis to theology and keen to preserve a "philosophical coherence" within Catholicism which he believed was lacking in other faiths (1999: 12-13). His attempt to establish "coherence" was formalised through the separation of theology into two categories: *theologia in se* (theology in itself) and *theologia nostra* (our theology). The first refers to knowledge available only to God; the second to that attainable through the human mind. While *theologia in se* lies beyond our cognitive power – and results in the belief, shared by Hopkins, that God can only, ultimately, be known through revelation – *theologia nostra* retains an intellectual aspect to theology which included, Cross explains, the "science", metaphysics, "responsible for yielding [limited] conclusions about the existence and attributes of God" (1999: 7, 10).

While *theologia nostra* reinforced Hopkins' belief that the establishment of 'truth' rested, up to a point, upon intellectual processes, there was, also, a striking correspondence with his scientific interests. Vos indicates a parallel with Victorian post-Romanticism when he writes that Scotus introduced "a new approach to *science*, *proof*, and *demonstration*" (2006: 11) which made an at least "modest" contribution to "new scientific revolutions in the sixteenth and seventeenth century" (2006: 392-3). In *The Physics of Duns Scotus* (1998) Cross argues, even more specifically, that ideas from physics are "scattered throughout" Scotus' writing (1998: 10) and that he played "a role in the development of some central concepts in physics" (see 1998: 2, 4-5). It is unsurprising, then, that Scotus' definition of physics correlates to the ontology Hopkins had been establishing in the journal:

> Bodily substance […] considered […] in so far as it has form, which is the principle
> of determinate operation, motion, and rest, has many passions inhering in it, which
> can be known by the way of sense. Therefore there will be […] a theoretical [science]
> regarding these things, which is called 'physics' or 'natural [science]'. (cited in Cross
> 1998: 3)

While this literal correspondence to Hopkins' interest in physics reinforced further the ideas established in the journal, Scotus' influence was
also to culminate in the shaping, consistent with that, of a theological
paradigm that brought Hopkins even closer to an ecological ontology.

   Scotus modified, Devlin points out, Aristotle's prioritising of the
intellect by positing its role not as "speculative" concerned, that is, with
"representations in the mind", but as practical, "drawn to an object
outside the mind" (SD: 346). He did this by means of an adaptation of St
Augustine's three stages of earthly life – memory, understanding and will –
which Hopkins subsequently took up in an adjustment to the levels of
comparison set out in the 'Health and Decay' essay. The first of these
stages, memory, is where, by focusing on individual species' "variegated
and differentiated beauties […] each distinct and individual and proclaim-
ing his own selfhood" (Pick 1942: 157), we begin to perceive the form
that underlies matter. At this stage, however, one cannot fully compre-
hend what it is that is being perceived so that memory might more
precisely be defined as a "state of indistinct knowing and desiring" (SD:
344). This is the point Hopkins was at when he described how the sprays
of the oak tree "shape out and as it were embrace greater circles".

   The subsequent distinction, of understanding from memory, has been
well summarised by Gardner:

> By a 'first act of knowledge' the mind has a direct but vague intuition of the individual
> concrete object as a 'most special image' […] it is through this knowledge of the singular
> that the mind, by abstracting and comparing in a 'second act', arrives eventually at its
> knowledge of the universal. (Hopkins 1982: xxiv)

Understanding occurs, therefore, when, through a cumulative process of
observation and verification, the observer begins to intuit God through
natural forms. While this is what occurred when Hopkins came to "know
the beauty of our Lord" by the bluebell, the process might also be seen as
ecological in that we gain knowledge by focusing both on distinct species
and on the flows of energy that maintain them. Hopkins believed,
however, that 'memory' and 'understanding' are, in themselves,
"incapable […] of an infinite object and do not tend towards it; they are
finite powers and can get each an adequate object" (SD: 138-9). The final

stage of the paradigm, 'will', was designed, therefore, to wed the two together in conscious affirmation.

This is a stage comprised of two components or (sub)stages: the 'affective' and the 'elective will'. According to the first of these Hopkins believed, closely following Scotus, that we "must always be affected towards the stem of good". What he means by this is that in perceiving, through the beauty of other inscapes, both God and the energy of his will we are 'affected' to see ourselves, also, as a "special image" of him. The elective will refers, in turn, to a subsequent 'act of election' that "project[s] the whole soul, by free choice, towards a supreme object of desire" (SD: 346).

Devlin describes the affective and elective will in terms of the difference between "inspiration" and prayer. The former he refers to as "a legitimate delight in the inspiration and exploration of the knowledge" gained from the perception of inscape, the latter as where "the soul goes all out for the object by an act of free will avowing the inspiration" (SD: 347). However, as he also makes clear, the act of election, certainly as it was seen by Hopkins, is not merely the outcome of that avowal but is also related to *theologia in se* in that it is, ultimately, an act of faith articulated in prayer and founded as much upon revelation as on a knowledge refined through the perception and conceptualisation of being. Akin, therefore, to the distinction between beauty and morality in 'The Origin of our Moral Ideas', problems would occur once Hopkins began to follow through the implications of this division between the affective and the elective will and, more to the point, when he began (as discussed in Chapter Six) to prioritise the latter. While this final sub-stage was, then, destined to become a fault line within the ecological character of Hopkins' thinking, for as long as the link between the affective and elective will was maintained Hopkins had, Gardner writes, "an aesthetic sanction and [...] moral justification for his inordinate attachment to poetry and the other arts" (1987: 340; and see also Pick 1942: 158; White 1992: 206).

According to the paradigm of memory, understanding and will, the study of inscape (being) cannot, then, in itself, bring us to a full knowledge of the "infinite". However, the "adequate object" also referred to by Hopkins was available. Amounting, in effect, to the ecological understanding of nature already apparent in the journal, that understanding was strengthened by Hopkins' discovery of Scotus as he continued to aspire towards a reconciliation of matter and the metaphysical:

> The study of physical science has [...] an effect the very opposite of what one would suppose. One would think it might materialise people [...] [however] they do not

believe in Matter more but in God less [...] in fact they seem to end in conceiving only
of a world of formulas [...] towards which the outer world acts as a sort of feeder,
supplying examples for literary purposes. (RWD 7/8/86: 139-40)

What has emerged, at this point, is a common epistemological framework in which equivalent categories shaped by Ruskin, Scotus and
Hopkins himself – the innocent eye, memory, inscape; response,
understanding, instress – correspond to the two central components of
ecological theory – individual species and the energy that holds them
together. Scotism, however, enabled Hopkins to reconcile his love of
nature with his Catholicism. And, having done so, this ecological
understanding became more prominent and took on a more distinctive
shape.

Holidays had always played a significant role in consolidating major
advances in Hopkins' understanding. It was on the Isle of Wight, for
example, where he stayed with his family in 1863, that he began to
practise drawing in accordance with Ruskinian principles (White 1992:
70-4); it was on his trip to the Alps, as we have seen, where Hopkins first
began to fully articulate and utilise the concept of inscape. Holidaying in
the Isle of Man, with the Jesuits, immediately after his discovery of
Scotus, we see in the journal entries recorded at the time, a renewed (and
greater) confidence in Hopkins' alignment of physics with Catholicism as
well as an enhanced ability to structure nature in his writing. This is
exhibited, on the whole, in descriptions of the sea around the Isle of Man, a
phenomenon, like clouds, that exemplifies the mutability of nature:

I noticed from the cliff how the sea foots or toes the shore and the inlets, now with a push
and flow, now slacking, returning to stress and pulling back

About all the turns of the scaping from the break and flooding of the wave to its run out
again I have not yet satisfied myself. The shores are swimming and the eyes have before
them a region of milky surf but it is hard for them to unpack the huddling and gnarls of
the water and law out the shapes and the sequence of the running: I catch however the
looped or forked wisp made by every pebble the backwater runs over—if it were clear
and smooth there would be a network from their overlapping, such as can in fact be seen
on smooth sand after the tide is out—; then I saw it run browner, the foam dwindling and
twitched into long chains of suds, while the strength of the backdraught shrugged the
stones together and clocked them one against another

The sea was breaking on all the stack and striking out all the ledges and edges at each
breaker like snow does a building. In the narrow channel between this outwork and the
main stack it was all a lather of foam, in which a spongy and featherlight brown scud bred
from the churning of the water roped and changed, riding this and that, but never got clear
of the channel. The overflow of the last wave came in from either side tilting up the

channel and met halfway, each with its own moustache. When the wave ran very high it would brim over on the sloping shelf below me and move smoothly and steadily along it like the palm of a hand along a table drawing off the dust. In the channel I saw (as everywhere in surfy water) how the laps of foam mouthed one upon another. In watching the sea one should be alive to the oneness which all its motion and tumult receives from its perpetual balance and falling this way and that to its level (JP 6/8/72: 221; 10/8/72: 223; 16/8/72: 225)

What emerges from this writing, as we can see, is a pronounced recognition of the extent to which mutable natural phenomena can be understood and explained in terms of the flow and operation of energy on matter. A further example occurs two years later, on another Jesuit holiday, this time in Devon. This passage describes "Heavy seas" experienced while walking along a seawall:

The wave breaks in this order—the crest of the barrel 'doubling' (that, a boatman said, is the word in use) is broken into a bush of foam, which, if you search it, is a lace and tangle of jumping sprays; then breaking down these grow to a sort of shaggy quilt tumbling up the beach; thirdly this unfolds into a sheet of clear foam and running forward in leaves and laps the wave reaches its greatest height upon the shore and at the same time its greatest clearness and simplicity. (JP 13/8/74: 251)

In this case, however, Hopkins extends the recognition that natural economy is shaped by the operation of energy so as to encompass a further principle, the interrelationship of all phenomena. He finds this both in nature in general, for example in "The colour of the breakers [that] registered the nature of the earth they were over—mostly brown, then a wandering streak or stain of harsh clayey red" and in humanity's embeddedness in that nature, represented here by a seawall "curved round to beetle over and throw back the spray without letting it break on the walk above" (JP 13/8/74: 251-2).

While speaking of "the unity of the whole", what Hopkins actually envisaged, as we can see from these passages, was an organic unity not of balance but of complexity, a unity which emerges from radically diverse elements and, more specifically, from the ecological process of energy exchange. As Nixon puts this "In inscape and instress—an ordering device and *vis viva* (living force), respectively—Hopkins saw a way through chaos. His discourse on inscape and the energy of inscape charges nature with creative, self-organizing processes" (2002: 139). Consequently, Hopkins ends the passage quoted above with a further, forceful alignment of physics and Scotist theology, and with the view, more generally, that matter moves within, as Goodwin suggests, complex "large-scale or global" systems:

The laps of running foam striking the sea-wall double on themselves and return in nearly the same order and shape in which they came. This is mechanical reflection and is the same as optical: indeed all nature is mechanical, but then it is not seen that mechanics contain that which is beyond mechanics. (JP 13/8/74: 251-2)

If, for Hopkins, what lay "beyond mechanics" was, ostensibly, the Christian God, there is, nevertheless, a recognition also of the "adequate object" that sits alongside the "infinite". What finally corroborates the unquestionably ecological character of that "adequate object" is that his descriptions in the journal also anticipate, explicitly, the notion of the earth as a living organism contained within the Gaia hypothesis. Indeed Hopkins even chose to encapsulate his recognition of this in imagery strikingly similar to the Gaia paradigm.

Devlin notes that Scotism bequeathed to Hopkins "a confused intuition of Nature as a living whole" (see Gardner 1987: 339). One of the forms this took in his journal was of recurring globular images. An example of this is the motif of the 'burl' which first appears in the 'Parmenides' notes. Both a verb (meaning 'to bubble') and a noun (referring, in part, to knots in wood) Hopkins' usage of 'burl' brings the two together and was designed to represent, Brown suggests, "a principle of determinate being which participates in a larger being, [or] a unified knot-like configuration of being that is integral to the larger ocean (or fabric) of being" (1997: 229). Exemplified when Hopkins wrote "there are ten thousand men to think and ten thousand things for them to think of but they are but names given and taken, eye and lip service to the truth, husks and scapes of it: the truth itself, the burl" (JP: 130) this was also seen, specifically, as a circular image, as is consistent with bubbles and knots, when Hopkins described "the eye-greeting burl of the Round Tower" at Windsor (JP 21/8/74: 256). Subsequently, this concentric motif, describing small circles of being that exist within a wider "burl" of truth, fed into further representations in which the ecological nature of existence was characterised by images of roundness.

In earlier studies of inscape Hopkins had posited the globe as, in effect, the inherent shape that underlies all natural phenomena. In a description, for example, of water running over an opening in a barrier or weir he writes that it "violently swells in a massy wave against the opposite bank, which, to resist its force, is defended by a piece of brick wall. The shape of wave of course bossy, smooth and globy"; likewise, he suggests, the "skeleton inscape of a spray-end of ash I broke at Wimbledon that summer is worth noticing for the suggested globe" (JP 1864: 19 (307); 25/8/70: 200). When, however, in the wake of his discovery of Scotus, Hopkins went on to offer instances of phenomena (both nonhuman and human) "warped" to the shape of the earth, such observations became transformed so as to articulate even more clearly the Gaian ontology by which Hopkins came to envisage "the entire range of living matter on earth" as constituting part of a "single living entity".

Aug. 8—Walked to Ramsey, and back by steamer. From the high-road I saw how the sea, dark blue with violet cloud-shadows, was warped to the round of the world like a coat upon a ball and often later I marked that perspective.

we sat on the down above Babbicombe bay. The sea was like blue silk. It seemed warped over towards our feet.

went up the hills towards Torquay, seeing all round me the sea and coast and valley of the Teign and getting fresh glimpses at every gate as I mounted. One dim horn on the left runs trending round into Dorset, past the mouth of the Exe, near which the red ends and chalk begins [...] Near below me the estuary and valley of the Teign; Teignmouth at the corner between river and sea, an irregular, not unpicturesque jaunt of white walls and lavender slate gables; the valley is backed and closed by Dartmoor, with several tors in sight. The sea striped with splintered purple cloud-shadows. I marked the bole, the burling and roundness of the world. (JP 8/8/72: 222; 18/8/74: 255; 11/8/74: 251)

7. Conclusion

In establishing an ecological "philosophy of nature" Hopkins' journal fulfilled the purpose that Mary Ellen Bellanca, in a recent study, sees as integral to the medium:

More than a repository of raw information, journals provided these writers with a versatile instrument for investigating not only nature but also themselves as perceiving subjects—for responding to experience and reconstructing discovery as well as fashioning modes of expression that would later inform other writings, including published work in other forms. (2007: 13)

There is, it should be said, no categorical evidence that subsequent parts of the journal are not waiting to be discovered, or were not destroyed (see JP: xxv-xxvi). However, the published journal does come to an end soon after Hopkins recorded the last of the two entries quoted above, while circumstantial evidence indicates that his practice of writing a daily journal probably did cease around this time. Assuming that to be the case the subsequent development of Hopkins' writing corroborates Bellanca's secondary point, that a reconstruction of one's view of nature would, invariably, give rise to new "modes of expression". In an 1882 poem, 'Ribblesdale', Hopkins would write:

> And what is Earth's eye, tongue, or heart else, where
> Else, but in dear and dogged man.

In the journal the observing "eye" had analysed, reconstructed, and given shape to the natural world. However, in what was, ultimately, his preferred medium, poetry, it was the "tongue" that would give voice to, and really bring to life, this newly ecological ontology.

Chapter 4

Finding a Voice:
The Development of a Sustainable Poetry

In a letter to his friend the clergyman and poet Richard Dixon, Hopkins acknowledged Wordsworth's profound influence on Victorian literary culture:

> There have been in all history a few, a very few men, whom all common repute [...] has treated as having had something happen to them that does not happen to other men, as having *seen something* [...] Or to put it as it seems to me I must somewhere have written to you or to somebody, human nature in these men saw something, got a shock; wavers in opinion, looking back, whether there was anything in it or no; but is in a tremble ever since [...] in Wordsworth when he wrote that ode ['Intimations of Immortality'] human nature got another of those shocks, and the tremble from it is spreading. This opinion I do strongly share; I am, ever since I knew the ode, in that tremble. (RWD 23/10/86: 147-8)

The precise nature of the "shock" to which Hopkins referred is implied in an earlier letter in which he identified, as had other Victorians such as Hazlitt and Ruskin (see Bate 1991: 53, 83; McKusick 2000: 149), that "Wordsworth's particular grace, his *charisma*, as theologians say" resided in his "spiritual insight into nature" (RWD 7/8/86: 141). That "insight" was, to be specific, to bring to the attention of human nature a sense of the integrity of and our interdependence on a nonhuman nature that is, as Wordsworth wrote, the "master-light of all our seeing" (156). This is, once again, a "timely utterance" (23) in the context of our own need to re-assert ecocentric sentiment.

A further element of Hopkins' appraisal was to consider the precise manner in which that "insight" was achieved or articulated. Writing earlier that year Hopkins had suggested that "It is true, if we sort things, so that art is art and philosophy philosophy, [that] it [Wordsworth's "insight into nature"] seems rather the philosopher's than the poet's: at any rate he had it in a sovereign degree" (RWD 7/8/86: 141). Appearing both to share in the distinction between poetic and enframing modes and to place Wordsworth as also in the latter category, Hopkins did, in actual fact, balance the two views. He writes, on the one hand, that:

> Wordsworth was an imperfect artist, as you say: as his matter varied in importance and as he varied in insight [...] so does the value of his work vary. Now the interest and importance of the matter were here of the highest, his insight was at its very deepest, and hence to my mind the extreme value of the poem.
>   His powers rose, I hold, with the subject. (RWD 23/10/86: 148)

Yet, on the other, he praises, at the more technical level, Wordsworth's powers of "execution": "The rhymes are so musically interlaced, the rhythms so happily succeed [...] the diction throughout is so charged and steeped in beauty and yearning" (RWD 23/10/86: 148). Hopkins' conclusion, therefore, was that Wordsworth had both "a 'divine philosophy' *and* a lovely gift of verse" (RWD 7/8/86: 141 (my italics)). This ideal, of a poetry executed so as to give voice to a particular philosophy of nature, was to be what Hopkins would aspire to in his own verse. Finding a suitable mode of expression proved, however, to be an elusive task.

1.   The search for a contemporary style of nature writing

While critics agree that Hopkins' juvenilia were largely imitative, few agree as to who it was he was imitating (see Poems: xix; Bergonzi 1978: 22; Peters 1948: xvi-xvii). Hopkins dabbled, in fact, in various styles of writing, the early poems providing evidence of a frustrated attempt to find an authentic poetic voice by which to represent nature. This is apparent, for example, in the contrast between two 1862 poems written only three months apart, the lush, Keatsian 'A Vision of the Mermaids' and the precise, Ruskinian 'A Windy Day in Summer':

some round the head
With lace of rosy weed were chapleted;
One bound o'er dripping gold a turquoise-gemm'd
Circlet of astral flowerets—diadem'd
Like an Assyrian prince, with buds unsheath'd
From flesh-flowers of the rock.
('A Vision of the Mermaids', 58-63)

The vex'd elm-heads are pale with the view
Of a mastering heaven utterly blue;
Swoll'n is the wind that in argent billows
Rolls across the labouring willows;

> The chestnut-fans are loosely flirting,
> And bared is the aspen's silky skirting;
> The sapphire pools are smit with white
> And silver-shot with gusty light;
> While the breeze by rank and measure
> Paves the clouds on the swept azure. ('A Windy Day in Summer')

Further, more obvious sources to which Hopkins turned were the pastoral and Romantic traditions, both of which appear in his unfinished *Richard* the fragments of which were written between 1864 and 1865.

As he would about Wordsworth, Hopkins enthused to his school friend Ernest Coleridge (grandson of Samuel Taylor Coleridge) about Moschus and Theocritus, the latter seen by many to be the originator of pastoral poetry (see Halperin 1983: 2; Segal 1981: 8-9): "they are lovely [...] say if there is anything so lovely in the classics. I believe I have said this before but I cannot say it too often" (FL (E. H. Coleridge) 3/9/62: 6). Yet there was, beyond his short-lived enthusiasm, little evidence to suggest that pastoral impacted in any significant way on his literary tastes or practice as this uncompleted poem highlights.

The fragments begin with a pastoral scene, a shepherd walking his sheep on the downs:

> As void as clouds that house and harbour none,
> Whose gaps and hollows are not browzed upon,
> As void as those the gentle downs appear
> On such a season of the day and year [...]
>
> there came one who sent his flock before him,
> Alone upon the hill-top, heaven o'er him. (I. 1-4; 7-8)

As Norman White suggests, the pastoral elements come across as "affected" for "Neither his heart nor mind were in this writing, filled with faint echoes of verses from another mind and time" (1992: 119, 122). To give one example, the dominant sense, conveyed in the first line in particular, is of emptiness, a notable contrast to the instressed clouds that Hopkins would shortly be depicting in his journal. The result of this is that we find him swiftly dismissing the arcadian pastoral vision as, in effect, false:

> Affinèd well to that sweet solitude,
> He was a shepherd of the Arcadian mood
> That not Arcadia knew. (I. 15-17)

With pastoral rejected, Hopkins sought an alternative model and transported his shepherd, 'Richard', to Oxford University which puts "graces on his country lip" and brings a "sense of gentle fellowship" (II. 3-4). With a new friend, Sylvester, Richard returns to the downs telling him "Come and see./You may quote Wordsworth, if you like, to me" (III. 7-8). Yet the Wordsworthian meditations, which appear in the final section, are themselves set aside. Richard identifies

> A spiritual grace
> Which Wordsworth would have dwelt on, about the place. (IV. 15-16)

invoking the "spiritual insight into nature" that Hopkins would later refer to. Yet there is also here a sentiment, "mingled […] 'Twixt resignation and content", as Ruskin had described Romanticism, that is portrayed by Hopkins as an unproductive feeling that

> Led Richard with a sweet undoing pain
> To trace some traceless loss of thought again. (IV. 17-18)

Consequently, though Sylvester then muses

> 'I like this […]

> I hope that all the places on our trip
> Will please us so.' (IV. 25; 27-8)

it is, as Ruskin wrote of Wordsworth, in "languid" inactivity that the fragments break up. Dissatisfied, then, with the literary modes most obviously available for representing nature, Hopkins still sought, at this stage, an authentic voice by which to articulate an essentially post-Romantic understanding.

The development of a suitable poetic style was, in effect, contingent upon the ecological philosophy of nature established in the journal and could not be realised until that happened. A clearer sense of what Hopkins was aiming towards can, however, be gained by considering his continued interest in poetic language. Hopkins' views on this were articulated, most notably, in frequent exchanges with Bridges that encompassed areas such as classicism, medievalism and the employment of archaisms. About each of these the writers were at odds. Hopkins mistrusted, for instance, the tendency of Victorian writers to retrieve classicism as a rejoinder to modernity. In fact, notwithstanding his brief enthusiasm for pastoral, and that his interest in classical literature has been the subject of a major critical study (see Bender 1966), Hopkins' opinion of it was somewhat dismissive. He remarked, for example, about the "stilted nonsense" of Greek tragedy (FL (E. H. Coleridge) 3/9/62: 6). His scepticism was most particularly directed, however, towards the utilisation of classical modes within Victorian literature, an attitude forcibly expressed in a merciless appraisal of Bridges' play *The Return of Ulysses* a partial dramatisation of the *Odyssey*. On, it would seem, moral and pragmatic grounds, Hopkins regarded the Greek Gods as "totally unworkable material". He writes "They are poor ignoble conceptions ennobled bodily only (as if they had bodies) by the artists, but once in motion and action worthless" and continues "What did Athene do after leaving Ulysses? Lounged back to Olympus to afternoon nectar. Nothing can be made of it" (RB 17/5/85: 216-18).

Hopkins was similarly ill-disposed towards a Victorian medievalism which represented, even more so than classicism, a reaction against modernity. Evaluating Tennyson, for example, he suggests

> When the inspiration is genuine, arising from personal feeling, as in *In Memoriam*, a divine work, he is at his best [...] But the want of perfect form in the imagination comes damagingly out when he undertakes longer works of fancy, as his Idylls: they are unreal in motive and incorrect [...] He shd. have called them *Charades from the Middle Ages*. (RWD 27/2/79: 24)

This dislike both of classicism and medievalism relates to the third of the examples that illustrate his literary disagreements with Bridges, a distrust of archaism. Hopkins criticised, for instance, "the archaism of the language" in *The Return of Ulysses* "which was to my mind overdone" (RB 17/5/85: 216-18). That distrust materialised most clearly, however, in an exchange with Bridges over an attempt by Charles Doughty to revitalise Victorian language. Bridges, it would appear, sympathised with Doughty who was seeking to re-introduce into the language what he saw to be a superior Elizabethan English (Phillips 1992: 140). Hopkins, however, maintained rather dogmatically that archaism "destroys earnest: we do not speak that way; therefore if a man speaks that way he is not serious, he is at something else than the seeming matter in hand" (RB 17/5/85: 218). Later, he challenged Bridges again: "is it not affectation to write obsolete English? You know it is" (RB 13, 14/9/88: 290).

Still seeking, then, an alternative basis from which to construct a post-Romantic poetic language, one potential source lay in philology, another of the intellectual interests apparent from the journal. James Milroy has pointed out that Hopkins lived through the heyday of English philology, in the 1850s and 1860s (1977: 35). He contends that Hopkins "owed virtually nothing to nineteenth-century conventions of poetic diction" (1977: 6) and that to understand the impulse behind Hopkins' poetic language "it is far more important to understand Hopkins' linguistic attitudes and interests [...] than to investigate his links with literary tradition" (13). While that perhaps overstates the case, it is nevertheless true that in the context of his dissatisfaction with existing literary language Hopkins initially turned to modes favoured, and made prominent, by contemporary philologists.

His interest in philology was mainly motivated by an interest in the materiality of language (see Banfield 2007: 189). This gave rise, for example, to a preference for Germanic over Latinate words and a fascination with onomatopoeia, particularly as it helped to infer the origin of words. In his early diaries Hopkins attempted, in numerous word lists, to relate the sounds of words to their meaning. So, in a list of words beginning "Gr" ('grit', 'greet', 'gruff', etc.) Hopkins deduced that the sound represents a "rubbing together" before then suggesting that "the onomatopoetic theory has not had a fair chance" (1863: 5); likewise, discussing the origins of "fl" words such as 'flick', 'fleck' and 'flake', he conjectures that a "connection is more clearly seen in the applications of the words to natural objects than in explanations" (1863: 11); and, in accordance with this, he also linked the names of Yorkshire rivers to natural phenomena: "Aire [...] Rapid stream. Calder [...] Woody water" (JP 1863-4: 14-15). Hopkins was similarly fascinated by regional or dialect speech. He enjoyed picking up on new words used by the "northcountry" laybrothers at Roehampton or Stonyhurst and quoted several examples in his journal (JP Spring 1869: 190-1 (402); June 1871: 211). These appear, furthermore, alongside words from African languages gathered from a book by John Hanning Speke (JP: 21). Much later in Ireland he enlists the help of students to submit material to Joseph Wright's *English Dialect Dictionary* apparently making 89 contributions to its 6 volumes (White 1992: 437).

Experts have suggested, reiterating the assessment both of his drawings and botanical descriptions, that Hopkins' interest in philology was "scholarly, but [...] also imaginative" and even that the wordlists "could be considered as verbal exercises [...] [and] miniature poetic compositions" (JP: 499; Milroy 1977: 97). Yet, as Milroy argues, the contribution of philology to his writing was more profound than such remarks suggest. It informed, in the first place, a critique of what Hopkins believed to be the inadequacies of "standard English". He complains, for example, to Bridges that "it is true this Victorian English is a bad business. They say 'It goes without saying' (and I wish it did) and instead of 'There is no such thing' they say a thing 'is non-existent'" (RB 7/9/88: 284). Earlier he had alluded directly to philology in writing "I cannot doubt that no beauty in a language can make up for want of purity" (RB 26/11/82: 163). This attack on "standard English" formed part of a more generalised critique in which he suggested that Victorian modernity, as encapsulated in its language, had lost touch with the land, with organic reality:

> How has so vague and inappropriate a word [acorn] superseded a proper one [ake-corn]? For of course people had some word for the fruit of the oak [my brackets].

> This seems in English a point craved for and insisted on, that words shall be single and specific marks for things [...] it is noticeable how unmeaning our topographical names are or soon become, while those in Celtic languages are so transparent. (FL (Baillie) 20/2/87: 280; RB 1/12/82: 165)

What such remarks indicate was that Hopkins was seeking a language designed to articulate a realist conception of nature and that, in doing so, he turned, like David Abram, to the language of rural or "indigenous peoples" seen to be "attuned [...] to the contour and scale of the local landscape". In Hopkins' case this took the form, principally, of an advocacy of the Dorset dialect poet William Barnes.

In books such as *An Outline of English Speech-craft* (with which Hopkins was familiar) and *Early England and the Saxon English*, Barnes had himself engaged in a critique of Victorian "standard English":

> English has become a more mongrel speech by the needless inbringing of words from Latin, Greek, and French, instead of words which might have been found in its older form, or in the speech of landfolk over all England, or might have been formed from its own roots and stems, as wanting words have been formed in German and other purer tongues. (1869: 101)

Seemingly expressing, like Barnes, a preference for Anglo-Saxon – it is, he told Bridges, "a vastly superior thing to what we have now" (RB 26/11/82: 162) – Hopkins' admiration for Barnes' came about because his use of dialect represented an alternative to standard Victorian English and, more specifically, because it "guarantees the spontaneousness of the thought and puts you in the position to appraise it on its merits as coming from nature and not books and education" (RB 14/8/79: 87-8). What he saw in Barnes was, in fact, a more general "embodiment" of a regional inscape whereby a clear link is forged between writer and environment:

It is his naturalness that strikes me most; he is like an embodiment or incarnation or manmuse of the country, of Dorset, of rustic life and humanity [...] It is true [...] [his images] are not far-fetched or exquisite (I mean for instance his mentions of rooks or of brooks) but they are straight from nature and quite fresh. His rhythms are charming and most characteristic: these too smack of the soil. (FL (Patmore) 6/10/86: 370-1)

Hopkins' interest in philology, and in particular onomatopoeia and dialect writing, opened up the possibility for a more concrete language grounded in an awareness of our affinity with the rest of nature. Yet Hopkins also understood the complexities of modernity well enough to recognise that Barnes, too, could offer no more than a "residual critique" and in the end he rejected this approach: "he does not see the utter hopelessness of the thing [...] The madness of an almost unknown man trying to do what the three estates of the realm together could never accomplish!" (RB 26/11/82: 162-3). The main significance, ecologically speaking, of Hopkins' dabbling in rural and dialect language lay, then, in his abandonment of it. We can gain a better sense of what, precisely, Hopkins was looking for by referring to a debate in twentieth-century literary criticism informed and prompted by Bridges and Hopkins' disagreement.

In his 1942 book *Robert Bridges: A Study of Traditionalism in Poetry* Albert Guérard praises Bridges for his "control of form and material" and writes that "This intellectual control—the detachment of the mind from what it contemplates—is the quality of Bridges' poetry which most distinguishes it from much contemporary poetry; it is the ultimate quality of the best art" (1942: 19, 104). Guérard invokes Bridges to defy the implication, which he had assigned to T. S. Eliot and F. R. Leavis, that "since society is loose one must write loose poetry" (1942: 104) and to argue, more specifically, that to counter this the poet should stand aside from society. Leavis believed in the opposite principle, namely that "the important poet" should be someone whose "interest in his experience is not separable from his interest in words" and who "by the evocative use of words" is able to "sharpen his awareness of his ways of feeling, so making these communicable" (1950: 13). For Leavis, Bridges represented a conventionalised Victorian poetry which "admits implicitly that the actual world is alien, recalcitrant and unpoetical, and that no protest is worth making except the protest of withdrawal" (1950: 15; and see 162) whereas Hopkins' so-called "experiments" with form, so disparaged by Bridges, exemplified an attempt to engage with and articulate Victorian modernity. Possibly occurring because philology had taught him about the evolutionary nature of language, thereby making it difficult to believe in permanence or standards of 'correctness' (Milroy 1977: 38), Hopkins' belief in the evolving contemporary nature of language is borne out in another letter to Bridges in which he clarified the principle governing his deployment of it:

> the poetical language of an age shd. be the current language heightened, to any degree heightened and unlike itself, but not (I mean normally: passing freaks and graces are another thing) an obsolete one. This is Shakespeare's and Milton's practice and the want of it will be fatal to Tennyson's Idyll's and plays, to Swinburne, and perhaps to Morris. (RB 14/8/79: 89)

The last of the writers cited here, William Morris, came to realise that in the context of his conversion to an essentially ecological socialism, the deployment of archaic language, in the form of his translations of Icelandic sagas, represented an attempt to "make a new tongue" though in a way, as E. P. Thompson puts it, that was "to disengage from, rather than to challenge, the sensibility of his time" (1977: 808). Believing, also, that "a perfect style must be of its age" (RWD 1/12/81: 99), Hopkins understood that an experience of modernity, which included, in his case, a dialectical conception of nature, would require an authentically modern poetic so as to be articulated. Scientific language, as we shall see, would help him towards the realisation of this as it had in the journal. Hopkins, however, reached the conclusion, given the condition of "Victorian English" and a lack of contemporary alternatives, that such a conception could not be articulated by language alone. He turned, instead, to another literary device, rhythm, and this became the most obvious feature of the (eco)poetic that would eventually emerge.

2. The development of a poetic style

Hopkins had, as it happens, stumbled across the beginnings of a preferred style in the Ruskinian mode of writing which, having appeared in 'A Windy Day in Summer', also found its way into the last two of the four fragments of *Richard*. Written twelve months after the first two (Poems: 304), and having since extolled (as seen in Chapter Three) Ruskin's techniques for drawing and his criticism to Baillie, we find, in these, detailed natural description

> a brush of trees
> Rounded it, thinning skywards by degrees,
> With parallel shafts,—as upward-parted ashes,—
> Their highest sprays were drawn as fine as lashes,
> With centres duly touch'd and nestlike spots,—

And oaks,—but these were leaved in sharper knots. (IV. 3-8)

complete with religious overtones

> The grass was red
> And long, the trees were colour'd, but the o'er-head,
> Milky and dark, with an attuning stress
> Controll'd them to a grey-green temperateness,
> Making the shadow sweeter. (IV. 11-15)

There is also, within these lines, a more detailed, scientific perspective in which the sense of vacancy, the pastoral "void" of the poem's opening, has been filled by an "attuning stress", namely the action of the atmosphere that has "controll'd" (regulated) the surrounding climatic environment. While any further development of that style appears to have been frustrated by the self-imposed suspension of his poetry, this was, as I have suggested, only really waiting upon the refinement in the journal of a fuller philosophy of nature. In that sense Hopkins' development of a suitable poetic style never really ceased.

Hopkins, we have seen, stopped writing poetry in May 1868 because he believed it would "interfere with my state and vocation". The resolution was not, however, as absolute as it at first appears. When he burnt his poems Hopkins asked Bridges to keep "corrected copies of some things which you have" and even promised to send updated versions so that "what you have got you may have in its last edition" (RB 7/8/68: 24). The reason for this continued attachment to poetry appears to have originated, aside from questions of personal taste, from the seriousness with which Hopkins viewed art. This again was influenced by Ruskin. In the first volume of *Modern Painters*, Ruskin laid out, as Sulloway points out, "three essential steps" for the artist: to see things unhindered by artistic convention, to respond, and to reproduce the object in accordance with a broader conception of "truth" (1972: 69). While the critical, moral dimension that Ruskin brought to art was the reason why Hopkins took writing so seriously, he also believed that poetry was the medium best equipped to the complex task of transferring, and articulating, observations of being into a wider meaning or understanding.

In an undergraduate essay on 'Poetic Diction' Hopkins stated that "poetry has tasked the highest power's of man's mind" (JP: 85), a point elaborated when he explained that "An emphasis of structure stronger than the common construction of sentences gives asks for an emphasis of expression stronger than that of common speech or writing, and that for an emphasis of thought stronger than that of common thought" (JP: 85). Not dissimilar to Jonathan Bate's belief that poetry expresses "the richest thoughts and feelings of a community" (2000: 247), such pronouncements might be read as implying, when taken in conjunction with Hopkins' other interests, the existence of new modes of understanding that would require, in turn, the "concentration" and "vividness of idea" that poetic form can alone offer (JP: 84); and, correspondingly, that "poetic orthodoxy" would have to be "abandoned [...] to confront experience in its complex and dynamic materiality" (Banfield 2007: 191).

It was, therefore, in the undergraduate essays that Hopkins first began to develop a mode of poetry capable of articulating a post-Romantic understanding of nature. The basic principle underlying that poetic was signalled, in the first place, in the 'Health and Decay' essay. It concerned the reconciliation of the Romantic notion that art can be "reached by intuition" and "genius" with a Victorian belief that "some scientific basis of aesthetical criticism is absolutely needed" (JP: 75). This was then substantiated in the dialogue 'On the Origin of Beauty'. Here the undergraduate, Hanbury, expresses the opinion that poetry and prose are basically equivalent in their effects. Testing that contention, Hopkins, in a precedent to the experiment conducted by Bate in *The Song of the Earth*, converts lines from Wordsworth's 'To the Cuckoo' into prose. The argument that emerges from this, expressed by the fictional Professor of Aesthetics, appears, on first reading, to typify Victorian "anti-Romanticism".

> I foresee I shall be told a string of sublime unlaborious definitions of poetry, that Poetry is this and Poetry is that, and that I am not to vex the Poet's mind with my shallow wit, for I cannot fathom it, and that the divine faculty is not to be degraded to the microscope and the dissecting knife, and that wherever a flower expands and dedicates its beauty to the sun there, there is Poetry, and that I am a Positivist [...] and botanise upon my mother's grave [...] (106-7)

While Hopkins appears to refute, in the Professor's sarcasm, romantic notions of the poet as possessed of "the deepest pathos and sublimity and passion and any other kind of beauty" (108), all he actually suggests is that "spiritual insight", which he concedes as necessary to poetry, should be harnessed to an ability to structure, or organise, that insight:

> genius works more powerfully under the constraints of metre and rhyme and so on than without [...] it is more effective when conditioned than when unconditioned [...] the concentration, the intensity, which is called in by means of an artificial structure

brings into play the resources of genius on the one hand, and on the other brings us to the end of what inferior minds have to give us. (108)

The aesthetic principle established in these works was then extended so as to encapsulate the ontological paradigm Hopkins was seeking at this time. This occurs in the notes on Greek philosophy where, as we have seen, Hopkins formulated a theory of material language designed to represent, simultaneously, both being and ontological unity, "the One". Hopkins establishes this in a section in which he explores the notion that "A word [...] has three terms belonging to it [...] its prepossession of feeling; its definition, abstraction, vocal expression or other utterance; and its application, 'extension', the concrete things coming under it" (JP: 125). In these terms Hopkins was referring, respectively, to the initial phenomenological stimulus; the being, or materiality, of the word itself; and the concept or understanding expressed. With relation to the first two, Hopkins, criticising a "less sane attitude" that prefers the "prepossession" to be "conveyed by the least organic" language, expresses the belief, as reiterated in his critique of 'standard English', that the material form, the word should incarnate the being being observed (JP: 126). With relation to the second two, Hopkins also believed that it was the province of art to fulfil the capacity of language to proceed from a materialisation of the perceived phenomena towards instructing us about 'truth'. Where "works of art [...] like words utter the idea" (JP: 126), he argued, more specifically, that our understanding of that idea was nevertheless dependent on the materiality of the language: the more the "prepossession flushes the matter [...] the more power of comparison, the more capacity for receiving that synthesis of [...] impressions which gives us the unity" (JP: 126).

Where the notes on Greek Philosophy signify, therefore, that Hopkins was attempting, through language, to work through the implications of a Darwinian relationship "between us and things", this becomes fully apparent in the 'Parmenides' notes. Here Hopkins writes, connecting words to the interrelation of "Being" and "truth":

> To be and to know or Being and thought are the same. The truth in thought is Being, stress, and each word is one way of acknowledging Being and each sentence by its copula *is* (or its equivalent) the utterance and assertion of it. (JP: 129)

Believing, as suggested above, that poetry would be the medium best served to articulate these ideas, how, specifically, this might occur was set out when Hopkins developed principles for an aural poetic practice when, between September 1873 and July 1874, he was assigned to Manresa House to teach Rhetoric to junior novices.

Hopkins established, in these lectures, two poetic principles that correspond to the respective emphases on being and meaning. The first was that poetry should be based primarily on sound and judged "by the ear not by reading and the eye" (JP: 273). This argument, for poetry as a principally aural means of communication, was elaborated through what Hopkins (like Abram) referred to as "speech":

> Definition of verse—Verse is speech having a marked figure, order/ of sounds independent of meaning and such as can be shifted from one word or words to others without changing. It is *figure of spoken sound* [...]
>
> Poetry is speech framed for contemplation of the mind by the way of hearing or speech framed to be heard for its own sake and interest even over and above its interest in meaning. Some matter and meaning is essential to it but only as an element necessary to support and employ the shape which is contemplated for its own sake. (Poetry is in fact speech only employed to carry the inscape of speech for the inscape's sake—and therefore the inscape must be dwelt on' [...]) (JP: 267, 289)

This emphasis on sound as "independent of meaning" and speech "contemplated for its own sake" indicates a phenomenological foundation in which "the poetic purpose is to stimulate contemplation and bring about the full exhibition of a statement. The meaning lies in the exhaustive presentation of it, rather than in a progression according to narrative or other intellectual logic" (Ball 1971: 113). Yet the sound-based principle established by Hopkins did not mean that there is no message or "meaning" in his poetry. As Gardner writes, Hopkins "seemed to place all the emphasis on significant form; yet he never underestimated the importance of meaning, and for him great poetry could never be entirely without moral significance" (Poems: xxii). This relates to the second principle established in his lectures, revealed as he carried out a detailed analysis of the "structural" aspects of poetry.

In the 'Health and Decay' essay Hopkins had previously speculated that "Conditions and restrictions", by which he means the rules of proportion of metre and rhyme, were "the unexpected cause [...] of all that we call poetry" (JP: 75). In the Roehampton lectures he settles, conclusively, on rhythm and rhyme as the two main "elements of verse" (JP: 288). Hopkins argues that rhythm confers unity on the constituent parts of a poem – the individual sounds, letters, syllables, feet, etc. (see JP: 275) – while rhyme is identified as chief amongst the "intermittent elements of verse" (also including, for example, the caesura). Designed to disrupt "the sameness of the rhythm" (JP: 283) these "intermittent" elements nevertheless serve, when properly understood, to strengthen or enhance the formal unity of the poem:

> It should be understood that these various means of breaking the sameness of the rhythm [...] do not break the unity of the verse but the contrary: they make it organic and what is organic is one [...] in everything the more remote the ratio of the parts to one another or the whole the greater the unity if felt at all [...] (JP: 283)

This emphasis, on a unity achieved by the interaction of rhythm and rhyme, relates back, in the first place, to a principle established in 'The Origin of Our Moral Ideas', where Hopkins wrote that "in art we strive to realise not only unity, permanence of law, likeness, but also, with it, difference, variety, contrast: it is rhyme we like, not echo, and not unison but harmony" (JP: 83). It also emanates, however, from the ecological paradigm established in the journal and, more generally, from the dialectical, diverse unity taught by the complexity sciences. For in Hopkins' poetic paradigm diverse species (inscape/rhyme) would be interlinked in an economy of energy exchange (instress/rhythm). Resting fundamentally on the latter, for it is rhythm that most characterises Hopkins' poetry, and encompassing a range of devices that included counterpointed and outriding rhythm, what, ultimately, epitomised a poetic refined so as to complement Hopkins' ecological philosophy of nature, was the establishment of one particular device, sprung rhythm, as central to his work.

3. Sprung rhythm

Though Hopkins did not specifically mention sprung rhythm in his Roehampton lectures, this was what he was referring to when later on he wrote to Dixon "I had long had haunting my ear the echo of a new rhythm" (RWD 5/10/78: 14). This can be seen, for example, in that an explanation to his students that "rhythm may be accentual or quantitative, that is go by beat or by time" (JP: 276) clearly foreshadows a later distinction that he made between sprung rhythm as a "sense-stress" rhythm and a conventional standard rhythm which Hopkins described as "common" or "running" rhythm (see Poems: 45; Ong 1949: 108). Establishing, further to this, any precise definition is, however, difficult not least because references to sprung rhythm in his writing are scattered, oblique, and undeveloped (Ong 1949: 94-5, 173).

Some sense does emerge, however, from attempts to explain his principle contained within a series of letters to Dixon and Bridges. "The essence of sprung rhythm", Hopkins told Dixon, was that "*one stress makes one foot*" (RWD 27/2/79: 14), a definition elaborated as follows: "To speak shortly, it consists of scanning by accents or stresses alone, without any account of the number of syllables, so that a foot may be one strong syllable or it may be many light and one strong" (RWD 5/10/78: 14). The essence of sprung rhythm was, therefore, that whereas "common" rhythm simply alternates stresses at "every second or third syllable", so Walter Ong notes in his long and instructive essay on sprung rhythm (1949: 170), the stress in "sense-stress" rhythm falls literally where the meaning (i.e. the sense) demands it. So, for example, in 'The Caged Skylark' Hopkins inserted 'a' twice in the opening line – "As a dare-gale skylark scanted in a dull cage" – in order to ensure that the natural stress emphasised a juxtaposition of the terms, "dare" and "dull", that he wished to accentuate.

Turning to this mode of language, regarded as "the normal tender for emotion" (Ong 172), sprung rhythm was consistent with the principle of "earnestness" Hopkins expected out of poetry. Related to this, it was also consistent, as implied in a reference to "stress with its belonging slack" (RWD 27/2/79: 22), with his ecological conception of natural economy. Sprung rhythm allowed for an almost unlimited deployment of 'stressed' or slack syllables. On the one hand, "the stress alone is essential to a foot and [...] even one stressed syllable may make a foot and consequently two or more stresses may come running, which in common rhythm can, regularly speaking, never happen"; on the other, "the stress being more *of* a stress, being more important, allows of greater variation in the slack and this latter may range from three syllables to none at all—*regularly*" (RWD 22/12/80: 39). The overall result was a greater freedom of rhythmic expression. As Hopkins himself wrote, sprung rhythm allowed for sudden changes "from a rising to a falling movement" which could be "strongly felt by the ear" (RWD 22/12/80: 40).

In one of the Roehampton lectures Hopkins had, however, balanced the capacity of rhythm to represent a full range of motion – climbing, rocking or falling – with a counter-emphasis on its "recasting [...] speech into sound-words, sound-clauses and sound-sentences of uniform commensurable lengths and accentuations" (JP: 274-5; 273). This counter aspiration, that rhythm should also confer structure, explains the continual, additional obligation that he felt to differentiate sprung rhythm from free verse (see RB 21/8/77: 44-5). He insisted, for example, not only that the retention of scanning (albeit by stress rather than syllable) would ensure that sprung rhythm was not itself "lawlessly irregular", but, specifically, that this was designed to provide a strictly regulated and structured aesthetic: "that piece of mine is very highly wrought. The long lines are not rhythm run to seed: everything is weighed and timed in them" (RB 18/10/82: 154-8). Further reinforced by the fact that much of Hopkins' sprung verse was contained within the relatively structured form of the sonnet (as discussed below), what he achieved from this interplay of movement with structure was a poetic mode of writing that embodied the flow of energy within the interrelated boundaries of the ecosystem, a mode which "nature", as he observed, "seems to prompt [...] of itself" (RWD 27/2/79: 21):

> It is a simple thing and capable of being drawn up in a few strict rules, stricter, not looser than the common prosody. But though the rules would be few and strict, the freedom of the motion in the rhythm gained under them would, as I believe, be very great. (FL (Patmore) 14/11/83: 335)

Sprung rhythm transformed Hopkins' descriptions of nature. Freed from the constraints of syllabic metre he was able, for example, to engage in more precise description – "High there, how he húng upon the réin of a wimpling wing" ('The Windhover', 4; and see Day Lewis, cited in Roberts 1987: 280); likewise, the principle of allowing "scanning to run on from line to line to the end of the stanza", even to the extent that it "runs on without break from the beginning, say, of a stanza to the end and all the stanza is one long strain", facilitated long passages of natural description (RWD 22/12/80: 40; Poems: 48) such as, for example, those of the ascent and song of the lark in 'The Sea and the Skylark' or the course of the burn in 'Inversnaid'. Its chief value, however, was to allow Hopkins to convey the motion that he saw as intrinsic to nature. In a description of the sea, starting with the assault of noise that begins 'The Sea and the Skylark', Hopkins captured, for example, the "push and flow" and "returning to stress and pulling back" described in his journal:

> On ear and ear two noises too old to end
> Trench—right, the tide that ramps against the shore;
> With a flood or a fall, low lull-off or all roar [...] (2-3)

Likewise, in what is, perhaps, his most famous poem, 'The Windhover', Hopkins utilised the possibilities of extended scansion so as to describe the movement and energy of the bird as it interacts with the air.

> Of the rolling level underneath him steady air, and striding
> High there, how he rung upon the rein of a wimpling wing
> In his ecstasy! then off, off forth on swing,

> As a skate's heel sweeps smooth on a bow-bend: the hurl and
>   gliding
> Rebuffed the big wind. ('The Windhover', 3-7)

In all these cases, whether in the precise description enabled by the
liberation of scansion, or in the motion that allowed Hopkins to convey,
rather than describe or explain, natural phenomena, sprung rhythm
exhibited the capacity to "let being be" creating a deep ecological sense of
the integrity of species that W. A. M. Peters has contrasted, in effect, to
poets who

> approaching nature through the imagination [...] interpret the emotions arising in
> themselves as due to a great poetic sensibility and not as due principally to any
> independent activity from the object itself [...] They cast round it an emotional
> atmosphere which the object possesses only in virtue of the poet's imagination. (1948:
> 20)

Sprung rhythm also, however, had a more pragmatic dimension, as a
device by which Hopkins would hold society to account for any detrimental
alterations to nature. For it enabled him, also, to portray disruptions to the
flow of energy, not least as a result of human activity. An obvious
example occurs in 'Binsey Poplars', examined in Chapter Five, where a
predominately aural description of the demise of aspen trees – "All félled,
félled, are áll félled" – is designed to imitate the labourer's blows. What,
then, Hopkins achieved through sprung rhythm was the poetic he himself
had ascribed to Wordsworth: in which direct insight into 'nature' was
complemented (rather than counteracted) by an intellectual framework;
and where that relationship would in turn be articulated by means of "a
lovely gift of verse".

Terry Gifford has argued that in Britain nature poetry became a
largely "pejorative term" in the twentieth century due to "the damage
done by Georgian pastoral poetry". He suggests that this might be
remedied by a contemporary "green poetry", by which he means "recent
nature poems that engage directly with environmental issues" (1996: 27-
8). Correspondingly, Leavis long ago speculated that had Hopkins' work
been appreciated earlier "we should not now be contemplating the futility
of the Georgian attempt to regenerate English poetry" (1950: 159). One
might argue here that in effectively short-circuiting Georgian poetry,
Hopkins' writing offers a historical precedent for the "green poetry" that
Gifford advocates. Derived from a convergence of the ecological
philosophy of nature established in the journal with the development of
rhythm, notably sprung rhythm, as the poetic mode most suitable to

articulating that philosophy, what his work offers, to be more precise, is a reconciliation of the ecocentric (phenomenological) and technocentric (enframing) dimensions which can broaden and enrich our understanding of the parameters of ecopoetry and, indeed, ecology itself. The remainder of this chapter will examine the ecological character of that poetry highlighting some key examples.

4. Formation of an ecopoetic

As indicated Hopkins' poetic model was premised, up to a point, on much the same phenomenological principles as those that have shaped the "ecopoetic" developed by Bate in *The Song of the Earth*. Indeed, his work literally maps onto the first two of the three principles governing Bate's model (as outlined in Chapter One). The first of these, that poetry should be activated by, and seek to convey, the phenomenological moment at which nature impacts upon the human consciousness, is apparent from the reflections on poetry which occur in his letters.

One of the ways in which Hopkins evaluated other poet's work was in terms of their faithfulness to the phenomenological moment. In describing, to give some examples, a poem of Dixon's as having a "directness" that "distinguishes it" (RWD 16/9/81: 57), or in remarking upon "the freshness and buoyancy and independence" of Bridges' poems (RB 22/2/79: 72), or by praising Barnes' imagery for being "straight from nature and quite fresh", Hopkins articulated a conviction that poetry should convey directly (i.e. without mediation) and immediately (in terms of its "freshness") the impact of an observed natural phenomenon on the individual consciousness. This belief, that the act of poetic creation "occurred", as Gardner explains, "when the poet's own nature (his own 'inscape') had been instressed by some complimentary inscape discovered in external nature" (Hopkins 1982: xxiv), was consequently carried through in a poetic practice that shared Bate's notion of inspiration.

Hopkins wrote, at the age of just twenty:

> The word inspiration need cause no difficulty. I mean by it a mood of great, abnormal in fact, mental acuteness, either energetic or receptive [...] This mood arises from various causes, physical generally, as good health or state of the air [...] the poetry of inspiration can only be written in this mood of mind. (FL (Baillie) 10/9/64: 216)

Drawing, here, on the full scope of the word, Hopkins suggests a linkage between the surrounding environment and the act of writing equivalent to what Bate means when he talks of the poet who "breathes in the being of the world" and whose poetry, "expiration", is designed to re-convey the ecological integrity of the "more-than-human" nature on which we depend. Indeed, Hopkins actually expanded upon this relationship between environment and composition by using it as a means of registering the condition of the environment, whether in affirmation or critique. So, the "fine scenery, great hills and 'fells'" around Stonyhurst stimulated rich journal descriptions, while the Welsh landscape about which Hopkins had enthused, prompted ten sonnets that emphatically responded to and praised nature. Conversely, his "muse turned utterly sullen in the smoke-ridden Sheffield air", in Liverpool, "of all places the most museless" (RB 2/4/78: 48; RWD 14/1/81: 42), Hopkins wrote only three poems in 19 months, while in Glasgow "inspiration" appeared to evaporate altogether:

> the vein urged by any country sight or feeling of freedom or leisure (you cannot tell what a slavery of mind or heart it is to live my life in a great town) soon dried and I do not know if I can coax it to run again. One night, as I lay awake in a fevered state, I had some glowing thoughts and lines, but I did not put them down and I fear they may fade to little or nothing. I am sometimes surprised at myself how slow and laborious a thing verse is. (RB 16/9/81: 136)

Connected to this basis of his verse was the elaboration of a sound-based practice, at Roehampton and then through sprung rhythm, which meant, in effect, that Hopkins' work conforms to the second of Bate's principles, that poetry, by virtue of its predominately aural quality, is uniquely equipped to recreate the phenomenological moment. Just as the recording of encounters with nonhuman nature had been a fundamental component of Hopkins' journal writing so too with his poetry, sometimes quite literally. His 1876 poem, 'The Woodlark', originates, for example, from a journal entry recorded ten years earlier. A further instance relates to an entry from 1873 in which Hopkins describes the song of the cuckoo: "Sometimes I hear the cuckoo with wonderful clear and plump and fluty notes: it is when the hollow of a rising ground conceives them and palms them up and throws them out" (JP 16/6/73: 232). Indicative of a sensitivity to the sounds and rhythms of nature, this became, so it would seem, the source behind "Repeat that, repeat", an undated fragment that is a good example of the phenomenological basis to Hopkins' work.

> REPEAT that, repeat
> Cuckoo, bird, and open ear wells, heart-springs, delightfully
>   sweet,

> With a ballad, with a ballad, a rebound
> Off trundled timber and scoops of the hillside ground, hollow
>   hollow hollow ground:
> The whole landscape flushes on a sudden at a sound.

What Hopkins describes in this poem is strikingly similar to a passage by which Abram illustrates the impact of the phenomenological moment:

> The raven's loud, guttural cry, as it swerves overhead, is not circumscribed within a strictly audible field—it echoes *through* the visible, immediately animating the visible landscape [...] My various senses, diverging as they do from a single, coherent body, coherently *converge*, as well, in the perceived thing [...]. (62)

In Hopkins' case the stimulus offered by the song, an expression of the cuckoo's inscape, prompts a response by the poet manifest, initially, in the opening of his "ear wells" and, thereafter, in the subsequent action, "heart-springs". What Hopkins articulates – in the recording of the moment in his journal and then in the poem – is an experience of being sensuously incorporated (of 'dwelling') within the environment, which then conveys to the reader precisely the sense of ecological "intersubjectivity" suggested by Abram. This gives rise, in turn, to deep ecological sentiment, a respect for the integrity of nonhuman life that was to become a prominent feature of Hopkins' poetry. An example of this, in the completed work, occurs in 'As kingfishers catch fire'.

Hopkins begins the poem, essentially a eulogy to inscape, with a sequence of phenomenological impressions in which what Scotus calls the *haecceitas* (individuality or "this-ness" (see SD: 283)) of each entity is conveyed by means of a characteristic mode of action.

> As kingfishers catch fire, dragonflies draw flame;
>   As tumbled over rims in roundy wells
>   Stones ring; like each tucked string tells, each hung bell's
> Bow swung finds tongue to fling out broad its name;
> Each mortal thing does one thing and the same:
>   Deals out that being indoors each one dwells;
>   Selves—goes itself: *myself* it speaks and spells,
> Crying *What I do is me: for that I came.* (1-8)

Hopkins draws attention, by the use of striking imagery, to the way in which each entity displays its individual characteristics – the "flame"-like colours of the kingfisher and dragonfly, the noise made by the stone falling down a well. In the succession of verbs employed – "catch fire", "draw flame", "fling out" – he goes on to illustrate the way in which the observer is attracted to the phenomenon described. Culminating in a declaration consistent with ecology's emphasis on the integrity of species (see Banfield 2007: 181) – for "Selves", used here as a verb, connotes a realisation of each species' individuality (Poems: 281) – 'As kingfishers catch fire' appears, then, to render a deep ecological poetry whose "business is to re-create the object, to present the qualities of phenomena as they strike the senses" (Ball 1971: 111). However, in the suggestion that each phenomenon not only "speaks" but "spells", we discover a contrary, enframing emphasis that runs throughout Hopkins' poetry – namely, the idea that inscape is designed to lead us to a perception of the truths' underlying nature.

It is in this final regard that Hopkins' writing departs from Bate's ecopoetic. For where Bate insists on the distinction of a phenomen-ological poetry from other, descriptive, representational or rhetorical modes, it was inevitable, in the light of his decision to become ordained, that Hopkins' inclination would be to build an ontological dimension into his verse. This tendency had, of course, already been apparent in the journal, where descriptions of natural phenomena holding the eye were perpetually complemented by an ongoing search for pattern. It was also, in fact, a feature from the beginning of his poetry. For Hopkins had always intended this to be another of the mediums by which he would seek to understand and synthesise a post-Darwinian, proto-ecological perspective on nature.

This dimension to Hopkins' work can be seen, for example, in some surviving, unfinished poems written at Oxford (see Beer 1996: 244-5). One of these, 'It was a hard thing to undo this knot' (1864) highlights the difficulty of bestowing structure on natural phenomena in a context in which science had posited a nature characterised by ceaseless change:

> It was a hard thing to undo this knot.
> The rainbow shines, but only in the thought
> Of him that looks. Yet not in that alone,
> For who makes rainbows by invention?
> And many standing round a waterfall
> See one bow each, yet not the same to all,
> But each a hand's breadth further than the next.
> The sun on falling waters writes the text
> Which yet is in the eye or in the thought.
> It was a hard thing to undo this knot. (1-10)

Hopkins conveys here the implausibility of individualised perception grasping broader truths, something captured, notwithstanding an implicit, ecological answer – that it is the sun that "writes the text" – in the question "who makes rainbows by invention?" Reiterated the following year in a fragment that begins "Confirmed beauty will not bear a stress;— /Bright hues long look'd at thin, dissolve and fly", the difficulty, at this stage, of grasping broader ontological truths was also expressed in some other, even more bewildered lines composed in 1865:

> What spirit is that makes stillness obsolete
> With ear-caressing speech? Where is the tongue
> Which drives this stony air to utterance?—
> Who is it? ('O what a silence is this wilderness', 16-19)

Written two years later, though still prior to his conversion, a further poem 'The earth and heaven, so little known', offers the beginnings of a solution.

> The earth and heaven, so little known,
> Are measured outwards from my breast.
> I am the midst of every zone
> And justify the East and West;
>
> The unchanging register of change
> My all-accepting fixèd eye,
> While all things else may stir and range,
> All else may whirl or dive and fly. (1-8)

Written around the time at which Hopkins had been compiling, in his journal, un-theorised lists of sense impressions, elements of this poem state, again, the difficulty of making sense of mutable natural phenomena. This is signified in the "all things" which "whirl or dive and fly" as well as when, later in the poem, he remarks upon a lack of "permanence in the solid world" and a nature perpetually "spent and ended" (16, 21). However, having adopted a post-Romantic approach, as expressed here in the Ruskinian concept of the "eye", Hopkins had by now altered his view as to the possibilities of individualised perception and so speculates that by registering and recording natural phenomena one might after all develop a "philosophy of beauty".

The way that is articulated in this particular poem, in the form of a (human) observer who can "in the midst of every zone […] justify the East and West", might be regarded as somewhat anthropocentric. Yet Hopkins was, at this same time, in the process of gradually stabilising the "flux of impressions" into the philosophy of nature established in the journal. This allowed him, as Isobel Armstrong suggests, "to say that 'things and us' *are*, to establish relationships and connections and to predicate the world of being" (1993: 422). It was once these "relationships and connections" had, via Scotus, completed their evolution into an essentially ecological conception of nature, that Hopkins was ready to articulate his philosophy through verse.

5. Sustainable poetry

Hopkins resumed writing poetry with the composition of 'The Wreck of the Deutschland' in 1875. Having been encouraged by a superior to write the poem – ostensibly about the death of five Franciscan nuns in the shipwreck but, more accurately, a statement of his theological position – he now felt able, for the time being at least, to put aside his scruples about poetry as "not belonging to my profession". While his ecological nature poetry took a short while longer to emerge, Hopkins did begin to develop this in two unfinished poems composed in the following year.

In the first of these, 'Moonrise June 19 1876', phenomenological description – of "The moon, dwindled and thinned to the fringe | of a fingernail" (2) – stimulates a response equivalent to Scotist 'understanding':

> This was the prized, the desirable sight | unsought, presented
>   so easily,
> Parted me leaf and leaf, divided me | eyelid and eyelid of
>   slumber. (6-7)

Where Hopkins had previously found it "a hard thing to undo" the "knot[s]" presented by nature, emboldened now by a scientific understanding refined in the journal, he is able – notwithstanding the elusiveness of a moon that has "dwindled and thinned" and which is, in the following line, "lustre-less" – to capture it "easily".

In 'The Woodlark', the second poem, an initially elusive phenomenon also becomes known to the observer.

> The cuckoo singing one side, on the other from the ground and unseen the wood-lark, as I suppose, most sweetly with a song of which the structure is more definite than the skylark's and gives the link with that of the rest of birds. (JP 3/6/66: 138 (353)

> *Teevo cheevo cheevio chee*:
> O where, what can thát be?
> *Weedio-weedio*: there again!
> So tiny a trickle of a sóng-strain;

> And all round not to be found […]
> Either left either right
> Anywhere in the sunlight. (1-5; 8-9)

The poem typifies what had been recurrent attempts by Hopkins to describe birds. For while such descriptions are relatively uncommon in the journal, compared to those of cloud formations or wave patterns, they do occur more frequently in the earlier poetic drafts and fragments. The lark itself had appeared, for example, in 1862's 'Il Mystico', in the '(Sundry Fragments and Images)' composed between October and November of 1864, and in two poems, 'When eyes that cast' and 'O what a silence is this wilderness', written in 1865. Heuser has suggested that a possible explanation for this is that birds indicated "spiritual direction and character" (1958: 60). This can be seen, for example, in repeated perceptions of the lark, known for its capacity to soar high in the sky, as close to heaven:

> When eyes that cast about the heights of heaven
> To canvass the retirement of the lark. ('When eyes that cast', 1-2)

> Or, like a lark to glide aloof
> Under the cloud-festoonèd roof,
> That with a turning of the wings
> Light and darkness from him flings. ('Il Mystico', 65-8)

A theological component is, therefore, inevitably present in 'The Woodlark' in which the bird represents a freedom of movement – "when the cry within/Says Go on then I go on" (34-5) – regulated by religious (or moral) sanction: "But down drop, if it says Stop" (37). Yet aside from this one allusion, the religious dimension is otherwise absent from the poem opening up the alternative possibility that Hopkins had fixed upon the species so as to demonstrate an ecological understanding of the natural environment.

Once the bird's identity has been exposed

> Well, after all! Ah but hark—
> 'I am the little woodlark […]' (10-11)

the poem continues by describing a bird's eye view of the beauty of an un-ripened wheat-field interspersed with poppies.

> To-day the sky is two and two

With white strokes and strains of blue.
The blue wheat-acre is underneath
And the corn is corded and shoulders its sheaf,
The ear in milk, lush the sash,
And crush-silk poppies aflash. (16-21)

Here Hopkins anticipated a key ecological concept. The "sunlight" (noted in line 9) is seen not only, in the adjective "lush", as having made the corn grow but also in further adjectives – "aflash" and (later) "Flame-rash" (23) – as having generated the energy which flows around the ecosystem. He also revealed, however, an even more extensive ecological understanding. For in the poem Hopkins moves beyond the phenomenological moment to depict an underlying philosophy of interrelationship – of landscape, bird, and (human) observer – that, though harmonious, conveys not so much a lifeless, static balance of nature but, rather, the idea of an entire landscape characterised by energy exchange.

The ecological imagery in these fragments remains, it must be said, rather fleeting. Nevertheless, the paradigm established here, of an initial phenomenological stimulus structured by empirical description into a depiction of energy exchange, was to characterise, and be fully realised within, a sequence of ten sonnets written at St Bueno's between February and September of 1877. It is with these that an ecological reading of Hopkins' poetry can really begin.

The most immediate example is, appropriately enough, 'Spring'.

Nothing is so beautiful as Spring—
  When weeds, in wheels, shoot long and lovely and lush;
  Thrush's eggs look little low heavens, and thrush
Through the echoing timber does so rinse and wring
The ear, it strikes like lightnings to hear him sing;
  The glassy peartree leaves and blooms, they brush
  The descending blue; that blue is all in a rush
With richness; the racing lambs too have fair their fling. (1-8)

Throughout the eight lines of the octave Hopkins largely eschews narrative description, a fact highlighted by the (literal) stress placed at the start of line 5 on "The ear" (see Poems: 264). This phenomenological quality is, then, most apparent in the description of the thrush's singing where he writes that the bird's song will "rinse and wring/The ear", meaning that the song will cleanse the mental blockages caused by conventionalised thinking. Hopkins implies, in turn, that this will alert us to an underlying "new realism" that "strikes like lightnings". While one might anticipate here that the description will, soon enough, be framed, as it is in the sestet, in reference to Catholic theology, an alternative realism (i.e. an "adequate object") is nevertheless apparent in that he also signals some key ecological themes. The opening line refers us, for example, to one such principle, renewal, while the second and third lines introduce another, the integrity of species (even weeds!). Also significant, in this respect, is the juxtaposition of "look little low" – which seems at first to describe an apparently insignificant phenomenon, thrush's eggs – with the added "heavens", which shifts the meaning to assert the bird's status within a creationist, or sacramental, theology. It is, however, the principle of movement, pervading the octave throughout, that instils into the reader an awareness of the octave's dominant theme, that of the landscape as an energy system.

Though written largely in standard rhythm the poem does experiment with sprung rhythm. Hopkins deploys what he calls "Sprung leadings" – (strong stresses placed on the first syllables of lines) to propel us into an economy of motion. "When weeds, in wheels" leads, for example, to a description of the shooting of those weeds in which the three adverbs "long and lovely and lush" run into each other thereby reinforcing the sense of motion. Hopkins goes on, from there, to represent the ecological principle which derives from that, of the unity intrinsic to motion. This is established by means of the devices he had called in his Roehampton lectures "half-rhymes". Particularly notable here are the assonant, strikingly active verbs which, stressed and/or placed at the end of the line – "wring", "strikes", "rush", "fling", "brush", "Spring" – resonate upon each other. He draws, likewise, on alliteration to accentuate, aurally, the interconnection of diverse inscapes. The alliterated "l" sound, describing both the thrush's eggs and the singing of the bird, matches that used to describe the weeds; "bl" connects the peartree (that "blooms") to the "descending blue" of the sky. The result is that Hopkins engenders a poetic embodiment of nature as it was seen in the journal, the dual deployment of rhyme and rhythm creating a structure characterised, ecologically, by shifting, unending, dialectical relationship.

Before we consider other examples of Hopkins' ecopoetry, a caveat needs to be added. 'Spring', in common with much of his verse, is, of course, a sonnet and draws upon a central element of that form, the eight-line octave, as an effective device for structuring or containing flux within a representation of dialectical natural economy. Sonnets are, of course, conventionally characterised by the shift from exemplum in the octave to argument in the sestet (see Spiller 1992: 18), a shift which sometimes gave rise, in Hopkins' work, to counter-ecological, orthodox theological elements. Signalled in the image of the "leaves and blooms" of the pear tree which, in common with the lark in 'When eyes that cast', reach towards heaven and "brush/The descending blue" (6-7), the ecological element in 'Spring' gives way, as the poem reaches the sestet, to a stern treatise about the Fall:

> What is all this juice and all this joy?
>   A strain of the earth's sweet being in the beginning
> In Eden Garden.—Have, get, before it cloy,
>
> Before it cloud, Christ, lord, and sour with sinning (9-12)

This is a pattern repeated in several of the poems, another notable example being 'As kingfishers catch fire', in which the phenomenological description of inscape in the octave also becomes abandoned for abstract theological notions – "I say more: the just man justices;/Keeps grâce" (9-10). There is, as Norman White puts it, a sharp division, in these poems, in which "it appears [...] as if a different, authoritarian voice, representative of tradition, has superimposed an alien framework" (1992: 268).

While that division will be examined further in Chapter Six, these poems may, nevertheless, be read in a way consistent with what Isobel Armstrong has called the Victorian "double poem". Describing Victorian literature as "belonging to a condition of crisis that had emerged directly from economic and cultural changes" (1993: 3), Armstrong locates that literature within a conundrum between a twentieth-century modernist sensibility that celebrates the elimination of meaning and a pre-modern desire to hold onto truth. Arguing that the Victorians, unlike the modernists, regarded that conundrum as a "problem", and that they therefore strove to give political, sexual, and ontological "content" to the potential elimination of meaning (see 1993: 7), Armstrong suggests that in the exploration of such ambiguities "what the Victorian poet achieved was often quite literally two concurrent poems in the same words" (1993: 12). This, in a sense, is how Claude Colleer Abbott, in his introduction to *The Letters of Gerard Manley Hopkins to Robert Bridges*, positions the St Bueno's poems. However, he goes further by also arguing that in many of Hopkins' nature poems the impressionism of the octave in effect overpowers the exemplum of the sestet:

They are poems written to the glory of God by a man who is looking on the world as charged with His grandeur and revealing His bounty and presence. But always as I read them I feel that the poet is primarily seized by the beauty of earth, and that though a man of exquisitely tempered and religious mind, his senses, not his religion, are in the ascendant. Let us grant the conviction that God made this loveliness and that it bears living witness to His affection. Hopkins says little more than this on the religious side of these poems, and he says this side with no particular distinction. On the other hand, his visions of earth and her creatures make a bevy of astonishing and new felicities rarely to be matched in English poetry [in which the] fusion of earthly beauty and exemplum is often so incomplete that the second is merely the addendum of a poet captive in the first place to the beauty besieging his senses. This loveliness is here for its own sake. (RB: xxvii-xxviii)

What I want to suggest, taking a lead from Abbott's argument, is that Hopkins' fidelity to "earthly beauty" often did override but could also complement the theological meaning of his poems; that, consistent with the sacramental and Scotist theology developed in the journal, Hopkins, on occasion, managed to reconcile the two. The remainder of this chapter will examine four poems that exemplify the ecological character of the nature writing that emerged. The first two, 'Pied Beauty' and 'Hurrahing in Harvest', both St Bueno's sonnets, exhibit the co-existence of ecological themes with theology enabled by Hopkins' discovery of Scotus; the second two, 'The Blessed Virgin compared to the Air we Breathe' and 'Inversnaid', examples of the less frequent nature writing that occurred after his ordination, demonstrate how the persistence of Hopkins' scientific interests contributed to the maintenance of an essentially ecological perspective.

> Glory be to God for dappled things—
>   For skies of couple-colour as a brinded cow;
>   For rose-moles all in stipple upon trout that swim;
> Fresh-firecoal chestnut-falls; finches' wings;
>   Landscape plotted and pieced—fold, fallow, and plough;
>   And áll trádes, their gear and tackle and trim.
> All things counter, original, spare, strange;
>   Whatever is fickle, freckled (who knows how?)
>   With swift, slow; sweet, sour; adazzle, dim;
> He fathers-forth whose beauty is past change:
>   Praise him.

'Pied Beauty' starts as a hymn of praise to dapple, a more basic instance of variety in nature which Hopkins had noted in his journal: "a dapple of rosy clouds blotted with purple" (JP 18/7/66: 146). Here, he bestows a phenomenological quality on such observations which in reversing the Cartesian emphasis on nature as inert engenders a sense of nature as 'alive'. The stippling described on the trout appears, for example, "only while the fish was still alive and swimming" (MacKenzie 1981: 86);

likewise, that of "fresh-firecoal" attached to the chestnut connotes, in the comparison with the red glow of burning coals, the notion of an inscape communicating its being. Yet the poem also offers an explicitly ecological paean to the diversity of species.

Understood as a scientific concept, biodiversity refers to three levels of biological organisation: the genetic diversity of individuals within any given species; organismal diversity, meaning the quantity and ratio (or spread) of different species in an ecosystem; and diversity of habitat, ecosystem or landscape (Gaston and Spicer 2004: 5; and see Allaby 2004: 380; Botkin and Keller 2005: G-2). While there is a debate as to the importance of biodiversity to the health of ecosystems (see Townsend, Begon, Harper 2003: 381-2), there also appears to be a consensus amongst ecological scientists as to its value in maintaining basic physical and chemical properties. This occurs by virtue of the necessity of biodiversity to processes such as soil formation, pollination, the chemical properties of water, the recycling of nutrients, protection against flood and drought, and the breaking down of waste (see Gaston and Spicer 2004: 98-9; Townsend, Begon, Harper 2003: 472). Understood, correspondingly, from a social perspective, biodiversity has been acknowledged, on the one hand, as important to humanity in areas that range from the provision of food, clothing or pharmaceuticals to benefits such as tourism, recreation, sport or leisure (Townsend, Begon, Harper 2003: 471-2); on the other, emphasis has been placed on the intrinsic value of species regardless of any direct or indirect use value to humans (see Gaston and Spicer 2004: 104).

Hopkins encapsulated all these understandings in 'Pied Beauty': implicit in the paean to dapple is the notion of genetic diversity, the phenomena he describes in lines 2 to 5 – the "stipple" upon the trout, the chestnuts as bright as glowing coals – also testifying to the genetic uniqueness of each individual creature; the poem celebrates, in its entirety, the diversity of species; while line 5 alludes to an affirmation of the diversity of landscape.

Foreshadowing, likewise, the philosophy of biodiversity, Hopkins captures the balance between humanity and other species within ecological theory. On the one hand, he comes close, in lines 5 and 6, to the perspective by which biodiversity encompasses those very "human activities that make conservation a necessity" (Townsend, Begon, Harper 2003: 472). He offers praise, for example, to animal and crop farming, even demonstrating an awareness (if we stretch a point) of sustainable farming by including "fallow" land. Indeed, he goes even further by suggesting, in the reference to "áll trádes" – and, specifically, in the stress on both words – that even the industrial activity connoted by "gear and tackle" (industrial equipment and tools) merits inclusion within a diverse economy of nature. The poem exhibits, in this way, not the idealism of feudalism, the "lost history and [...] undemocratic social order" that Armstrong finds (1993: 426), but a sympathy for industrial labour that we shall see again in Chapter Five. Finally, Hopkins also develops, in the sestet, the theme of biodiversity for its own sake in giving praise to the principles of oppositeness, individuality, and instability in nonhuman nature. With the first valorised, in the line "swift, slow; sweet, sour; adazzle, dim", Hopkins articulates the intrinsic, non-utilitarian value of species by extolling not only individuality (the "original") and eccentricity (the "strange") but also "All things counter [...] spare" – species in conflict with or useless to humankind – as exemplifying God's "glory".

The ecological themes raised in the poem are enhanced and supported by the poetic devices that Hopkins employs. Critics have noted that 'Pied Beauty' epitomises his idea that "in art we strive to realise not only unity [...] but also, with it, difference, variety, contrast" and that "it is rhyme we like, not echo, and not unison but harmony" (JP: 83; and see Bergonzi 1978: 177). While biodiversity has sometimes been equated to outmoded notions such as balance, stability or the climax community (Allaby 2004: 126), Richard Kerridge has suggested that one of those principles, harmony, potentially connotes "a much more dynamic and interactive process than mechanical (and perhaps ultimately static) balance" (see Garrard 2007: 24). It is on this, alternative basis that Hopkins realised an ecological conception of biodiversity which occurs through the interplay of rhythm and rhyme. For in a poem written in "sprung paeonic rhythm", he conveys an economy of species individualised by rhyme but then interrelated, first by assonance – dappled, couple, stipple, tackle, fickle, freckled, adazzle (see MacKenzie 1981: 87) – and then by the rhythm which confers structural unity. Depicting "a world unified 'past change'" what Hopkins conveys is an ecological celebration of diversity and flux brought together, dialectically, in the rhythm.

Having, then, avoided a pre-modern conception of nature, Hopkins also eludes the potentially more counter-ecological connotations of biodiversity. The equation, noted above, of biodiversity to balance or stability has been attributed to the Christian concept of plenitude (Keller and Golley 2000: 105-6). Given that the poem was written at the time of Hopkins' theological training, that might well have been the understanding offered in 'Pied Beauty'. Yet this is not the case. To achieve, for him, the somewhat difficult feat of writing a poem "primarily seized by the beauty of earth" Hopkins utilised a secondary poetic device, the flexibility of the sonnet form. Phillis Levin locates that flexibility in the division between octave and sestet, or, in other words, at the volta (turn) of the poem (see 2001: xxxviii-ix). The use, in this poem, of the shortened, curtal sonnet appears to encourage Hopkins to construct his volta not, as in several other poems, around a turn to theological argument but, remaining focused on nature, in terms of a shift from phenomenological observation to an argument in support of biodiversity. Only in the last two lines does Hopkins introduce a theological dimension.

> He fathers-forth whose beauty is past change:
>   Praise him.

Yet even here the exhortation, "Praise him", only brings about a reconciliation of the ecological and the theological. In fact, in relegating theology to the coda, 'Pied Beauty', as Abbott writes, can only be regarded as "a devotional poem [...] in the way that all poems witnessing to beauty are devotional" (RB: xxviii). The belatedness serves, that is, to reinforce the predominant ecological message of the poem.

A co-existence of theology and ecology also occurs in the next poem Hopkins wrote, 'Hurrahing in Harvest'.

> Summer ends now; now, barbarous in beauty, the stooks rise
> Around; up above, what wind-walks ! what lovely
>   behaviour
> Of silk-sack clouds ! has wilder, wilful wavier
> Meal-drift moulded ever and melted across skies?
>
> I walk, I lift up, I lift up heart, eyes,
> Down all that glory in the heavens to glean our Saviour;
> And, éyes, heárt, what looks, what lips yet gave you a
> Rapturous love's greeting of realer, of rounder replies?
>
> And the azurous hung hills are his world-wielding shoulder
> Majestic—as a stallion stalwart, very-violet-sweet!—
> These things, these things were here and but the beholder
> Wanting; which two when they once meet,
> The heart rears wings bold and bolder
> And hurls for him, O half hurls earth for him off under his
>   feet.

The opening statement – "Summer ends now" – evokes an earlier poem, 'The Summer Malison' (1865), that teems with images of decaying nature – broken hedges, an oppressive sun, barley turning to weed, corn beaten flat. The intention on that occasion had been theological, Hopkins renouncing earthly beauty for a heavenly salvation that he symbolised through harvest. Yet, here, with his love of nature sanctioned by his Scotism there is no renouncement. And, in what might have been referred to as his most *environmentally* benign poem – "the outcome of half an hour of extreme enthusiasm as I walked home alone one day from fishing in the [River] Elwy" (RB 16/7/78: 56) – the "enthusiasm" can be seen, in fact, to derive from an *ecological* mode of perception, one charged, additionally, by the use of sprung rhythm.

From the beginning, with the repetition of "now", we get not the images of decay which had marked the earlier poem but a sense of motion that continues even at the summer's end. The reader is then prompted towards an ecological awareness by the use of active verbs to describe an instressed environment, flush with beauty and energy. "Up above" clouds are "wind-walks"; below, the "stooks" (wheat-sheaves), more conventionally assembled in static groups, "Rise/ Around". Most fundamentally, and remembering Hopkins' earlier studies of clouds, we find individual inscapes characterised by the dialectical relationship between structure and flux, the "wilder, wilful wavier" meal-drift becoming "moulded ever" and "melted across skies".

Yet the significance of the poem lies not only in its conveying an ecological sense of natural economy, but also in the affirmative statement by which the poet sees himself as embedded within that ecosystem. This begins to occur in lines 5 to 8 where Hopkins highlights his own sensory act of response in the "éyes, heárt" that "greet" God in affirmative gestures. In the journal, as we have seen, Hopkins followed Ruskin's practice of deploying the "innocent eye" so as to discern the economy of nature; conversely, the heart, for Hopkins, connoted a "beauty of character", a "handsome heart" for which Christ was the standard (RB (22/10/79): 95-6; SD: 37-8). This relationship was, ultimately, theological: the eye registering nature (memory, understanding), the heart affirming God (will). While, as examined in Chapter Six, the heart often took precedence, here, as signified by the matching stress ("éyes, heárt") and the amendment from an earlier title, 'Heart's Hurrahing in Harvest', the eye achieves an equality; Hopkins does not, that is to say, subordinate an ecological to a theological perspective.

The ecopoetic formula is complete when, having registered the conjunction of eyes and heart, his "lips", the reading of the poem, give voice to a sacramental theology. This becomes apparent in the sestet in which the eye registers a physically and metaphysically interdependent system, sky and land intermingling in the "azurous hung hills" that offer to God a "world-wielding shoulder". Where, in the earlier stages of the journal, Hopkins had puzzled over inscape, by this point "these things" of nature had been met (understood) and incorporated by the "beholder". And, crucially, while the threat of retraction from an ecological perspective remains, in the act of dedication (election), it does not, in this instance, result in withdrawal from nature. For while Hopkins "lift[s] up" his heart towards God ("our Saviour") he also, simultaneously, looks "Down" at the earth. While he, himself, is lifted up, as his "heart rears wings", the earth under his feet is only "half" hurled, his spiritual existence remaining connected to the physical environment (MacKenzie 1981: 89) thereby confirming the convergence of Scotist theology and an ecological sense of human integration in the landscape.

The St Bueno's poems were composed in a flush of "extreme enthusiasm" engendered by a combination of the Welsh landscape, Hopkins' impending ordination and his recent discovery of Scotus. The sacramental theology this brought about would not, again, be so prominent in his poetry, but later works did continue to offer an ecological perspective that was further informed by an interest in science that had been enhanced by a second period spent at Stonyhurst, an institution with a "considerable scientific reputation" (see Nixon 2002: 134; Zaniello 1988: 61, 97), between September 1882 and February 1884. The remainder of this chapter looks at two such poems, 'The Blessed Virgin compared to the Air we Breathe' and 'Inversnaid'. These offer, respectively, an analogy between pure air and the spiritual sustenance offered by the Virgin Mary and what would now be recognised as an ecological perspective on wetlands.

The central analogy Hopkins makes in 'The Blessed Virgin compared to the Air we Breathe' was, in fact, signalled, in an earlier (1878) poem 'The May Magnificat'. That poem begins with Hopkins questioning why May has conventionally been dedicated "Mary's month" – "I/Muse at that and wonder why" (1-2) – and with the speculation, "Is it only its being brighter/Than the most are that must delight her?" (9-10). This, in turn, leads to what becomes a notable example of the phenomenological basis to his work.

> When drop-of-blood-and-foam-dapple
> Bloom lights the orchard-apple

> And thicket and thorp are merry
> With silver-surfèd cherry
>
> And azuring-over greybell makes
> Wood banks and brakes wash wet like lakes
>   And magic cuckoocall
>   Caps, clears, and clinches all— (37-44)

In these lines Hopkins responds to the visual stimuli in the environment, in particular to the bloom that "light[s]" the "orchard-apple" and "azuring-over", a memorable depiction of the "greybell" opening into a bluebell (Poems: 272). While "wash wet" refers, literally, to the woods awash with bluebells, it connotes, also, the general process being described here, in which one's perception of the surrounding environment becomes rinsed "clear" of conventionalised thinking.

As in "Repeat that, repeat", it is the call of the cuckoo that "clears, and clinches all". Yet, unlike that poem, what these lines "clinch" is not the phenomenological impression itself but, rather, the theological point of reference that underlies it. This is articulated in the following, closing stanza of the poem:

> This ecstasy all through mothering earth
> Tells Mary her mirth till Christ's birth
>   To remember and exultation
>   In God who was her salvation. (45-8)

While this demonstrates the tendency to enframe that habitually possessed Hopkins' writing, the poem, in effect a further affirmation of his Scotism, also elaborates an analogous perception of the environment as an energy system.

For Hopkins ultimately rejects the superficial answer initially offered to his question – "its being brighter" – in favour of May's embodiment of "Growth in everything" (16). This results, in turn, in a reiteration of the view, expressed in the journal, that spring offers "a new world of inscape":

> Question: What is Spring?—
> Growth in everything—
>
> Flesh and fleece, fur and feather,
> Grass and greenworld all together;
>   Star-eyed strawberry-breasted
>   Throstle above her nested

> Cluster of bugle blue eggs thin
> Forms and warms the life within;
>   And bird and blossom swell
>   In sod or sheath or shell. (15-24)

Associating (by means of the em-dash) the magnification of each inscape with the fact that Mary does, also, "Magnify the Lord" (32), what appears here is a depiction of the economy of nature in which initially straightforward images of harmony ("all together") are curtailed by the semicolon so as to give way to a more detailed ecological imagery. Represented by the throstle, shown forming and sustaining the life of her young, Hopkins develops this, in the next stanza, into a generalised observation wherein a more static understanding of harmony is supplanted in favour of the "dynamic and interactive process" envisaged by Kerridge where natural phenomena – whether birds, blossom or grass – are seen, explicitly, to be formed and sustained by energy exchange. It is this analogy, between the Virgin Mary and an ecological understanding of natural economy, that Hopkins, in the later poem, goes on to develop.

'The Blessed Virgin' is premised, as is 'Inversnaid', on the ecological concept of "wildness", a concept that is most easily understood by means of a contrast with its preservationist equivalent, "wilderness". That distinction has been famously analysed by the environmental historian William Cronon. Identifying wilderness as a "human creation" (1995: 69-70) derived historically from the Romantic and American transcenddentalist reaction against modernity, Cronon, in the words of his influential article, sees the "trouble with wilderness" as the establishment of a dualism that allows us to imagine that "we can flee into a mythical wilderness to escape history and the obligation to take responsibility for our own actions" (90). Arguing that we need to be "broadening our sense of the otherness that wilderness seeks to define and protect" (87) he advocates the replacement of "wilderness" with "wildness", a more ecological concept.

'Wildness' has been famously articulated by Gary Snyder who defines it, in *A Place in Space*, as referring to a notion of "nature *as* process rather than as product or commodity" (1995: 168) and, in more detail, as follows:

'Wild' alludes to a process of self-organization that generates systems and organisms, all of which are within the constraints of—and constitute components of—larger systems that again are wild, such as major ecosystems or the water cycle in the biosphere. Wildness can be said to be the essential nature of nature. (1995: 174)

To this basic definition other dimensions have been added. Cronon himself introduces an ethical, social component. Because, he argues, wildness, unlike wilderness, "can be found anywhere" (89), it reminds us continually of the need to respect the autonomy and otherness of the nonhuman life that surrounds us and on which we depend: "Learning to honor the wild [...] means looking at the part of nature we intend to turn toward our own ends and asking whether we can use it again and again and again—sustainably—without its being diminished in the process" (89-90).

As part of the attempt to inculcate such values, Snyder has also produced a subsidiary theory of language as "wild". This posits language as functioning both phenomenologically and conceptually, much like the ecopoetic outlined in this chapter:

> language does not impose order on a chaotic universe, but reflects its own wildness back.
>   In doing so it goes two ways: it enables us to have a small window onto an independently existing world, but it also shapes—via its very structures and vocabularies—how we see that world. (1995: 174)

Hopkins drew upon a very similar notion of the wild so as to signify a "more-than-human" nature that he juxtaposed to human nature – the "wild nest" (11) of 'The Caged Skylark', for example, or the "wild wooddove" (1) of 'Peace'. The more specific, ecological notion of wild, as flux and as a "process" organising itself into larger systems, can also be attributed, however, to Hopkins who, as it happens, used the term in this way as well to describe the autonomy of non-human nature's growth and organisation. An instance of this occurs, as we have seen, in 'Hurrahing in Harvest' where the "wilder, wilful wavier" clouds signify a sacramental economy of nature. It is, however, 'The Blessed Virgin' and 'Inversnaid' which most clearly exemplify, and enact, the three interconnected components noted above: of nature (and human nature) as "wild"; of a language that articulates and "reflects [...] wildness back"; and of the need for a social philosophy that takes account of that "wildness". Each of the poems supplements such an understanding by means of a conceptual framework provided by science.

'The Blessed Virgin compared to the Air we Breathe' begins as follows:

> Wild air, world-mothering air,
> Nestling me everywhere,
> That each eyelash or hair

> Girdles: goes home betwixt
> The fleeciest, frailest-flixed
> Snowflake; that's fairly mixed
> With, riddles, and is rife
> In every least thing's life;
> This needful, never spent,
> And nursing element;
> My more than meat and drink,
> My meal at every wink;
> This air, which, by life's law,
> My lung must draw and draw
> Now but to breathe its praise,
> Minds me in many ways
> Of her. (1-17)

Though recalling, momentarily, the puzzlement of his earlier poems, in the description of the air as "fairly mixed/With, riddles", Hopkins nevertheless establishes in these lines a complex understanding of air as "Wild" as well as, in a development from 'The May Magnificat', "world-mothering" (nurturing). This understanding corresponds, furthermore, to the dialectical, Darwinian mode of tension that, at the time, was shaping an incipient scientific ecology. Air is seen, on the one hand, as the basis for all existence, the "law" that nestles, girdles, nurses every single "eyelash or hair" and "every least thing's life", even that of the snow-flake. Yet while Hopkins believes this "needful [...] element" to be sustainable, "never spent", there is, also, a clear message about the vulnerability such dependence bestows, a message that ought to resonate with the contemporary reader. This is implied, for example, when the image of air as humanity's "nursing element" becomes reinforced by the lines

> This air, which, by life's law,
> My lung must draw and draw
> Now but to breathe its praise

These lines have a breathless quality, created by the commas and extended by means of the interruption between (the notably repeated) "draw and draw" and the urgent and insistent "Now". A further instance of this can be found in an analogy, later in the poem, in which Mary – "She, wild web, wondrous robe" who "Mantles the guilty globe" (38-9) – is described as protecting humankind, "like air's fine flood" from "the deathdance in his blood" (51-2). Through Mary, Hopkins suggests, "Men here may draw like breath/More Christ and baffle death" (66-7). While, in the second example, he is ostensibly concerned with the immortality of the soul, the physicality of the rhythm, in the first in particular, confers upon each of these examples (quite literally embodying) a corporeal sense of human integration within, and dependence upon, the abiotic environment. This carries the poem's ecological significance beyond a mere thematic analogy between science and theology, a point reinforced if we consider the relationship between Hopkins' scientific interests and the emergence, later in the poem, of further ecological ideas.

A passage in the middle of the poem demonstrates an acquaintance with the recently established theory of Rayleigh scattering, the reflection and scattering of light waves by particles in the air that produces the blue of the sky.

> Again, look overhead
> How air is azurèd […]
>
> The glass-blue days are those
> When every colour glows,
> Each shape and shadow shows.
> Blue be it: this blue heaven
> The seven or seven times seven
> Hued sunbeam will transmit
> Perfect, not alter it […] (73-4; 83-9)

One of the areas of physics Hopkins was most interested in was spectroscopy. While this largely involved the analysis of light generated by matter through a prism, and the separation of colours on a photographic plate so as "to form a series of spectral lines", Roger G. Newton notes that the German physicist, Joseph von Fraunhofer had also discovered dark lines in the spectrum of the sun caused, in this case, by the absorption rather than emission of light (2007: 224). Given that this discovery led directly to the debates about wave particles that "raged" in Britain in the 1820s and 1830s (see Heilbron 2005: 305), it is unsurprising that Hopkins, writing three or four decades later, followed the same course.

Hopkins argued, in an undergraduate essay, 'The Tests of a Progressive Science', that the real contribution of spectroscopy would lie in studying "the chemical composition of non-terrestrial masses" (sun, moon, stars etc.) and by "analyzing", as Zaniello explains, "the spectrum or component bands of light emitted or reflected by these bodies" (1988: 133). We find, thereafter in his writing, a fascination with light, and, specifically, with the colour and condition of the sky. This can be seen in the journal. From Stonyhurst he notes a sky "blue […] like that blue of vase-glass" and, the year after, "a sky of blue 'water'" (JP 28/4/71: 207; 12/12/72: 228). Earlier, he had suggested that in the absence of a clear blue sky sunlight or the sun's rays would be dulled: "sky round confused pale green and blue with faint horned rays" (JP 18/7/66: 146). This fascination also underlay his desire to write "a sort of popular account of Light and the Ether" and, in particular, the four letters to *Nature* which really corroborate Hopkins' interest in the relationship between sunlight and the atmosphere. While the letters, in particular, seem perhaps more concerned with aesthetic effect than scientific explanation, it is nevertheless likely that Hopkins had developed a firm knowledge of the science of scattering through an acquaintance with the work of John Tyndall.

Tyndall explained scattering in 'On the Scientific Use of the Imagination' (1870), the published version of an address first presented to the British Association (see Beer 1996: 264). This essay was published in various places, for Tyndall disseminated his ideas, like many of his scientific contemporaries, in more general periodicals and journals (see Beer 1996: 243; Thompson 1981: 154). Beer assumes, on the evidence that Tyndall published in journals with which Hopkins was familiar, that Hopkins must have been aware of the theory of scattering (see 1996: 263-6). Indeed in the poem '(On a Piece of Music)' Hopkins had compared the moral neutrality of a "good" that is "neither right nor wrong" to a sky "No more than red and blue", Tyndall having posited, in the address, that "different light-waves produce different colours. Red, for example, is produced by the largest waves ... blue, of the small waves". In this poem, another of Tyndall's statements, that the limits of the imagination lead us to identify just the seven colours of the rainbow when there might in fact be "seven or seven times seven" (see Beer 1996: 265, 266), is echoed in the lines

> [...] this blue heaven
> The seven or seven times seven
> Hued sunbeam will transmit

Such lines demonstrate that the unification of "material" (science) with ideal (theology) occurred largely without detriment to the former. The chief significance, however, in this context, of Hopkins' interest in spectroscopy is that it also prompted an instinctive move from physics to ecology.

> Whereas did air not make
> This bath of blue and slake

> His fire, the sun would shake,
> A blear and blinding ball
> With blackness bound, and all
> The thick stars round him roll
> Flashing like flecks of coal,
> Quartz-fret, or sparks of salt,
> In grimy vasty vault.
> Through her we may see him
> Made sweeter, not made dim,
> And her hand leaves his light
> Sifted to suit our sight. (94-102; 110-13)

Placed in a literal relationship to ecological theory, this passage could be said to anticipate anxieties about the perceived hole in the ozone layer. Maureen Christie notes that the presence of ozone in the atmosphere had first been detected in 1879 (four years before the poem was written) and that its role in "shielding the earth's surface from solar ultraviolet light" became apparent shortly afterwards (2001: 9). While it is by no means likely that Hopkins would have been aware, specifically, of such ideas, Christie's subsequent identification of a connection to spectroscopy – she writes "missing frequencies observed in the spectrum of sunlight" would have made it difficult for scientists not "to deduce that gases in the earth's atmosphere must be responsible" (2001: 9) – does offer one explanation for the anticipation of ecology apparent in this passage.

For what Hopkins describes, building on the scientific insights articulated earlier in the poem, is a further understanding of the ecology of "Wild air", namely that the protection offered by the ozone layer provides conditions suitable to growth. Daniel Brown argues that in Hopkins' work blue sky frequently symbolised "vigour and growth" (1997: 244). He offers examples from the poems such as the "Blue-beating" of the May sky in 'The Wreck of the Deutschland' (st.26) and the "descending blue [...] all in a rush" in 'Spring'. We also find this, in more detail, in the journal passage (cited in Chapter Three) that begins "Cowslips capriciously colouring meadows in creamy drifts". For this progresses from a "Sky sleepy blue without liquidity" to an observation of growth activated by a sun safely filtered through the blue of the sky:

On further side of the Witney Road hills, just fleeced with grain or other green growth, by their dips and waves foreshortened here and there and so differenced in brightness and opacity the green on them, with delicate effect. On left, brow of the near hill glistening with very brightly newly turned sods [...] Copses in grey-red or grey-yellow—the tinges immediately forerunning the opening of full leaf. Meadows skirting Severn-bridge road voluptuous green. Some oaks are out in small leaf. Ashes not out, only tufted with their fringy blooms. Hedges springing richly [...] Sun seemed to make a bright liquid hole in this. (JP 3/5/66: 133-4)

Having foreshadowed, then, in this poem and other works, an ecological understanding of the role played by the atmosphere, both in regulating sunlight and in fostering growth, what occurs in the passage quoted above is a contrary perception that any reduction in the protection offered from the glare of the sun will result in an apocalyptic scenario, that of the sun returning to the "black body spectrum" which would occur in any environment where the process of scattering had been prevented or reduced (Bloomfield 2001: 386).

If 'The Blessed Virgin compared to the Air we Breathe' demonstrates, then, the transition Hopkins made from phenomenological impressionism to a scientifically informed, ecological mode of representation we can also see in it shades of the next, logical progression, towards a related social critique. For while social commentary appears explicitly only once in the poem, in the reference to "the guilty globe" (39), it is implied throughout. This is apparent in the development from an elemental "Wild air" that is seen to sustain life ("Nestling me everywhere") to the depiction of a lifeless atmosphere, the "blear and blinding ball/With blackness bound", but also if we take into account thematic parallels to passages that appear elsewhere. For example, in an 1879 sermon Hopkins had compared the "blue sky, which for all its richness of colour does not stain the sunlight" to "smoke and red clouds [which] do" (SD: 29). More substantially, the critical implications of the lines quoted above, where the stress on "Whereas" arguably compels the reader to consider the consequences should we, humanity, unsettle the blue sky, are borne out by the recurrent association Hopkins made between "blackness" and the disintegration of society, in images, for example, where "the black West", as he calls it in 'God's Grandeur', is seen as responsible for the "blear and blinding ball" described above. Though perhaps only alluded to here, this development, in Hopkins' poetry, from an ecological writing about nature to social critique did go much further as will be discussed in Chapter Five.

In certain places the theology of this poem does not always sit so neatly with ecological paradigms. Earlier, for example, where Mary is seen to "sift" the force of God's love, she is also described as having a power "Great as no goddess's/Was deemèd, dreamed" (27-8). A reference, it would appear, to the Greek goddess Gaia (MacKenzie 1981: 157), this indicates the habitual tendency in some of Hopkins' verse to give pre-eminence to orthodox theology over ecology. Yet while

Hopkins, interestingly, disliked both 'The May Magnificat' and 'The Blessed Virgin' on precisely these (religious) grounds – he saw "little good" in the former and described the latter as "a compromise with popular taste" (RB 29/1/79: 65; RB 11/5/83: 179) – the development, in this poem, from detailed anticipation of ecological science to the beginnings of a social-ecological critique does offer a detailed and fulsome example of Victorian ecology that can be corroborated, furthermore, by reference to the final poem to be considered in this chapter.

No Hopkins poem has received as much renewed impetus from the 'green movement' as 'Inversnaid'. Hitherto critically ignored (it is not referred to once, for example, in Roberts' *Critical Heritage* edition) it has lately become in Robert Bernard Martin's words, "something of a manifesto for the forces of conservation" (1991: 335). Yet such popularity rests on a misreading. For while 'Inversnaid' appears to offer a preservationist lament for wilderness it is, quite specifically, an ecological poem about wildness.

> This darksome burn, horseback brown,
> His rollrock highroad roaring down,
> In coop and in comb the fleece of his foam
> Flutes and low to the lake falls home.
>
> A windpuff-bonnet of fáwn-fróth
> Turns and twindles over the broth
> Of a pool so pitchblack, féll-frówning
> It rounds and rounds Despair to drowning.
>
> Degged with dew, dappled with dew
> Are the groins of the braes that the brook treads through,
> Wiry heathpacks, flitches of fern,
> And the beadbonny ash that sits over the burn.
>
> What would the world be, once bereft
> Of wet and of wildness? Let them be left,
> O let them be left, wildness and wet;
> Long live the weeds and the wilderness yet.

Hopkins wrote the poem on a two-day break in Loch Lomond having completed a period of exhausting parochial work in Glasgow. In this context it is, perhaps, unsurprising that 'Inversnaid' has attracted predominately romantic readings. Martin suggests, for example, that it counteracted a feeling that "cities dried him up spiritually and poetically" (1991: 335-6). Norman MacKenzie, drawing on Mill's *Principles of*

Political Economy, argues that 'Inversnaid' advocates solitude – the "cradle", in Mill's words, "of thoughts and aspirations" – and that it extols what Mill called "the spontaneous activity of nature" (1981: 147). White interprets the emphasis on weeds as a Ruskinian injunction to avoid "all very neat things" (1992: 76). Each accentuates, therefore, the concept of wilderness, emphasising notions of spontaneity and creativity. Yet the empirical mode of analysis forged in the journal, not to mention the impatience with thoughtful solitude demonstrated in *Richard*, suggests that such a mode was alien to Hopkins, a fact borne out by closer examination of the poem.

Hopkins' focus was, in the first place, not on wilderness but, as can be seen from the final stanza in particular, on wildness. In that respect 'Inversnaid' exhibits precisely the difference of emphasis suggested by Cronon. An even more significant variation comes when Hopkins, consistent with the concept of the wild, replaces a pronounced stress on wilderness in the first draft.

> O where is it, the wilderness,
> The wildness of the wilderness?
> Where is it, the wilderness?
>
> And wander in the wilderness;
> In the weedy wilderness,
> Wander in the wilderness.

with the emphasis on wetness that predominates in the final draft. It is in this alteration that Hopkins produced a distinctively post-Romantic work that parallels, furthermore, contemporary writing on wetland ecology.

Ecological scientists have established two fundamental contributions that water makes to life on earth: the regulation of temperature and climate (Tudge 1991: 23); and the movement of energy and nutrients (carbon, nitrogen, phosphorus etc.) around the ecosystem. (Townsend, Begon, Harper 2003: 389-91; Tudge 1991: 24-5). With regard to the second, a key component underlying the ecological value attributed to water is its liquidity and the principle of motion this helps instil into any given ecosystem. As Colin Tudge has put this, "the movements of water affect the surface structure of the land (its topography); the overall climate; and the day-to-day weather" (1991: 23). This perspective, and a connected point that, after earth movements, "the movement of water is the chief sculptor of landscape" (1991: 25) was one anticipated, as it happens, by Ruskin.

Eulogising about water in the first volume of *Modern Painters* Ruskin suggests that the "transporting agency of water", its "guiding influence", underlies "the structure of the framework of the earth" a point he elaborates at the start of Section 5, 'Of Truth of Water':

> Of all the inorganic substances, acting in their own proper nature, and without assistance or combination, water is the most wonderful [...] we [can] think of it as [...] the instrument by which the earth we have contemplated was modelled into symmetry and its crags chiselled into grace. (1903-12 (3): 494)

Believing that "all plains capable of cultivation are deposits from some kind of water" (1903-12 (3): 428) Ruskin saw one of the primary responsibilities of what he regarded as humanity's stewardship of the land to be the management and utilisation of water. In letter nineteen of *Fors Clavigera*, for example, he advises Italian peasants to embank their hill-sides so as to gather the rain flow, and counsels them also to learn "a little hydraulics" (1903-12 (27): 326, 330). In a later letter he outlines, more generally, six principles of "good human work", modelled on the six days it took God to create the world. Including "the disciplining of falling waters" and "the separation of earth from water" (to illustrate which point he praises Dutch land reclamation) (1903-12 (28): 175-6), these became, in turn, the principles by which Ruskin identified water as one of the "three Material things, not only useful, but essential to Life" from which he shaped his political philosophy.

Yet while water was central to an essentially ecological conception of nature, the parallels with contemporary ecological theory begin to dissolve, as with all of Ruskin's writing, once this perspective becomes subsumed into the moral and religious framework implicit when he speaks of "crags chiselled into grace". This took the form, in particular, of moralistic juxtapositions between pure highland mountainous water and "lowland" water such as "streams" which "in [...] level land crept in dark eddies by unwholesome banks" (1903-12 (6): 120). Exhibiting a particular dislike of wetland areas – marshes, swamps, bogs, which he saw as contrary to the "good human work" of separating earth from water – it is here where Ruskin departs from an ecological science which, in fact, has placed a great deal of emphasis on reasserting (or reclaiming) the importance of wetland areas.

Botkin and Keller list the vital and varied ecological importance of wetlands in terms of the following qualities: the capacity to act as a "sponge" reducing flooding in times of high rainfall and replenishing water supplies in periods of dry weather; as a nursery ground for the diversity of species; as natural filters that, in trapping toxins, purify the water supply; the recycling of nutrients and chemicals; and the storage of organic carbon sources (2005: 420). More generally, Rod Giblett, in his 1996 study *Postmodern Wetlands*, links wetland areas both to Tudge's notion of water sculpting the landscape and to the hydrological cycle. Of the first, Giblett suggests

> Without the wetland, the world would fall apart [...] there would be nothing to replen-ish the skeletal system of the dry land, the backbones of mountain ranges, the ribs of ridges, the limbs of peninsulas and capes, and the fingers of land reaching into the sea all of which (including the marrow of the wetlands) supply and make possible the fertile plains, prairies and steppes on which agriculture takes place, on which industry depends, on which cities 'live', or more precisely which they parasitically suck dry. (1996: 234)

Of the second, he writes that while wetlands have been associated pejoratively with bowels they are, quite literally "connected to the bowels of the earth via the underground aquifer of which they are often the expression and on which the city is reliant for domestic water supplies". He cites in this context Mitsch and Gosselink's valuable description of wetland areas as the "kidneys of the landscape" (1996: 136).

Having outlined the ecological value of wetland areas, the other main aspect to Giblett's book, the attempt to posit wetlands as postmodern, works, amongst other things, to highlight the ecological value of cultural, or literary, association. Wetlands, he suggests, are postmodern because they are "neither strictly land or water" (1996: 3). Contrasting this understanding to an earlier, modernist opposition, traced back to Ruskin, in which wetlands were seen, negatively, as places of darkness or nothingness (1996: 23), the point Giblett makes is that wetlands will "not be regarded as ecologically valuable until they are seen as aesthetically pleasing" (1996: 12). He notes, however, that such a shift "would entail rethinking the whole category and function" of the modernist landscape aesthetic, but argues for wetlands as places in which "to celebrate the ambivalence and fluidity of the postmodern" in opposition to the modern state of mind under which they were "drained, or filled, or polluted" (1996: 20-1). 'Inversnaid' can be seen, in that it anticipates such a perspective, as offering precisely the positive aesthetic representation that Giblett advocates.

The opening of the poem derives, probably, from a journal entry re-corded seven years earlier in which Hopkins, observing a horse on Wimbledon Common, compared its "likeness [...] to a breaker, a wave of the sea curling over" (JP 6/4/74: 242). While Hopkins was, as we know, particularly interested in the motion of water, the poem expands upon the descriptions in the journal by drawing on the possibilities afforded by rhythm and rhyme. It begins with an emphasis on wild nature encapsulated by the "darksome burn" and the metaphor of the wild horse "roaring down". This, however, is promptly subsumed into a central ecological metaphor as Hopkins' description highlights the fundamental importance of water to this particular ecosystem.

He gives the ecosystem a specific (wild) inscape, interrelating its different components. This is conveyed, in part, through colloquialism – "highroad"; "windpuff-bonnet"; "beadbonny ash" – and, more centrally, through the ongoing metaphor of the wild horse that symbolises the energy conveyed by the burn. While the burn, in stanza one, rollercoasts over "coops" (hollows) and "comb's" (crests) of rock, it nevertheless "falls" into order as the water "flutes" into grooves. The use, once again, of the active verb is notable, conveying – as with the "moulded" of 'Hurrahing in Harvest', or Tudge's metaphor of sculpting – a sense of the determinate action, instress, that underlies conceptions of both divine and ecological order. Maintaining this theme the poem nevertheless switches direction in stanza two where Hopkins draws upon his knowledge of thermodynamic theory to warn of an alternative possibility, that energy will become disordered (entropic). This he conveys through the image of the water that "féll-frówning" into a "pool so pitchblack", an image embodied within the broken rhythm of the lines. However, exploiting the variations possible within sprung rhythm, he again bypasses this picking up the rhythm in stanza 3 to recommence the description of the course of the burn. It is here that the poem really captures the fundamental importance of water to sustaining the ecosystem and sculpting the landscape. The braes which the brook "treads through" are "degged" (sprinkled) (Poems: 280) and (note) "dappled" with dew which, though partly aesthetic (the light catching the dew), is also symbiotic: the river "degs" the brae with dew while the hill-sides are, themselves, the source from which the burn draws its water (MacKenzie 1981: 147). In the bodily reference (line 10) to "the groins of the braes" Hopkins does, furthermore, incorporate the water into a landscape – of heather ("heath-packs"), fern, and ash – nourished, throughout, by it.

The fact that 'Inversnaid' is not a sonnet enabled Hopkins to avoid the temptation to split the poem into sacramental and orthodox components. He is able to offer, therefore, a thoroughly ecological poem. He does, however, instigate a different type of juxtaposition in which alternate stanzas serve, respectively, to convey, first, ecological order (1 and 3) and then possible disruptions to that (2 and 4). Where the second stanza had warned of entropic decline, the fourth and final stanza counsels against the depletion of wetlands through human activity.

Discussing the earlier draft Hopkins told Bridges that he had written "something [...] on the decline of wild nature" but that he had been struggling with the poem: "if I cd. only seize it" (RB 22/2/79: 73-4). He appears to have done so once he forsook the romantic notion of wilderness. For in the final version of the poem wilderness is mentioned only in the last line and even there, seemingly, as just one example, like "weeds", of a more general (ecological) principle of wildness. The completed version does convey the loss of the land – in the stilted movement and artificial action, that contrasts so effectively with the natural energy of the burn – but it warns, not against the loss of wilderness, in a preservationist sense, but against an equivalent loss of wetness, that is of the energy and sustenance essential to the surrounding ecosystem. The final irony is that it is the priest, Hopkins, who produces a poem devoid of the religiosity and anthropomorphism of Ruskin, and who offers, in this description of water, a literary precursor that can, indeed, help shape an ecological appreciation of wetlands.

The poems discussed above, 'The Blessed Virgin' and 'Inversnaid', focus on two of the "three Material things", air and water, advocated by Ruskin as the basis for a new political economy. They shadow, therefore, at least by implication, the trajectory of Ruskin's work from nature writing to social critique. In fact this was a transition Hopkins himself began to make as, post-ordination, he turned his attention increasingly from nature, in the general sense, to human nature. A further example of this appears in 'The times are nightfall' a draft for the poem that eventually became 'Spelt from Sibyl's Leaves'.

> The times are nightfall, look, their light grows less;
> The times are winter, watch, a world undone:
> They waste, they wither worse; they as they run
> Or bring more or more blazon man's distress.
> And I not help. Nor word now of success [...] (1-5)

Hopkins utilises in these lines an entropic imagery of darkness ("nightfall") which, in common with similar imagery in the "Blessed Virgin" and "Inversnaid", is designed to depict a social "world" unravelling ("undone"), the "waste" and "wither[ing]" acting as a signifier ("blazon") for the moral, social and ecological "distress" of humankind. The injunctions "look" and "watch" characterise, of course, the utilitarianism of the Victorian impulse to act against this. While Hopkins was, in this regard, deeply self-critical – as the blunt admission, "And I not help", demonstrates – the evolution in his poetry towards a focus on the negative social and environmental impacts of Victorian political economy does represent, as will now be considered, the other important way in which Hopkins might help inform our own ecological thinking.

Chapter 5

Hopkins in the Victorian World:
From a Social to a Human Ecology

One consequence of Hopkins' poems not being published until thirty years after his death was that he became "a writer emancipated from time and tradition" (Roberts 1987: 69). As Sulloway puts it Hopkins has "been lifted out of his age as his own contemporaries have not" (1972: 5). Yet he was deeply interested in the Victorian world, about which, one can say, his attitude was one of ambivalence rather than outright hostility. He enjoyed and was fascinated by consumer goods and innovative technologies ranging from soothing syrups to photography to the gelatine process (an early form of photocopying) (RB 14/12/85: 223; FL (Baillie) 1/5/88: 290-1; RB 21/10/82: 158 and 6/11/87: 264). Neither was he entirely opposed, it would seem, to industrial activity and economic progress. Sjaak Zonneveld records that at the St Bueno's Debating Club Hopkins spoke against a motion that "the advancement of material civilization is injurious to true progress". Although, as Zonneveld points out, we cannot be entirely sure that he was speaking from personal conviction, given the nature of the debating club, such a position is consistent with that occasionally expressed in his letters (1992: 41). Writing, for example, from highly industrialised Bedford Leigh, near Manchester, Hopkins told Baillie "Trade is slack but reviving. Today I saw two barge-loads of some salt—'chemicals'—going to one of the mills; so I hope Lord Beaconsfield was right" (FL (Baillie) 19/11/79; 243).

Yet like many of his contemporaries, Hopkins was also frequently scathing about Victorian modernity. Sometimes on its own terms – "Nov. 26 1882. And 'in spite of the boasted civilisation of this so-called nineteenth century' this letter cannot even start from here for more than 24 hours nor reach you before Tuesday morning" (RB 26/11/82: 161) – more generally, he believed, like Carlyle or Ruskin, that, intrinsically, Victorian 'progress' added up to very little. As he tells a congregation in Liverpool:

the means of travelling and the speed of it have increased prodigiously; communication between men, by print, by letter, by telegraph, and by other ways, has been made easy in a still more extraordinary degree; the realm of nature has been laid bare and our knowledge of it widened beyond measure [...] Yet after all these are not the things that make much difference to human nature. (SD: 104)

Given such ambivalence one might argue that what Hopkins objected to was not modernity *per se* but the particular direction Victorian modernity was taking. Possessed of both "critical bite" and the "romance of construction" it is unsurprising, as I will demonstrate in this chapter, that Hopkins immersed himself in, and engaged with, Victorian society, and that his writing "idiosyncratic that it is [...] transcends private idiosyncrasy to speak of Victorian concerns" (Sulloway 1972: 5). While Sulloway's study has done much to stimulate later readings into the critique that emerged (see also Phelan 2005; Zonneveld 1992) no one, as yet, has addressed the ecological component of that critique.

1. Hopkins as a Victorian ecological critic

Hopkins encapsulated the "Victorian Temper" as it was defined by Buckley. While that was partially characterised by the "romance of construction" it was also subject to Buckley's contradictory paradigm of the "two voices". In this context there were, then, two responses Hopkins might have made towards Victorian modernity: withdrawal or engagement.

He did exhibit a tendency towards withdrawal which often took the form, from an early age, of a disparagement of "worldliness". Arranging to meet Ernest Coleridge in 1863 he speaks of wanting to be "far from Cyril", the only one of his five brothers to have followed in Manley's business, "and other pomps and vanities of this wicked world" (FL 22/3/63: 15). He concurs, likewise, with the dissatisfaction expressed by another friend, Edward Urquhart, that eternity should depend upon something "so trivial and inadequate as life is"; and he describes to Baillie how "the *sordidness* of things, wh.[ich] one is compelled perpetually to feel" works as an "inducement" to Catholicism wherein, he continues, this feeling is both "(objectively) intensified and (subjectively) destroyed" (FL (Urquhart) 22/1/66: 19-20; (Baillie) 10-12/9/65: 226-7). This element in Hopkins' thinking would result, on occasion, in blank theological rebuttals of earthly reality. In later writings, for example, he frequently described the world as Satan's domain and Satan as having put himself above the world "wreathing nature and as it were constricting it to his purposes" (SD: 198). In the same vein he tells a congregation in Bedford Leigh "This life is night, it is night and not day; we are like sleepers in the nighttime, we are like men that walk in the dark [...] The truth of things is either dimly seen or not seen at all. The thoughts in men's hearts are dark" (SD: 39). Such ideas do concur with elements in Catholic thinking. Yet in summarising this – "The contrast between things as they are and as they ought to be! Catholicism darkens the view of the world because it is seen as it is, and yet it gives a new vision, a vision of the world as it should be" (1942: 75) – what John Pick foregrounds is, in fact, the reverse side of the "two voices", an impulse towards social engagement. Consequently, while Hopkins would never entirely shake off the tendency towards social withdrawal, and the melancholy encouraged by misanthropic elements in his thinking, his life and work do demonstrate a conscious, pragmatic social critique that was, furthermore, encompassed within both his vocations, that of priest and poet.

Hopkins' Catholicism was motivated, to a not inconsiderable degree, by the impulse towards social engagement. His conversion had been governed, as we know, by principles of permanence, continuity and hierarchy, conservative principles nurtured by his interest in architecture and subsequent involvement in the High Church movement at Oxford. The primary factor in Hopkins' decision to convert had been the identification of what he called an "Anglican logical break-down" (FL (E. W. Urquhart) 31/12/67: 48), a belief, in accordance with the creed of apostolic succession, that only the Catholic Church truly represented the principle of conservatism: "I can hardly believe anyone ever became a Catholic because two and two make four more fully than I have" (FL (H. P. Liddon) 7/11/66: 31; see also FL (J. H. Newman) 28/8/66: 22; (Father) 16/10/66: 92). Yet, at the same time, as Sulloway suggests, "Each conversion was the response of a specific man at a specific time in his country's history", and "a way of dealing not only with crises of the self but crises in the society" (1972: 6). The impulse that derived from this, towards addressing the social and environmental ills of Victorian society, took the subsequent form, in this context, of his decision to become a Jesuit.

The consensus appears to be that Hopkins' main reason for joining the Jesuits, and then for entering the priesthood, was an attraction to the order and discipline of Jesuit life. Its basis in the practical teaching of 'The Spiritual Exercises of St. Ignatius', a series of meditations and prayers designed to reform and consolidate the repentance of the sinner, offered the potential for directing his introspective tendencies to more vocational ends (see Martin 1991: 175; White 1992: 186). The nature of those voca-

tional ends becomes clearer if we consider Hopkins' decision in relation
to the role played by the Jesuits in Victorian society.

Hopkins spent seven months subsequent to his conversion teaching at
Cardinal Newman's Oratory School in Birmingham, but decided not to
stay. Informed by the Romantic tradition the Newmanite strand represented,
in broad terms, an attempt to integrate Catholicism into an intellectual
opposition to Victorian modernity represented in secular society by
Matthew Arnold (Holmes 1978: 112). Conversely, the Jesuits, who were
flourishing during Hopkins' adult lifetime, were prominent in
Ultramontanism (see Aveling 1981: 315-17), a movement that regarded the
Newmanite tendency, in Cardinal Manning's words, as "a patristic, literary,
Oxford tone transplanted into the church" (see Holmes 1978: 127).
Ultramontanism preferred to locate its opposition to the commercial values
of Victorian society in an ultra conservative emphasis on papal authority as
well as in a communitarian model which viewed the church not "as the
servants of the plutocracy" but as "the guides and guardians of the poor"
(Holmes 1978: 185; Norman 1985: 86). Epitomised by Manning, who in his
role as Archbishop of Westminster campaigned in areas such as temperance,
housing, anti-vivisection and child labour (Holmes 1978: 176; Norman
1985: 86), such a position was similar to the contemporary environmental
justice movement in its belief, which Hopkins came to share, that moral and
religious improvement was impossible without, amongst other things,
improvements in the physical environment of the urban poor (Holmes 1978:
158). Connected, therefore, to a post-Romantic sense of social responsibility
that Hopkins felt deeply, he chose, as Norman White neatly puts it, "a
Counter-Reformation order [rather] than a pre-Reformation one" (1992:
111); as Hopkins himself wrote, "Cowardly it would be and a wretched
inconsistency in a knight to decline a glorious campaign from dislike of
the hardships to be borne in securing its success" (SD: 163). Much the
same motivation extended to Hopkins' other vocation, poetry.

In pronouncements about the roles and responsibilities of poetry
Hopkins came down in favour of pragmatic, social engagement. It was a
belief founded, like most of his literary attitudes, on a stance taken
towards the Romantic writers, most notably, on this occasion, Keats.
From an extended dialogue with Patmore, we know that Hopkins held
Keats in exceptionally high regard. He described his "genius" as
"astonishing, unequalled at his age and scarcely surpassed at any" and
even suggested that, had he lived, Keats' reputation might even have
rivalled Shakespeare (RWD 13/6/78: 6). Yet Hopkins concurred, nevertheless, with a contention of Patmore's that Keats' writing was overly

sensual and, indeed, developed this line of argument further in noting what he perceived to be a failure by Keats to apply his insight to some form of values or social purpose.

Hopkins apprehended precisely what E. P. Thompson found in regard to Keats' influence on Morris, namely that "art as a means of escape" only leaves one "forlorn" (1977: 12-13):

> It is impossible not to feel with weariness how his verse is at every turn abandoning itself to an unmanly and enervating luxury. It appears too that he said something like 'O for a life of impressions instead of thoughts!' It was, I suppose, the life he tried to lead. The impressions are not likely to have been all innocent and they soon ceased in death. His contemporaries, as Wordsworth, Byron, Shelley, and even Leigh Hunt, right or wrong, still concerned themselves with great causes, as liberty and religion; but he lived in mythology and fairyland the life of a dreamer. (FL 6/5/88: 386)

Ultimately, however, Hopkins sought to redeem Keats. He argued that he was "made to be a thinker, a critic, as much as a singer or artist of words" and claimed that he began to "feel and see in him the beginnings of [...] an interest in higher things and of powerful and active thought" (FL 6/5/88: 387). Whether criticising or defending Keats, the greater relevance of this dialogue lies in its common thread, the articulation of a post-Romantic belief that "active thought", and the pursuit of "higher things" or "great causes", ought to be the fundamental purpose of poetry.

These ideas extended both to judgements about Victorian literature and to the development of his own poetic practice. Hopkins believed, in the first place, that writers should be "in earnest". He praised Arnold for possessing this quality and criticised Browning and Carlyle for lacking it (RWD 24/9/81: 59; RB 2/8/71: 27; FL (Edward Bond) 4/8/73: 58). On that basis he frequently assessed literary works in terms of their utilitarian value, complaining, to give one example, that "practical suggestions" in Carlyle's *Shooting Niagara* were "so vague that they should rather be called '*too* dubious moonstone-grindings and on the whole impracticable-practical unveracities'" (RB 2/8/71: 27). Sometimes going so far as to question altogether the value of a literary vocation – he tells Bridges, for instance, "I should be sorry to think you did nothing down there but literary work: could you not be a magistrate?" (RB 26/9/82: 152) – Hopkins believed in the end that writers had a responsibility to develop a public role. As a consequence, he implored both Bridges and Patmore to strive to get their poems more widely known:

> That is why I hold that fine works of art [...] are really a great power in the world, an element of strength even to an empire.

A great work by an Englishman is like a great battle won by England. It is an unfading bay tree [...] It is then even a patriotic duty *to be active in producing poetry* and to secure the fame and permanence of the work. (FL 4/6/86: 368; RB 13/10/86: 231 (italics translated from the Greek))

To Patmore, a fellow convert, Hopkins offered the more specific suggestion that the basis of "civilisation" and "empire" should be "Catholic truth" and that "The great end of Empires" should be to "be Catholic and draw nations into their Catholicism" (FL 4/6/86: 367). He articulated, therefore, in these exchanges, a belief that pragmatically inclined religious and poetic vocations could work in tandem, a view Hopkins sought to enact in his own work even while he remained troubled by doubts about a literary vocation.

This belief in the pragmatism of both his vocations was also, as it happens, articulated in the poetry itself. The first example of this is the under-regarded 1865 poem 'The Alchemist in the City', written during a period of uncertainty two years after Hopkins had entered Oxford and eighteen months before his conversion. Documenting both a scepticism about modernity and an anxiety concerning his place in the world, the poem opens with commonplace Wordsworthian images of flux and movement that equate the city to modernity.

> My window shews the travelling clouds,
> Leaves spent, new seasons, alter'd sky,
> The making and the melting crowds:
> The whole world passes; I stand by. (1-4)

The feeling of torpor, which arises from a sense of alienation from modernity, is extended in the following stanza in which Hopkins measures himself against the productivity of others:

> They do not waste their meted hours,
> But men and masters plan and build:
> I see the crowning of their towers,
> And happy promises fulfill'd. (5-8)

Imagining, briefly, the possibility of producing something from his own labour, Hopkins nevertheless concludes, at an alarmingly early age, that he lacks the energy for such a purpose:

> But now before the pot can glow
> With not to be discover'd gold,
> At length the bellows shall not blow,

The furnace shall at last be cold.

Yet it is now too late to heal
The incapable and cumbrous shame
Which makes me when with men I deal
More powerless than the blind or lame. (13-20)

In later parts of the poem, Hopkins indicates that this sense of power-lessness is less an individual weakness and more the inevitable symptom of changes, towards an industrial and mercantile society, that have left him and his like-minded peers marginalised. He voices, for example, the despondent anticipation that the knowledge he'd acquired at Oxford would have little place in the modern Victorian world. Articulated in the clever central metaphor of the weary alchemist unable, in an indifferent society, to exercise potentially magical powers Hopkins suggests that, where, in "prediluvian age", the "The labours I should then have spent/Might so attain their heritage" (10-12), in Victorian society such learning is, simply, "thankless lore/[...] That holds no promise of success" (22; 34). Later on such a recognition would lead to a Carlylean protest about the need for alternative social values. This poem, however, merely culminates with further stanzas in which we find that the only solution Hopkins can envisage is a "forlorn" withdrawal from modernity.

No, I should love the city less
Even than this my thankless lore;
But I desire the wilderness
Or weeded landslips of the shore [...]

Then sweetest seems the houseless shore,
Then free and kind the wilderness,

Or ancient mounds that cover bones (21-4; 35-7)

John Robinson suggests, in reference to this poem, that Hopkins had "the wistfulness of a solitary [...] of someone in retreat who has recourse to nature as a sanctuary from what is in humanity unmanageable or disagreeable" (1978: 83). Had Hopkins' poetic philosophy remained with the conclusions suggested in these lines – in the image, that is, of the poet walking away from the city – then it would, indeed, have conformed to Rogers' residual "romantic discourse" which posits "no common measure between [...] the poet's vision and the everyday". Similarly, such engagement as there was might well have taken the form of a deep ecological poetic premised upon the capacity of the imagination to return us to a state of 'naïve' being. Yet, as is alluded to in the "ancient mounds that cover bones", such a response would only have led to symbolic death, of the active self and of meaningful poetry, an outcome to which Hopkins never, in fact, subscribed.

A month after writing 'The Alchemist in the City' Hopkins composed another poem, 'Myself, Unholy', that served, as Wendell Stacy Johnson has pointed out, to "express the Victorian need of Carlyle, Mill, Tennyson, Arnold, and others to escape from melancholy and from isolation, to find an external object of faith which gives meaning to self" (1968: 26). In the poem, Hopkins describes how a state in which he is "confusèd, struck, and shook", and in which he "Yields to the sultry siege of melancholy" (7-8), might be resolved by means of a commitment to Christ:

> No *better* serves me now, save *best*; no other
> Save Christ: to Christ I look, on Christ I call. (13-14)

In the construction offered here, of a faith designed to follow the example of Christ's sacrifice, Hopkins put forward what was to be the rationale for his priesthood – as a vocation which, with the intention of bringing meaning to the self, would also contribute to society. This ideal was re-stated in two poems written shortly after his ordination, when Hopkins returned to Oxford as a priest in December 1878.

The first of these, 'Peace', outlines and corroborates a sense of responsibility to engage with Victorian society though it begins with a plea not dissimilar to that of 'The Alchemist in the City'.

> When will you ever, Peace, wild wooddove, shy wings shut,
> Your round me roaming end, and under be my boughs?
>
> [...] I yield you do come sometimes; but
> That piecemeal peace is poor peace. What pure peace allows
> Alarms of wars, the daunting wars, the death of it? (1-2; 4-6)

Here, however, the image of "war" and the preceding juxtaposition between a "poor" and "pure peace", signals a change in emphasis that had come about with Hopkins having resolved the frustrations and anxieties documented in the earlier poem. Posing the question of how, in Victorian society, one can expect to find "pure peace", and rejecting the "peace" offered by escape or withdrawal because it is incomplete ("piecemeal"), Hopkins advises that real peace has to wait. Offering, "in lieu", "patience"

(7-8), he suggests that "peace" will only "plume" into a fully-fledged "pure peace" (9) (see Poems: 278) in the wake of evidence of tangible works:

> And when Peace here does
> house
> He comes with work to do, he does not come to coo,
> He comes to brood and sit. (9-11)

The suggestion that an individual "with work to do [...] does not come to coo" might be read as a belittling of poetry and, up to a point, it was, given this was a sentiment that Hopkins occasionally repeated in remarks about his poetic vocation (as we see in Chapter Six). Yet the statement, taken as a whole, also serves to articulate what was to become perhaps the primary basis of his (post-ordination) poetic practice, the articulation of a social and ecological critique.

Where Hopkins had conceived, in 'Peace', a principally utilitarian role for poetry, a more specific sense of that role was established in a second poem, 'Andromeda'. This poem, Bernard Bergonzi points out, is unique in Hopkins' work for drawing upon classical myth (1978: 184). In the Greek legend the king of Aethiopia, whose country, having incurred the wrath of Poseidon, is ravaged by floods and a sea-monster, agrees to sacrifice his daughter, Andromeda, to the monster so as to prevent further devastation to the land. Chained to the cliffs, she is saved by Perseus who, having returned from slaying the Gorgon Medusa, sees and falls in love with her.

The myth was pervasive within Victorian culture having also been adapted by Browning, Kingsley and Ruskin and as with each of these writers Hopkins' rewriting of the legend was, characteristically, contemporary. Beginning with the lines

> Now Time's Andromeda on this rock rude,
> With not her either beauty's equal or
> Her injury's (1-3)

Hopkins, in the second stanza, expands upon the critique of Victorian England implicit in "this rock rude" (Poems: 277)):

> Time past she has been attempted and pursued
> By many blows and banes; but now hears roar
> A wilder beast from West than all were, more
> Rife in her wrongs, more lawless, and more lewd. (5-8)

For Hopkins, the dragon, that "wilder beast from West […] more/Rife in her wrongs", was a Victorian modernity which had brought with it unprecedented levels of risk. Contrary, however, to the withdrawal articulated in 'The Alchemist in the City', he advocates, on this occasion, confrontation. Each of the writers who had been drawn to the myth offered alternative interpretations of Perseus that were indicative of their differing approaches towards countering Victorian society. Browning's was St George, Kingsley's humanist Greek values, Ruskin's the Guild of St George (see, respectively, MacKenzie 1981: 130; White 1992: 314; Heuser 1958: 114). For Hopkins the challenge to Victorian modernity would come from Christ (or, specifically, the Church), who, he envisages at the end of the poem, will "alight" and "disarm" Victorian society, a reference either to the second coming or, more likely, the hoped for conversion of England to Catholicism (Poems: 277). While on this occasion Perseus was embodied in the figure of the priest Hopkins nevertheless appeared to believe, not least from the evidence of his own writing, that he might also appear in the figure of the poet.

Several critics have noted that the poetry written after Hopkins' ordination indicates a greater preoccupation with society and the self. Robinson suggests that "Hopkins' picture of man began to separate itself from his picture of nature", Devlin that "his interest shifted increasingly from the presence of God's design or inscape (that is, Christ) in inanimate nature to the working-out of that design—by stress and instress—in the minds and wills of men" (Robinson 1978: 99; SD: 109). Yet contrary to the implications of both those remarks, some at least of Hopkins' post-ordination poetry, rather than turning away from nature, channelled this new focus into a criticism of what was being done to it; this, then, related to a concern about the impact society was having on its (human) population. These two things constitute, as Sulloway has indicated, the main foundation of the social engagement that entered a writing that would come to typify Victorian literary culture:

> Hopkins's poems and prose are as full of these public crises as the works of Carlyle, Tennyson, Ruskin, Newman, or either of the Arnolds. His work reflects the anguish of religious strife, abuse of labour, the scandal of privileged cruelty, the horrors of rampant industrialism pouring its scum and smoke all over England, the search for national prescriptions. (1972: 6)

The remainder of this chapter considers Hopkins' engagement with Victorian modernity in the context of Clark's social ecology of the imagination. Looking, in detail, at an essentially social-ecological critique of Victorian political economy, the chapter concludes by considering Hopkins' parallel adherence to the second of Clark's criteria "the creation of an ecological imaginary" which arose in the context of his "search for national prescriptions".

2. Poems of ecological protest

We saw in relation to two of the poems considered in Chapter Four, 'The Blessed Virgin compared to the Air we Breathe' and 'Inversnaid', Hopkins addressing the impact of Victorian political economy on two of Ruskin's "three material things, not only useful, but essential to Life", water and air. It was, however, in relation to the third, "Earth", that his nature poetry most clearly translated into social-ecological critique.

One instance of Hopkins' ambivalence, rather than hostility, to modernity, was that he did not, as a matter of course, bemoan modern forms of human intervention on the land. He concurred, for example, in the journal, with Ruskin's remarks about Turner's 'Pass of Faido'. Noting that the painting had been prompted by the dream of a great storm, Ruskin had written that whereas "Most persons [...] regret that there is any living thing in it; they say it destroys the majesty of its desolation", he himself believed that "The torrent was wild, the storms were wonderful, but the most wonderful thing of all was how we ourselves [...] ever got here. By our feet we could not—by an ivory gate we could not—in no other wise could we have come than by the coach road" (see JP 14/9/71: 215 (413-14)). Hopkins, similarly, was often surprisingly non-committal about the presence of humanity, even industry, in the landscape. We see this, for example, in remarks about smoke. On returning from a holiday in Devon he remarks ruefully that "As we approached Windsor the London smoke met us rolling up the valley of the Thames" (JP 21/8/74: 256). Yet he was unperturbed, on the Isle of Man, by the smoke of the steamers which "overhung" the town, as he was at Stonyhurst where the clouds "must be full of soot, for the fleeces of the sheep are quite black with it" (JP 14/8/72: 224; FL (Baillie) 10/4/71: 234-5). He also seems to accept industrial encroachment (that had emanated from trans-national capitalism) in Wales:

All the landscape had a beautiful liquid cast of blue. Many-coloured smokes in the valley, grey from the Denbigh lime-kiln, yellow and lurid from two kilns perhaps on the shoulders of a hill, blue from a bonfire, and so on

Portmadoc half a mile off is still more modern: my landlord remembers when there
were only three houses there. It is rising, but fashion has not found it. Bretons come
here in jerseys, earrings, and wooden shoes to sell vegetables, and Portmadoc and all
N. Wales seem to live upon slate, to get which they are quarrying away great
mountains: nowhere I suppose in Europe is such a subjection of nature to man to be
witnessed. The end is that the mountains vanish, but in the process they take a certain
beauty midway between wildness and art. (JP 24/9/74: 260; RB 2/10/86: 226)

The ambivalence expressed in these observations appears to stem
from an interest in aesthetic effect that would sometimes take precedence
over scientific understanding or environmental concern. Yet Hopkins was
somewhat less ambivalent in relation to environments in which he more
clearly perceived the pervasive impact of industrialised modes of
production and where he felt compelled to question the un-sustainability
of such practices. The critique this engendered is exemplified in two
poems, 'God's Grandeur', which addresses the consequences of soil
pollution, and 'Binsey Poplars', a critique of deforestation.

> The world is charged with the grandeur of God.
>   It will flame out, like shining from shook foil;
>   It gathers to a greatness, like the ooze of oil
> Crushed. Why do men then now not reck his rod?
> Generations have trod, have trod, have trod;
>   And all is seared with trade; bleared, smeared with toil;
>   And wears man's smudge and shares man's smell: the soil
> Is bare now, nor can foot feel, being shod.
>
> And, for all this, nature is never spent;
>   There lives the dearest freshness deep down things;
> And though the last lights off the black West went
>   Oh, morning, at the brown brink eastward, springs—
> Because the Holy Ghost over the bent
>   World broods with warm breast and with ah! bright wings.

'God's Grandeur' opens with a juxtaposition between the intensity of
nature's energy (instress), conveyed throughout the poem by familiar
signifiers – "charged", "flame[s]", "springs", "shining […] shook foil" –
and the nullifying energy of human activity on the land. Hopkins' feelings
about the latter are clear from a later complaint to Bridges (quoted below)
about the work of "navvies or daylabourers" disfiguring the earth (see RB
10/2/88: 273). Along the same lines Sulloway speculates that this poem
might well relate to a description of Ruskin's of the most "absolute type of
impurity [...] the mud or slime of a damp, over-trodden path, in the outskirts
of a manufacturing town" (1972: 85-6). Yet, in embodying these contra-

dictory energies in poetic form, the sense, it seems to me, runs much deeper than this.

In an extension to Williams' description of the "Romantic Artist" who experiences industrialism "on the senses", Hopkins represents these impacts ecologically. On the original draft he had recorded that the poem was "To be read [...] slowly, strongly marking the rhythms and fetching out the syllables" (Poems: 263). Consistent with that Hopkins conveys unsustainable human energy through assonance – the verbs "seared", "bleared", "smeared" inferring, as Michael Moore has suggested,[1] the violence wrought by industrial processes – and, in particular, through rhythm. Read in the way Hopkins suggests, the poem, in a striking inversion of phenomenological ecopoetics, allows the reader to feel (rather than simply understand) the impact of industry, for this lies in the very structure, scape, of the poem. In the brutal repetition, for example, of "have trod, have trod, have trod" Hopkins succeeds in conveying industrial impacts rhythmically, not just "on the ground" but *in* the ground, the underlying ecosystem, more than just an abstract environment, "disfigure[d]" or altered by a human dominance threatening to create a monoculture ("wears man's smudge and shares man's smell").

Hopkins goes on to signal, in the last line of the octave, a change of emphasis which extends, rather than undercuts, the poem's critique. Writing that though the land is bare "nor can foot feel, being shod", he suggests that humanity has become desensitised to nature and implies that the loss is, foremost, a human loss. While this becomes, as he develops his theme in the sestet, straightforward social critique – in the references, similar to those in other poems, to "the black West" or the "bent/World" – the overall argument also leads to a more specific, ecological point when Hopkins writes, in line 9, that "for all this, nature is never spent". Immediately reiterating this, in the assertion that "freshness" lies "deep" in nature and that renewal ("morning [...] springs") will endure, we find that the central message of 'God's Grandeur' is, in fact, that of the Gaia hypothesis: that if we alter the ecosystem it will be humanity that suffers. While darkness may come to us, nature, understood as Gaia, as Earth, will go on with its perpetual adaptation, renewal and re-birth, regardless of human society and its industrial practices, and even when the "last lights" have disappeared from the "black West".

Trees, as we know, were central to the philosophy of nature developed in the journal. For Hopkins the destruction of a tree, which he regarded –

---

[1] I am grateful to Dr Moore for having sent me a copy of his paper, 'Pleading for the Tongueless Earth: Gerard Manley Hopkins and Victorian Eco-Poetics'.

deep ecologically – as an "unselving" of inscape (see Johnson 1968: 102), was an act of sacrilege:

> April 8—The ashtree growing in the corner of the garden was felled. It was lopped first: I heard the sound and looking out and seeing it maimed there came at that moment a great pang and I wished to die and not see the inscapes of the world destroyed anymore. (JP 8/4/73: 230)

While Hopkins didn't always discriminate between natural or human damage – he observes, for example, at Roehampton how "a grievous gap has come in that place with falling *and* felling" (JP 6/12/68: 189 (my italics)) – where he did come across instances caused by human activity he invariably took these to be an indictment of Victorian society:

> They have cut down the beautiful beech in the Garden Quad, which stood in the angle of Fisher's buildings, because it was said to darken their rooms. This is a wicked thing; such a beech no doubt has not its like in Oxford, beech being a rare tree here. Its destruction is owing to the Fellows Green and Newman. The former is of a rather offensive style of infidelity, and naturally dislikes the beauties of nature. It is said the Fisher building[s] are to be pulled down [...] I wish they could have pulled them down first, and let the tree stand. (FL 19/10/63: 83)

In one of his first letters on returning to Oxford as a priest, Hopkins lamented to Dixon the gradual disappearance of the landscape he had known as an undergraduate. He comments it is "already abridged and soured and perhaps will be put out altogether" and, in a postscript to the letter, which took him several days to complete, adds "I have been up to Godstow this afternoon. I am sorry to say that the aspens that lined the river are everyone felled" (RWD 27/2/89: 20, 26). 'Binsey Poplars' was composed on the same day.

Binsey Poplars

felled 1879

My aspens dear, whose airy cages quelled,
Quelled or quenched in leaves the leaping sun,
All felled, felled, are all felled;
Of a fresh and following folded rank
Not spared, not one
That dandled a sandalled
Shadow that swam or sank
On meadow and river and wind-wandering bank
weed-winding bank.

O if we but knew what we do
When we delve or hew—
Hack and rack the growing green!
Since country is so tender
To touch, her being só slender,
That, like this sleek and seeing ball
But a prick will make no eye at all,

Where we, even where we mean
To mend her we end her,
When we hew or delve:
After-comers cannot guess the beauty been.
Ten or twelve, only ten or twelve
Strokes of havoc únselve
The sweet especial scene,
Rural scene, a rural scene,
Sweet especial rural scene.

According to Martin, the trees at Godstow were "cut down for use as brake blocks, or 'shoes', for the locomotives of the Great Western Railway" (1991: 307). While there is no evidence that Hopkins knew this, he was, nevertheless, particularly watchful at this time about felling in the name of social utility, having recently read a poem of his father's ('The Old Trees') that attacked proposals to fell a line of trees in the name of improvements to the Well Walk estate in Hampstead (2006: 191). Jude V. Nixon, in an analysis of the controversy at Hampstead, demonstrates that opposition to the proposals for Well Walk was largely motivated by preservationist sentiment which encompassed, as suggested in Chapter One, cultural significance, in this case the "heritage of the walk" and its association with Dr Johnson, Keats, and Constable (2006: 204). This is apparent in Manley's poem which epitomises, as well, the somewhat defeatist quality of preservationism in that he places the felling of the trees in the context of a seemingly unstoppable "Progress" effected by those who seek to "modernise a by-gone age,/Unreverent to what has been" (39-40):

All, now, we ask, a little space
Ere these trees fall beside their race [...]

Grant us, sweet heaven, that one more Spring
May glad our eyes with old delight;
Greeting the birds' returning wing [...]
(23-4; 31-3; and see Nixon 2006: 195)

Given the dedication, "felled 1879", with which Hopkins opens the poem, 'Binsey Poplars' might also be seen as elegiac, preservationist protest. Yet the opening demonstrates, in fact, a tension between preservationist sentiment and ecological science as "My aspens dear" immediately gives way to an embodiment of photosynthesis, fundamental to the ecological process.

By means of photosynthesis plants, bacteria and algae extract energy from the sun and convert water and carbon dioxide into the materials, oxygen and carbohydrates, that enable growth and reproduction in living organisms. This not only "provides the energy for the whole of the living world" but, as a constantly renewable source, works against the entropic tendency of the laws of thermodynamics thereby enabling organisms, up to a point, to "become independent of the limitations imposed by other energy sources" (see Lawlor 2001: 1-2). While his familiarity with scientific periodicals might lead us to assume that Hopkins must have been aware of what had been, since the beginning of the century, an acknowledged biological concept (Sebastian 2001: 263-4), a number of allusions in the journal indicate, more substantially, Hopkins' acquaintance with photosynthesis.

On holiday in 1866, with university friends in the Sussex Downs, Hopkins observes, standing by a stile, that "a spray of the ash stood forward like a bright blind of leaves drawing and condensing the light" (JP 24/7/66: 147). Two years later, at the Royal Academy, he noted George Watt's "remarkable" bust representing the legend of Clytie, who, having revealed Apollo's consummated love, "sat nine days in starvation, yearningly turning her head to the sun in his course, and was then slowly changed into the heliotrope plant" (JP 17/6/68: 167 (389). Most notably, is his recording that

> My eye was suddenly caught by the scaping of the leaves that grow in allies and avenues: I noticed it first in an elm and then in limes. They fall from the two sides of the branch or spray in two marked planes which meet at a right angle or more. This comes from the endeavour to catch the light on either side, which falls left and right but not all round. (JP September 1869: 192. See also 22/8/67: 151; 18/7/73: 233)

Here, however, photosynthesis is rendered poetically in lines that once again demonstrate the ecopoetic qualities of sprung rhythm. At the beginning of the poem the rhythmic stresses aurally embody, rather than verbally describe, the process of photosynthesis, in the "quelling" and – in a hungry, alimentary image – "quenching" of the sun's energy by the leaves of the trees. In line 3, by contrast, Hopkins 'stresses', uncompromisingly, the finality of the felling, the sprung rhythm enabling him to imitate the labourer's blows so that the stunting of the rhythm mirrors the stark ecological consequences of the loss. The critique, carried emphatically by the rhythm, of a photosynthetic process (literally) undercut by human activity, is broadened in lines 6-8 where Hopkins embodies the ecological economy that had existed hitherto, one nourished by the organic rhythms of a growth governed by the sun's energy. This fact is apparent in the music of "meadow and river and wind-wandering bank", but also by the protection offered by the trees which had "dandled a sandalled/shadow", filtering the direct glare of sunlight from the other life-forms inhabiting the surrounding meadow and river bank. The protest, in these opening eight lines, derives, that is to say, from a scientific understanding of the implications of tree-felling on the entire, surrounding ecosystem.

In the second and third stanzas Hopkins amplifies his critique through, in the first place, the diction employed in lines 10 and 11 – "delve" (dig deeply), "hew" (chop or cut with an axe), "hack" (chop roughly), "rack" (subject to pain) – which all signify, as does, later, "strokes of havoc", a violence equivalent to that depicted in 'God's Grandeur'. Conferring, here, a strong emphasis on human culpability, the full extent of this critique emerges, as we move towards the final stanza, in the re-introduction of the motif of the eye.

Hopkins argues, in what becomes an extended metaphor, that Victorian society lacks the Ruskinian aesthetic eye required to truly understand nature. Ignorant, so he argues, of the fact that even the most seemingly insignificant action (e.g. the cutting down of a group of trees) will effect irreparable damage – "But a prick will make no eye at all" – he then expands upon the image to suggest, offering little solace, that so *blind* are his contemporaries to nature that even attempts at conservation, at the management of the earth's resources, are characterised by incompetence and destined to fail: "even where we mean/To mend her we end her". The poem offers, then, a powerful rhythmic embodiment both of the ecological processes governing nature and of the risk engendered in a society blind to those processes.

'Binsey Poplars' does, however, exhibit some preservationist elements. Apparent, for instance, in the descriptions of nature as "tender" and "slender", we find this most obviously in the conclusion, an uncharacteristic lament for the "sweet especial rural scene". Yet without disregarding a certain unevenness to the poem, the elucidation, in the final stanza, of an implied self-imposed threat to humanity, does, nevertheless, retain its predominantly ecological message.

There is, at least in comparison to many of his poems, relatively little explicit theological reference in 'Binsey Poplars'. At the same time, though, our vulnerability to ecological processes is reinforced by the haunting, religious connotations that underlie the poem. The fact that the aspen is known as the "trembling poplar" not only because of its "quivering leaves" but also because its wood was reputedly used in the crucifixion gives to these warnings a sharp existential force underwritten by the allusion to Christ's words on the cross – "they know not what they do". Corresponding to this the lines

> After-comers cannot guess the beauty been.
> Ten or twelve, only ten or twelve
> Strokes of havoc únselve

have a quality of foreboding, emphasised by the colon with which they are prefaced, that emanates from the signification, in this context, of beauty. For the word is employed here not in a conventional romantic sense but in the more precise manner derived from Scotus. As suggested in the journal, Hopkins meant that if inscape leads us to an 'understanding' of a reality simultaneously Christian and ecological, then continued human "havoc" will mean, conversely, that Victorian society has consigned itself and "After-comers" (future generations) to a permanent blindness that would leave us bereft of the capacity to "guess", let alone understand, both the existence of God and our place in the natural economy. It is a blindness, one might argue which in our time is, in the latter sense at least, increasingly close to realisation.

Len Scigaj suggests, as we have seen, that a poetry informed by environmental science can help us "understand, respect, and cooperate with the laws of nature that sustain us". Such a vision is essential, he continues, to "promote environmental awareness and active agency" (1999: 22). This formula forms the basis for a pragmatic, sustainable poetry that might help us ensure humankind does not "perish". Informed by the concepts and theories that shaped scientific ecology, Hopkins' nature poetry meets Scigaj's criteria. Indeed, with the addition of these two "Earth" poems to the "Air" and "Water" poems examined in Chapter Four, Hopkins arrived, as indicated above, at a critique of Victorian society's impact on nature consistent with the "three Material things" identified by Ruskin as the basis for a new (ecological) political economy. Yet Hopkins also, ultimately, moved beyond Ruskin both in the extensiveness of his critique and in bringing to it an active, distinctively social-ecological flavour. Supporting Berman's point that a more socially advanced Victorian literature was activated by the urban environment, this critique took on a more definite shape in the light of Hopkins' experience of the industrial city, to where the Jesuits moved him in 1879.

3. Hopkins, the city, and social ecopoetry

Hopkins' attitude towards the urban environment mirrored his ambivalence to modernity more generally. He tended, in certain respects, towards a standard, romantic aversion to the city. Writing from the Isle of Wight, for example, he quotes Tennyson's 'The Daisy' to Baillie:

> Shanklin is a delightful place. If you were here you would have soon
>
> > —forgot the clouded Forth,
> > The gloom that saddens heaven and earth,
> > The biting East, the misty summer
> > And grey metropolis of the North.
>
> where I do not envy you. (FL 10/7/63: 200)

Similarly, in letters to Bridges, he noted, having escorted two Frenchman around London, that "frost fog red with smoke made it so dark that we could scarcely be said to see" and regrets, on an earlier occasion, being forced to observe nature in the context of the city: "The sun was eclipsed today. I saw it all up the City Road, to such a pass have natural phenomena come" (RB 1/2/82: 142; 8/10/66: 12). Such remarks were balanced, however, by the fact that Hopkins had grown up, been educated, and trained for ordination in London and Oxford. This engendered an appreciation of the qualities of cities, not least as repositories of culture. Of London, notwithstanding a reference to its "bad and smokefoul air", he tells Baillie that "in summer its air is a balmy air, certainly in the West End. Then it [...] is cheerful and quietly handsome, with many fine trees, and [...] so many resources, things to go to and hear and see and do. Everything is there". Likewise, after Bridges had moved to the countryside, Hopkins wrote "I am glad that you will be back at pastoral Yattendon, but do not understand why you should be unhappy in London" (FL 1/5/88: 292-3; RB 12/1/88: 268).

In theory, therefore, Hopkins believed that cities were characterised by certain positive traits. Indeed, he went so far as to set out a blueprint for this in 1879's 'Duns Scotus' Oxford', a poem that represents the idealised city.

TOWERY city and branchy between towers;
Cuckoo-echoing, bell-swarmèd, lark-charmèd, rook-racked,
    river-rounded;
The dapple-eared lily below thee; that country and town did
Once encounter in, here coped and poisèd powers;

Thou hast a base and brickish skirt there, sours
That neighbour-nature thy grey beauty is grounded
Best in; graceless growth, thou hast confounded
Rural rural keeping—folk, flocks, and flowers.

Yet ah! this air I gather and release
He lived on; these weeds and waters, these walls are what
He haunted who of all men most sways my spirits to peace;

Of realty the rarest-veinèd unraveller; a not
Rivalled insight, be rival Italy or Greece;
Who fired France for Mary without spot.

The poem establishes, in the first instance, that Hopkins was attracted to cities characterised by an intermingling of 'natural' and built components. Indeed, in the letter to Dixon lamenting the felling of the Binsey poplars what Hopkins had described as "abridged and soured" was a "landscape the charm of Oxford, green shouldering grey" (RWD 27/2/79: 20). This apparent approval for the suburban environment is repeated throughout the opening quatrain of 'Duns Scotus' Oxford': in the "branchy between towers"; in the combination of sounds represented by the cuckoo and the church bells; most of all, in the suggestion of "coped and poisèd powers" by which country and town are "set off one against the other and well matched" (Poems: 273). In the second quatrain we find references to the debasement described in his letter, for instance to the city's "base and brickish skirt". Yet in what is a reference to the development of unattractive modern housing, Hopkins was criticising not urban development *per se* but, specifically, the aesthetically "graceless" quality of a modern growth that had destroyed this hitherto mutually interrelated environment. It is, one can note, the "neighbour-nature" of country and town, the "grey beauty" which has been "soured". In that respect, the two poems, 'Binsey Poplars' and 'Duns Scotus' Oxford', which Hopkins worked on in the same month, articulate a complementary protest, concerning the extent to which the industrial mode of production that characterised Victorian political economy had reconstituted 'natural' and urban landscapes alike.

This more positive representation of a particular type of urban environment is then expanded in the sestet as Hopkins makes the conventional switch to explanatory mode. This is designed to demonstrate, in the first place, the relationship between an interest in architecture and the built environment and the conservative principles that underpinned his Catholicism, a point Hopkins imparts by contrasting the Victorian Oxford described in the octave to the medieval Oxford of Scotus. Regarding Scotus as "Of realty the rarest-veinèd unraveller", Hopkins, who in 'The Loss of the Eurydice' had spoken of when "So at home, time was, to his truth and grace" (100), implies here that his values, even today, can be breathed in from the surrounding environment ("this air I gather and release"), by which he means both "weeds and waters" and (as emphasised by the comma preceding "these walls") its "built" components. Accordingly – and notwithstanding the passing ruralism of the reference to "folk, flocks, and flowers" – what Hopkins was positing was the role of the city in harbouring progressive social values something already implicit when, during his time at university, he had described "home" as "uncivilized" (see FL (Baillie) March 1864: 207). While Hopkins may have despaired, then, of what Oxford had become, he nevertheless suggests, in a poem that extols the relevance of the proto-ecological Scotus, a generalised ideal of the city as a much-needed locus of "truth and grace". Clearly Victorian industrial cities were perceived to have fallen some way short of such ideals. Yet while Hopkins concurred with that, he did so with an even-handedness brought about by having actually experienced the urban environment.

Between 1879 and 1881 Hopkins was posted to Liverpool, also spending brief periods in Bedford Leigh and Glasgow. Within days of arriving in Lancashire his letters were describing the environment in a graphic detail that combined romantic horror, Dickensian imagery, Victorian social investigation and environmental impact assessment. Leigh was "a darksome place, with pits and mills and foundries" (FL (Baillie) 19/11/79: 243); St Helen's he regarded as "probably the most repulsive place in Lancashire" (RB 8/10/79: 90); while Liverpool was a "hellhole" where, in contrast to London, "one can not see the sun" (FL (Francis de Paravicini) 15/6/81: 63). Coloured, no doubt, by the strain of parochial work, this perception of the city was frequently extended to its working-class population. Alongside the "mean" houses and "darksome [...] pits" there appear, accordingly, accounts of the poor physical appearance of the people, such as here when he describes to Bridges a procession in Liverpool:

> While I admired the handsome horses I remarked for the thousandth time with sorrow and loathing the base and bespotted figures and features of the Liverpool crowd.

When I see the fine and manly Norwegians that flock hither to embark for America walk our streets and look about them it fills me with shame and wretchedness. I am told Sheffield is worse though. (27/4/81: 127-8)

Yet Hopkins' feelings towards these northern, industrial cities, both the environment and the people, were more ambivalent than such remarks suggest. He concedes that "For Liverpool [...] something can be said" (FL (Francis de Paravicini) 15/6/81: 63). While the point is not elaborated, a sense of what he might mean can be gathered from a later description of Glasgow as "repulsive to live in yet there are alleviations: the streets and buildings are fine and the people lively" (FL (Baillie) 6/5/82: 248). In fact, Hopkins frequently cited the vitality of the urban working class as an antidote to the poor physical and social environment. In Leigh, for example, the people are "hearty" and warm, while he remarks, more generally, that "these Lancashire people of low degree or not of high degree are those who most have seemed to me to welcome me and make much of me" (see RB 8/10/79: 90; RWD 24/10/79: 29; FL (Baillie) 22/5/80: 244-5). While Hopkins' attitude did, in truth, vacillate between "loathing" – "the drunkards go on drinking, the filthy, as the scripture says, are filthy still: human nature is so inveterate. Would that I had seen the last of it" (RB 26/10/80: 110) – and warmth, the second, when it appeared, did translate into a genuine pastoral compassion (see Zonneveld 1992).

One thing to emerge from Hopkins' somewhat ambivalent attitude to the Victorian industrial city was a social-ecological critique that stretched to encompass the humanist dimensions of that philosophy. Drawing on the work of Beck, Kevin Fitzpatrick and Mark LaGory have recently described the city in terms of what they call "risk spaces" – the places where hazards and risk are maximised (2000: 11-12). They also identify, borrowing a term from Michael Greenberg, an "urban health penalty", the greater imposition of that risk on the urban poor (2000: 6). Hopkins' critique, drawn from the evidence of his ministry, coalesced around these two themes: the state of the environment, specifically the air; and the impact of urban environmental hazards in increasing the "social risk position" experienced by the Victorian working class.

Botkin and Keller note that one of the primary "adverse effects" of air pollution is the "aggravation of chronic illnesses in people" (2005: 518) and that one of its earliest forms was the "sulphurous" smog associated with the early industrial city (2005: 520). Hopkins noticed both immediately. In Leigh, where there were "a dozen mills or so, and coalpits also" he found that "the air is charged with smoke as well as damp" (RB

8/10/79: 90); and, further to the description of St Helen's quoted above, he goes on to describe an environment characterised by smog:

> I was yesterday at St. Helen's, probably the most repulsive place in Lancashire or out of the Black Country. The stench of sulphuretted hydrogen rolls in the air and films of the same gas form on railing and pavement. (RB 8/10/79: 90)

In passages such as these Hopkins transcended conventional environmental critique. For, here, the aesthetic description ("the most repulsive place") is immediately substituted by an ecological mode of analysis seen in the air "charged" by the "stench" and "films" of gas and in the dampness and the smoke which permeate and pollute the entire surrounding ecosystem. Yet Hopkins also observed that the pollution "form[s]", analogously, on human, built components, the railings and the pavement, and from such observations he begins to consider the impact of industrial processes on, specifically, human health. It is around this that we find perhaps his most powerful critique of the ecological impact of Victorian political economy.

4. Hopkins, the body, and environmental health

Underlying Hopkins' interest in health was a marked sensitivity to the fact that our own human being is primarily experienced within the corporeal dimension, that is within the "living body". As noted in Chapter One, this is also what recent cultural researchers have suggested we need to rediscover so as to properly understand the material, ecological nature of our existence. Such work, well exemplified by Brian Massumi's *Parables for the Virtual* (2002), can be summarised as an attempt "to put matter unmediatedly back into cultural materialism, along with what seemed most directly corporeal back into the body" (Massumi 2002: 4). Suggesting that these perspectives have been written out of cultural theory on the grounds that they are seen to appeal to "unmediated experience" or a "naïve subjectivism" (2002: 2), Massumi, like Soper, begins by attempting to challenge the prevailing concept of the body as socially constructed.

The main basis for this is an argument that an understanding of bodies as "frameworks of culturally constructed significations: male versus female [...] gay versus straight" etc. (2002: 2), is generally static in that it fails to offer any account of the material transformations the body goes through. To counter that perspective, Massumi divides those transformations into two categories arguing that, on the one hand, the body can "perform its way out of a definitional framework" in changes that might encompass anything from fashion to surgery and, on the other, that the body is subjected to physical and material changes as a result of external forces (2002: 2-3). Seeking, however, to avoid any retreat into essentialism, or a simplistically materialist analysis, Massumi argues that "Far from regaining a concreteness, to think the body in movement thus means accepting the paradox that there is an incorporeal dimension of the body. Of it, but not it. Real, material, but incorporeal" (5). Further describing this, in a term borrowed from Foucault, as an "incorporeal materialism" (2002: 5), a central aspect of that is the continual transmutation of physical being by external factors, not least the surrounding environment, something we see when Massumi refers, in this respect, to energy and matter (2002: 5) in a way that corresponds to Tansley's definition of ecosystems theory as a network of relationships structured by the "material exchange of energy and […] chemical substances".

Massumi's work offers a theoretical basis for reconciling a sense of the material and ecological foundation of human nature with a dialectical emphasis on the capacity of society or the individual to act upon that nature. His other useful argument in this regard, taking us from the realm of the body to that of the senses, is a notion of "*the felt reality of relation*". Massumi suggests that through the senses we can perceive the transformations shaping ourselves (and, indeed, others or the environment around us). That experience comprises of two dimensions, the sensory occurrence itself (the act of taste, hearing, seeing, etc.) and one's perception of this, what he calls "the feeling of having a feeling". While the second is located in a consciousness which is at least partially socially and culturally constructed, Massumi argues that at the moment of the sensory occurrence we experience a "feeling of transition by nature" (2002: 13-14, 15) which offers, in turn, a glimpse of that reality of the self as materially embedded in nature: "the sensation is the first glimmer of a determinate experience […] A first glimmer of definable self-experience" (2002: 16). What is being suggested here is, in one regard, simply the attention to the senses being advocated by phenomenological philosophers and literary critics. Yet Massumi also rejects any categorical distinction between the social and the pre-social because the concept of "incorporeal materialism" clearly extends to the constitution of the body by political economy or social organisation, factors themselves, which act on and are shaped by the ecosystem, "in mutual movement into and through each other", and which represent, he argues, "a dynamic unity of reciprocal variation" (2002: 11). This suggests the possibility that the sensory nature of phenomenological perception might be extended so as to ascertain the conditions under which human nature may have been shaped, as Martin Ryle puts it, by the "negative reality of destructive economic and social forces and practices". This greater understanding of the full extent to which "incorporeal materialism" shapes human nature is the perfect lens through which to examine the ecological character of Hopkins' later, social poetry.

Hopkins' had a pronounced sense of corporeality. This can be illustrated through another one of the St Bueno's poems 'The Caged Skylark'.

> As a dare-gale skylark scanted in a dull cage
>   Man's mounting spirit in his bone-house, mean house,
>   dwells—
>   That bird beyond the remembering his free fells,
> This in drudgery, day-labouring-out life's age.
>
> Though aloft on turf or perch or poor low stage,
>   Both sing sometimes the sweetest, sweetest spells,
>   Yet both droop deadly sometimes in their cells
> Or wring their barriers in bursts of fear or rage.
> Not that the sweet-fowl, song-fowl, needs no rest—
> Why, hear him, hear him babble and drop down to his nest,
>   But his own nest, wild nest, no prison.
>
> Man's spirit will be flesh-bound when found at best,
> But uncumberèd: meadow-down is not distressed
>   For a rainbow footing it nor he for his bones risen.

In the poem's central analogy Hopkins compares the caged skylark to the soul imprisoned in a body which constrains its impetus towards ascension. In part this is, then, a religious poem that bemoans humanity's corporeality, most notably in the distinctive image "bone-house" (possibly drawn from the "prison-house" of Wordsworth's 'Intimations of Immortality' (V. 10)) and the (doubly stressed) "bónes rísen" which ends the poem with an emphasis, contrary to 'Hurrahing in Harvest', where the ascendant self only "half hurls earth" from "under his feet". However, in the line "Man's spirit will be flesh-bound when found at best,/But uncumberèd", Hopkins also affirms a central component of the Scotist theology with which he had recently familiarised himself, that physical, bodily being was a necessary pre-requisite to the act of election.

Elsie Phare described Hopkins' position accurately when she argued, in a 1933 biography, that he "never separates soul and body, never casts off his flesh like a garment in an attempt to emerge all spirit" (see

Roberts 1987: 253-4; also Pick 1942: 69-70). For however ambivalent his feelings may have been about the body, it is the case, in this poem and elsewhere, that Hopkins succeeded very well in conveying this core element of the human condition. It is captured, here, in the early lines in particular: "mean house" reinforces but also, in halting the flow of the rhythm, embodies the sense of imprisonment; likewise, the unstressed syllables of "day-labouring-out" succeed in prolonging a related sense of "drudgery". This, furthermore, extends the analogy to an implication of humanity's present social condition, one which Hopkins juxtaposes to the bird who inhabits, in a freedom carrying romantic connotations of nature and individuality, its "own nest, wild nest".

Hopkins wrote 'The Caged Skylark' in the "fresh and wholesome" surroundings of North Wales. However, both its implicit social critique and the heightened sense of imprisonment in the body which an 'un-healthy' Victorian society brought about, was reinforced once he came to experience the Victorian city. For here he perceived, even more clearly, Massumi's second point, that a fundamental element of the "incorporeal materialism" that shapes the body's constant movement and transforma-tion was the interplay between social and environmental forces. Derived from his own preoccupation with the body and bodily health, it was a perception consistent, furthermore, with Victorian preoccupations.

What Peter Dickens has described as "the real or material connections between people and nature and the social relations involved in the modification of nature and of the body" (1992: 159) is the essence of social-ecological philosophy. This is illustrated further by the urban ecological writers Nik Heynen, Maria Kaika and Eric Swyngedouw who draw on Marx's metaphor of "socio-metabolic processes which are productive and that generate the thing in and through the process that brings it into being". Offering, as examples, "commodities, cities, or bodies" (2006: 7) they argue, specifically, that the organisation and social space of the city brings about "the continuous production of new urban "natures", [and] of new urban social and physical environmental conditions" (2006: 4), a fact, they acknowledge, which "occur[s] in the realms of power" (4). This "metabolic" metaphor is, then, designed to literally embody the dialectical relationship between political economy, physical environment and human nature.

Heynen, Kaika and Swyngedouw also suggest (with echoes of Ber-man) that "Throughout the nineteenth century, visionaries of all sorts lamented the 'unsustainable' character of early modern cities and proposed solutions and plans that would remedy the socio-environmental dystopias that characterized much of urban life" (2006: 4). One reason why the metabolic metaphor can be found in Hopkins' poetry, and why, in turn, that poetry typifies the visionary nature of a writing that "lamented the 'unsustainable' character of early modern cities", was a preoccupation with health and corporeality derived (in part) from wider Victorian culture. In *The Healthy Body and Victorian Culture* Bruce Haley argues not only that "no topic more occupied the Victorian mind" than health but also that it was as dominant a concept to them as nature had been for the Romantics (1978: 3). This, he makes clear, was a preoccupation which stemmed from a perceived link between health and the environment. In fact, Haley even relates this, implicitly at least, to the emergence of an ecological consciousness by borrowing a quote from René Dubos' book *Man Adapting* (1965) just at the time at which Dubos was coming to prominence as co-author of the UN sponsored *Only One Earth: The Care and Maintenance of a Small Planet* (1972). For the Victorians, Haley writes, in the citation from Dubos, the body was "the summation of all the constituents and properties of the organism, including their individual relations to the total environment" (19 (my italics)).

Hopkins, as I have already implied, perceived this link between the human body and the surrounding environment, particularly (though not exclusively) through the state of the air. George Rosen suggests that "the atmosphere was considered [by the Victorians] an important factor in the etiology of disease" (1973: 643). This was a notable theme in Hopkins' letters from the city:

> I have been knocked up, the work of Easter week (worse than Holy Week) was so hard, and I had happened to catch a bad cold, which led to earache and deafness: I felt wretched for some time. Neither am I very strong now and as long as I am in Liverpool I do not see how I can be; not that I complain of this, but I state it. There are many Italians here, organ grinders and so on; I do not know how they can bear such an air and sky. No, I see nothing of the spring but some leaves in streets and squares. It is good, and all advise it, to get out of town and breathe fresh air at New Brighton or somewhere else, but I find it almost impossible. (FL (Mother) 30/4/80: 157)

One needs to point out here that Hopkins was something of a hypochondriac (see RB 10/9/88: 289; 13, 14/9/88: 290; 19/10/88: 296), which, incidentally, was a further feature of the period, Haley suggests, also apparent in Carlyle, Eliot, Tennyson and Ruskin (11, 13). While, aside from bouts of diarrhoea and vomiting, there is little suggestion that his physical health was significantly worse in Liverpool than it had been elsewhere, Hopkins did, nevertheless, have some grounds for complaint about this and, significantly, it was these concerns that served to engender further ecological understanding.

Brought on by the strain of his vocation, we find in Hopkins' writing repeated complaints about the need for energy:

> The tax on my strength has been greater than I have felt before: at least now at Teignmouth I feel myself weak and can do little.
>
> The parish work of Liverpool is very wearying to mind and body [...]
>
> it seems to me that I could lead this life well enough if I had bodily energy and cheerful spirits. However these God will not give me.
>
> It seems to me I cannot always last like this: in mind or body or both I shall give way [...] all I really need is a certain degree of relief and change; but I do not think that what I need I shall get in time to save me. (JP July 1874: 250; RWD 14/5/80: 33; SD: 262; RB 7/9/88: 282)

Many of these complaints related, as we can see, to Hopkins' mental rather than physical state. Yet the "weariness" was genuine, endemic, in fact, to the unsustainable demands made by the markedly pragmatic nature both of Jesuitical Catholicism and Victorian post-Romanticism. Martin cites, in this connection, a rather disturbing 1868 survey which revealed that in contrast to a national average of 61 the average life expectancy for a man entering the Jesuit order at 21 was 44 (1991: 213-14). More generally, Hopkins himself questioned, in 'The Leaden Echo and The Golden Echo',

> O why are we so
> haggard at the heart, so care-coiled, care-killed, so fagged,
> so fashed, so cogged, so cumbered. (26)

Most conclusively of all, while he may not appear to have shared the "social risk position" that afflicted the urban working class, Hopkins, as noted at the start of this book, did die from a Victorian environmental hazard, at the age of 44. Demonstrating (albeit rather starkly) the real, material basis to Hopkins' concerns about health what these complaints also engendered was what one might call a corporeal ecology, a notion he then applied in his social critique.

This corporeal ecology emerged from a correspondence between a theological notion of being centred around 'pitch' and an equivalent, corporeal notion developed out of his interest in energy physics. That emanated, in turn, from the derivation of Hopkins' central paradigm, instress, from the term 'stress' in mechanics, the physical pressure exerted on a material object. What this meant was that while instress was, at one level, simply a metaphorical representation of the presence or absence of grace, it also encompassed a literal awareness of the extent to which energy upholds human, physical being. We see this if we examine Hopkins' parallel use of the term to describe different aspects of human being.

Grace is posited, in the first place, as a binding force that bestows "organic unity" on the individual. This was central to Hopkins' theology, as indicated by his assertion of it at the beginning of 'The Wreck of the Deutschland', a poem explicitly designed to set out the grounds of his faith.

> Thou mastering me
> God ! giver of breath and bread;
> World's strand, sway of the sea;
> Lord of living and dead;
> Thou hast bound bones and veins in me, fastened me with flesh,
> And after it almost unmade, what with dread,
> Thy doing: and dost thou touch me afresh?
> Over again I feel thy finger and find thee. (I. 1-8)

Having seen grace in corporeal terms, as something that binds and fastens our bones and veins and flesh, Hopkins also believed that the self could be "unmade" by the absence of grace:

> the ideal, the one, is our only means of recognising successfully our being to ourselves, it unifies us, while vice destroys the sense of being by dissipating thought. (JP: 83)

> personality playing in its freedom not only exerts and displays the riches and capacities of his one nature but unhappily disunites it, rends it, and almost tears it to pieces. (SD: 171)

While all this refers to our spiritual being Hopkins also employed instress to describe, analogously, bodily health for this, like "all things", is "upheld by instress" (JP: 127) (as "bound bones and veins" implies). At moments of illness and mental stress Hopkins described himself, then, almost literally, as unravelling. Apparent early on in the journal

> being unwell I was quite downcast: nature in all her parcels and faculties gaped and fell apart, *fatiscebat*, like a clod cleaving and holding only by strings of root. But this must often be.

the body no longer swayed as a piece by the nervous and muscular instress seems to fall in and hang like a dead weight on the chest. (JP 16/8/73: 236; September 1873: 238)

this is most prominent thereafter in the 'Terrible Sonnets', a group of poems probably written in 1885 (Poems: 288), and which, deriving from "the life I lead now […] one of a continually jaded and harassed mind" (RB 1/9/85: 221), appear to document a spiritual crisis which occurred in Ireland towards the end of his life.

> I am gall, I am heartburn. God's most deep decree
> Bitter would have me taste: my taste was me;
> Bones built in me, flesh filled, blood brimmed the curse.
> ('I wake and feel the fell of dark, not day', 9-14)
>
> Not, I'll not, carrion comfort, Despair, not feast on thee;
> Not untwist—slack they may be—these last strands of man
> In me ór, most weary, cry *I can no more*. ('(Carrion Comfort)', 1-3)

That crisis, and its impact on Hopkins' ecological vision, is discussed further in Chapter Six. However, if we look beyond these examples of occasional self immersion, what we also find is that Hopkins' extreme corporeal sensitivity brought new depths to his awareness of the dialectical relation between self, nature and society.

While dismay at "the base and bespotted figures and features of the Liverpool crowd" might have stemmed from occasional "loathing", and from the moral judgements Hopkins would sometimes impose on the urban poor, an outraged perception that urban environmental hazards were having an equivalent, and disproportionate, impact on the health of its working-class population can, at the same time, be clearly discerned:

What I most dislike in towns and in London in particular is the misery of the poor; the dirt, squalor, and the illshapen degraded physical (putting aside moral) type of so many of the people, with the deeply dejecting, unbearable thought that by degrees almost all our population will become a town population and a puny unhealthy [...] one. (FL (Baillie) 1/5/88: 293)

The particular way, however, in which Hopkins articulated this truth that the body is the "summation of […] individual relations to the total environment" was through the consideration of labour.

From a Marxist perspective Heynen, Kaika and Swyngedouw suggest that

In the most general sense, "labouring" is seen exactly as the specifically human form through which the metabolic process is mobilized and organized [...] To the extent that labour constitutes the universal premise for human metabolic interaction with nature, the particular social relations through which this metabolism of nature is enacted shape the form this metabolic relation takes. (2006: 7-8)

This was, again, recognised in the nineteenth century. Noting just such a sense of metabolic relationship, Haley suggests that for the Victorians "Bodily health imparts a sense of physically belonging, of being at home with physical things and laws" (1978: 253-4) that was expressed in a "useful, creative labour" within which "the self and the environment are conceptually created in personal action" (21, 254). From their own metabolic perspective there came about, therefore, a Victorian recognition that while labour in the service of a sustainable political economy brings about human health, the same labour in a toxic economy might well result, conversely, in some form of health penalty. Hopkins' own perception of this, while sometimes articulated in exaggerated references to himself, also carried through into two diametrically opposed poems about the human labouring subject.

5. A humanist ecopoetic

These two poems, each of which utilise the capacities of rhythm, enable us to feel the metabolic process for ourselves. The first, 'Harry Ploughman', is an ideal, if perhaps idealised, representation of human labour operating in a sustainable environment.

> HARD as hurdle arms, with a broth of goldish flue
> Breathed round; the rack of ribs; the scooped flank; lank
> Rope-over thigh; knee-nave; and barrelled shank—
>   Head and foot, shoulder and shank—
> By a grey eye's head steered well, one crew, fall to;
> Stand at stress. Each limb's barrowy brawn, his thew
> That onewhere curded, onewhere sucked or sank—
>   Soared ór sánk—,
> Though as a beechbole firm, finds his, as at a rollcall, rank
> And features, in flesh, what deed he each must do—
>   His sinew-service where do.
>
> He leans to it, Harry bends, look. Back, elbow, and liquid
>   waist
> In him, all quail to the wallowing o' the plough. 'S cheek
>   crimsons; curls
> Wag or crossbridle, in a wind lifted, windlaced—

See his wind- lilylocks -laced;
Churlsgrace too, child of Amansstrength, how it hangs or
    hurls
Them—broad in bluff hide his frowning feet lashed ! raced
With, along them, cragiron under and cold furls—
            With-a-fountain's shining-shot furls.

There are several ways to read this poem, which possibly originates from Hopkins having watched a ploughman at work in Ireland (see MacKenzie 1981: 192). It might be seen as an idealisation of the pastoral environment, a pre-Heideggerian advocacy of immanence over alienation (see Soper 1995: 237). It might, alternatively, be read as a sacramental poem, a description of labour performed in the service of God (see Johnson 1997: 86; Pick 1942: 151). The juxtaposition, for example, in the "Soared ór sánk—,/Though as a beechbole firm" between motion and an organisation and purpose dictated by one fixed principle ("one crew, fall to") re-states an ontological relationship central to Hopkins' theology. The poem might also represent – given its close attention to the "broth of goldish" hair and to "wind- lilylocks -laced" (meaning, according to Gardner and MacKenzie "fair as lilies, laced, plaited by the wind" (see Poems: 293)) – an idealisation of masculinity, or even repressed sexual desire (see Alderson 1998: 122-3; Saville 2000: 184-5). Julia Saville has detected, for example, "libidinal energy and orgasmic effects" in various drafts of the final line (184). Indeed, with the exception of this last point, these readings might even be brought together: the ploughman's masculinity, in a traditional rural occupation, being directed towards the theological concept of labour as religious service, an instressing of the spiritual energy within his body. Such a sense would be traceable through the apparent influence of the painter Frederick Walker whose work Hopkins regarded as "divine" (RWD 30/6/86: 134). For we might note here the similarity of this poem to his evaluation of Walker's 'The Harbour of Refuge':

> The young man mowing was a great stroke, a figure quite made up of dew and grace and strong fire: the sweep of the scythe and swing and sway of the whole body even to the rising of the one foot on tiptoe while the other was flung forward was as if such a thing had never been painted before, so fresh and so very strong. (JP Winter 1873-4: 240)

However, elements within that appraisal – "the sweep of the scythe and swing and sway of the whole body", the foot "flung forward" – also indicate a further possible reading, one that might foreground the representation of the ploughman's literal, physical energy.

One criticism levelled, throughout the years, at 'Harry Ploughman' concerns the perceived de-humanisation of its subject. Phare, for example, compared it to 'The Windhover' in describing it as the representation of "a creature who is intent on exercising all the powers with which he is endowed and who merely as a by-product flashes off beauty, unbeknown to himself, giving intense pleasure to the eye of the beholder" (see Roberts 1987: 252). White, more recently, argues that the poem is "successful precisely because Harry is dehumanized, turned into a connected series of natural phenomena" (1992: 439). While Hopkins does, admittedly, walk a fine line here, I would offer, as mitigation, the poem's depiction of a physical, muscular energy that embodies the consumption, production, and exchange of energy between the human labourer and the wider ecosystem.

Surveying, in the first place, the production and circulation of energy throughout the ploughman's body, Hopkins begins the poem with a roll-call in which, it becomes apparent, each component of that body – the ribs, flank, thigh, knee, shank – has something to contribute ("features, in flesh, what deed he each must do"). From highlighting each individual action Hopkins goes on to describe visible manifestations of the energy generated. Implied in the golden hair ("flue") "breathed round" his arms, and in the absence of the religious connotations (e.g. of "grace" or "fire") imposed on Walker's painting, this can be seen in the "curding" (bunch-ing) of the "thew" (muscle), in the motion by which the muscle "Soared ór sank", and, of course, when the "cheek crimsons". Having described, initially, this circulation of energy as fluid, in the extended metaphor that evokes the descriptions of water in the journal – i.e. "curded", "sucked", and "sank" – Hopkins nevertheless moves on to suggest that this is determinate and structured. As Milroy has put it, "the tensions between liquid and solid, soft texture and hard, curved shapes and slender, form the underlying pattern of the poem" (1977: 173-4).

Drawing, therefore, on the conventional Hobbesian analogy of the commonwealth as a human body, in this case "steered" by the plough-man's "grey eye", that determination is implied in the theologically connoted "Soared", accented to read almost as two syllables (Poems: 293), and made explicit in the "sinew-service" that "each must do". Hopkins utilises, furthermore, another convention to emphasise the point, an equation of theological with military motifs also seen in "Stand at stress". However, this unusual sonnet, in which the (indented) 'burden-lines' serve as additions to the usual fourteen-line structure, concludes not, as is customary, with theological interpretation – nor in what might have been, in another poet, the idealisation of a pastoral commonwealth – but in an extension to the ecological portrayal in which we see that the energy generated by Harry is passed on to produce the freshly ploughed "shining" soil. For having described how the "Back, elbow, and liquid waist" of the ploughman "all quail to the wallowing o' the plough", Hopkins ends the poem, in the obscure final lines (17-19), by drawing a parallel between the movement of Harry's feet and the line of the ploughed furrow, an organised interaction of body and environment that results in a depiction of productive energy exchange.

'Felix Randal', which like 'Harry Ploughman' encompasses multiple themes – the dignity of labour, social class, masculinity, doctrines of pastoral care and responsibility – can also be read as a poetic embodiment of energy exchange between the labourer and his environment. The subject of the poem is a parishioner of Hopkins' in Liverpool, a thirty-one year old farrier, Felix Spencer, who was one of five parishioners to have died that week alone (MacKenzie 1981: 135-6). A victim of a death rate twice the average for England at that time (see Lampard 1973: 21), Felix Spencer contracted pulmonary tuberculosis, a disease "continually present in", and largely exclusive to, the urban community and which spread as a combination of the very factors – overcrowded living conditions, lack of clean air, seclusion from sunlight (see Rosen 1973: 628, 642-4) – that Hopkins had complained about in his letters.

In 'Harry Ploughman' we experienced a "felt reality of relation" between the human subject and a rich, resourceful environment that that subject helped to sustain. This poem begins, conversely, with a depiction of the labourer's energy wasting away, a depiction that captures the malaise of the urban environment in Felix's body.

> Felix Randal the farrier, O is he dead then? My duty all
>   ended,
> Who have watched his mould of man, big-boned and hardy-
>   handsome
> Pining, pining, till time when reason rambled in it and some
> Fatal four disorders, fleshed there, all contended?
>
> Sickness broke him. (1-5)

While there is, also, a deterioration in the mind ("reason rambled"), we mainly feel, in the stunted rhythm of the first quatrain, the farrier's physical deterioration. Having been the embodiment of powerful ("hardy") physical presence, an archetype of labouring masculinity, Felix has now become a mere shell ("mould"). Referring thereafter to the convergence of infections that characterises tuberculosis, the decay is enacted materially, the "fatal four disorders, fleshed there". Usurpers from the wider ecosystem, we literally *feel*, in the rhythm, the infections dissipate the energy which had once sustained his physical being, weakening him further as they fight each other ("all contended"). Whereas, then, in 'God's Grandeur' Hopkins depicted industrial processes infiltrating the earth, here they infiltrate the body.

A powerful embodiment of the metabolic metaphor the poem also incorporates, consistent with the analogous notion of stress, a religious dimension. Hopkins finds a variety of spiritual consolations in Felix's death: the farrier's growing faith, the "heavenlier heart [that] began some/Months earlier" (6-7); the communion of pastoral care including what he, as a priest, gains from the relationship – "seeing the sick endears them to us, us too it endears" (9); the redemption promised by the Catholic faith. Yet there is not, here, the same shift as in 'The Caged Skylark' from exemplum (the fundamental corporeal reality of human being) to argument (a countering reality of eternal life promised by the church). Rather, by dividing the sestet into two tercets Hopkins restricts the theological component to the first of these while the second, conversely, overrides this to reintroduce, as Charles Williams suggests, "the outer world with […] an overmastering noise of triumph over the spiritual meditation" of what went before (Roberts 1987: 175). Here then, in a marked juxtaposition to the beginning of the poem, Hopkins resurrects the physical vigour of

>   thy more boisterous
>   years,
> When thou at the random grim forge, powerful amidst peers,
> Didst fettle for the great grey drayhorse his bright and battering
>   sandal! (12-14)

Physical strength resounds in these lines: "the repeated 'ay' sounds ('great grey dray') ring out", in Norman MacKenzie's words, "like blows on the anvil" (1981: 139); the commas either side of "powerful amidst peers" emphasise the farrier's strength; the double stress on "forge" and "powerful" (see Poems: 279) allows the physical act to leap from the page.

While all this only serves to emphasise the environmental injustice of Felix's mortal illness, 'Felix Randal' nevertheless defies the dictum that "inspiration" could only come from "good health or state of the air". For while Liverpool might have been "of all places the most museless", this poem, literally inspired by the poor state of the air, offers an exceptional, perhaps unique, poetic extension of the phenomenological emphasis on the body as situated in place.

Discussing Keats' 'To Autumn' Jonathan Bate suggests that the poem carries the shadow of Keats' tuberculosis. His need for good weather, clean water and decent air, found on the Kent coast at Margate, underlie, Bate explains, the poem's concern about the weather while "The good summer and clear autumn of 1819 very literally gave a new lease of life" (2000: 104-5). While 'Felix Randal' also relates the ecosystem to tuberculosis there is the realisation that a "good summer and clear autumn" was impossible both in an urban environment where "one can not see the sun" and because Felix's social and economic (risk) position did not allow him to evade the city's particular environmental consequences. What the poem offers, then, is an awareness, and embodiment, of toxic environmental degradation, and of Greenberg's "urban health penalty", suffered by the Victorian working class, an awareness which, in turn, motivated the critique of society that began to appear in Hopkins' work.

6. Development of, and retraction from, an ecological social philosophy

Victorian writers, as Haley indicates, regarded poor health much in the same way as the Romantic writers regarded negative impacts on nature – as an indictment of society. Gissing, for example, laments, in *The Nether World*, the impoverishment imposed upon an (urban) population consigned to "sit [...] through all the years of the life that is granted them, who strain their eyesight, who overtax their muscles, who nurse disease in their frames, who put resolutely from them the thought of what existence *might* be" (1974 [1889]: 11); the Christian socialist writer F. D. Maurice voiced that critique in explicitly ecological terms when he connected human nature to the impact on nature as a whole:

> We ought to feel that all God's judgments by fever and cholera are judgments for neglect of His physical laws, but that *they* will not be obeyed till men obey His moral laws, by ceasing to live to themselves, by feeling that it is their business to care for their fellows and for the earth. (cited in Haley 1978: 255)

The issue of health provoked Hopkins, also, to call into question "'the boasted civilisation of this so-called nineteenth century'".

> Our whole civilisation is dirty, yea filthy, and especially in the north; for is it not dirty, yea filthy, to pollute the air as Blackburn and Widnes and St. Helen's are polluted and the water as the Thames and the Clyde and the Irwell are polluted? The ancients with their immense public baths would have thought even our cleanest towns dirty. (RB 23/2/89: 299)

> My Liverpool and Glasgow experience laid upon my mind a conviction, a truly crushing conviction, of the misery of town life to the poor and more than to the poor, of the misery of the poor in general, of the degradation even of our race, of the hollowness of this century's civilisation: it made even life a burden to me to have daily thrust upon me the things I saw. (RWD: 1/12/81: 97)

The political opinions which resulted were by no means consistent, exhibiting, rather, a mass of contradiction typical of the disoriented Victorian experience of modernity. Nevertheless, Hopkins did develop some form of political position which, furthermore, can be mapped against social ecology. Two elements, in particular, coincide with that philosophy: an advocacy of a more sustainable subsistence economics; and the recognition, supported by a communitarian element in his thought and practice, that this might be achieved through egalitarian politics.

The first of these took the form of a Carlylean critique of the pursuit of wealth for its own sake not unrelated, though inevitably given greater theological emphasis, to the understanding of quality of life that Mill and Morris have passed down to social ecology. Hopkins spelt this out most clearly when preaching at Oxford on the Sermon on the Mount (see SD: 21-3). Identifying what he sees as the competing claims of God and Mammon, he declares "We cannot [...] serve God and do what he asks of us if our first thought is of money or other worldly goods". We have a responsibility to work, he continued, "since St. Paul plainly says / If a man will not work neither shall he eat" but only so as to "Provide for necessities": "To the question then / How much we may take of money and worldly goods / we have Christ's answer / Seek first etc. that is where God's service and the world's clash. God is the master, not the world, God must be obeyed, the world neglected" (SD: 22-3). Hopkins ends the sermon by questioning, on this basis, the pursuit of commodities beyond those required for basic subsistence. "Life must be kept up by food, [and] the body protected by clothing" but, he instructs his congregation, "the food is for the life, not the life for the food [...] When therefore we have necessary food and clothing we have enough: Having food and clothing, the Apostle says, let us be content" (SD: 23). At certain points this position became radicalised much closer to the socialism that permeates social ecology. Though his experience of the city was influential in this regard Hopkins' views were, in fact, most explicitly set out in the so-called "red letter" written to Bridges while he was still training for the priesthood (RB 2/8/71: 27-8).

Hopkins tells Bridges, early in the letter, "I am always thinking of the Communist future", and, later, that he foresees "some great revolution is not far off". Believing such a situation to have occurred because of a lack of substantive opposition to the direction taken by Victorian modernity, and a void in leadership exemplified when he singles out Carlyle (RB 2/8/71: 27), Hopkins chose to announce, to the deeply conservative Bridges, that "in a manner I am a communist" (RB 2/8/71: 27-8).

Hopkins continues the letter by elaborating on the social conditions which, he feels, might prompt a revolution:

> it is just.—I do not mean the means of getting to it are. But it is a dreadful thing for the greatest and most necessary part of a very rich nation to live a hard life without dignity, knowledge, comforts, delight, or hopes in the midst of plenty—which plenty they make. (RB 2/8/71: 27-8)

And he goes on to expand the point:

> As it at present stands in England it is itself in great measure founded on wrecking. But they got none of the spoils, they came in for nothing but harm from it then and thereafter. England has grown hugely wealthy but this wealth has not reached the working classes; I expect it has made their condition worse. (RB 2/8/71: 28)

In arguing that society has a responsibility towards providing basic material subsistence to all, Hopkins moves here into the realms of socialist political philosophy. Indeed his remarks have an interesting echo in statements Morris was to make in the midst of his conversion to an ecological socialism:

> If civilization is to go no further than this [...] if it does not aim at getting rid of this misery and giving some share in the happiness and dignity of life to *all* the people that it has created … it is simply an organized injustice, a mere instrument for oppression.

> I do not want art for a few, any more than education for a few, or freedom for a few. (cited in Thompson 1977: 255, 253)

Following Morris' lead, we can connect Hopkins' emphasis on art ("delight") and education ("knowledge") to the re-conceptualisation of a quality of life that might encourage less materialistic, more sustainable patterns of consumption. Furthermore, we can note the parallel between the anxieties expressed in the "red letter" and those expressed elsewhere, in similar language, about the environmental impact of Victorian modernity (possibly alluded to in the reference to "wrecking"). In all of these regards, Hopkins came close, then, to the green politics encapsulated by Morris. While it would be easy to dismiss the "red letter" as the posturing of a relatively young man (he was 26) baiting his conservative friend (who, in fact, ceased correspondence for two years), the recognition contained in his letters of a connection between 'natural' and social sustainability did, nevertheless, rest upon a belief in a less acquisitive, more socially just society which Hopkins carried through in his ministry and articulated in his poetry.

In the hymn, 'Thee, God, I come from, to thee go', composed in 1885, Hopkins asks the rhetorical question of how best he might serve God as a priest. While the belatedness of the poem alerts us to feelings of dissatisfaction and doubt that gradually began to beset his vocation, Hopkins answered clearly enough on this occasion. In a rejection of social withdrawal, he suggests – in the reference to his parishioners as "my brother", "mate", or "counterpart" – a communitarian model of priesthood more Ultramontane than Newmanite.

> I have life left with me still
> And thy purpose to fulfil;
> Yea a debt to pay thee yet:
> Help me, sir, and so I will.
>
> But thou bidst, and just thou art,
> Me shew mercy from my heart
> Towards my brother, every other
> Man my mate and counterpart. (17-24)

The clearest evidence that Hopkins put this into practice came when he worked, in Liverpool, as chaplain to the recently established Society of St. Vincent de Paul, an Ultramontane charity set up to "guide its members in personal holiness and to encourage them in their work" (1992: 58). Hopkins, as Zonneveld demonstrates, enthusiastically supported the society, which "he felt convinced [...] had a great future" (1992: 59). Working actively to alleviate urban poverty, this included, amongst other things, providing grants of clothing, money, coal or tools to help men find employment. Zonneveld goes so far as to conjecture that a "sharp increase in membership" in Hopkins' parish in 1880 "was in all probability partly due to his work" and even points out that his obituary in the Jesuit journal 'Letters and Notices' made reference to Hopkins having shown "beautiful love of the poor and the young, and devotion to the Society of St Vincent de Paul wherever he went" (1992: 58-9).

His understanding of the extent of the "social risk position" experienced by the urban working class, which Hopkins sought to mitigate in his charitable work, and the realisation that this was interconnected to the environmental problems afflicting Victorian society, was encapsulated in the difficult 1887 poem 'Tom's Garland' (Hopkins was obliged to produce a "crib" so that Bridges and Dixon could understand it (RB 10/2/88: 272-4)). Written, Saville notes, in a "year of severe economic depression" (2000: 188), and concurrent, in fact, with the emergence of Gould's "early green politics", this poem utilises the devices both of rhythm and the sonnet structure in order to help the reader understand those risks. He also, thereafter, envisages their alleviation by proposing a potential political solution.

> Tom—garlanded with squat and surly steel
> Tom; then Tom's fallowbootfellow piles pick
> By him and rips out rockfire homeforth—sturdy Dick;
> Tom Heart-at-ease, Tom Navvy: he is all for his meal
> Sure, 's bed now. Low be it: lustily he his low lot (feel
> That ne'er need hunger, Tom; Tom seldom sick,
> Seldomer heartsore; that treads through, prickproof, thick
> Thousands of thorns, thoughts) swings though. Commonweal
> Little I reck ho! lacklevel in, if all had bread:
> What! Country is honour enough in all us—lordly head,
> With heaven's lights high hung round, or, mother-ground
> That mammocks, mighty foot. But nó way sped,
> Nor mind nor mainstrength; gold go garlanded
> With, perilous, O nó; nor yet plod safe shod sound;
>   Undenizened, beyond bound
> Of earth's glory, earth's ease, all; no one, nowhere,
> In wide the world's weal; rare gold, bold steel, bare
>   In both; care, but share care—
> This, by Despair, bred Hangdog dull; by Rage,
> Manwolf, worse; and their packs infest the age.

It would be easy, as does Martin, to contrast 'Harry Ploughman', a "lyrical embodiment of the harmony of beautiful countryman and the earth of which he is part" with Tom, a "product of the depressed urban classes" (1991: 232). Yet Hopkins drew attention, in fact, to the "resemblance" between the two poems "conceived", he wrote, "at the same time". He describes this, jokingly, as "a fault in me the sonneteer" and cites Aeschylus: "he is always forgetting he said a thing before. Indeed, he never did, but tried to say it two or three times—something rich and profound but not by him distinctly apprehended" (RB 12/1/88: 271). What is "rich and profound" in both poems is a complex, ecological understanding that a harmony of "physical" and "moral state" is possible, even in an urban environment, if productive human energy can be harnessed to the service of an equitable and sustainable "social state".

The "kinetic strength and grace" that Martin goes on to attribute to 'Harry Ploughman' is also depicted in the early part of this poem where we see a clear admiration for the industrial labourer. It begins with a description that testifies to the labouring classes being what Hopkins would call the "mainstrength" of the nation. Apparent from the opening line, where the sense of "garlanded" – ornament or decoration – suggests that their labour is 'prized', it continues in the subsequent celebration of vigorous energy connoted, for example, by the alliterative force of "rips out rockfire" and in the adjective "sturdy". Further on, Hopkins advocates, in more general terms, the desirability of a social state in which the comfort and subsistence of the working population – measured by the provision of basic energy sources, the "low lot" of home, food, sleep, health – is assured in exchange for their labour, a principle which extends so as to encompass, consistent with the "red letter", an expectation that these labourers might enjoy their leisure time untroubled, neither hungry, sick, "heartsore", or troubled by "thorns" of "thoughts" or "care" (8; 17). There is no sense, though, that "Tom's" labour is imbued with goodness or right purpose; in fact its end product is condemned by Hopkins. Yet what does occur alongside an ensuing critique of what is being done to the environment is the realisation expressed in his letters that the utilisation of human energy towards ugly and unsustainable environmental consequences would be matched by equally ugly, unsustainable social consequences.

The environmental consequences of industrialisation, though not to the forefront of the poem, are, nevertheless, clearly implicit in the imagery that 'Tom's Garland' shares with 'God's Grandeur'. References to the "ground" torn to pieces by a "mighty foot" (11-12) that "plod safe shod" (14) recall, in diction, rhyme and rhythm, the "Generations" of the earlier poem which "trod, have trod, have trod" and "seared" and "smeared" the earth. As with much about 'Tom's Garland' this can be clarified by referring to Hopkins' "crib". What the poem is saying, he writes, is that

> it is the navvies or daylabourers who, on the great scale or in gangs and millions, mainly trench, tunnel, blast and in other ways disfigure, 'mammock' the earth and, on a small scale, singly, and superficially stamp it with their footprints. (RB 10/2/88: 273)

While the repetition here of the motif of the footprint resonates, of course, with the contemporary notion of the 'ecological footprint', Hopkins' own concern about this is evident in the violence of the image by which the ground is torn apart. It is not, though, environmental protest that underpins the poem, but, as in 'God's Grandeur', a Gaian, ecological sense that nature will survive its disfigurement. The point is made when Hopkins suggests that the wealth of natural resources, such as gold and steel, are extracted at "earth's ease" (16-17). The message is, then, that it will be "the black West", society, that suffers the consequences of an exploitative political economy. Where, in the earlier poem, Hopkins had described this in terms of a possible extinction of the human race, here there is a further, parallel recognition of the 'risk' that stems from the social exclusion of the unemployed, a different emphasis, but one rooted, nevertheless, in the economy of energy exchange.

The parallel social critique comes most clearly with the change of emphasis as we approach the two codas to the poem. In the sonnet proper, the body of the labourer is conventionally incorporated into the body politic (see Alderson 1998: 123-5). While such a scenario might engender a harmonious society, this is clearly under threat as we see when Hopkins repeats the argument of the "red letter" that Victorian society is intrinsically at risk ("perilous") because, he explains to Bridges, "the curse of our times is that many do not share it, that they are outcasts from it and have neither security nor splendour" (RB 10/2/88: 273). The elaboration of this particular argument is triggered by the word, "Undenizened", with which the codas begin. Describing the unemployed as "outcasts" both from "earth's glory" (riches) and its "ease" (subsistence), Hopkins argues that they have been denied their right to dwell in the industrial society to which they belong. He offers, in this, a conception of dwelling that extends far beyond the Heideggerian position evoked in recent ecocriticism, one that remains ecological, but is premised upon a concern not to transcend society but to engage with the dual principle of social and environmental justice.

The extent to which Hopkins felt the former (human exclusion) as deeply as he did the latter (damage to nature) is indicated in the sophisticated way in which he embodies the plight of the unemployed within the structure and rhythm of the poem: the separation of the two codas from the sonnet equates, of course, to an exclusion of the unemployed from the main body of society; a stress on the first syllable ("Un-") of line 15, "independent of the natural stress of the verse" (Poems: 290), functions as a sound signifier which, circumventing the somewhat strangled syntax (see Roberts 1987: 19-20, 28-9), accentuates this condition; finally, key words – "Commonweal", "mother-ground", "Rage" – are placed for emphasis at the end of a line, the separation of "beyond bound" from "earth's glory" or "no one, nowhere" from "world's weal" serving, in particular, to re-affirm the displacement of the unemployed.

When Hopkins goes on to elucidate, in the second of the two codas, the extent of the risk posed by the social exclusion of the unemployed, he renders this, however, in distinctly ecological terms. This occurs with an extension of the idea of the body politic which takes it beyond its metaphorical aspect and into the scientific understanding that we are all incorporated (or not) within society on the basis of the energy embodied in and exchanged through our labour. As in 'Harry Ploughman', the labourer in 'Tom's Garland' contributes his energy to society and redistributes it productively. Hopkins offers no judgement on this other than to condemn the particular way in which Victorian political economy utilises that energy. Returning, in the closing lines, to this same theme Hopkins suggests that one of two things will arise from unemployment, from, that is, the frustration of the labourers' energy. On the one hand, it may induce an entropic state. This is apparent from the repetition of "Despair" a word Hopkins had used in 'Inversnaid' to describe the possibility that the energy of the burn might become disordered and dissipate into a "pool so pitchblack, féll-fró́wning/It rounds and rounds Despair to drowning". Alternatively, frustrated human energy might also be converted, or unleashed, into the "Rage" of social revolution, the "Manwolf", whose "packs infest the age", acting back on the society that has excluded him. The poem represents, in this light, the culmination of a process in which Hopkins had applied his apprehension of energy exchange as the basis for all life towards a recognition of the fact that a functioning political economy rests upon the productive exchange and harnessing of energy. While, then, like 'Felix Randal', 'Tom's Garland' draws upon ecological understanding to offer a powerful critique of Victorian risk society, on this occasion that perspective was also developed in a more pragmatic direction. It was, however, at precisely this point that Hopkins diverged from the "early green politics" which had appeared to underwrite his critique.

Hopkins returned to a philosophy of conservatism which had always, in fact, been his default political position. This was a principle encapsulated in a ministry that can be symbolised through Hopkins' interest in the Doctrine of the Sacred Heart, a nineteenth-century adaptation of a traditional, popular devotion to the physical heart of Jesus. Initially advocated by the Jesuits, the Doctrine of the Sacred Heart was adopted into official Catholic culture as a belief in offering "reparation for the outrages committed against the Divine love" (see Cross/Livingstone 1997: 1437). These "outrages" might well have included concerns similar to those expressed by Hopkins, the destruction of nature and the inequitable treatment of the urban poor. Yet notwithstanding such communitarian implications, Hopkins, in keeping with Ultramontanism, chose to address such concerns by blending compassion with a parochial model of authority fashioned after Christ (who he had described as both "gentle" and "stern" (see SD: 17, 37)). In this light, as Zonneveld points out, even Hopkins' involvement in the Society of St Vincent de Paul can be seen as an assertion of leadership and the principle of hierarchy as an alternative to centralised (state) intervention in offsetting the threat of social revolution (1992: 143). Applied in the context of his ministry this conservative principle was also articulated in the metaphor of the "Commonweal" that lies at the centre of 'Tom's Garland'.

Hopkins had explored and conceptualised the idea of the commonwealth in a series of three sermons delivered in Liverpool on consecutive Sundays in January 1880. Here he explained that the notion of the commonwealth is founded upon a contract in which God's "Providence", the guarantee to humanity of "health, food, generation, and pleasures" (SD: 59, 166), is offered in return for "eternal praise and glory from his subjects" who, in sequence, gain "Eternal life […] in mind and body for the efforts made" (SD: 59-60). Derived, however, from Scotus' speculation that Christ may have assumed bodily presence at the beginning of creation, Hopkins goes on to conjecture (see SD: 57) that what was called, until the Fall, "God's first kingdom" or "first commonwealth", might also have been extended to encompass the Earth. Elaborating what, in that scenario, the Earth might have looked like, he offers a model intriguingly close to the social-ecological commonwealth of Morris' *News from Nowhere*.

Hopkins believed that "as men multiplied man was to spread over the earth […] and reclaim it piece by piece to the condition of Paradise". This he envisaged as a pristine environment free from hazards such as "drought and storm, plague, blight, or locust" (SD: 60). He then goes on to consider the possible "laws of this kingdom" and conjectures, in passing, that ownership might have been common (SD: 61), a suggestion expanded when he conceives that in this 'earthly paradise' "a whole people" could have been "selfgoverning and selfgoverned" or, at the very least, that the "common good" may have been determined by "constitution" (i.e. democratically) (SD: 55-6). Hopkins visualises, that is, the economy of "God's first kingdom" as a utopian society in which a sustainable use of natural resources would have existed hand in hand with an equitable, communitarian society.

The Fall represents the loss of this particular 'earthly paradise'. For where, he tells his congregation, "man was put into Paradise to dress and keep it and […] bidden to increase and multiply and fill the earth and subdue it" the failure marked by original sin meant that "far from turning the waste wilderness of the outside earth into a Paradise he was cast from paradise out into the waste wilderness" (SD: 60). Consequently, in place of the fallen "first kingdom" there came about, as Hopkins describes it at the end of the first of the sermons, "God's second kingdom", an alternative commonwealth established through and regulated by the Catholic church.

Hopkins initially defines this as:

> the meeting of many for their joint and common good, for which good all are solemnly engaged to strive and being so engaged are then in duty bound to strive, the ruler by planning, the ruled by performing, the sovereign by the weight of his authority, the subject by the stress of his obedience. (SD: 58)

This hierarchical philosophy is substantiated a year later in notes recorded while Hopkins, on retreat, was making the Spiritual Exercises of St Ignatius.

> The sovereign and the subject enter (by free contract or otherwise) into relations and this makes a polity or commonweal, commonwealth. There is joint action, a common end in view, and a common good. The common good is shared either according to some constitution or terms of the contract or else by the disposal of some judge, usually the sovereign power; in the case of God and man altogether by the disposal of the sovereign. It is equitable that it should be in proportion to the work done. Besides the common good to be obtained by common action there is status, the status of sovereign and the status of subject. To the status belongs duty or function, in the

sovereign to legislate, command; in the subject to obey, but in the sense of consenting. This consent is primary, I mean that in it consists obedience rather than, or prior to, the execution. (SD: 164-5)

While, as he says here, the establishment of the "common good" might still have remained a democratic process – in that it could, theoretically, have been determined "according to some constitution" – Hopkins nevertheless appears to conclude, given the 'fallen' nature of the second commonwealth, that it would necessitate governance by means of a conservative, hierarchical philosophy, one in which the "common good" would be at "the disposal of some judge, usually the sovereign power".

Though Hopkins framed the concept of the commonwealth theologically it was, nevertheless, pregnant with obvious political connotations (SD: 165). It is these that are expounded in 'Tom's Garland', mainly between lines 8 and 12.

Commonweal

> Little I reck ho! lacklevel in, if all had bread:
> What! Country is honour enough in all us—lordly head,
> With heaven's lights high hung round, or, mother-ground
> That mammocks, mighty foot.

While the reference is, once again, obscure, light is shed on these lines by his explanation of the poem to Bridges where Hopkins makes it clear that he is drawing out the political implications of the analogy between society and the human body (RB 10/2/88: 272). What we find here is that Hopkins failed to follow through the radical connotations of his own re-thinking of the body politic – the conclusions that Marx (and contemporary ecologists) have drawn from a metabolic understanding of energy flow in which society, nature and human nature are interrelated – and instead retreated to the more conventional, Hobbesian use of this corporeal metaphor as a representation of hierarchy. In the letter Hopkins offers the blunt distinction on which his philosophy rests: "The head is the sovereign, who has no superior but God and from heaven receives his or her authority [...] The foot is the daylabourer, and this is armed with hobnail boots, because it has to wear and be worn by the ground" (RB 10/2/88: 273). Conceding the inequality that lies behind this concept, Hopkins chose to address this by arguing that while the labourer lacks "one advantage, glory or public fame, [he] makes up for it by another, ease of mind, absence of care" (RB 10/2/88: 273), a view, clarifying lines 4-8, which amounts to the belief that the working man does not aspire towards social revolution: "the labourer—surveys his lot, low but free from care; then by a sudden strong act throws it over the shoulder or tosses it away as a light matter. The witnessing of which lightheartedness makes me indignant with the fools of Radical Levellers" (RB 10/2/88: 273). One can, of course, suggest here that Hopkins could not have been aware of an "early green politics" which might, perhaps, have made him more sympathetic to socialism. At the time this was only just beginning to germinate and even then in radical circles and discourses to which he would not, in all likelihood, have had access. Yet such a perspective was, in fact, available to him by means of an interest in the American poet Walt Whitman.

Hopkins read George Saintsbury's review of Whitman's *Leaves of Grass* in the *Academy*. This described Whitman's "gospel", in distinctly social-ecological terms, as one that united a respect for non-human nature with social democracy. Whitman, we are told, was led "both by natural inclination and *in the carrying out of his main idea*, to take note of 'the actual earth's equalities', he has literally filled his pages with the song of birds, the hushed murmur of waves, the quiet and multiform life of the forest and the meadow" (RB: 313 (my italics)). Furthermore, we learn from Saintsbury, Whitman believed in "the necessity of the establishment of a universal republic, or rather brotherhood of men", a "Utopia [...] which shall be open to everybody" (RB: 311-12).

Hopkins, commenting on Whitman to Bridges, notes various similarities in theme and (superficially) in the deployment of rhythm but remarks that

> I always knew in my heart Walt Whitman's mind to be more like my own than any other man's living. As he is a very great scoundrel this is not a pleasant confession. And this also makes me the more desirous to read him and the more determined that I will not. (RB 18/10/82: 154-5)

While such comments were almost certainly prompted by what Saintsbury had referred to as "the prominence [...] of the sexual passion" in Whitman's work (see SD: 215-16), it is also likely, as some critics have suggested, that they relate in part to Hopkins' politics (see Bergonzi 1978: 112-13; Martin 1991: 350-1). Either way, the analysis he makes of Whitman's work (see RB 18/10/82: 154-8) serves to confirm that Hopkins was aware of, and chose to reject, the connection, made by Whitman, between natural and human "equalities".

Notwithstanding the view that the "too intelligent artisan is master of the situation", Hopkins did not, in the end, possess Morris' faith in the transformative potential of the working class. On the contrary, one element of his attitude towards them was a marked condescension which occasionally comes across in his poetry. "Tom", representative of the labourer, is untroubled, for example, by reflection or analysis, "prickproof" from "Thick/thousands of thorns, thoughts"; 'Harry Ploughman' has a "churls [peasant's] grace" and is described as a "child of Amansstrength"; Felix Randal is "child, Felix, poor Felix Randal" (11). Possessed, in addition, of both an Ultramontane faith in social hierarchy and that movement's deep suspicion of socialism (see Norman 1985: 86) Hopkins believed, as suggested above, that any impetus towards revolution would come not from the working class itself – with whom, in the light of his own experience, he did retain some sympathy – but from "Socialists and other pests of society" (RB 10/2/88: 274). As Bergonzi succinctly puts it, Hopkins' "critique was that of a Tory radical rather than a socialist: he wanted the working class to be given their rightful place in the existing social order rather than see that order overthrown" (1978: 71).

I argued in Chapter Two that the temptation to retreat into pre-modern political solutions seems a somewhat inadequate response to nineteenth-century ecological problems given both the presence of new democratic movements in which the working class pro-actively voiced ecological concerns and the already existing failure of feudalistic solutions such as Ruskin's Guild of St George. It is a lesson worth recalling when a contemporary writer such as Wendell Berry feels inclined to retrieve the notion that "Among all creatures there are hierarchies of ability, intelligence, and power [...] which *exist by nature*" and then to extend that towards a related advocacy of "*just* hierarchy" (1983: 148-9), an idea which appears furthermore, in the UK, to underwrite Prince Charles' possibly well-meaning but ill-founded incursions into ecological debate and policy (Cohen 2008). The intention here, however, is not to censure Hopkins, merely to suggest that it is in the retreat away from something akin to Morris' early socialist "commonwealth" that a contemporary, social-ecological reading needs to withdraw from him.

This notion, that we have to know where to disconnect as well as connect with our literary and historical predecessors, is part of a wider argument with which, up to a point, I will end the book: the impossibility of conferring what Buell calls "environmental sainthood" on literary figures. Following on from this I will consider in Chapter Six the degree to which the paradigm of the commonwealth, as it was further articulated in Hopkins' spiritual writings, brought about an ontological separation from the rest of nature that almost succeeded in alienating him both from other species and from a more general ecological sense of interconnectedness and interdependence. It is, however, worth stating that none of this need detract from what the poems considered in this chapter, and in Chapter Four, offer. For though Hopkins never quite succeeded in developing a blueprint for "an ecological imaginary", the transition in his work from an ecocentric, phenomenological nature poetry to a technocentric, socially aware verse – in which we feel the environmental impacts of Victorian political economy in, simultaneously, the decimation of the photosynthetic process and the physical deterioration of its human subjects – does engender a small but significant body of work that conforms, and demonstrates poetry's applicability to, the other side of John Clark's social ecology of the imagination – the "concrete and experiential investigation of the existing imaginary".

Chapter 6

Bewitched by the "Spell of the Sensuous": A Disenchanted Ecological Imagination

In an early poem, 'Easter', written shortly before his conversion to Catholicism, Hopkins suggested that we should "Take a lesson from the ground" (14). In a St Bueno's poem, 'The Starlight Night', where the octave, typically, presents a rush of phenomenological impressions, he counselled the reader seeking truth to "Look at the stars! Look, look up at the skies!" (1) and "Down in the dim woods" (4) and "the grey lawns cold where gold, where quickgold lies" (5). The theology embedded in these passages, that in perceiving the beauty within nature we can perceive and 'understand' the truth of God, was the basis of the ecopoetry examined in Chapter Four. However, there was, in parts of his work, another contradictory impulse that separated the realm of earth from that of heaven.

That desire broadly corresponds to the way in which, as Lynn White Jr. famously argued, in "The Historical Roots of our Ecologic Crisis", Christianity can be seen to counteract ecological ideas by having de-sanctified nature and by being, in the words with which Roger Gottlieb describes White's argument, "the product of a transcendent, immaterial 'sky God'" (2006: 22). Hopkins articulated this as early as 1865 in the poem 'My prayers must meet a brazen heaven' where he makes a quite literal distinction – "My heaven is brass and iron my earth" (9). Thereafter, he would, from time to time, draw upon imagery in which natural phenomena were seen to point towards a primary reality existing beyond the earth, the tree groping towards heaven in the poem '(Ashboughs)', for example, or, here, in 'The earth and heaven so little known':

> The sky is blue, and the winds pull
> Their clouds with breathing edges white
> Beyond the world [...] (22-4)

Connected to this turning aside from the beauties of nature were related attempts by Hopkins to quell the senses by which he assimilated the natural world. This is evident in the 1866 poem "The Habit of Perfection", also composed prior to his conversion, where Hopkins "exhorts his sense-organs one by one to turn away from the world and delight instead in the pleasure of a holy life" (Vinge 1975: 174). A series of injunctions in the poem includes those senses, the eye and the ear, by which Hopkins would later understand and articulate an essentially ecological perspective on nature:

> Elected silence, sing to me
> And beat upon my whorlèd ear,
> Pipe me to pastures still and be
> The music that I care to hear.
>
> Shape nothing, lips; be lovely-dumb (1-5)

Corresponding to this self-willed rejection of the phenomenological stimulus there is, in the third stanza, a welcoming of darkness:

> Be shellèd, eyes, with double dark
> And find the uncreated light:
> This ruck and reel which you remark
> Coils, keeps, and teases simple sight. (9-12)

Hopkins explicitly rejects here a world of sensation because, he says, it "teases simple sight" and confuses ("coils") our understanding of the true reality governing earth. In denying the senses he deliberately shut himself off, therefore, from receptivity and connectedness with the natural world. While this strain in his thinking was overcome, for some considerable time, by the Scotism that legitimated Hopkins' love of nature, it did resurface later on when it increasingly cut across the ecological dimension to his ideas and poetry. This chapter begins by examining, in turn, the two key elements that prompted this: orthodox Catholic theology and an over-emphasis on the utilitarian dimension of Victorian post-Romanticism.

1. The factors undermining an ecological philosophy

Present from the beginning of the development of his ideas, the religious counter-emphasis to his ecological philosophy was articulated, most notably, in the undergraduate essay 'The Origin of Our Moral Ideas'.

Written, as we have seen, for Pater, aspects of the essay do reiterate the proto-ecological ontology Hopkins set out in his other undergraduate writing. It is here, for example, that he puts forward the principle of diverse unity, later realised in 'Pied Beauty', when he writes that "in art we strive to realise not only unity, permanence of law, likeness, but also, with it, difference, variety, contrast: it is rhyme we like, not echo, and not unison but harmony" (JP: 83). However, Hopkins also argued for "a point of divergence" between beauty and "moral excellence" (JP: 80) subordinating, in doing so, the Romantic equation of truth and beauty to a "prior" principle of morality. He argued that because the "logic" of the mind steers it towards both virtue and vice, relative standards have to be eschewed in a morality which should be governed not by "difference, variety, contrast" but with reference to unwavering standards: "in morality the highest consistency is the highest excellence". This was based, in turn, on adherence to law, or to an "ideal", in Hopkins' case that of the Catholic church: "the desire for unity, for an ideal, is the only definition which will satisfy the historical phenomena of morality"; therefore, "the desire of unity is prior to that of difference" (see JP: 83).

This strain ran through Hopkins' nature writing in certain poems that were characterised by a schism between effusive, ecological description of nature and stark redemptive theology. Observed, in Chapter Four, in relation to the sonnets composed at St Bueno's, the impact of this can be illustrated, most graphically, in probably the most famous of all those poems.

The Windhover:

To Christ our Lord

I caught this morning morning's minion, king-
    dom of daylight's dauphin, dapple-dawn-drawn Falcon, in
        his riding
    Of the rolling level underneath him steady air, and striding
High there, how he rung upon the rein of a wimpling wing
In his ecstasy! then off, off forth on swing,
    As a skate's heel sweeps smooth on a bow-bend: the hurl and
        gliding
    Rebuffed the big wind. My heart in hiding
Stirred for a bird,—the achieve of, the mastery of the thing!
Brute beauty and valour and act, oh, air, pride, plume, here
    Buckle! AND the fire that breaks from thee then, a billion
Times told lovelier, more dangerous, O my chevalier!

No wonder of it: shéer plód makes plough down sillion

> Shine, and blue-bleak embers, ah my dear,
>   Fall, gall themselves, and gash gold-vermilion.

Described by Hopkins as "the best thing I ever wrote" (RB 22/6/79: 85) 'The Windhover' illustrates the close attention to detail that characterises the best of his nature poetry. The octave exemplifies both a phenomenological poetic, "Stirred" by the act of perception, which reminds us of the integrity of species, and, at the same time, a scientific work that articulates a proto-ecological conception of dialectical nature. It is, as so often, sprung rhythm that enabled such co-existence. On the one hand, Hopkins conveys, rather than describes, both the bird's flight – "off, off forth on swing" – and its moments of stasis, halting the rhythm so as to create an impression of the falcon hovering on "the rolling level underneath him steady air". On the other, it is, specifically, an ecological sense of the bird's energy that is "caught" in these first six lines as Hopkins depicts the falcon working with and against the wind. The octave represents, therefore, in the fullest possible sense, an example of an ecopoetry that unifies eco- and technocentric perspectives.

Yet the ecology embodied within the poem co-exists with a contrary, theological dimension. Implied from the beginning, in the precise analogy in which the "minion" becomes "the symbol or analogue of Christ, Son of God, the supreme Chevalier" (Poems: 267), in the octave the two dimensions work to complement each other. However, in the transition from understanding to will, heralded by the sestet, the emphasis shifts, counteracting the ecological component of the poem. Two things, in particular, occur here. The first is that beauty, by virtue of its transience, is seen to have dangerous potential. Implied in the adjective "Brute beauty" this is developed further through the verb (as it is here) "Buckle!" Elisabeth Schneider has argued that "buckle" cannot possibly offer both its meanings – "fasten together" and "give way under pressure" – but it seems to me that in the context of the poem's ambiguous response to nature it does exactly that (1968: 147; 150-1). The "brute beauty, and valour and act", produces the spiritual energy of the "fire". This can either "fasten together", in the dedication of the beauty to God, thereby becoming "a billion/Times [...] lovelier", or it can "give way under pressure", becoming "dangerous" and corrupting and leading to moral decay.

The second shift is a differentiation between the human observer and the non-human creature that has been summarised, as follows, by Sulloway: "The sonnet celebrates things as they ARE in nature, or that windhover as he IS in nature, without any judgement of *him*. But this vision is deliberately paired with a far more trustworthy Ignatian vision of man as he ought to be" (1972: 108). Though (not insignificantly) this is delayed until the final tercet, the differentiation is, nonetheless, strikingly apparent. The bird, no longer "incarnated", becomes morally neutral, the phrase "No wonder of it" designed to indicate the inconsequentiality of beauty for its own sake. Correspondingly, Hopkins argues, human beauty, which is not neutral and is morally corruptible, needs to be quelled. Following, again, what he sees as the example of Christ, this is done by sacrificing beauty to duty, the poem turning to advocate an abnegation of beauty for toil: it is, Hopkins says, the "shéer plód [which] makes plough down sillion/Shine"; the "blue-bleak embers", *not* the fire, that hold eternal life (see Bernard Kelly, cited in Roberts 1987: 314; MacKenzie 1981: 84).

One can argue, following Claude Colleer Abbott, that in poems like 'The Windhover' "primarily seized by the beauty of earth", the theology acts almost as an "addendum". After all, its introduction in this case is delayed until the final three lines. Later on in his life Hopkins' religious position hardened, however, bringing him closer to an acceptance of orthodoxy. And as will now be discussed, it was the elements noted in connection with 'The Windhover' – distrust of beauty, the hierarchical separation of humanity from the rest of nature, the subjugation of beauty for duty – that increasingly began to prevail. The extent to which Hopkins' later poetry represented a drift away from a proto-ecological perspective can best be understood, however, by measuring his earlier work against both contemporary notions of "ecotheology" and the obstacles Christian orthodoxy presents to ecology.

One of the key writers to have conceptualised the grounds for a better form of relationship between ecology and Christianity is Sally McFague. Criticising the fact that metaphors of God as king, lord and master have meant that "still the most prevalent" paradigm for humanity's relationship with the Earth is one of dominion, or what she calls "the world as king's realm" (see 1993: 138-9), McFague has argued that this "monarchical model" should be replaced with an alternative "organic model" captured in her book title *The Body of God* (1993: 140). Gottlieb has helpfully summarised this view as the belief that "Nature is permeated by a Divine Spirit", the Holy Spirit, which, he notes, is frequently depicted in the Bible as a natural presence – a bird or fire or wind. He cites, in this connection, the Protestant theologian Mark Wallace's unmistakeably ecological statement that "All things are made of spirit *and* are part of the continuous biological flow patterns that constitute life on our planet" (see 2006: 36-7, 42). In suggesting, furthermore, that reverence for the natural world and knowledge of God might be extended by means of a more scientifically informed understanding of nature (2006: 38-9) Gottlieb indicates that the ecotheological notion of "the world as God's body" is broadly consistent with the scientifically informed ontology of nature established by Hopkins.

McFague points out, though, that in isolation the organic notion of "the world as God's body" is pantheistic. She suggests, therefore, that it needs to be conjoined with an "agential model" that posits a still transcendent God, an "energy empowering the whole universe" as, furthermore, an "actor and doer, creating and redeeming the world" (see 1993: 140, 150). Making the point that such a conjunction is necessary so as to align ecotheology with orthodox Christianity (without which it would be meaningless) – "The agential model preserves transcendence, while the organic model underscores immanence" (1993: 141) – the supporting notion, that, as an agent, God's "intentions and purposes are realized in history, *especially human history*" serves to highlight the "profound ethical" implication of ecotheology, that humanity is entrusted with a stewardship of the immanent world (see 1993: 139-40 (my italics)).

This emphasis, formulated in the context of a conscious response to environmental anxieties, has helped re-shape a Christian understanding of how we should act towards the "more-than-human" world. Informed both by a duty of care to the land and by cautionary warnings about the consequences should we fail in this (Gottlieb 2006: 25), other green theologians have addressed the precise nature of that duty by placing the example of Christ at the centre of the resultant reconfiguration of Christian doctrine. Noting the "connection between human sin and ecological disaster" which recurs throughout the Old Testament in stories such as the punishment of Cain or the flood (1990: 121-3), Sean McDonough suggests, for example, that this also operates in reverse in that the incarnation, "an outpouring of God's love for the world" (1990: 160) can remind us of his immanence. Accordingly, the Eucharist has been seen as a symbolical revelation and perpetual reminder both of God's presence in creation and of his/her act of creating and redeeming humanity. Lodge and Hamlin have argued, for instance, that "connection to God is mediated by connection to the nature of which we are a part" (2006: 293) an interpretation of the Eucharist that compels us, in turn, to bring salvation to the earth by working communally with it (see Cooper 1990: 164; McDonough 1990: 140-3). In this context ecotheology feeds into a further concept, "ecojustice", premised upon ideas such as sustainability, democracy, sufficiency, and "solidarity with all of life"

(Gottlieb 2006: 45). Seeking "to ensure that the creative powers of God's creation are not permanently impaired through agrochemicals, soil erosion, elimination of food plants" and, at the same time, to challenge the economic and political structures that keep people hungry (McDonough 1990: 142), this emphasis relates, correspondingly, to Hopkins' social philosophy. In other words, the work of Hopkins considered up until this point broadly conforms to the contemporary understanding of ecotheology.

This frankly marginal tradition of Christianity runs into difficulties, however, when encountering mainstream orthodox theology. To take one example, the retention of the idea of a "transcendent and infinitely powerful Deity" means continuing to accept, in line with White Jr's argument, "that in some sense, God is outside of time and space, and not a creature of earth" (Gottlieb 2006: 54). McFague concedes, similarly, that an emphasis on dominion remains staunchly at the heart of mainstream Christianity (1993: 138-9). The theological and metaphysical reasons for this, and its ecological consequences, have been examined by another writer, Philip Sherrard.

Sherrard argues that the establishment of a more sacramental theology would rest upon the "recognition of the actual imminence of nature in the divine" (1987: 111). Equating this, like Gottlieb, to the Holy Spirit, which he describes as an "ever-present, indwelling" principle "animating these energies [...] of every existing thing", Sherrard concludes, nevertheless, that it is because the doctrine of the Holy Spirit has never been fully affirmed in Latin Christendom that such an understanding is lacking (111). This, he suggests, is, in turn, a consequence of the gradual emergence in mainstream Christian theology of a philosophical separation between form and matter, and a distinction between grace and nature, which Sherrard traces back to St Augustine and St Thomas Aquinas, precisely the tradition affirmed in the theological training Hopkins received from the Jesuits.

According to St Augustine, though created beings are created as an "uttering of their ideas in the Logos of God" they remain themselves ontologically distinct from the deity. There is, as Sherrard puts it, no "ray of divine light within the creature". Philosophically this results in an understanding in which God, the uncreated being, represents a "formal and active principle" whereas matter, all of which is created by God, is characterised by a "principle of formlessness and potentiality" (1987). On this basis, all creatures, lacking grace unless God deems otherwise, tend towards "nothingness and non-existence" (or non-being). An entropic inevitability in the case of nonhuman species, this is merely a potential outcome for humans who are, like angels, recipients of grace. Humanity is possessed, furthermore, of an ability both to recognise its own state of grace and to conceive of itself, intellectually, as an idea in God's mind. This, according to St Augustine, comes either through divine light or "traces of the divine visible in creation". Such a paradigm, though premised firmly upon hierarchical separation, thereby retains some semblance of value for nonhuman existence in so far as it can lead humanity towards a recognition of God.

Aquinas initially extends the separation made by St Augustine by means of an argument that God remains essentially unknowable. He did believe, however, that a limited understanding of God's existence could be gleaned from the natural world (108-9). Aquinas effectively understood nature in a way akin, therefore, to Scotus' distinction between *theologia in se*, knowledge that can be known only by God, and *theologia nostra*, knowledge attainable by humans. He attempted, furthermore, to lessen the impact of St Augustine's theological paradigm by seeking "to substitute for any genuine relationship between the sphere of nature and the sphere of theology the principle of analogy". Aquinas saw nature as having an existence independent of God which was, Sherrard continues, "autonomous and independent within its own terms of reference, operating according to its own laws, premises and purposes", laws which would be "sufficient, in themselves, for understanding how nature works" (107-8). However, Sherrard indicates, while this view retained some degree of integrity for nonhuman nature, albeit confined to a separate, material realm, deeper problems arose in the light of subsequent theological developments that neglected to consider Aquinas' careful distinctions.

In the first place, the human ability to recognise grace, whether by divine light or through "visible [...] creation", was removed within much theological thinking as the result of an increasingly redemptive theology centred around the Fall. According to that, humankind was, subsequent to the Fall, reliant upon the medium of the Church in order to obtain such an understanding. Unless controlled and directed by the Church, love of beauty (and nature) became "linked with evil", a possibility which troubled Hopkins considerably (104-5). Furthermore, Sherrard asserts, later philosophers seemed to remember only that God "was no longer present as an imminent, ever-working principle of energy in the natural world" rather than the counter principle that nature had its own "laws, premises and purposes". Such an understanding came, therefore, to sanction a scientific and (ultimately) economic practice justified by the belief that humankind "may decipher, articulate and eventually dominate it [nature] as a self-sufficient entity by the use of his individual reason in disregard of, if not in contradiction to, the truths of the Christian revelation" (109). These two things represent, then, the ultimate outcome of a theology, established by Augustine and extended by Aquinas, premised upon the differentiation and separation of human from nonhuman nature.

By embracing the work of Scotus, Hopkins had initially eluded the theological orthodoxies that alienated Christian doctrine from a prototypical ecological philosophy and had developed, correspondingly, a position that broadly accorded with Sherrard's suggestion that what Christianity needs to recover is an earlier tradition of spirituality in which "in creating what is created, it is himself that God creates" and where "In creation He becomes His own image" (93-4). Unfortunately, while, as Jill Muller points out, Hopkins' Scotism "pointed him towards a reconciliation of Christianity and evolutionism that was unavailable to his more orthodox contemporaries", it also "coincided with a period of rigid Thomism in Jesuit theological studies and cost him his career as a theologian" (2003: 8). In July 1877 Hopkins, described by a contemporary, Joseph Rickaby, as "too Scotist for his examiners" (see White 1992: 284), failed an oral examination in dogmatic theology and was denied the opportunity, further to his ordination that September, to continue his studies into a fourth and final year. Mollified by this experience, he began to feel the pull of a more conventional theology and consequently moved towards a philosophical separation of humankind from the rest of nature that would divorce him from romanticism, Scotus, and what would now be called an ecotheological position.

The most critical period in terms of this development came when Hopkins returned to Roehampton in October 1881 to undertake a twelve month tertianship prior to making his final vows. This was designed, he explained to Dixon, "to enable us to recover that fervour which may have cooled through application to study and contact with the world" (RWD 12/10/81: 75). It was during the tertianship that Hopkins developed, in spiritual writings related to the Spiritual Exercises, a more orthodox position (see SD: 107). This was first signalled in retreat notes recorded a year earlier on the 'First Principle and Foundation', a preliminary to the main Exercises (see SD: 161).

*

2. Theological writing

At the start of these notes Hopkins comments that "I have been thinking about creation" and aspects do at first appear to re-affirm his belief in a sacramental, Scotist theology. Writing that God created the world "to give him praise, reverence, and service: *to give him glory*" (SD: 238), Hopkins posits, for example, that each phenomenon in nature is created, specifically, to represent a particular quality of God: "The birds sing to him, the thunder speaks of his terror, the lion is like his strength, the sea is like his greatness, the honey like his sweetness" (SD: 239). Hence, "This world [...] is word, expression, news of God [...] Its end, its purpose [...] to name and praise him" (SD: 129). Yet a gradual shift away from Scotism was, at the same time, prompting Hopkins towards an orthodox separation between humans and other creatures. These notes mark the point at which Hopkins discharged the nonhuman from his theological framework.

What emerges are two particular ideas both of which contradict a hitherto proto-ecological ontology: the development of a hierarchical chain-of-being theology; and the intensification of a redemptive focus on his own individuality. With regard to the first, Hopkins, consistent with a distinction between creatures who do and those who do not possess grace, suggests that, far from signifying an incorporation of instress or grace, the "praise" described above merely serves to express "news" of God. All creatures "give him glory, but they do not know what they do, they do not know him, they never can, they are brute things that only think of food or think of nothing. This then is poor praise, faint reverence, slight service, dull glory" (SD: 239). In contrast:

> AMIDST THEM ALL IS MAN, man and the angels [...] man can know God, *can mean to give him glory*. This then was why he was made, to give God glory and to mean to give it; to praise God freely, willingly to reverence him, gladly to serve him. Man was made to give, and mean to give, God glory.
> I WAS MADE FOR THIS, each one of us was made for this. (SD: 239)

This section of Hopkins' notes endorses, then, the hierarchical distinction between humankind and other species made in the 'First Principle and Foundation' itself:

> Man was created to praise, reverence and serve God our Lord, and by so doing to save his soul. And the other things on the face of the earth were created for man's sake and to help him in the carrying out of the end for which he was created. Hence it follows that man should make use of creatures so far as they help him to attain his end and

withdraw from them so far as they hinder him from so doing. For that, it is necessary to make ourselves indifferent in regard to all created things in so far as it is left to the choice of our free will and there is no prohibition. (SD: 122)

The second markedly new element in these notes was an increasing preoccupation with reflections on self and individuality. Comprising their bulk, these extend the sense of estrangement from the rest of nature. This is founded, in the first place, upon a formularisation of the ontological separation between God, humankind and other species. In the relevant passage Hopkins designates God, "unlike me or any other one thing", as "X", the "One" that brings all things together by virtue of being a "composition" of those things. X, Hopkins writes, can be "compounded with A, B, C, D etc" so as to "have its being in a series" (represented as "AX, BX, CX, DX etc"). Contrastingly, neither A and B nor AX and BX can be brought together into any equivalent series of unified being (SD: 127). What, then, Hopkins established out of this individualisation of phenomena is a principle of hierarchical unity which he advances in preference both to ecological (A compounded with B) and creationist (AX with BX) unity.

This equation formalises a fundamental change in Hopkins' view of other (i.e. nonhuman) phenomena in which he turned away from a sense of interconnectedness with, and interest in, other species: "when I compare my self, my being-myself, with anything else whatever, all things alike, all in the same degree, rebuff me with blank unlikeness" (SD: 122-3). This was motivated, in the first place, by a reaffirmation of the hierarchical differentiation between humanity and nonhuman species. He regards "human nature", for example, as "more highly pitched, selved, and distinctive than anything in the world" and suggests that it must have developed "not [...] by the working of common powers but only by one of finer or higher pitch and determination than itself and certainly than any that elsewhere we see" (SD: 122-3). The change is also premised, however, on a bleak conceptual rejection of interrelationship summarised when he writes that "searching nature I taste *self* but at one tankard, that of my own being" (SD: 123).

Hopkins increasingly dwelt, as a consequence of this, on his own individuality and a uniqueness, described, in a memorable image, as "more distinctive than the taste of ale or alum, more distinctive than the smell of walnutleaf or camphor" (SD: 123). Writing, also, that "Nothing else in nature comes near this unspeakable stress of pitch, distinctiveness, and selving, this selfbeing of my own [...] there is no resemblance" (SD: 123), Hopkins was, at this point, dwelling on a "selfbeing" that is "more important to myself than anything I see" (SD: 122). Encompassing, more generally, a change of emphasis "from the presence of God's design or inscape (that is, Christ) in inanimate nature to the working out of that design—by stress and instress—in the minds and wills of men" (SD: 109-10), this shift towards an increasingly redemptive theology was formalised and extended in further spiritual writings recorded during the tertianship itself, most notably his reflections 'On Personality, Grace and Free Will'.

In these notes Hopkins continued the development of an anti-materialist understanding of individuality by developing the concept of "pitch" – which, as noted in Chapter Three, refers to the degree of formal definition an individual being has achieved – away from its equation, elsewhere in his writing, to energy physics. Explaining the term in its specific relation to human being, Hopkins writes that "self is prior to its being", by which he means it pre-exists our earthly life, so that, as Devlin explains, "individuality is not constituted by the mere fact of existence; existence is the state in which an individual finds himself" (SD: 341). By such an understanding the soul can be seen as undertaking a journey. We are created in God's mind and given life as an opportunity to find our way back to him through the exercise of "free-will" (see SD: 338), a process of self-determination necessary to the fulfilment of our pitch.

This belief – that pitch, as Hopkins writes, only "truly comes into being when the self, the person, comes into being with the accession of nature" (SD: 151) – explains why, notwithstanding the pre-eminence afforded to individuality and freedom of the will, it is a Scotist notion (see Cross 1998: 1; Vos 2006: 7). Yet, as Hopkins refined the concept he increasingly modified a materialist dimension that was always retained by Scotus. Accepting physical being as essential to the fulfilment of pitch, Hopkins nevertheless reasserts its overriding, non-materialist dimension, in focusing, increasingly, on the process by which it is free-will that returns us back to God. Prior to the Fall, he explains, "man was created in grace, that is / in the elevated, the supernatural / state, and his will addressed towards God". This was a state of "creative grace" in which human beings, without sin, were automatically pre-destined to find their way back to God. After the Fall, however, there came about a "'medicinal', corrective, redeeming / grace" (see SD: 158) comprised of the affective and the elective will. The two, as we know, are connected by Scotus for whom, Devlin points out, it is "very clear that while the free choice [the act of election] is the nobler part of the will […] the affective act is the one that comes first, because without it there would be no guarantee that the whole soul was involved"; "in *praxis* (which is the projection of the whole soul towards God)", Devlin adds, "the first movement must be spontaneous" (SD: 347, 348). Hopkins, however, having already dismissed the capacity of nonhuman phenomena to "help me to understand" my "selfbeing", was now moving inexorably towards a prioritising of the elective over the affective will. We begin to see this in notes recorded directly before the two discussed so far, 'A Meditation on Hell' in which he insists that "the tendency in the soul towards an infinite object comes from the *arbitrium*", the elective will, which embodies the "freedom of play [...] given by the use of a nature, of human nature, with its faculties" (see SD: 138-9).

This change in emphasis appears to have been prompted by an interest in the French visionary Marie Lataste who Hopkins had discovered three years earlier. Lataste was told by Christ that "there are two movements in man: that of his being, created by God, towards existence, and that of his existing being towards God" (SD: 289). Resulting in the theory that there are two strains of existence, the creative and the redemptive, the latter defined as "the personal choice of free agents", Devlin suggests that Hopkins "leaped to the conclusion that redemption or sacrifice of some sort, so as to give an opportunity of love by free choice, would have been necessary even had there been no sin" (SD: 110). This is a view expounded in the notes 'On Personality, Grace and Free Will' in which Hopkins "exaggerated", Devlin argues, "Scotus's distinction between nature and individuality" (SD: 120) by placing too much emphasis on the anti-natural will. Disregarding the affective will as largely irrelevant and concluding, instead, that the act of election was the permanent, most fundamental component of human being, this is captured most clearly, in these notes, in the insistence that "There must be something which shall be truly the creature's in the work of corresponding with grace: this is the *arbitrium*, the verdict on God's side, the saying Yes" (SD: 154).

The pre-eminence given to the elective will as the central, perhaps only, constituent of pitch, brought to its logical conclusion Hopkins' movement away from a conception of the will as affected by beauty and other creatures. It replaced it with precisely the separation of mind and matter that has been seen as having obstructed the development of a Christian ecotheology. Foregrounding, from this point on, a largely redemptive theology, one notable symptom of this was to enhance the prioritisation of morality over beauty first signalled in 'The Origin of Our Moral Ideas'.

In the notes 'On Personality, Grace and Free Will', the argument is made, in the first place, by means of an analogy with the points of a compass.

> The will is surrounded by the objects of desire as the needle by the points of the compass [...] It has in fact, more or less, in its affections a tendency or magnetism towards every object and the *arbitrium*, the elective will, decides which: this is the needle proper. (SD: 157)

Hopkins then suggests that since the Fall humanity has required a "corrective", "purifying" or "mortifying" grace that operates through the example of Christ or, as it is in practice, the teachings of the Catholic Church (SD: 157-8). Taken together, a heightened emphasis on morality and a keener sensitivity to the teachings and practice of the Church inform the second key element in these notes, Hopkins' extension of the incorporeal aspect of "pitch" by means of a primarily redemptive theology.

Hopkins believed that the purpose of free-will was to give the individual an opportunity, by their own actions, to conform to the "personality" (pitch) envisaged for them. He answers the question of what, precisely, is meant by "free-will" when he posits it as a quality of "simple positiveness [...] with precision expressed by the English *do*" (SD: 151). "Pitch" is fulfilled by doing and is, on this basis, a dynamic principle, a series of actions or decisions by which the person either does or does not ascend to the personality God has intended for them (see SD: 339). As Hopkins puts this, "*the doing* be [...] and the thread or chain of such pitches or 'doing-be''s [...] is self, personality" (SD: 151). In this equation he formalises, therefore, a theological preference for duty over beauty – through duty we can "give God glory and mean to give it" – a principle which, prior to this, had been only half, and half-heartedly, articulated in 'The Windhover'.

The separation between humanity and other species, captured conclusively in the operation of the elective will, is equivalent to the conservative prognosis arrived at in Hopkins' social and political thinking. Sharing the same theological premise, that of a 'Fall' into "God's second kingdom", they represent, together, a retreat into a (premodern) medieval chain-of-being that has been seen, subsequently, as incompatible with an ecological philosophy which, whether understood scientifically or socially, is borne out of modernity (see Pepper 1996: 180). The specific ways in which this shift towards a hierarchical and redemptive theology undermined the ecological character of Hopkins' nature writing will be examined shortly. Before this, however, it needs also to be noted that the second of these developments, the movement towards an increasingly redemptive theology, had another source – the overly utilitarian nature of Victorian post-Romanticism.

Devlin states that while Hopkins "exaggerated Scotus's distinction between nature and individuality" (SD: 120), by disregarding the "affective will", he also ignored similar teachings by more orthodox figures, including St Augustine and St Ignatius, that moral choice has to be stimulated by desire, as seen in the passage from John's gospel famously commented on by St Augustine – "Nobody can come to me without being *attracted* by the Father who sent me" (John 6:44). He took, in other words, the redemptive element in Christianity further even than it is normally taken. Suggesting, then, that "it is certain that Hopkins's stress on a naked, anti-natural, non-affective will does not come from Scotus or from St Ignatius", Devlin attributes this instead to Hopkins' cultural context, and, specifically, the severity of "religious ideals" which exaggerated the contrast in Jesuitism between "nature and grace" particularly with regard to a "dichotomy between inclination and duty" (SD: 120). Sulloway appears to agree, for she suggests that Hopkins' moralistic, utilitarian obligation to repudiate beauty derived not so much from Catholicism as from Ruskin's adaptation of Christian ethics. Later to declare that "all great art is praise", Ruskin had commended, in *Modern Painters* III, the artist that "disdains" art, nature, and beauty for "wisdom of purpose" (1972: 104-5). This was a principle he would refer to, in *The Seven Lamps of Architecture*, as the "Levitical Sacrifice", defined by Ruskin as "self-denial for the sake of self-discipline […] acted upon in the abandonment of things loved or desired" and, additionally, as "the desire to honour or please some one else by the costliness of the sacrifice" (1903-12 (8): 31). Quoting the Book of John – "Neither will I offer unto the Lord my God of that which doth cost me nothing" – Ruskin regarded the Levitical Sacrifice as the most "acceptable condition in all human offerings" to God (1903-12 (8): 31).

Hopkins, in effect, incorporated that idea into his theology by means of reference to 'The Great Sacrifice' of Christ. He tells his parishioners in Oxford that "Religion is the highest of the moral virtues and sacrifice the highest act of religion" (SD: 14) and afterwards writes, in "further notes" on the 'First Principle and Foundation', that "man, should after its own manner give God being in return for the being he has given it […] This is done by the great sacrifice. To contribute then to that sacrifice is the end for which man was made" (SD: 129). For all then that his post-

Romanticism prompted Hopkins towards an ecological perspective, it also, eventually, undermined this. For in the process of carrying out the sacrifice advocated by Ruskin, Hopkins, in his utilitarian, pragmatic, dutiful vocation almost destroyed his love for nature by becoming fundamentally alienated from other species.

To conclude, the three ways, specifically, in which this combination of orthodox theology and excessive Victorian utilitarianism served to undermine a hitherto ecological ontology were the adoption of a hierarchical chain-of-being ontology that prioritised human over nonhuman; and a sacrificing of beauty, first to morality (severing the Romantic link between truth and beauty); and then to duty. These were, inevitably, worked through in his poetry as we see if we take each in turn.

3. Unsustainable poetry

An example of the first can be seen in 1882's 'Ribblesdale' in which Hopkins constructed a version of humanity's relationship to the rest of nature premised not on the modern paradigm of interdependent, dialectical energy exchange, but on the pre-modern notion of a chain-of-being.

> EARTH, sweet Earth, sweet landscape, with leavès throng
> And louchèd low grass, heaven that dost appeal
> To, with no tongue to plead, no heart to feel;
> Thou canst but only be, but dost that long—
>
> Thou canst but be, but that thou well dost; strong
> Thy plea with him who dealt, nay does now deal,
> Thy lovely dale down thus and thus bids reel
> Thy river, and o'er gives all to rack or wrong.
>
> And what is Earth's eye, tongue, or heart else, where
> Else, but in dear and dogged man?—Ah, the heir
> To his own selfbent so bound, so tied to his turn,
>
> To thriftless reave both our rich round world bare
> And none reck of world after, this bids wear
> Earth brows of such care, care and dear concern.

Hopkins' previous work was founded upon the phenomenological principle that each creature, rather than merely passing on "word, expression, news of God", has "tongue to fling out broad its name". Here, reflecting the change in his ideas, Hopkins contrasts humankind – "Earth's eye, tongue, heart" – to a nature that has "no tongue" and requires humanity to speak for it. While exhibiting, in this, one ecotheological notion, that of humanity as steward acting on behalf of an "agential" God, Hopkins had, nevertheless, lost the complementary "organic model" of God's immanence within the "continuous biological flow patterns that constitute life on our planet".

What occurs, as a result, is a corresponding loss of sacramental energy. An energetic verb "Throng" is employed statically, for example, as an adjective ("dense", "thick") while sprung rhythm – the mode which always signified in his work the presence of an ecological perspective – is jettisoned. Accordingly, though the poem retains some of the sense of the earlier poems, and the journal, of God's energy structuring nature – the grass "louchèd low" is bent back while "reel" (line 7) suggests a pattern made by wavelets on the river (see Poems: 282) – the employment of a more conventional rhythmic form reduces the landscape to an abstract, pastoral, designation indicated, as at the end of 'Binsey Poplars', by the weak adjective "sweet". "The dynamic unanswerable force" of 'God's Grandeur', has, in the words of John Robinson, "declined into the ineffectual maternalism of 'Ribblesdale'" (1978: 99).

The sestet changes direction and considers the fact that humanity is responsible for having created all this "rack or wrong". Hopkins develops the point, in part, after the em dash where the imagery employed produces a critique as powerful as that of any of his other poems: "reave" offers, for example, an impressive aural embodiment of the stripping or despoliation of the land (see Poems: 282); the blunt description of a human subject "selfbent so bound, so tied to his turn" leads, correspondingly, to Hopkins signalling the potential consequence of these "thriftless" social values, "none reck of world after" a reference to the afterlife which might also refer, in this context, to the natural resources of future generations (Martin 1991: 348-9). Yet having attributed to humanity a responsibility analogous to the philosophy of stewardship the poem also rests, nevertheless, on an anthropocentric assumption that the remainder of the ecosystem is dependent upon its so-called dominant species, a significant retraction from the Gaian critique of 'God's Grandeur'. For where, in that poem, "nature", despite all Victorian Britain's industrial activity, "is never spent", the consequences rebounding instead on humanity, here we are awarded a power to harm a largely defenceless Earth, in the ability to render "our rich round world bare". What we ultimately find in this poem is, then, the substitution of one paradigm for another. A conventional rhythm embodying hierarchical theology and a stewardship philosophy has replaced the sprung rhythm,

sacramental theology and anticipation of Gaia found elsewhere in
Hopkins' writing. The further implications of this shift in his theology
demonstrate, even more, the retraction from an ecological perspective
that occurred in his work.

Hopkins' adoption of a hierarchical theology was premised, as we
have seen, on a revised belief in the ontological insignificance of other,
nonhuman species which he regarded as lacking grace. Increasingly
Hopkins saw the nonhuman as characterised by transience and inevitable
dissolution. This view took two specific forms in his poetry: a belief in
the categorical meaninglessness of nonhuman species which made them
ontologically irrelevant to humankind; and the idea that the beauty of
'nature' was, by virtue of that meaninglessness, dangerous and linked to
evil.

Both were, as it happens, an occasional feature of Hopkins' early pre-
conversion verse which exhibited the post-Romantic preoccupation with
seasonal change and the passing of time that Wendell Stacy Johnson has
attributed to anxieties engendered by evolutionary theory and the
'disappearance of God' (1968: 99). There is, for example, an ambivalence
and "sweet sadness" about summer's beauty in 'A Vision of the Mermaids' (117) which emanated from an awareness of its impending
dissolution and that recurred in poems such as 'The Summer Malison'
and 1864's, 'Now I am minded', "a song to the decaying year". In this
later example Hopkins described a chestnut bud breaking "So late there is
no force in sap or blood" and "The fruit on the wall/[that] Loose on the
stem has done its summering" (11-13). Correspondingly, in 1863's
'Spring and Death' he had personified autumn as Lucifer marking
flowers in spring "With a subtle web of black" (19-20). Creative energy
leads not here to renewal, as would be the case from a purely ecological
perspective, but to a decay and degenerative flux that prefaces warnings
about the Fall. Such ideas, while not eradicated, were certainly marginalised in the light of a conversion to Catholicism which enabled Hopkins,
via Scotus, to channel his attraction to beauty to God. However, they
begin to re-appear in his later work once the link between the transience
of nature and evil had been established in the tertianship notes where, for
example, Hopkins wrote of the devil as having introduced "the law of
decay and consumption in inanimate nature, death in the vegetable and
animal world, moral death and original sin in the world of man" (SD:
199).

This contrast between the moral and religious imperatives that dictate
or govern human action and a categorically meaningless nonhuman

nature derives, in part, from what Devlin describes as "one of Scotus's less beneficent teachings—upon 'indifferent acts'", which essentially means acts not sinful in themselves but lacking any positive, God (or Church)-given sanction (SD: 216). Referring, then, to actions, as described by Hopkins, that are "positively good but quantitatively nothing" (SD: 168) this mode of thinking is most evident in the 1888 poem 'That Nature is a Heraclitean Fire and of the comfort of the Resurrection', a poem in which Hopkins returned both to sprung rhythm and, initially at least, in the depiction of clouds in a high wind, an essentially ecological understanding of nature structured by energy exchange:

> Cloud-puffball, torn tufts, tossed pillows flaunt forth, then
>   chevy on an air-
> built thoroughfare: heaven-roysterers, in gay gangs | they
>   throng; they glitter in marches.
> Down roughcast, down dazzling whitewash, | wherever an
>   elm arches,
> Shivelights and shadowtackle in long | lashes lace, lance, and
>   pair.
> Delightfully the bright wind boisterous | ropes, wrestles, beats
>   earth bare
> Of yestertempest's creases; | in pool and rutpeel parches
> Squandering ooze to squeezed | dough, crust, dust; stanches,
>   starches
> Squadroned masks and manmarks | treadmire toil there
> Footfretted in it. Million-fuelèd, | nature's bonfire burns on. (1-9)

In the passage immediately following the opening lines, Hopkins expands the ecological description. The reference to "beats earth bare" (5) depicts a process of energy redistribution in which the wind first sponges water from the ground, forming "Squandering ooze", before, in conjunction with the sun's own transforming energy, drying this back into earth, the "dough, crust, dust" of line 7 (see Poems: 294; Banfield 2007: 184). He even integrates humanity into this landscape, the reference to "manmarks" on the wet mud implying that alteration to the land extends to encompass human activity. And he asserts, finally, both that "nature's bonfire burns on" (9) and an alternative possibility, dissolution, which, signalled in the succession of stressed syllables that comes three lines below – "Both are in an unfa-thomable, all is in an enormous dark" (12) – offers, in the sheer difficulty of reading the line out loud, a particularly effective embodiment of entropy. Hopkins infers, that is, both the human condition of embeddedness in nature and, more specifically, a Gaian understanding that, if we don't attend to this, nature will carry on without us. Yet rather than pursue the ecological implications of these lines, the poem switches to a theological separation between nature's inevitable decay and a potential human immortality.

Larry Rasmussen has suggested that sacramentalist theology represents a celebration of flux (2006: 272). By inference, therefore, Hopkins' turn towards a redemptive theology would be liable to result in a rejection of this and of the nonhuman species celebrated in his earlier nature poetry. That is, indeed, how he concludes this poem after he has steadied the flux, as Banfield notes, by means of the injunction, "Enough!" (16) (see 2007: 184). For, having, in fact, described nonhuman phenomena, given such deep ecological integrity in the St Bueno's poems, as showy, frivolous or superficial – in the image of cloud formations that "flaunt forth", "chevy", and "glitter" – here we find that her "bonniest, dearest […] clearest-selvèd spark/Man" (10-11) is, in theory, exempt from dissolution, able, alone, in the 'Resurrection/A heart's clarion!', to look towards (and become) Christ.

> In a flash, at a trumpet crash,
> I am all at once what Christ is, | since he was what I am, and
> This Jack, joke, poor potsherd | patch, matchwood, immortal
>   diamond,
>   Is immortal diamond. (21-4)

In the act of election, Hopkins is saying, the human subject who follows Christ will circumvent dissolution and achieve everlasting life, becoming, in the memorable phrase that closes the poem, an "immortal diamond".

'That Nature is a Heraclitean Fire' is the culmination of several other poems in which Hopkins also renounced earthly beauty for heavenly salvation. This is, for example, symbolised through harvest in a fragment written after he had moved to Ireland in 1884 – "tell Summer No,/Bid joy back, have at the harvest, keep Hope pale" ('Strike, churl; hurl, cheerless wind', 3-4). Another, better known example is 'Spring and Fall'. Here the narrative, beginning with the lines quoted at the start of this book

> Márgarét, áre you gríeving
> Over Goldengrove unleaving? (1-2)

contrasts a child weeping for the leaves falling in autumn with a mature, adult realisation that nature's inexorable decay is shared, in mortal terms, by humanity:

> Sórrow's springs áre the same […]

> It ís the blight man was born for,
> It is Margaret you mourn for. (11; 14-15)

Notwithstanding this apparent acceptance of the human physical condition, Hopkins returned to the idea that salvation rests in the act of election in a two-part dramatic poem, 'The Leaden Echo and The Golden Echo' (1958: 59), described by Heuser as a "Christian answer" to Pater.

In the first, 'Leaden Echo', section of the poem, Hopkins searches for some "bow or brooch or braid or brace, láce,/latch or catch or key to keep/Back beauty [...] from vanishing away" (1-2) but concludes, bluntly, "there's none" (5). In the 'Golden Echo' section, however, he suggests that a beauty "too apt [...] to fleet" (11) can be "fastened", can achieve an "everlastingness" (12-13), if we opt, "long before death", to "deliver" it to God ("beauty's giver" (19)). If we do so we will find that "not a hair is, not an eyelash, not the least lash lost" (20).

Elaborating on this, Hopkins, who had explained to Bridges, in connection with this poem, that (romantic) "words like *charm* and *enchantment* will not do" to describe his understanding of beauty (RB 26/11/82: 162), concludes by suggesting that beauty is located not on the earth, or "within seeing of the sun". Repeating, here, the separation noted at the start of this chapter, the reader is, instead, petitioned to follow:

> Where kept? Do but tell us where kept, where.—
> Yonder.—What high as that! We follow, now we follow.— [...]
>
> Yonder. (30-2)

If this seals the need to turn away from nature, and in turn from an ecological sense of interrelationship, a secondary implication of the poem was that any continued attachment to it would, at best, amount to a neglect of our spiritual duties and at worst be sinful. Hopkins briefly indicates this in "The Golden Echo" when he suggests that if we continue to dwell on earth, in nature's beauty, which is, he writes, "dearly and dangerously sweet" (9) – and do not "Give beauty [...] back to God" (19) – then consequences may follow, as captured in the injunction that we should "sign", "seal" and "deliver it [beauty], early now, long before death" (16; 18). This strand in his writing, which came to the forefront as Hopkins increasingly began to reflect upon his individuality and redemption, was further enhanced by anxieties about beauty which had always threatened to undermine the ecological dimension to his ideas.

Hopkins' fear was of becoming bewitched by the "spell of the sensuous". Such ideas had brought him to one crisis point at Oxford where Hopkins became infatuated by Digby Dolben, a friend of Bridges', whom he met just once in February 1865. Notwithstanding the brevity of their association, this meeting appears to have been "closely bound up with" Hopkins' conversion in that it brought about, House conjectures, "a religious crisis which led to his first confession and the beginning of the daily spiritual notes" (Poems: 249-50). While, thereafter, religious morality, and in particular the structure afforded by rigorous Jesuit discipline, enabled Hopkins to stabilise, possibly even transcend, the latent homosexual tendencies which his attraction to beauty appeared to enflame – one might note here, for example, the word association (quoted earlier) in the journal between trees and "bones sleeved in flesh [and] Juices of the sunrise" – such tendencies re-emerge later where they are seemingly exacerbated by Hopkins having imposed a theological foundation on his suspicion of beauty.

This newly theologised sanction against beauty was conceptualised, as indicated above, in relation to the Devil. In further tertianship notes, 'Creation and Redemption: The Great Sacrifice', Hopkins expressed a belief that when Satan saw the "humiliation" for Christ and all creatures that would be involved in the sacrifice to God in the "first kingdom" he "rebelled" and "flung himself direct on beatitude, to seize it of his own right or merit" (SD: 197-8); having done this he "resolved that [...] man should be brought to fall" (SD: 63). This, as Hopkins explained to no doubt mystified parishioners in Liverpool, was what brought about the end of the first commonwealth. The agent for humanity's fall was, in other words, beauty something Hopkins connected, conventionally enough, to Eve but articulated, less conventionally, in somewhat eroticised terms:

> When some child, one of Eve's poor daughters, stands by a peachtree, eyeing the blush of colour on the fruit, fingering the velvet bloom upon it, breathing the rich smell, and in imagination tasting the sweet juice, the nearness, the mere neighbourhood is enough to undo her, she looks and is tempted, she touches and is tempted more, she takes and tastes. (SD: 65)

That such tendencies persisted, and continued to undermine Hopkins' attraction to nature, can be demonstrated with reference to a late, 1888 poem 'Epithalamion' (1991: 392). Here, again, description of natural profusion ("leafwhelmed" (2)) located in a "Southern dean or Lancashire clough or Devon cleave" (4) briefly returns us to a poetry "echoing-of-earth" (45) and premised upon the ecological and sacramental principle of energy sculpting the landscape. Hopkins describes, for example, "a gluegold-brown/ Marbled river" which

> boisterously beautiful, between
> Roots and rocks is danced and dandled, all in froth and water-
> blowballs, down. (6-7);

and, later, a "basin" (Poems: 317) of rock into which

> [...] the water warbles over [...] filleted | with glassy grassy
> quicksilvery shivès and shoots
> And with heavenfallen freshness down from moorland still
> brims,
> Dark or daylight on and on. (38-40)

However, with the overstated language of a phrase like "water blowballs" betraying a drift away from more precise ecological description, such passages ultimately give way to the poem's central narrative, of a "listless stranger" (14) stimulated into "sudden zest" (20) when he observes some boys bathing. Faced with this apparent "tendency or magnetism" towards the male form, Hopkins retreated from such a scenario, including the hitherto ecological depiction, and leaves the poem trailing off, unfinished.

With an always problematic attraction to beauty heightened by his amended theological position, Hopkins increasingly felt inclined to subjugate an affective relationship to beauty to the moral demands of the elective will. In the poem 'To what serves Mortal Beauty?' he arbitrates between his earlier belief in a romantic beauty that "keeps warm men's wits to the things that are: what good means" (2-3) and the moralistic understanding that beauty is "dangerous" (1). Hopkins suggests here, as a means of evading beauty's double-edged quality, a distinction between a "glance" which acknowledges beauty but moves on and a "gaze" (3-4) which dwells on beauty and which even when it seeks to understand it, as in his journal, runs the risk of being corrupted. He concludes, at the end of the poem, that only if "Home", the core of our being, is situated "at heart" – i.e. in one's internal moral "compass" – can we truly "own [...] heaven's sweet gift":

> What do then? how meet beauty | Merely meet it; own
> Home at heart, heaven's sweet gift; | then leave, let that alone. (12-13)

Other poems, though also exhibiting a continued preoccupation with beauty, are more closely tied to the last of the three factors that were to alienate Hopkins from an ecological ontology, the operation of a redemptive theology. The two features specifically identified in the tertianship notes as characteristic of a stress on the elective will – the replacement of beauty with a moral "compass" and the subsequent direction offered by that compass, in the emphasis on "doing" – are signalled in an 1879 poem, '(On a Piece of Music)', when Hopkins makes what Gardner describes as an "important distinction between formal beauty or 'the good' on the one hand, and moral beauty, or 'the right', on the other" (see 1987: 337).

> For good grows wild and wide,
> Has shades, is nowhere none;
> But right must seek a side
> And choose for chieftain one. (25-8)

Articulating, even extending, his retraction from beauty, Hopkins ends the poem by dismissing several of the things which had once captivated him: "wild" nature (in this instance the honey created by bees), music, architecture, and (in the allusion to optics noted in Chapter Five) the insights of science which in his earlier, sacramental phase had opened Hopkins' eyes to the creative operation of God.

> Therefore this masterhood,
> This piece of perfect song,
> This fault-not-found-with good
> Is neither right nor wrong
>
> No more than red and blue,
> No more than Re and Mi,
> Or sweet the golden glue
> That's built for by the bee.
>
> [Who built these walls made known
> The music of his mind,
> Yet here he has but shewn
> His ruder-rounded rind.
> His brightest blooms lie there unblown,
> His sweetest nectar lies behind.] (29-42)

The final, most Victorian element, of this newly redemptive theology, the emphasis on "doing" implied in the statement that "right must seek a side", is ultimately articulated, also in 1879, when Hopkins re-conceptualises the idea of beauty itself.

Hopkins formulated a notion of three levels of beauty in a letter to Bridges and a sermon delivered at Bedford Leigh. Each of these levels, the first of which was "beauty of the body", was epitomised through Christ (see RB 22/10/79: 95-6; SD: 34-8). Hopkins describes Christ as possessed of "perfect" health and as having all the attributes "that can make man lovely and loveable". He sees him, in more detail, as "moderately tall, well built and tender in frame, his features straight and beautiful"; of "his bearing", he writes, "how majestic, how strong and yet how lovely and lissome in his limbs, in his look how earnest, grave but kind". Yet, Hopkins adds tellingly, while "no one can admire beauty of the body more than I can do [...] this kind of beauty is dangerous". He goes on, then, to elaborate a second level, beauty of the mind. Telling his parishioners that Christ "was the greatest genius that ever lived", Hopkins suggests that no stories, parables, or proverbs compare with those of Christ. For instance, "Nowhere in literature is there anything to match the Sermon on the Mount" while an even "greater proof of his genius and wisdom" can be found in the "ranks and constitution [...] rites and sacraments" of the Catholic church. Ultimately, however, "far higher than beauty of the body, higher than genius and wisdom the beauty of the mind, comes the beauty of his character, his character as man". Seeking to explain this to Bridges, Hopkins identifies qualities "of sincerity or earnestness, of manliness, of tenderness, of humour, melancholy, human feeling" (RB 22/10/79: 96); in the sermon, similarly, he attributes to Christ qualities such as compassion for humanity and a sense of justice comprised of both tenderness and sternness (SD: 37-8) before going on explicitly to relate "beauty of character" to the doctrine of the Sacred Heart. He believes, as he puts it in a later sermon, that "the heart is of all members of the body the one which most strongly [...] expresses [...] what goes on within the soul" (SD: 103). This equation of "beauty of character" to the Sacred Heart was the culmination of a process in which Hopkins redefined beauty into a moral rather than aesthetic quality. It was enacted in poetic terms in the paradigm Hopkins called the "handsome heart".

What occurred in some later poems that articulated this concept was a shift in the order of priority from one aesthetic concept, the Ruskinian aesthetic of the eye – which, for Hopkins, had always been central to registering and understanding the economy of nature – to another, the (moral/ Catholic) notion of "the handsome heart". Where, in earlier, sacramental poems, notably 'Hurrahing in Harvest', the eye and heart had existed in harmonious interrelationship – the eye registering nature, the heart affirming God the creator – in later works, reflective of the subsumption of the affective by the elective will, the motif of the heart began to dominate. We see this, for example, in 'On the Portrait of Two Beautiful Young People' where the eye, by which one can only 'understand' nature, is substituted by the "heart's eye" (1) which can "stead" us in the 'truth' of Christ. Subsequent significant strands of this later, post-ordination poetry include a handful of sentimental, even mawkish, poems that articulate a "beauty of character", manners, and sibling love, as in 'Brothers', moralistic poems such as the one entitled 'The Handsome Heart', which depicts a "wild and self-instressed" Christian nature that, of far greater significance than a "handsome face" (9), always returns, like a carrier pigeon, to "its own fine function", and, implied in this last quotation, poems which encapsulate the sense of responsibility or duty that comes with an adherence to the elective will. These include 'The Bugler's First Communion' and a late poem 'St. Alphonsus Rodriguez' written to honour the canonisation of a Jesuit laybrother "who for forty years acted as hall-porter to the College of Palma in Majorca" (RB 3/10/88: 292-3).

In subjugating beauty to morality and by then redefining it into the notion of a "handsome heart" characterised by function and duty, Hopkins ruptured the conventional Romantic equation between truth and beauty. The irony was that at the very point at which he theorised this ascetic emphasis on duty he was becoming increasingly disillusioned with his vocation. This was prompted, it would seem, by frequent, insensitive deployment by the Jesuits and compounded by the trauma and weariness of his time spent in the Victorian industrial city. Yet it actually worsened with his dual appointment in 1884 as Professor of Greek at University College, Dublin and Fellow in Classics at the Royal University of Ireland. For there those feelings intensified into a full blown spiritual crisis, a combination of the "drudgery" of marking hundreds of examination papers and of working in institutions sympathetic to and implicated in Irish Home Rule to which the politically conservative and patriotically English Hopkins, though he could see its logic, was deeply antipathetic (FL (Mother) 2/3/87: 181).

The degree and intensity of this disillusionment is documented in retreat notes recorded at Tullabeg, the novitiate of the Irish Jesuit province, on New Year's Day in 1889. Taking stock of his vocation and "Deeply concerned", Gardner and MacKenzie write, "with his own personal and vocational 'imitation of Christ'" (Poems: 268), Hopkins tested himself against unachievable standards, and fell short, which culminated in a substantial degree of self-accusation:

I do not feel then that outwardly I do much good [...] Five wasted years almost have passed in Ireland. I am ashamed of the little I have done, of my waste of time, although my helplessness and weakness is such that I could scarcely do otherwise.

I say to myself that I am only too willing to do God's work and help on the knowledge of the Incarnation. But this is not really true: I am not willing enough for the piece of work assigned me. (SD: 263; see also SD: 261-2; FL (Mother) 5/7/88: 184-5)

A consequence of Hopkins' disillusionment might well have been, and to a degree was, a questioning of his vocation. Another outcome, however, was that "indifference" to other species turned into resentment, a resentment which almost brought about the total eradication of his ecological vision. One poem that demonstrates this is 'Thou art indeed just, Lord'. Written two months after the retreat at Tullabeg, Hopkins brutally and jealously juxtaposed his perception of professional failure with nature's unending productivity.

4. Disenchantment

> Thou art indeed just, Lord, if I contend
> With thee; but, sir, so what I plead is just.
> Why do sinners' ways prosper? and why must
> Disappointment all I endeavour end?
>
> Wert thou my enemy, O thou my friend,
> How wouldst thou worse, I wonder, than thou dost
> Defeat, thwart me? Oh, the sots and thralls of lust
> Do in spare hours more thrive than I that spend,
>
> Sir, life upon thy cause. See, banks and brakes
> Now, leavèd how thick! lacèd they are again
> With fretty chervil, look, and fresh wind shakes
>
> Them; birds build—but not I build; no, but strain,
> Time's eunuch, and not breed one work that wakes.
> Mine, O thou lord of life, send my roots rain.

A somewhat disheartening echo of 'The Alchemist in the City', 'Thou art indeed just, Lord' records Hopkins' professional "disappointment", "defeat", and "thwart[ed]" aspirations in the context of what had been, at this point, twenty years of "endeavour". It draws significantly (as we see later) on his earlier nature writing in that the chervil "lacèd" bank by which Hopkins exemplifies profusion quite possibly relates back to a journal entry from 1868: "Fine and summer-like [...] Chervil and wood-sorrel out" (JP 15/3/68: 162). However, in the context of his growing disenchantment Hopkins turns this, in the sentence that bridges octave and sestet, into a striking parallel between profusion and the prospering of "sin" and "lust" that articulates the correspondence between categorical 'indifference' and evil foregrounded in his writing on Lucifer. This serves, in so doing, to corroborate the near total rejection of a sacramental theology while the other key natural analogy in the poem, with the activity of birds, further underlines the reversal of his previous correlation between theology and ecology. For where birds, taking into account the dual meaning of instress, had once signified grace and energy, here there is only a sense of resentment articulated in the complaint that "birds build—but not I build; no". The poem appears then to bring to a bleak conclusion the gradual eradication of inscape from Hopkins' ontological framework.

A further example of how these shifts in his thinking impacted on what remained of Hopkins' nature poetry can be seen in 'Spelt from Sibyl's Leaves', a poem begun in 1884.

> EARNEST, earthless, equal, attuneable, | vaulty, voluminous
> . . . stupendous
> Evening strains to be tíme's vást, | womb-of-all, home-of-all,
> hearse-of-all-night.
> Her fond yellow hornlight wound to the west, | her wild
> hollow hoarlight hung to the height
> Waste; her earliest stars, earlstars, | stárs principal, overbend
> us,
> Fíre-féaturing heaven. For earth | her being has unbound; her
> dapple is at end, as-
> tray or aswarm, all throughther, in throngs; | self in self
> steepèd and páshed—qúite
> Disremembering, dísmémbering | áll now. Heart, you round
> me right
> With: Óur évening is over us; óur night | whélms, whélms,
> ánd will end us.
> Only the beakleaved boughs dragonish | damask the tool-
> smooth bleak light; black
> Ever so black on it. Óur tale, O óur oracle! | Lét life, wáned
> ah lét life wind
> Off hér once skéined stained véined varíety | upon, áll on twó
> spools; párt, pen, páck

Now her áll in twó flocks, twó folds—black, white; | right,
    wrong; reckon but, reck but, mind
But thése two; wáre of a wórld where bút these | twó tell, each
    off the óther; of a rack
Where, selfwrung, selfstrung, sheathe- and shelterless, | thóughts
    agaínst thoughts ín groans grínd.

The description of evening in the opening lines serves as a metaphor for entropic decline ("Waste") in which "dapple", the biodiversity celebrated in 'Pied Beauty', has dissipated, as represented in the image "aswarm" (6). Hitherto sharply defined, the closely studied individual inscapes of other poems have become, here, beaten ("pashed") into a shapeless mass, representing the retraction away from a deep ecological affinity with nature. What has also been lost, as Hopkins described and apparently accepted this transition to an "earthless" state as the inevitable "home-of-all" being (14), is any notion (as implied in "shelterless") that humanity dwells on the earth. The depiction represents, that is, the outcome of an increasingly redemptive theology, a "disremembering" of ecological concepts – biodiversity and dwelling – that has occurred in the context of the transition from acts of memory to a single, all-important act of election. Rejecting the eye, Hopkins seeks solace in the heart, "Heart, you round me right", and asserts that it has counselled him correctly because when nature inevitably decays, when night ultimately (over)whelms and will "end us", then we will need the heart to lead us towards the consoling, orthodox absolutes of "black, white; | right, wrong". He ends the poem, on this note, by counselling the reader to "[be]ware" of any world other than that in which "these | twó tell, each/off the other".

Beer reads the poem as indicative of the extent to which an interest in and anxiety about thermodynamics and thermodynamic decline had transformed Victorian perceptions. By means of a redemptive theology Hopkins sought to mitigate what she describes as "the discussions and the dreads [...] released by the[se] laws" (1996: 262). Yet if this is supposed to have afforded Hopkins spiritual consolation – if Nixon is right to suggest that 'Spelt from Sibyl's Leaves', uniquely amongst his poems, "entertains no diurnal return" (2002: 138, 147) – one can, nevertheless, detect a persistent dissenting voice. For leaving aside the sense of resignation when he writes "Lét life [...] wind/Off hér once skéined stained véined varíety", a sense emphasised by the stress and repetition within these lines, Hopkins can hardly be said to have found solace in accepting or embracing entropy. On the contrary, the trees that in 'Spring' "brush[ed] the descending blue" have become, in Norman MacKenzie's words, "cruel as the beaks of flying dragons, etched against a steel-grey [...] sky" (1981: 162); while what remains of the distinctive shapes of nature are now threatening, the "beakleaved boughs dragonish" warning of the devil (see SD: 189). The sense of dissension is enhanced, furthermore, by elements within the poem that carry an implicit social critique, most apparent in the relationship between line 5 – "earth | her being has unbound" – where Hopkins evokes the goddess Gaia and line 7 where the coupling of "disremembering" with the residual, angrily connoted "dismembering" reminds us that loss of memory (and, consequently, understanding) is liable to lead, as suggested in 'Binsey Poplars', to a cultural blindness that will threaten nonhuman and human nature alike. If such a connection appears tenuous the social implications become clearer when one remembers that "The times are nightfall" was, in all probability, a draft of this poem (see Poems: 314). For there, as we saw, more or less the same entropic signifiers – nightfall, winter, waste – were used to indicate a contemporary "times" characterised by social and ecological risk.

Both his own sense of alienation and the implied social critique suggest, then, that Hopkins took no solace in spiritual immortality. Indeed, having turned to Catholicism to quell the "dreads" of modernity, he remained, in the end, curiously attuned to the ecological processes governing nature. This is most apparent in that those processes are embodied within the rhythm and structure of the poem itself. Consistent with his principles, Hopkins had insisted that the "performance" of the poem should rest upon "not reading with the eye but loud, leisurely, poetical (not rhetorical), recitation, with long rests, long dwells on the rhyme and other marked syllables", that it should "be almost sung" (RB 11/12/86: 246). As a result, the thermodynamic decline is felt, literally, by the reader. We feel the dying of the day, "evening straining", as Leavis put it, "to become night, enveloping everything, in the movement, the progression of alliteration, assonance and rime" (1950: 183). Hopkins, likewise, embodied this potential dissolution in the form merging the poem together so as to leave "quatrains and tercets melting at the edges, and the octave flowing into the sestet in line 7" (MacKenzie 1981: 161).

In this representation of entropic decline Hopkins offers, then, a further dimension to the 'song of the earth' which, disturbing though it may be, testifies to the persistence of an ecological element within his thinking. Ultimately resisting the eradication of other species, more fundamentally, because of what Beer calls his "passionate apprehension of entropy" (262), he never lost his understanding of the other half of ecological theory, that the flow and exchange of energy (instress) sustains all life, not least human life. While the principles which in earlier poems had signalled creative energy – fire and light – are, here, in danger of dissolution they do, nevertheless, remain. Precisely at the point, therefore, at which he was most alienated from nature Hopkins demonstrated an acute, even enhanced, sense of energy as the central fact of existence.

Chapter 7

Re-enchantment

The argument with which I concluded the previous chapter, that even at his most alienated Hopkins retained an underlying ecological vision, concludes, almost, the ecocritical reading offered in this book. This is the point, therefore, at which we might stop to summarise that reading.

To begin with, Hopkins' proximity both to the scientific ideas that shaped ecology and to an "early green politics" makes him a prime example of the 'Victorian ecology' described in Chapter Two. Having absorbed those ideas in the practice of his journal, that acquaintance went on to transform romantic descriptions of nature in his juvenile work into a mature poetry shaped by a dialectical understanding of a nature characterised by energy exchange. Tracing, thereafter, the development from this understanding of ecosystems theory to a social philosophy premised upon sustainability, initially through a critical nature poetry, we find, most radically, Clark's social ecology of the imagination in works that embody what Peter Dickens has called "the real or material connections between people and nature and the social relations involved in the modification of nature and of the body" (1992: 159). At a more technical level, Hopkins utilised a phenomenological ecopoetic designed to 'let being be' towards social-ecological depictions that assist us to feel the extent to which toxic, unsustainable practices in Victorian society impacted on the human body as much as they did on trees, rivers or wilderness. In all this his work offers, then, an extended, ecocentric and technocentric, understanding of the ways in which poetry, that most cerebral of forms, might shape an ecological awareness. This reconciliation, in Hopkins' work, between the two components of ecological theory remains the single most important argument for presenting him as an ecopoet.

The problem, however, is that, while Hopkins resisted the eradication of inscape in 'Spelt from Sibyl's Leaves', alienation from nonhuman nature remained, all the same, a prominent feature of his later verse, a fact which threatens to undermine the notion of Hopkins as a proto-ecological poet.

What, in turn, this should remind us is that, notwithstanding the premise of this book, to assert a more technocentric ecological literary criticism, it is only in the conjunction of eco- and technocentric tendencies that a fully-realised ecological theory can emerge. This, as it happens, is the final thing that a contemporary ecology might learn from Hopkins.

The value of an ecocentric perspective is frequently acknowledged by contemporary writers even where they are sensitive to the social dimension of ecology. Richard Mabey has reminded us, for example, that "compassion for and delight in the natural world are what turn people to act in its defence in the first place" (cited in Evans 1997: 4); Martin Ryle suggests that "no one […] will regard themselves as an 'ecocritic' unless they feel some sense of the power of the best writing about nature to delight and instruct" (2002: 12). This is, furthermore, one of the lessons to be learnt from Victorian ecology. For while Morris' alignment of romantic sentiment to Marxist theory brought about an early social ecology demonstrative of the value of supplementing ecocentric with technocentric approaches, the converse example of Mill highlights the opposite. Mill's recovery from a "mental crisis" brought about by his remorselessly utilitarian upbringing lay, as we saw, in reading Wordsworth. In cultivating a love for nature and poetry which put him back in touch with "the very culture of the feelings […] I was in quest of" (1964: 115-16), Mill was led to re-shape his political and economic philosophy in a way that would accommodate a variety of proto-ecological ideas. Hopkins, conversely, having chosen a pragmatic vocation, lost sight of his own ecocentric understanding. And, in losing his "delight" in nature, his poems lost much of their ability, ecologically speaking, to "instruct".

Typifying the utilitarianism of Victorian post-Romanticism, Hopkins had become increasingly sceptical of the value of a literary vocation. Describing his artistic endeavours as "luxuries or rather bywork", compared to the "necessity" of his scholastic studies (RB Early October 1882: 153), he argued, in accordance, it would appear, with Jesuit tradition (Aveling 1981: 24-5), that literature was justifiable "only as a means to an end" and that "[Jesuit] history and [...] experience shew that literature proper, as poetry, has seldom been found to be to that end a very serviceable means" (RWD 1/12/81: 93). Regarding literature, then, as "out of keeping with my present duties", and professing to believe that he could not "in conscience spend time on poetry" (RWD 29/10/81: 87; RB 15/2/79: 66), Hopkins provoked Dixon, also a clergyman, to plead "Surely one vocation cannot destroy another" (RWD 4/11/81: 90). His answer, lengthy and dismissive, encompassed a rejection of the "dazzling

[…] attractions" of literature in favour of the handsome heart: "we [Jesuits] cultivate the commonplace outwardly and wish the beauty of the king's daughter the soul to be from within" (see RWD 1/12/81: 92-6).

Yet Hopkins never entirely forsook literature. In the first place, his letters continued to be characterised by a familiarity with and knowledge of contemporary fiction as well as by long, detailed criticism of his friends' poetry. More significantly it becomes apparent that complaints about lacking the energy to "breed one work that wakes" actually related as much to an inability to compose poetry as to any failure to fulfil his religious duties. The complaint, for example, that the "parish work of Liverpool is […] wearying to mind and body" connects to a remark that it "leaves me nothing but odds and ends of time. There is merit in it but little Muse, and indeed 26 lines is the whole I have writ[ten] in more than half a year" (RWD 14/5/80: 33); similarly, when he suggests to Bridges, in an echo of sentiments expressed in 'Thou art indeed just, Lord', that "There is a point with me in matters of any size when I must absolutely have encouragement as much as crops rain", it immediately becomes apparent that these "matters of any size" refer not to his religious vocation but to a poetic vocation which "I am in my ordinary circumstances unable, with whatever encouragement, to go on with" (RB 17/5/85: 218-19).

In an early fragment, 'Summa', composed in 1866, Hopkins, writing perspicaciously of a time of "care" when "The city tires to death" (11-12), had suggested that "There must be something to supply/All insufficiencies" (7-8) (see Nixon 2002: 134). What is also to be found in Hopkins' response to Dixon is the answer to this – that a return to poetry might just restore his energy and bring about, in turn, at least a partial rediscovery of an ecological perspective. For notwithstanding his otherwise pious and belligerent response, Hopkins did hold out the hope, in this letter, that his writing might have some worth – "if you value what I write, if I do myself, much more does our Lord. And if he chooses to avail himself of what I leave at his disposal he can do so with a felicity and with a success which I could never command" (RWD 1/12/81: 93). The sentiment is reiterated in some retreat notes written two years later: "in some med[itations] today I earnestly asked our Lord to watch over my compositions […] that he should have them as his own and employ or not employ them as he should see fit. And this I believe is heard" (SD: 253-4). This gradual reconciliation towards his poetry brought about, at least sporadically, a corresponding return to both a deep ecological affinity with other species and a dialectical sense of nature as an energy system.

Seen, for instance, in the brief flourishes of sacramental, ecological description that appear in 'That Nature is a Heraclitean Fire' and 'Epithalamion', Sulloway also notes that for all its antipathy towards nonhuman nature 'Thou art indeed just, Lord' exhibits something of a return to a "fresh, teeming world [...] intensely moving because [...] so unexpected" (1972: 153-4). This can be found in the brief Ruskinian passages that describe riverbanks and thickets "lacèd [...] again/With fretty chervil" and which convey, in precise terms, nature's capacity for renewal and interrelation.

In *Nature Cure* Mabey suggests that the renewal of a "delight in the natural world" can occur in conjunction with a return to mental or psychological health (see 2005: 224). This is, in fact, what we find in Hopkins, albeit in the most unexpected of places. The six poems that constitute the Terrible Sonnets appear to mark, for all their desolation, an attempt by Hopkins to write his way out of a spiritual crisis. In this context there emerges in 'My own heart let me more have pity on', the sonnet that draws the sequence to a close, the clearest indication of how a renewed ecocentrism, marked here by a reconciliation with his poetry, can, indeed, bring about a return to an ecological perspective.

> My own heart let me more have pity on; let
> Me live to my sad self hereafter kind,
> Charitable; not live this tormented mind
> With this tormented mind tormenting yet.
>
> I cast for comfort I can no more get
> By groping round my comfortless, than blind
> Eyes in their dark can day or thirst can find
> Thirst's all-in-all in all a world of wet.
>
> Soul, self; come, poor Jackself, I do advise
> You, jaded, let be; call off thoughts awhile
> Elsewhere; leave comfort root-room; let joy size
>
> As God knows when to God knows what; whose smile
> 's not wrung, see you; unforeseen times rather—as skies
> Betweenpie mountains—lights a lovely mile.

The poem begins with Hopkins counselling the need to show himself pity. In a qualification of his recent emphasis on the elective will, lines 3 and 4 deal with the consequences of having over-*stressed* a redemptive theology, the phrase "tormented mind tormenting yet" depicting a mind – parallel to the corporeal "untwist[ing]" described in '(Carrion Comfort)'

– that "reduplicates itself as a series, continually reversing the 'tormented' and 'tormenting' position of subject and object" (Armstrong 1993: 437). In '(Carrion Comfort)' Hopkins had also, in a fleeting moment of positive thought, followed the lament "me […] most weary, cry *I can no more*" with the defiant "I can;/Can something, hope, wish day come, not choose not to be" (3-4). Here that "something" is elaborated on as he develops a strategy for self-survival.

Hopkins suggests that the fulfilment of "pitch" rests not only on doing but also by attending to the "world within" by means of rest and personal renewal. Though not a common theme in his poetry, similar sentiments had appeared in 'The Caged Skylark', where Hopkins had recognised that the bird's capacity to fly "free" and "sing […] the sweetest, sweetest spells" is sustained by "rest", and in an entreaty in 'The Candle Indoors' – "your fading fire/Mend first" (9-10). Here, despite having initially discounted – in the images of thirst and blindness (5-8) – any immediate prospect of "comfort", Hopkins nevertheless demands rest – emphasised in the stress on "let" in "let be" (Poems: 290) – so as to revive energies thereafter given "room" to "root". Also developing "Soul, self" into a jaded "Jackself" – which, in its connotations of work, amounts to a criticism of over-utilitarianism – what is most noticeable is the impact that rest and kindness to the self has. It brings about a renewed openness to nonhuman nature embodied in the structure of the poem itself.

The division, on this occasion, between octave and sestet reverses the movement from sacramental to redemptive theology that had characterised the majority of Hopkins' poetry. Allowing himself rest and "comfort", in having "call[ed] off thoughts awhile", there is a renewal of grace achieved by a return to the theology of Scotus. Hence, the "heart" in line 1, which initially appears to be the 'Handsome Heart' of the elective will, turns out, instead, to be the romantically-inflected heart of an affective will responding to beauty. This renewal of grace is, in turn, complemented by the re-discovery of a feeling for inscape. Where in 'The Wreck of the Deutschland' his conversion had been met with "the jay-blue heavens appearing/Of pied and peeled May!" (26. 3-4), and in 'God's Grandeur' the Catholic conversion of England had been represented by "brown brink eastward, springs" (12), here personal renewal, rewarded at one level by the (re)appearance of God's "smile" in line 12, is also signified, correspondingly, by the sun emerging from between the mountains, lighting up the sky and illuminating dapple as Hopkins re-discovers his own intimate connection with the "more-than-human" world.

Bibliography

Hopkins: Key Texts

The following abbreviations have been used for citations from the primary sources.

FL   Abbott, Claude Colleer (ed.). 1956. *The Further Letters of Gerard Manley Hopkins*. London: Oxford University Press.

JP   House, Humphry and Graham Storey. 1959. *The Journals and Papers of Gerard Manley Hopkins*. London: Oxford University Press.

Poems   Gardner, W. H. and N. H. MacKenzie (eds). 1970. *The Poems of Gerard Manley Hopkins* (4th edition). Oxford: Oxford University Press.

RB   Abbott, Claude Colleer (ed.). 1935. *The Letters of Gerard Manley Hopkins to Robert Bridges*. London: Oxford University Press.

RWD   Abbott, Claude Colleer (ed.). 1935. *The Correspondence of Gerard Manley Hopkins and Richard Watson Dixon*. London: Oxford University Press.

SD   Devlin, Christopher (ed.). 1959. *The Sermons and Devotional Writings of Gerard Manley Hopkins*. London: Oxford University Press.

NB: References to letters and journal entries appear in parentheses after the citation and include the abbreviation and (if necessary) the date. Letters to correspondents aside from Bridges and Dixon are in the *Further Letters*. References taken from this include, where not apparent, the recipient of the letter inserted between the abbreviation and the date e.g. (*FL* (J. H. Newman) 28/8/66: 22). Other page numbers in parentheses, in references from *The Journals and Papers*, refer to the editor's note e.g. (*JP* 1864: 21 (310)). Two further notes: Hopkins had a policy of not using full-stops at the end of paragraphs both in his journal and theological writings (see editor's note, *JP*: xxx). This explains why occasional references in my text do not contain the expected full-stop; secondly, all italics in this text appear in the original unless otherwise indicated.

Other Sources

Abram, David. 1996. *The Spell of the Sensuous: Perception and Language in a More-Than-Human World*. New York: Vintage Books.

Adamson, Joni, Mei Mei Evans and Rachel Stein (eds). 2002. *The Environmental Justice Reader: Politics, Poetics and Pedagogy*. Tucson: The University of Arizona Press.

Alderson, David. 1998. *Mansex Fine: Religion, Manliness and Imperialism in Nineteenth-Century British Culture*. Manchester and New York: Manchester University Press.

Aldington, Richard (ed.). 1948. *Walter Pater: Selected Works*. London: William Heinemann.

Allaby, Michael. 2000. *Basics of Environmental Science*. London: Routledge.

— (ed.). 2004. *A Dictionary of Ecology*. Oxford: Oxford University Press.

Appiah, Kwame Anthony. 1992. *In My Father's House: Africa in the Philosophy of Culture*. London: Methuen.

Armstrong, Isobel. 1993. *Victorian Poetry: Poetry, Poetics and Politics*. London and New York: Routledge.

Arnold, Matthew. 1965. *The Poems of Matthew Arnold* (ed. Kenneth Allott) (Longmans Annotated English Poets). London: Longmans.

Aveling, J. C. H. 1981. *The Jesuits*. London: Blond and Briggs.

Ball, Patricia M. 1971. *The Science of Aspects: The Changing Role of Fact in the Work of Coleridge, Ruskin and Hopkins*. London: The Athlone Press.

Banfield, Marie. 2007. 'Darwinism, Doxology, and Energy Physics: The New Sciences, the Poetry and the Poetics of Gerard Manley Hopkins' in *Victorian Poetry* 45(2): 175-94.

Barnes, William. 1869. *Early England and the Saxon English; With Some Notes on the Father-Stock of the Saxon-English, The Frisians*. London: John Russell Smith.

Batchelor, John. 2000. *John Ruskin: No Wealth but Life*. London: Chatto & Windus.

Bate, Jonathan. 1991. *Romantic Ecology: Wordsworth and the Environmental Tradition*. London: Routledge.

— 2000. *The Song of the Earth*. London: Picador.

Beck, Ulrich. 1992a. *Risk Society: Towards a New Modernity*. London: Sage.

— 1992b. 'From Industrial Society to the Risk Society: Questions of Survival, Social Structure and Ecological Enlightenment' in Featherstone, Mike (ed.) *Cultural Theory and Cultural Change*. London: Sage.

— 1995. *Ecological Politics in an Age of Risk*. Cambridge: Polity Press.

Becker, Egon and Thomas Jahn (eds). 1999. *Sustainability and the Social Sciences*. London and New York: Zed Books.

Beer, Gillian. 1985. *Darwin's Plots: Evolutionary Narrative in Darwin, George Eliot and Nineteenth-Century Fiction*. London: Ark.

— 1996. *Open Fields: Science in Cultural Encounter*. Oxford: Clarendon Press.

Bellanca, Mary Ellen. 2007. *Daybooks of Discovery: Nature Diaries in Britain, 1770-1870*. Charlottesville and London: University of Virginia Press.

Bender, Todd. 1966. *Gerard Manley Hopkins: The Classical Background and Critical Reception of his Work*. Baltimore: John Hopkins Press.

Bergonzi, Bernard. 1978. *Gerard Manley Hopkins*. London: Macmillan.

Berman, Marshall. 1982. *All That is Solid Melts Into Air*. London: Verso.

— 1984. 'The Signs in the Street: A Response to Perry Anderson' in *New Left Review* 144: 114-23.

Berry, Wendell. 1983. *Standing by Words*. San Francisco: North Point Press.

Biehl, Janet. 1998. *The Politics of Social Ecology: Libertarian Municipalism*. Montreal: Black Rose Books.

Bloomfield, Louis A. 2001. *How Things Work. The Physics of Everyday Life*. New York: John Wiley & Sons, Inc.

Bookchin, Murray. 1980. *Toward an Ecological Society*. Montreal: Black Rose Books.

— 1987. *The Modern Crisis*. Montreal and New York: Black Rose Books.

— 1988. 'Social Ecology versus Deep Ecology' in *Socialist Review* 18(3): 9-29.

— 2003 [1994]. 'Will Ecology become "The Dismal Science"?' repr. in VanDeVeer and Pierce (2003): 273-7.

Botkin, Daniel B. 1990. *Discordant Harmonies: A New Ecology for the Twenty-First Century*. New York: Oxford University Press.

— and Edward A. Keller. 2005. *Environmental Science: Earth as a Living Planet*. Hoboken, New Jersey: John Wiley & Sons, Inc.

Bramwell, Anna. 1989. *Ecology in the Twentieth Century: A History*. New Haven and London: Yale University Press.

Brennan, Andrew. 1995. 'Ecological Theory and Value in Nature' in Elliot, Robert (ed.) *Environmental Ethics*. Oxford: Oxford University Press.

Brown, Daniel. 1997. *Hopkins' Idealism: Philosophy, Physics, Poetry*. Oxford: Clarendon Press.

Bryson, J. Scott. 2002. *Ecopoetry: A Critical Introduction*. Salt Lake City: The University of Utah Press.

Buckley, Jerome Hamilton. 1969. *The Victorian Temper*. Cambridge, MA: Harvard University Press.

Buell, Lawrence. 1995. *The Environmental Imagination: Thoreau, Nature Writing, and the Formation of American Culture*. Cambridge, MA and London: The Belknap Press.

— 2001. *Writing for an Endangered World. Literature, Culture, and Environment in the U.S. and Beyond*. Cambridge, MA and London: The Belknap Press.

— 2005. *The Future of Environmental Criticism*. Oxford: Blackwell.

Butler, Marilyn. 1981. *Romantics, Rebels and Reactionaries: English Literature and its Background 1760-1830*. Oxford: Oxford University Press.

Campbell, Chris and Erin Somerville (eds). 2007. *What is the Earthly Paradise? Ecocritical Responses to the Caribbean*. Newcastle-upon-Tyne: Cambridge Scholars Publishing.

Carlyle, Thomas. 1845. *Past and Present*. London: Chapman and Hall.

— 1869. 'The State of German Literature' in *Critical and Miscellaneous Essays* 1. London: Chapman and Hall. 23-73.

— 1869. 'Characteristics' in *Critical and Miscellaneous Essays* 2. London: Chapman and Hall. 193-227.

— 1869. 'Varnhagen von Ense's Memoirs' in *Critical and Miscellaneous Essays* 3. London: Chapman and Hall. 227-52.

Carroll, Joseph. 2004. *Literary Darwinism: Evolution, Human Nature, and Literature*. New York: Routledge.

Chandler, Alice. 1971. *A Dream of Order: The Medieval Ideal in Nineteenth-Century Literature*. London: Routledge & Kegan Paul.

Chapman, Raymond. 1968. *The Victorian Debate: English Literature and Society 1831-1901*. London: Weidenfeld and Nicolson.

Christie, Maureen. 2001. *The Ozone Layer: A Philosophy of Scientific Perspective*. Cambridge: Cambridge University Press.

Clark, John. 1997. 'A Social Ecology' in *Capitalism, Nature, Socialism* 8(3): 3-33.

Cobley, Paul (ed.). 2001. *The Routledge Companion to Semiotics and Linguistics*. London and New York: Routledge.

Cohen, Michael P. 1988. *The History of the Sierra Club, 1892-1970*. San Francisco: Sierra Club Books.

— 2004. 'Blues in the Green: Ecocriticism under Critique' in *Environmental History* 9(1). Online at: <http://www.historycooperative.org/journals/eh/9.1/cohen.html> (consulted 10.06.2004).

— 2006. 'Handles, Grounds, and Patterns: Questions for Ecocritical Theory' in *Green Letters* 7: 14-22.

Cohen, Nick. 2008. 'Charles, A Very Modern Marie Antoinette' in *The Observer* (17 August 2008).

Coleman, B. I. 1973. *The Idea of the City in Nineteenth-Century Britain*. London: Routledge & Kegan Paul.

Cooper, Tim. 1990. *Green Christianity*. London: Spire.

Coupe, Laurence (ed.). 2000. *The Green Studies Reader: From Romanticism to Ecocriticism*. London and New York: Routledge.

Creese, Walter L. 1977. 'Imagination in the Suburb' in Knoepflmacher, U. C. and G. B. Tennyson (eds) *Nature and the Victorian Imagination*. Berkeley and London: University of California Press.

Cronon, William (ed.). 1995. *Uncommon Ground: Toward Reinventing Nature*. New York and London: W. W. Norton & Company.

Cross, F. L. and E. A. Livingstone (eds). 1997. *Dictionary of the Christian Church* (3rd edn.). Oxford: Oxford University Press.

Cross, Richard. 1998. *The Physics of Duns Scotus: The Scientific Context of a Theological Vision*. Oxford: Clarendon Press.

— 1999. *Duns Scotus*. New York and Oxford: Oxford University Press.

Cunningham, William P. and Barbara Woodworth Saigo. 1997. *Environmental Science: A Global Concern*. Boston: WCB McGraw-Hill.

Dale, Peter A. 1989. 'Thomas Hardy and the Best Consummation Possible' in Christie, John and Sally Shuttleworth (eds) *Nature Transfigured: Science and Literature, 1700-1900*. Manchester: Manchester University Press. 201-21.

Day, Aidan. 1996. *Romanticism*. London: Routledge.

DeLoughrey, Elizabeth M, Renée K. Gosson and George B. Handley (eds). 2005. *Caribbean Literature and the Environment: Between Nature and Culture*. Charlottesville and London: University of Virginia Press.

Desmond, Adrian, James Moore and Janet Browne. 2007. *Charles Darwin*. Oxford: Oxford University Press.

Dickens, Charles. 1985 [1857]. *Little Dorrit* (ed. John Holloway) (Penguin Classics). London: Penguin.

Dickens, Peter. 1992. *Society and Nature: Towards a Green Social Theory*. Hemel Hempstead: Harvester Wheatsheaf.

Disraeli, Benjamin. 1980 [1845]. *Sybil* (ed. R. A. Butler) (The Penguin English Library). Harmondsworth: Penguin.

Dixon, Terrell. 1996. 'The Literature of Toxicity from Rachel Carson to Ana Castillo' in Di Giulio, Richard T. and Emily Monosson (eds) *Interconnections Between Human and Ecosystem Health*. London: Chapman and Hall. 237-58.

Dobson, Andrew. 2000. *Green Political Thought*. London: Routledge.

Earth Summit '92: The United Nations Conference on Environment and Development. 1992. London: The Regency Press Corporation.

Eckersley, Robyn. 2004. *The Green State: Rethinking Democracy and Sovereignty*. Cambridge, MA and London: The MIT Press.

Eichler, Margrit. 1999. 'Sustainability from a Feminist Sociological Perspective: A Framework for Disciplinary Reorientation' in Becker and Jahn (1999): 182-206.

Elder, John. 1985. *Imagining the Earth: Poetry and the Vision of Nature*. Urbana: University of Illinois Press.

Elkin, Tim and Duncan McLaren with Mayer Hillman. 1991. *Reviving the City: Towards Sustainable Urban Development*. London: Friends of the Earth with the Policy Studies Institute.

Elliot, Robert (ed.). 1995. *Environmental Ethics*. Oxford: Oxford University Press.

Evans, David. 1997. *A History of Conservation in Britain*. London: Routledge.

Fitzpatrick, Kevin and Mark LaGory. 2000. *Unhealthy Places: The Ecology of Risk in the Urban Landscape*. New York and London: Routledge.

Fletcher, Ian. 1971. *Walter Pater*. Harlow: Longmans, Green.

Gardner, W. H. 1958. *Gerard Manley Hopkins. A Study of Poetic Idiosyncrasy in Relation to Poetic Tradition* (2 vol.). London: Oxford University Press.

— 1987 [1936]. 'A Note on Hopkins and Duns Scotus' repr. in Roberts (1987): 337-44.

Garforth, Lisa. 2002. 'Ecotopian Fiction and the Sustainable Society' in Parham (2002): 100-13.

Garrard, Greg. 2004. *Ecocriticism*. Abingdon: Routledge.

— 2007. 'Yes But. A Reply to Terry Gifford' in *Green Letters* 8: 23-5.

Gaskell, Elizabeth. 1985 [1848]. *Mary Barton* (ed. Stephen Gill) (Penguin Classics). London: Penguin.

Gaston, Kevin J. and John I. Spicer. 2004. *Biodiversity. An Introduction*. Oxford: Blackwell.

Giblett, Rod. 1996. *Postmodern Wetlands: Culture, History, Ecology*. Edinburgh: Edinburgh University Press.

Gifford, Terry. 1995. 'Conclusion' in Wheeler, Michael (1995): 187-94.

— 1996. 'The Social Construction of Nature' in *ISLE: Interdisciplinary Studies in Literature and Environment* 3(2): 27-35.

— 1999. *Pastoral*. London: Routledge.

— 2006. 'What is Ecocriticism for? Some Personal Reflections in Response to Two Recent Critiques' in *Green Letters* 7: 6-13.

Gissing, George. 1974 [1889]. *The Nether World: A Novel* (ed. John Goode). Brighton: The Harvester Press.

— 1982 [1886]. *Demos, A Story of English Socialism* (ed. Pierre Coustillas). Brighton: The Harvester Press.

Glotfelty, Cheryll. 1996. 'Ecocriticism: Literary Studies in an Age of Environmental Crisis' in Di Giulio, Richard T. and Emily Monosson (eds) *Interconnections Between Human and Ecosystem Health*. London: Chapman and Hall. 229-36.

Goodbody, Axel. 2007. *Nature, Technology and Cultural Change in Twentieth-Century German Literature: The Challenge of Ecocriticism*. Basingstoke: Palgrave Macmillan.

Goodwin, Brian. 1994. *How the Leopard Changed its Spots: The Evolution of Complexity*. London: Weidenfeld & Nicolson.

Gottlieb, Roger S. 2006. *A Greener Faith: Religious Environmentalism and Our Planet's Future*. New York: Oxford University Press.

Gould, Peter. 1988. *Early Green Politics: Back to Nature, Back to the Land and Socialism in Britain 1880-1900*. Brighton: Harvester.

Goyder, Jane and Philip Lowe. 1983. *Environmental Groups in Politics*. London: George Allen & Unwin.

Green Party (UK). 'Statement of Core Principles'. On line at: <http://policy.greenparty.org.uk/values.html> (consulted 07.11.2008).

Grumbine, Edward. 1995. 'Wildness, Wise Use, and Sustainable Development' in Sessions (1995): 376-96.

Guérard, Albert. 1942. *Robert Bridges: A Study of Traditionalism in Poetry*. Cambridge, MA: Harvard University Press.

Haley, Bruce. 1978. *The Healthy Body and Victorian Culture*. Cambridge, MA and London: Harvard University Press.

Hall, Stuart. 1977. 'Culture, the Media and the "Ideological Effect"' in Curran, James (ed.) *Mass Communication and Society*. London: Edward Arnold. 315-48.

Halperin, David M. 1983. *Before Pastoral: Theocritus and the Ancient Tradition of Bucolic Poetry*. New Haven and London: Yale University Press.

Hampson, Norman. 1984. *The Enlightenment: An Evaluation of its Assumptions, Attitudes and Values*. London: Penguin.

Hardy, Thomas. 1978 [1891]. *Tess of the D'Urbervilles* (ed. David Skilton) (Penguin Classics). Harmondsworth: Penguin.

— 1993 [1886]. *The Mayor of Casterbridge*. London: Everyman.

Harrison, Robert Pogue. 1992. *Forests: The Shadow of Civilization*. Chicago and London: The University of Chicago Press.

Hay, Peter R. 2003 [1988]. 'Ecological Values and Western Political Traditions: from Anarchism to Fascism' in Pepper, Webster and Revill III (2003): 7-18.

Hayward, Tim. 1995. *Ecological Thought: An Introduction*. Cambridge: Polity Press.

Heilbron, J. L. 2005. *The Oxford Guide to the History of Physics and Astronomy*. Oxford: Oxford University Press.

Heuser, Alan. 1958. *The Shaping Vision of Gerard Manley Hopkins*. London: Oxford University Press.

Hewison, Robert. 1996. ''Paradise Lost': Ruskin and Science' in Wheeler, Michael (1996): 29-44.

Heyck, T. W. 1982. *The Transformation of Intellectual Life in Victorian England*. London: Croom Helm.

Heynen, Nik, Maria Kaika and Erik Swyngedouw (eds). 2006. *In the Nature of Cities: Urban Political Ecology and the Politics of Urban Metabolism*. Abingdon: Routledge.

Holmes, J. Derek. 1978. *More Roman than Rome: English Catholicism in the Nineteenth Century*. London: Burns and Oates.

Hopkins, Gerard Manley. 1982. *Poems and Prose of Gerard Manley Hopkins* (ed. W. H. Gardner). Harmondsworth: Penguin.

Houghton, Walter. 1957. *The Victorian Frame of Mind: 1830-1870*. New Haven and London: Yale University Press.

Howes, David (ed.). 2005. *Empire of the Senses: The Sensual Culture Reader*. Oxford and New York: Berg.

International Institute for Sustainable Development. 'What is Sustainable Development?' On line at <http://www.iisd.org/sd/> (consulted 18.08.2009).

Johnson, E. D. H. 1963. *The Alien Vision of Victorian Poetry*. Connecticut: Archon Books.

Johnson, Margaret. 1997. *Gerard Manley Hopkins and Tractarian Poetry*. Aldershot: Ashgate.

Johnson, Wendell Stacy. 1968. *Gerard Manley Hopkins: The Poet as Victorian*. New York: Cornell University Press.

Keller, David R. and Frank B. Golley. 2000. *The Philosophy of Ecology: From Science to Synthesis*. Athens and London: University of Georgia Press.

Kerridge, Richard. 2002. 'Narratives of Resignation: Environmentalism in Recent Fiction' in Parham (2002): 87-99.

Kitchen, Paddy. 1978. *Gerard Manley Hopkins*. London: Hamish Hamilton.

Kroeber, Karl. 1994. *Ecological Literary Criticism: Romantic Imagining and the Biology of the Mind*. New York: Columbia University Press.

Lampard, Eric E. 1973. 'The Urbanizing World' in Dyos, Jim and Michael Wolff (eds) *The Victorian City* (vol. 1). London and New York: Routledge. 3-57.

Larrissy, Edward. 1999. *Romanticism and Postmodernism*. Cambridge: Cambridge University Press.

Lawlor, David W. 2001. *Photosynthesis*. Oxford: Bios.

Leavis, F. R. 1950. *New Bearings in English Poetry: A Study of the Contemporary Situation*. London: Chatto & Windus.

Legler, Gretchen. 1998. 'Body Politics in American Nature Writing. "Who May Contest for What the Body of Nature will be?"' in Kerridge, Richard and Neil Sammells (eds) *Writing the Environment: Ecocriticism and Literature*. London & New York: Zed Books. 71-87.

Lerner, Lawrence. 1975. 'What did Wordsworth Mean by Nature?' in *Critical Quarterly* 17(4): 291-308.

Levin, Phillis (ed.). 2001. *The Penguin Book of the Sonnet*. New York: Penguin.

Levine, George. 1988. *Darwin and the Novelists: Patterns of Science in Victorian Fiction*. Cambridge, MA and London: Harvard University Press.

Light, Andrew (ed.). 1998. *Social Ecology after Bookchin*. New York and London: The Guilford Press.

Lindholdt, Paul. 1996. 'Literary Activism and the Bioregional Agenda' in *ISLE: Interdisciplinary Studies in Literature and Environment* 3(2): 121-37.

Lodge, David M. and Christopher Hamlin (eds). 2006. *Religion and the New Ecology: Environmental Responsibility in a World in Flux*. Notre Dame: University of Notre Dame Press.

Love, Glen A. 2003. *Practical Ecocriticism: Literature, Biology and the Environment*. Charlottesville and London: University of Virginia Press.

Lovelock, James. 2000. *Gaia: A New Look at Life on Earth*. Oxford: Oxford University Press.

— 2000b. *The Ages of Gaia: A Biography of our Living Earth*. Oxford: Oxford University Press.

Luke, Timothy W. 1997. *Ecocritique: Contesting the Politics of Nature, Economy and Culture*. Minneapolis and London: University of Minnesota Press.

Mabey, Richard. 2005. *Nature Cure*. London: Chatto & Windus.

MacKenzie, Norman H. 1981. *A Reader's Guide to Gerard Manley Hopkins*. London: Thames and Hudson.

— 1993. 'Hopkins and Science' in Hollahan, Eugene (ed.) *Gerard Manley Hopkins and Critical Discourse*. New York: AMS Press. 81-95.

Martin, Robert Bernard. 1983. *Tennyson: The Unquiet Heart*. Oxford: Clarendon Press.

— 1991. *Gerard Manley Hopkins: A Very Private Life*. London: HarperCollins.

Massumi, Brian. 2002. *Parables for the Virtual: Movement, Affect, Sensation*. Durham and London: Duke University Press.

Mathews, Freya. 2000. 'CERES: Singing up the City' in *PAN: Philosophy, Activism, Nature* 1: 5-15.

McDonough, Sean. 1990. *The Greening of the Church*. New York: Geoffrey Chapman.

McFague, Sallie. 1993. *The Body of God: An Ecological Theology*. Minneapolis: Fortress Press.

McIntosh, Robert P. 1985. *The Background of Ecology: Concept and Theory*. Cambridge: Cambridge University Press.

McKusick, James C. 2000. *Green Writing: Romanticism and Ecology*. Basingstoke and London: Macmillan.

— 2003. Review of Winter (1999) in *Nineteenth-Century Contexts* 25(3): 287–90.

Merchant, Carolyn. 1982. *The Death of Nature: Women, Ecology and the Scientific Revolution*. London: Wildwood House.

Midgley, Mary. 2006. *Science and Poetry*. London: Routledge.

Mill, John Stuart. 1920 [1848]. *Principles of Political Economy with Some of their Applications to Social Philosophy* (ed. W. J. Ashley). London: Longmans, Green, & Co.

— 1964 [1873]. *Autobiography of John Stuart Mill* (Signet Classics). New York: The New American Library of World Literature.

— 1969 [1874]. *Collected Works of John Stuart Mill: Essays on Ethics, Religion and Society* 10 (ed. J. M. Robson). Toronto and London: University of Toronto Press and Routledge. 373-402.

Milroy, James. 1977. *The Language of Gerard Manley Hopkins*. London: Andre Deutsch.

Moore, Michael D. 1997. 'Pleading for the Tongueless Earth: Gerard Manley Hopkins and Victorian Eco-Poetics'. Paper presented at *Literature and Natural Environment* conference (University of Wales: Swansea, 25-27 March 1997).

Morris, William. 1993. *News from Nowhere and Other Writings* (ed. Clive Wilmer) (Penguin Classics). London: Penguin.

Muller, Jill. 2003. *Gerard Manley Hopkins and Victorian Catholicism*. New York and London: Routledge.

Myers, Greg. 1989. 'Nineteenth-Century Popularizations of Thermodynamics and the Rhetoric of Social Prophecy' in Brantlinger, Patrick (ed.) *Energy and Entropy: Science and Culture in Victorian Britain*. Bloomington and Indianapolis: Indiana University Press. 307-38.

Naess, Arne. 1995. 'The Deep Ecological Movement: Some Philosophical Aspects' in Sessions (1995): 64-84.

Najarian, James. 2002. *Victorian Keats: Manliness, Sexuality, and Desire*. Basingstoke: Palgrave.

Newton, Roger G. 2007. *From Clockwork to Crapshoot: A History of Physics*. Cambridge, MA and London: The Belknap Press.

Nixon, Jude V. 2002. '"Death blots black out": Thermodynamics and the Poetry of Gerard Manley Hopkins' in *Victorian Poetry* 40(2): 131-55.

— 2006. 'Fathering Graces at Hampstead: Manley Hopkins' "The Old Trees" and Gerard Manley Hopkins' "Binsey Poplars"' in *Victorian Poetry* 44(2): 191-211.

Norman, Edward. 1985. *Roman Catholicism in England*. Oxford: Oxford University Press.

Olsen, Donald J. 1976. *The Growth of Victorian London*. Harmondsworth: Penguin.

Ong, Walter. 1949. 'Hopkins' Sprung Rhythm and the Life of English Poetry' in Weyand, Norman (ed.) *Immortal Diamond: Studies in Gerard Manley Hopkins*. London: Sheed & Ward.

O'Riordan, Tim. 1981. *Environmentalism*. London: Pion.

O'Shea, Alan. 1996. 'English Subjects of Modernity' in Nava, Mica and Alan O'Shea (eds) *Modern Times: Reflections on a Century of English Modernity*. London: Routledge. 7-37.

Parham, John. 1999. Review of *Culture and Environmentalism* conference (Bath Spa University, 3-5 July 1998) in *Key Words: A Journal of Cultural Materialism* 2: 122-6.

— (ed.). 2002. *The Environmental Tradition in English Literature*. Aldershot: Ashgate.

— 2003. 'Green Man Hopkins: Gerard Manley Hopkins and the Ecological Imagination' in *Nineteenth-Century Contexts* 25(3): 257–76.

— 2007. 'What is (ecological) "nature"? John Stuart Mill and the Victorian Perspective' in Becket, Fiona and Terry Gifford (eds) (2007) *Culture, Creativity and Environment: New Environmentalist Criticism*. Amsterdam and New York: Rodopi. 37-54.

— 2008. 'The Poverty of Ecocritical Theory: E. P. Thompson and the British Perspective' in *New Formations* 64: 25-36.

Park, Chris C. 1987. *Acid Rain: Rhetoric and Reality*. London and New York: Methuen.

Pater, Walter. 1986 [1873]. *The Renaissance: Studies in Art and Poetry* (ed. Adam Phillips) (Oxford World's Classics). Oxford: Oxford University Press.

Pepper, David. 1996. *Modern Environmentalism: An Introduction*. London: Routledge.

Pepper, David with Frank Webster and George Revill (eds). 2003. *Environmentalism: Critical Concepts* (5 vol.). London: Routledge.

Perry, Seamus. 1998. 'Romanticism: The Brief History of a Concept' in Wu (1998): 3-11.

Peters, W. A. M. 1948. *Gerard Manley Hopkins: A Critical Essay Towards the Understanding of his Poetry*. London: Oxford University Press.

Phelan, Joseph. 2005. *The Nineteenth-Century Sonnet*. Basingstoke: Palgrave Macmillan.

Phillips, Catherine. 1992. *Robert Bridges: A Biography*. Oxford: Oxford University Press.

Phillips, Dana. 2003. *The Truth of Ecology: Nature, Culture, and Literature in America*. Oxford and New York: Oxford University Press.

Pick, John. 1942. *Gerard Manley Hopkins: Priest and Poet*. London: Oxford University Press.

Porter, Roy. 2003. *Flesh in the Age of Reason*. London: Allen Lane.

Praz, Mario. 1970. *The Romantic Agony*. London and New York: Oxford University Press.

Rasmussen, Larry. 2006. 'Ecology and Morality: The Challenge to and from Christian Ethics' in Lodge and Hamlin (2006): 246-78.

Redclift, Michael and Ted Benton (eds). 1994. *Social Theory and the Global Environment*. London and New York: Routledge.

Rigby, Kate. 2004. *Topographies of the Sacred. The Poetics of Place in European Romanticism*. Charlottesville and London. University of Virginia Press.

Roberts, Gerald (ed.). 1987. *Gerard Manley Hopkins. The Critical Heritage*. London: Routledge & Kegan Paul.

Robertson, James. 1998. *Beyond the Dependency Culture: People, Power and Responsibility in the 21ˢᵗ Century*. Westport and London: Praeger.

Robinson, John. 1978. *In Extremity: A Study of Gerard Manley Hopkins*. Cambridge: Cambridge University Press.

Roe, Nicholas. 2002. *The Politics of Nature: William Wordsworth and Some Contemporaries*. Basingstoke: Palgrave.

Rogers, Raymond. 1994. *Nature and the Crisis of Modernity: A Critique of Contemporary Discourse on Managing the Earth*. Montreal and London: Black Rose Books.

Rosen, George. 1973. 'Disease, Debility, and Death' in Dyos, Jim and Michael Wolff (eds) *The Victorian City* (vol. 2). London and New York: Routledge. 625-67.

Ruskin, John. 1903–12. *The Complete Works of John Ruskin* III (eds E. T. Cook and Alexander Wedderburn). London: George Allen.

— 1903–12. *The Complete Works of John Ruskin* V (eds E. T. Cook and Alexander Wedderburn). London: George Allen.

— 1903–12. *The Complete Works of John Ruskin* VI (eds E. T. Cook and Alexander Wedderburn). London: George Allen.

— 1903–12. *The Complete Works of John Ruskin* VIII (eds E. T. Cook and Alexander Wedderburn). London: George Allen.

— 1903–12. *The Complete Works of John Ruskin* XXVII (eds E. T. Cook and Alexander Wedderburn). London: George Allen.

— 1903–12. *The Complete Works of John Ruskin* XXVIII (eds E. T. Cook and Alexander Wedderburn). London: George Allen.

— 1903–12. *The Complete Works of John Ruskin* XXXIV (eds E. T. Cook and Alexander Wedderburn). London: George Allen.

Ryle, Martin. 2000. 'Place, Time and Eco-Criticism' in *Green Letters* 2: 11-12.

— 2002. 'After "Organic Community": Ecocriticism, Nature, and Human Nature' in Parham (2002): 11-23.

Saville, Julia F. 2000. *A Queer Chivalry: The Homoerotic Asceticism of Gerard Manley Hopkins*. Charlottesville and London: University Press of Virginia.

Schneider, Elisabeth W. 1968. *The Dragon in the Gate: Studies in the Poetry of G. M. Hopkins*. Berkeley and Los Angeles: University of California Press.

Schumacher, E. F. 1974. *Small is Beautiful*. Abacus: London.

Scigaj, Leonard M. 1999. *Sustainable Poetry: Four American Ecopoets*. Lexington: University Press of Kentucky.

Sebastian, Anton. 2001. *A Dictionary of the History of Science*. London and New York: The Parthenon Publishing Group.

Segal, Charles. 1981. *Poetry and Myth in Ancient Pastoral: Essays on Theocritus and Virgil*. Princeton: Princeton University Press.

Sessions, George (ed.). 1995. *Deep Ecology for the Twenty-First Century*. Boston and London: Shambhala.

Sherrard, Philip. 1987. *The Rape of Man and Nature*. Ipswich: Golgonooza.

Simmons, I. G. 1993. *Interpreting Nature: Cultural Constructions of the Environment*. London: Routledge.

Small, Ian. 1979. *The Aesthetes: A Sourcebook*. London: Routledge & Kegan Paul.

Small, Robin (ed.). 2001. *A Hundred Years of Phenomenology: Perspectives on a Philosophical Tradition*. Aldershot: Ashgate.

Snyder, Gary. 1980. *The Real Work: Interviews and Talks 1964-1979*. New York: New Directions Books.

— 1995. *A Place in Space: Ethics, Aesthetics, and Watersheds*. Washington, DC: Counterpoint.

Soper, Kate. 1995. *What Is Nature?: Culture, Politics And The Non-Human*. Oxford: Blackwell.

Spiller, Michael R. G. 1992. *The Development of the Sonnet*. London: Routledge.

Stein, Rachel. 2002. 'Activism as Affirmation: Gender and Environmental Justice in Linda Hogan's *Solar Storms* and Barbara Neely's *Blanche Clears Up*' in Adamson, Evans and Stein (2002): 194-212.

Sulloway, Alison G. 1972. *Gerard Manley Hopkins and the Victorian Temper*. London: Routledge & Kegan Paul.

— 1984. 'The Nature of Art, Nature, and Human Nature' in North, John S. and Michael Moore (eds) *Vital Candle: Victorian and Modern Bearings in Gerard Manley Hopkins*. Waterloo, Ontario, Canada: University of Waterloo Press. 61-78.

Syer, G. N. 1971. 'Ahead of their Time' in *The Ecologist* 1(7): 13-14.

Tallmadge, John. 1998. 'Beyond the Excursion: Initiatory Themes in Annie Dillard and Terry Tempest Williams' in Branch, Michael P. (et al.) *Reading the Earth: New Directions in the Study of Literature and Environment*. Moscow, Id: University of Idaho Press. 197-207.

Tennyson, Alfred Lord. 1991. *Selected Poems* (ed. Aidan Day) (Penguin Classics). London: Penguin.

Thompson, D. 1981. 'Contributions to Scientific Education and the Teaching of Science' in Brock, W. H, N. D. McMillan and R. C. Mollan (eds) *John Tyndall: Essays on a Natural Philosopher*. Dublin: Royal Dublin Society. 145-56.

Thompson, E. P. 1977. *William Morris: Romantic to Revolutionary*. London: The Merlin Press.

Tobias, Michael (ed.). 1988. *Deep Ecology*. San Diego: Avant Books.

Townsend, Colin R, Michael Begon and John L. Harper. 2003. *Essentials of Ecology*. Oxford: Blackwell.

Tudge, Colin. 1991. *Global Ecology*. London: Natural History Museum Publications.

VanDeVeer, Donald and Christine Pierce (eds). 2003. *The Environmental Ethics and Policy Book*. Belmont and London: Thomson/Wadsworth.

Vinge, Louise. 1975. *The Five Senses: Studies in a Literary Tradition*. Lund: C. W. K. Gleerup.

Vos, Antoine. 2006. *The Philosophy of John Duns Scotus*. Edinburgh: Edinburgh University Press.

Wall, Derek (ed.). 1994. *Green History*. London: Routledge.

Wallace, Jennifer. 1997. 'Swampy's Smart Set' in *The Times Higher Education Supplement* (4 July 1997).

Watson, David. 1996. *Beyond Bookchin: Preface for a Future Social Ecology*. Brooklyn, NY: Autonomedia; Detroit, MI: Black & Red; Fifth Estate.

Westling, Louise. 2002. 'Introduction' in Parham (2002): 1-8.

Wheeler, Michael (ed.). 1995. *Ruskin and Environment*. Manchester: Manchester University Press.

— (ed.). 1996. *Time and Tide: Ruskin and Science*. London: Pilkington Press.

Wheeler, Wendy. 2006. *The Whole Creature: Complexity, Biosemiotics and the Evolution of Culture*. London: Lawrence & Wishart.

White Jr., Lynn. 1967. 'The Historical Roots of our Ecologic Crisis' in *Science* 155(3767): 1203-7.

White, Norman. 1975. 'Hopkins as Art Critic' in R. K. R. Thornton (ed.) *All My Eyes See: The Visual World of Gerard Manley Hopkins*. Sunderland: Ceolfrith Press. 89-106.

— 1992. *Hopkins: A Literary Biography*. Oxford: Clarendon Press.

Williams, Raymond. 1979. *Politics and Letters: Interviews with New Left Review*. London: NLB.

— 1980. *Problems in Materialism and Culture: Selected Essays*. London: NLB.

— 1983. *Towards 2000*. London: The Hogarth Press.

— 1984. *Keywords: A Vocabulary of Culture and Society*. London: Flamingo.

— 1985 [1973]. *The Country and the City*. London: The Hogarth Press.

— 1987 [1958]. *Culture and Society: 1780-1950*. London: The Hogarth Press.

Wilson, Eric. 2000. *Romantic Turbulence: Chaos, Ecology, and American Space*. New York: St. Martin's Press.

Winter, James. 1999. *Secure from Rash Assault: Sustaining the Victorian Environment*. Berkeley and London: University of California Press.

Wordsworth, William. 1973. *Poetical Works* (ed. Ernest de Selincourt). London, Oxford and New York: Oxford University Press.

— 1977 [1835]. *Wordsworth's Guide to the Lakes* (ed. Ernest de Selincourt). Oxford: Oxford University Press.

Worster, Donald. 1994. *Nature's Economy: A History of Ecological Ideas*. Cambridge: Cambridge University Press.

— 1995. 'The Shaky Ground of Sustainability' in Sessions (1995): 417-27.

Wu, Duncan (ed.). 1998. *A Companion to Romanticism*. Blackwell: Oxford.

Zaniello, Tom. 1988. *Hopkins in the Age of Darwin*. Iowa City: University of Iowa Press.

Zonneveld, Sjaak. 1992. *The Random Grim Forge: A Study of Social Ideas in the Work of Gerard Manley Hopkins*. Assen/Maastricht: Van Gorcum.

Index